POLICE AGAINST THE MOVEMENT

Politics and Society in Modern America

Gary Gerstle, Elizabeth Hinton, Margaret O'Mara,
and Julian E. Zelizer, Series Editors

For a full list of books in this series, see http://press.princeton.edu/ series/ politics-and-society-in-modern-america

Police Against the Movement

The Sabotage of the Civil Rights Struggle and the Activists Who Fought Back

Joshua Clark Davis

PRINCETON UNIVERSITY PRESS

PRINCETON AND OXFORD

Published by Princeton University Press
41 William Street, Princeton, New Jersey 08540
99 Banbury Road, Oxford OX2 6JX

press.princeton.edu

All Rights Reserved

ISBN 978-0-691-23883-8
ISBN (e-book) 978-0-691-23884-5

Library of Congress Control Number: 2025933884

British Library Cataloging-in-Publication Data is available

Editorial: Dave McBride and Alena Chekanov
Production Editorial: Kathleen Cioffi
Jacket Design: Katie Osborne
Production: Erin Suydam
Publicity: Maria Whelan and Kathryn Stevens
Copyeditor: Elisabeth A. Graves

Jacket image: Charles Moore Photographic Archive, camh-dob-030838, The Dolph Briscoe Center for American History, The University of Texas at Austin

This book has been composed in Adobe Text and Gotham

Printed in the United States of America

10 9 8 7 6 5 4 3 2 1

For Jess

CONTENTS

ACKNOWLEDGMENTS

No single person can take credit for nearly eight years of researching and writing a book—not even an author. This work is no exception. It would have been impossible without the help and support of so many people. Ultimately, it was a collective effort.

A historian is nothing without their sources. Before this was a book, it was a research project. There are too many archivists and librarians to name who assisted me in this process, but I should name several who went above and beyond in guiding me. Rossy Mendez was tireless as she fielded my nonstop questions about the New York Police Department intelligence squad collection at the New York City Municipal Archives. At the National Archives, Megan Dwyre and Haley Maynard Birnbaum worked with me for more than five years as they processed my many requests for Federal Bureau of Investigation records. Allen Fisher at the LBJ Presidential Library, Shannon O'Neill at New York University, and the staffs of the University of California, Los Angeles, Library Special Collections; the Birmingham Public Library's Department of Archives and Manuscripts; and the Houston Public Library's Houston History Research Center also played a key role in making this project possible. Donna Wade offered her internal guidance in navigating the records of the Los Angeles Police Department.

The most important research institution for this book has been the University of Baltimore's Robert L. Bogolmony Library. Without the help of Sean Hogan and Delores Redman in the Intercampus/Interlibrary Loan office, this would have been impossible. The same would have been true without librarians Tammy Taylor, Erin Toepfner, Sarah Gilchrist, and Debbie Li, all of whom made sure

I got the hundreds of books I requested. Even during a global pandemic, this group left the confines of their office to come out to the street, masked and bearing boxes and oversized ziploc bags filled with books. And thanks go to Jeffrey Hutson and Tim Commo, who filled my interminable requests for book purchases, and to Aiden Faust, who assisted me in Special Collections with materials from the Baltimore Police Department.

One other library deserves special recognition. In the last several grueling years of writing this book, the Waverly Branch of the Enoch Pratt Free Library in Baltimore served as my office away from home and campus, a place where I could drop in and write without distraction. So many staff at the branch indulged my repeat appearances and checked me into one of their two Quiet Rooms: Darryl Cook, Lolita Little-Staten, Neelam Prasad, Danielle Markham, Jessi Leister, Maria Elliott-Richburg, and several other staff who wish to remain unnamed.

I have been fortunate to work with a group of exceptionally gifted students at the University of Baltimore who have doubled as research assistants for this book, thanks to the Federal Work-Study program. In the early stages of this project, Abraham Rodriguez and Regina Gray Rodriguez transcribed interviews and dove into databases, with research assistance from Jacob Abraham. More recently, Annie Allan assisted with research, as did Lexzander Ernst, who played a critical role in assembling the images for this book.

Two other researchers—and good friends—have gone above and beyond in contributing to this project. One is Joseph Lacey, who helped with my unceasing and at times quixotic effort to obtain as many Federal Bureau of Investigation records on the individuals described in this work as possible from the National Archives. The other is Andrew Holter, who not only aided me in these adventures with the Freedom of Information Act but offered tremendous assistance as I tried to make the most out of database research for this book, especially during the height of the pandemic in 2020 and 2021, when archives were closed across the country. Other friends gave me places to stay on research trips, asked me about my writing progress, and just generally supported me, including Chris Dietrich,

Veronica Jiménez Vega, Danny Zeiger, Sandya Viswanathan, Asher Burk, Jason Perlmutter, Hollie Jones, Raphael Ginsberg, Emily Coward, Ari Berenbaum, Laughlin Siceloff, Tamra Higgs, Annie Farmer, Jon Grover, and Sebastian Stockman.

My colleagues at the University of Baltimore supported me as well, particularly BoRam Yi, Nicole Hudgins, Ian Power, Steven Leyva, Jennifer Keohane, and Toni Martsoukos. I am grateful as well to my dean, Chris Spencer, who encouraged my work and advocated for the value of history for our students. Claudette Booth has supported me at every turn, booking travel and processing reimbursements for me and basically making my research trips possible.

I've been lucky to have an outstanding circle of friends here in Baltimore as I've worked on this book, many of whom are interested in and work on issues that appear in this book: Steph Saxton, Brandon Soderberg, Stuart Schrader, Christy Thornton, Sarah Fouts, Kate Drabinski, Niki Fabricant, Max Berger, Nicole Stanovsky, Jaisal Noor, Nicole King, Osita Nwanevu, Baynard Woods, Michelle Stefano, Nathan Connolly, Eli Pousson, Courtney Hobson, Kelly King, Jackson Gilman-Forlini, Andy Dahl, Marissa Dahl, Lester Spence, Caitlin Goldblatt, Jes Godinez, and Anneke Dunbar-Gronke.

So many scholars listened to me discuss this work and offered constructive feedback, including several named above as well as Derek Musgrove, Simon Balto, Marisol LeBron, Nishani Frazier, Anne Gray Fischer, Todd Moye, Max Krochmal, Seth Kotch, Brandon Winford, Johanna Fernández, DeAnza Cook, Peter Pihos, Kerry Taylor, asmin Young, Menika Dirkson, Keith Riley, Robert Chase, Natalie Ring, Jermaine Thibodeaux, Brandon Jett, Jacob Bruggeman, and Chloe Hawkey.

A few scholars in particular who intervened in this project to make it much stronger were my reviewers at Princeton University Press, Dan Berger and Melanie Newport. I am indebted to these two thinkers for making my book better. Stuart Schrader offered invaluable feedback on several parts of this manuscript. Thanks are due as well to Elizabeth Hinton in her role as series editor for lending her eyes to this manuscript.

This book would not have been possible without my agent Alison Lewis of the Frances Goldin Literary Agency. Alison believed in this work before virtually anyone else, and she was tireless in bringing it to auction and finding a good home for it. She was a constant source of encouragement and sound advice as I slowly turned my manuscript into a book.

I've been delighted to work with Princeton University Press on this book. More than anyone, Bridget Flannery-McCoy helped to transform my scattered Word documents into a book. Her line edits combined with big-picture editorial notes to make this book more lucid, more convincing, and much more readable. Bridget read draft after draft, helping me see the forest for the trees and chart a path forward even when I was close to being overwhelmed by the mass of edits in each chapter. I'm lucky to have worked with her for the second time and wish her the best of luck at her new position at Grove Atlantic. Major thanks are in order to Eric Crahan and Dave McBride, who joined this project at a critical juncture, guiding it through the production process in the year leading up to publication. And I'm grateful for Alena Chekanov, who has done so much throughout this project to help me pull together loose ends and get the details right, especially as we worked together in the production phase to combine words and images to turn this into a book. Elisabeth Graves did an expert job copyediting this manuscript.

I am hugely thankful to the movement veterans who have offered me advice, support, and friendship through this long process. They include Daphne Muse, Judy Richardson, Jennifer Lawson, Marc Steiner, and Courtland Cox. I am very grateful to have known Betty Garman Robinson, who passed away far too soon and who I wish could have seen this project come to fruition.

I was fortunate to publish some of my preliminary research with the assistance of two very skilled editors: Atossa Araxia Abrahamian at *The Nation* and Rebecca Onion at *Slate*.

I'm also indebted to the individuals who shared their personal histories with me and agreed to be interviewed for this book: Khaleel Sayyed, Walter Bowe, Adraenne Bowe, Floyd Nichols, Trazawell Franklin, Stu Wechsler, Tony Bouza, Gethsemane Campbell, Kelly

Wood, Sol Herbert, Nan Murrell, Mack Parker, Billie Williams, Bobby Caldwell, Connell Linson, Omowale Lithuli-Allen, Fred Hofheinz, Bob Cash, Don Byrd, and Frank Joyce. I am especially thankful to Sean Hannon, who not only let me interview him but entrusted me with his father's personal papers, letting me borrow a one-of-a-kind archival collection that was foundational for my chapter on Michael Hannon.

I have had the great fortune to receive financial support for my work as I wrote my book. More than any organization, the National Endowment for the Humanities made this work possible by awarding me a Public Scholars grant, which allowed me to extend my sabbatical by an additional semester. This book may likely not have been possible without that extra half year of time away from teaching. I'm very grateful to the Robert B. Silvers Foundation for the Work in Progress grant they awarded me, as well as for the Rubys Artist Award that I received from the Robert W. Deutsch Foundation. Generous grants from the LBJ Presidential Library; the University of California, Los Angeles, Library Special Collections; the Getty Research Institute; and the College of Arts and Sciences at the University of Baltimore made visits to out-of-state archives possible. Last but not least, the Wildacres Retreat in Little Switzerland, North Carolina, hosted me twice for its Residency Program, treating me to two weeklong stays where I was able to concentrate on my writing, including in the final months of producing my manuscript.

Family have been a huge source of support throughout this work. They asked about my project again and again as it dragged on over the years. When I've traveled to Atlanta and Oakland, my dad Jeff, his wife Tricia, my sister Rosemary, and my brother John have all let me stay with them. My aunt Elizabeth, my uncle Casey, and my aunt Dede have done the same.

Finally, there is one person above all else who has encouraged and endured me as I've toiled on this years-long project, and that's Jessica Douglas. More than anyone, Jess has been with me on this journey, joining me on research trips across the country and putting up with this undertaking as it demanded much more time than I could have ever imagined. As an archivist, she's explained things to me that I could barely fathom, helping me immensely as I struggled with court records and finding aids and ArchivesSpace. She hasn't been afraid to point out when my expectations for court clerks or archives detached from reality. But more than anything, she has supported me and believed in this project and talked with me about so many aspects of this research as I tried to transform it into a book that people would want to read.

Jess, I love you, and I could not have done this without you. I dedicate this to you.

POLICE AGAINST THE MOVEMENT

Introduction

Law enforcement officials loom large as villains in the history of the civil rights movement. J. Edgar Hoover and the Federal Bureau of Investigation (FBI) stifled activists with covert surveillance, while Birmingham commissioner of public safety Bull Connor attacked them with German shepherds and fire hoses. Some segregationist Southern sheriffs even plotted the murders of civil rights workers. These men deserve the scorn they have received. But too many Americans have found false comfort in treating them as anomalies whose pathological abuses were reined in by federal authorities, a national devotion to fairness and democracy, and an equitable justice system outside the South. It is a myth that law enforcement gladly promotes.

To understand the roots of racism and violence in policing in the twenty-first century, we need to look beyond Hoover's FBI and the most sadistic segregationist sheriffs, the avowed enemies of Martin Luther King Jr. Behind them lies a deep history of local police not just in Alabama and Mississippi but in the cities of the North, West, and purportedly progressive New South—everywhere from New York to Los Angeles, Houston to Philadelphia. While they invoked the "color-blind" pursuit of "law and order" in public pronouncements, local police sabotaged the work of civil rights activists with calculated stealth.

Birmingham and Selma guaranteed that the image of officers beating Black protesters would prevail as symbols of police violence for decades to come. On the one hand, photographs and film footage exposed brutality by white law enforcement against Black people; they roused thousands to march against white supremacy. It is not an exaggeration to credit them with generating much of the political momentum that propelled the Civil Rights Act of 1964 and the Voting Rights Act of 1965 to passage.

And yet, just as these captured images ignited political firestorms— like today's cell phone videos of law enforcement misdeeds—they also narrowed the public's conception of police violence. Both then and now, they have been misinterpreted as evidence that police violence is always recognizable by its physical brutality, something that can be documented on film or video that will strike all decent people as wrong, if disseminated.

But what about police violence that is not easily caught on camera, abuses that have escaped the attention of many Americans? We might think of these as instances of "slow violence." These are unhurried acts of harm, the products of painstaking design that exact damage in a such a subtle and drawn-out manner as to not appear violent at all, at least not to many observers. Examples include many of the insidious weapons police used against civil rights organizers in the 1960s: retaliatory felony prosecutions; the infiltration of activist groups by undercover officers; widespread surveillance, which many in the movement suspected at the time but could not prove; and a campaign of vilification aimed at destroying activists' reputations and halting their organizations' gains. These tactics were gradual in both their execution and their effect. These slow but violent acts committed by police against the civil rights movement—and the activists who fought back against them—are the subject of this book.[1]

––––

One of the most persistent and pernicious myths about the movement was that it endured police violence without fighting it. More than a few contemporary commentators have claimed that a meaningful national movement against police violence did not materialize in America until the Movement for Black Lives emerged in the 2010s. The *Washington Post* argued in 2015, for instance, that "the Black Lives Matter [BLM] movement is picking up the unfinished work of activists who fought for equal voting rights five decades ago." And the *Los Angeles Times* noted in the wake of the summer of 2020 that "the unfinished work of the civil rights movement was laid bare" by that year's protests. Indeed, this framing of police violence as an issue that the civil rights movement failed to address—presumably because the problem was too intractable, or because activists did not understand it, or because the movement was too busy with other issues—has proved all too common since the emergence of BLM.[2]

In fact, civil rights organizers did not at all leave the fight against racist police violence "unfinished." Rather, activists were steadfast in their efforts to combat repressive law enforcement. But the organizers who dared to protest police abuses against Black citizens found themselves the targets of tremendous and ultimately overwhelming violence that derailed, discouraged, and discredited the movement. These attacks took physical, psychological, economic, and legal forms. Far from surrendering to this onslaught, civil rights organizers waged a defiant counterattack on the array of violence perpetrated by police against Black people, including assaults aimed at the movement.

By the middle of the 1960s, some activists—especially in two of the civil rights movement's more radical organizations, the Congress of Racial Equality (CORE) and the Student Nonviolent Coordinating Committee (SNCC)—insisted on confronting police abuses. The National Association for the Advancement of Colored People (NAACP) clung to a decades-old legalistic strategy of suing police departments in selective instances of egregious physical violence against Black citizens. Dr. King's Southern Christian Leadership Conference meanwhile singled out the most unapologetically abusive police departments—such as those in Birmingham and Selma—with campaigns for desegregation and voter registration designed to prod them into violent overreactions, as part of a strategy to attract national media attention. But neither group made organizing against law enforcement abuses a significant part of their efforts.

The organizers of CORE and SNCC, by contrast, took direct action against police violence. They picketed law enforcement outside city halls and department headquarters, staged sit-ins in precinct stations, and stopped traffic on busy streets to protest police misdeeds. CORE organizers developed a theory of "police malpractice" to cover the wide array of abuses by law enforcement, including false arrests and political prosecutions, not just physical attacks on protesters. SNCC, in turn, came to understand police abuses as manifestations of structural racism and state repression that presaged the onset of fascism. On the West Coast, CORE and SNCC organizers helped establish street teams to monitor police in African American neighborhoods as early as 1965, pioneering an approach that the Black Panther Party later made famous. While the Panthers and other Black Power groups of the late 1960s tended to dismiss earlier civil rights activists as too moderate, their own work built on these previous efforts by the movement's radical critics of police power.

Over time, SNCC and CORE expanded their work against physical brutality to focus on political policing, namely, the monitoring and legal harassment of activists for organizing activities regarded as criminally subversive. Although political ideology informs all varieties of policing, this approach to law enforcement explicitly targets those who are politically active. In the late nineteenth and early twentieth centuries, political police targeted leftists and labor organizers with backgrounds as European immigrants. As Marcus Garvey's Universal Negro Improvement Association emerged as a mass movement in the 1920s and African Americans joined the Communist Party in growing numbers in the 1930s and 1940s, police began to set their sights on Black activists, too. But only by the start of the 1960s, after the pervasive repression of the Red Scare had decimated the Communist Party, did the ascendant struggle for racial justice—or the "long civil rights movement"—capture the full attention of political police.[3]

Within this context, political policing took shape as a potent but underrecognized variety of what scholars have termed the anti-Black punitive tradition. In a body of literature that has ballooned in the last two decades, researchers have explored criminalization and incarceration as white supremacist tools of social control imposed on African Americans throughout U.S. history. And yet, the very slowness of the covert methods and legalistic weapons deployed by police against Black activists has functioned as camouflage. This is especially true for local police, whose sparse recordkeeping and widespread destruction of surveillance files have posed particular challenges for historians, in contrast to the extensive paper trails left behind by even the most secretive federal law enforcement agencies.[4]

By placing political policing at the heart of the anti-Black punitive tradition, this narrative returns localized state repression and activism against police violence to the center of the civil rights movement. Political policing of the movement is often remembered as the work of the federal government. Indeed, a common misperception is that while the FBI attacked activists with the sophisticated tools of surveillance and slander, local police were content to assault them with the primitive weapons of clubs and dogs. But local police were far more experienced in spying on and sabotaging activists than we have acknowledged—so much so that COINTELPRO, the FBI's notorious counterintelligence program against "Black extremists" launched in August 1967, should be recognized for federalizing efforts that local police departments had already undertaken to disrupt the civil rights movement.[5]

———

Local law enforcement pioneered political policing. At the start of the twentieth century, before the FBI was founded, police in New York and Chicago formed political surveillance units tasked with monitoring local radicals, and in the decades between the two world wars, departments in almost every major American city followed suit. Colloquially known as "red squads," these secretive detective divisions committed themselves to ferreting out communists and other Marxists. By the middle of the 1950s, they began to shift their focus to the burgeoning Black freedom movement. Red squads photographed protesters at rallies, monitored activists' communications and travels, and amassed countless filing cabinets of information on their political and private lives. Time and again, they noted peaceful, orderly, and legal activities in their surveillance reports, yet they continued to spy on civil rights organizers as though the safety of their cities depended on it. Decades before police utilized text mining and predictive algorithms, these intelligence units were the original pioneers of "big data surveillance" in law enforcement.[6]

By some measures, the scale of political policing by municipal departments exceeded that of the Bureau's operations against activists. Because they were closer to the ground and embedded more deeply in their communities than federal authorities, local departments enjoyed an advantage in collecting information on organizers. As the civil rights movement swelled in the early and middle 1960s, police departments in New York, Philadelphia, Houston, and Nashville reimagined their existing red squads or formed new units to track a new generation of activists. The fewer than sixty FBI field offices covering the United States had far more area to cover than the roughly five hundred police departments that operated their own political intelligence units. The best estimates available indicate that while the FBI devoted three thousand of its agents to political intelligence by the end of the 1960s, America's local police departments assigned more than 4,700 individuals to this work.[7]

Red squads attacked civil rights organizers in ways that even the FBI did not. Although the Bureau engaged private citizens to spy as volunteer or paid informants, it did not assign its own agents to carry out undercover work in Black activist organizations. A major reason for this was that the Bureau lacked the staff for infiltration. As late as 1968, barely one-half of 1 percent of the FBI's agents were Black, which federal authorities admitted was a major impediment to collecting intelligence on Black activists. Although major city police departments were also overwhelmingly white, their share of Black officers ranged between 3 and 10 percent.[8] In addition, Hoover banned his agents from going undercover, and the only documented cases in which his subordinates flouted the prohibition were in infiltrating white antiwar groups—but not Black-led organizations. Hoover feared that any undercover FBI agents discovered spying on activists would harm the agency's reputation and raise charges of entrapment and political prosecution. Paid informants were simply easier to disavow than salaried federal employees.[9]

Local police displayed no such qualms in their attempts to sabotage the movement. Red squads in New York, Los Angeles, and Houston, for example, assigned officers to assume false identities and masquerade as activists so that they could infiltrate SNCC and CORE. In each of these instances recounted in detail later in this work, undercover agents were dispatched to spy on activists who had protested police brutality. In one case, an officer admitted under oath that he encouraged three activists to blow up the Statue of Liberty with dynamite and even helped them obtain the explosives. His testimony secured the trio's conviction and sentencing to federal prison. In another incident, a civil rights organizer passed a single joint of marijuana to an undercover officer who later testified that the activist had effectively sold him weed, resulting in a thirty-year prison sentence for the organizer. Over the course of the 1960s, police departments in Houston, Philadelphia, Atlanta, and Nashville indicted dozens of SNCC organizers on felony charges of inciting riots or other violent plots. Although virtually every one of these charges ended up falling apart in court or being dropped altogether by prosecutors, police largely succeeded in stymieing SNCC's activities in these cities, particularly their work against police abuses.

Over and over, red squads were firsthand observers of the movement's defining moments, if not direct participants in them. Undercover detectives watched as Klansmen attacked Freedom Riders in Alabama in 1961, and they stood in the audience of the March on Washington in 1963 on the National Mall. Police intelligence monitored King when he campaigned against housing segregation in Chicago in 1966 and when he arrived in Memphis two years later to support the city's striking Black sanitation workers. And, perhaps most disturbingly, red squad officers stood mere feet from both King and Malcolm X at the moments they were murdered.[10]

———

At the start of the 1960s, polling suggested that most Americans considered political protest to be ineffective. A significant majority disapproved of early civil rights actions such as the Freedom Rides. And the idea of protesting the police lay not only far outside the political mainstream but beyond what most left-wing organizations considered prudent. At the time, opinion surveys showed that an overwhelming majority of Americans had deep respect for police and simply did not believe that officers assaulted citizens in their own communities. White Americans especially doubted that police brutality occurred in the cities and towns where they lived. And for those who did criticize police—mostly African Americans and a small segment of the white Left—the idea of protesting them on the street seemed like a reckless invitation for harassment, if not worse. In some communities, citizens were charged with resisting arrest, assaulting officers, or filing false reports in retaliation for making formal complaints against police abuses.[11]

One source of resistance to activists' efforts was the widespread belief in law enforcement's fairness. In a poll completed in 1960, for example, 85 percent of respondents—a number that came notably close to the proportion of the U.S. population that was white— asserted that if they "had some trouble with the police," they believed that they would be treated the same as anyone else. The overwhelming majority of Americans, it seemed, could not conceive that law enforcement might interact with one group of people differently than another. Widespread, deep-seated bias in favor of the law and those who enforced it was only further exacerbated by the rise of "law and order" politics later in the decade, championed by Richard Nixon and George Wallace in response to uprisings in Black communities, spiraling crime rates, and proliferating street protests, all of which they were eager to blame on the supposed disorder and disobedience advanced by the civil rights movement.[12]

To challenge the police was to attack one of the country's most cherished myths: the notion that the law was impartial. The activists doing this work understood that legal desegregation was not going to end police violence against Black people, as they recognized the limitations of the segregation-versus-integration framework that white media and officials embraced for assessing the movement's activities. For many liberals, the solution to the country's crisis of racial inequality was to create federal laws that superseded discriminatory state and local statutes in the South (and they did think that the problem of racism was mostly in the South). But if America was a "nation of laws, not of men," as many liberals claimed, what good was it if those charged with law enforcement could do as they pleased, without facing any punishment for violating laws themselves? What was the use of civil rights legislation if it failed to address the police who discriminated and brutalized, not only in the South but in all parts of the United States? That the answers to these questions proved so vexing highlights why the fight against police violence was among the civil rights movement's most radical undertakings—and why that fight continues to inspire sustained attacks from law enforcement and elected officials to this day.

———

In the wake of the brutal Birmingham police response to protests in 1963, many civil rights organizers zeroed in on police repression. That August, the famed Black psychologist Kenneth Clark interviewed SNCC executive secretary James Forman for a public television documentary. Asked what challenges the movement faced in registering Black voters in Alabama and Mississippi, Forman answered without hesitation. "Police brutality is the number one problem in the South," he declared, citing weekly harassment and attacks by officers on SNCC organizers.[13]

"What the dogs and guns and hoses have proved is that the entire power structure of the South must be altered," Lorraine Hansberry wrote later that year in *The Movement: Documentary of a Struggle for Equality*, a book published by SNCC that paired Hansberry's original writings on civil rights work with photographs by Danny Lyon and other SNCC staffers. The book's cover featured a shot of a white Atlanta police officer placing Black high schooler Taylor Washington in a headlock as he arrested him at a protest (see figure I.1). "The original demand for equal treatment on buses and at lunch counters has had to broaden and sharpen, to strike at the political base of Negro oppression," Hansberry told readers, arguing that police violence

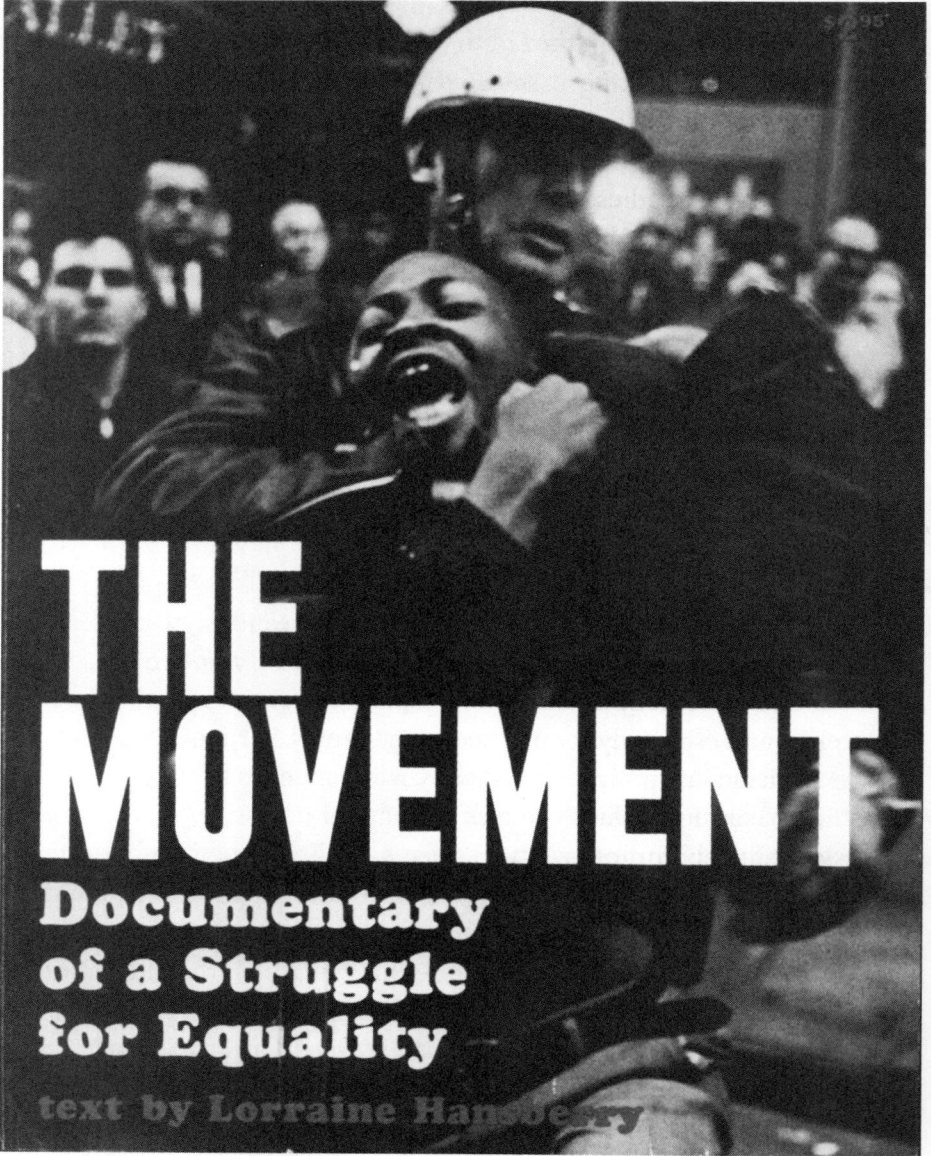

FIGURE I.1. Authored by Lorraine Hansberry, *The Movement* was published by SNCC and featured multiple photographs of police taken by staff photographers Danny Lyon and Matt Herron. Courtesy of the SNCC Legacy Project.

had helped organizers identify the ultimate source of the racism confronting them. Months later, in April 1964, CORE director James Farmer made a strikingly similar observation: "The feeling in the Negro community, especially in the North, is stronger against police brutality than anything else."[14]

A handful of studies have explored the history of activism against police violence. Indebted to these scholars' work, I offer this book as a retelling of the national civil rights struggle through its work against police violence—and the police who attacked the movement with surveillance, undercover agents, and retaliatory prosecutions. Focusing on a cast of figures whose entanglements with law enforcement were both representative and exceptional, this book tells the story of police and civil rights organizers as it played out on the ground across the United States.[15]

Many of the individuals in this work are largely forgotten today. Although King is remembered for his eloquent denunciation of police brutality at the March on Washington, he was not at the forefront of organizing efforts against police violence. As our perspective on law enforcement and the movement has narrowly focused on the FBI and especially its abuses against King, we have lost view of the work against police violence by noted civil rights leaders such as Ella Baker, Fred Shuttlesworth, and Fannie Lou Hamer; we have almost entirely forgotten once-prominent organizers devoted to combating police abuses such as Herb Callender, Mike Hannon, and Lee Otis Johnson; and we have failed to recognize how an activist such as Angela Davis, whom we do not typically remember as part of the civil rights movement, challenged police power during her time with SNCC and later built an alliance against state repression with Ralph David Abernathy and the Southern Christian Leadership Conference. Far from being an exhaustive list, these individuals represent a selection of activists who placed the fight against police violence at the center of their work, even as they themselves endured sustained state repression.

Civil rights activism against police violence predated the famed Montgomery Bus Boycott of 1955, which popular memory credits with launching the movement. A prime example is Ella Baker's work as the head of New York City's NAACP chapter in an extended campaign against police assaults on unarmed Black citizens in 1953, at the height of the Red Scare. But when New York Police Department officials and the police union struck back with furious accusations that the NAACP was perpetrating a communist plot to defame the department, they effectively rendered the issue of police brutality radioactive for Black activists, both in New York and nationally, by hinting that protests against police could attract scrutiny from federal law enforcement or even Congress's House Un-American Activities Committee. Not surprisingly, the NAACP—which had endorsed anticommunism in 1950—shifted away from direct action protests and community organizing against police violence. Instead, they employed a more cautious approach of filing civil lawsuits on behalf of the victims of egregious police violence and lobbying federal officials to prosecute the most flagrant abuses by local departments.[16]

In contrast to the NAACP's national leadership, activists like Baker who collaborated with current or former socialists and communists did not shy from organizing direct action protests against police violence. For decades, communists had articulated an analysis of police violence as political repression and spent more time than any other group campaigning against it, especially through organizations such as the International Labor Defense, the Civil Rights Congress, and the National Lawyers Guild. But because this work carried the taint of leftist radicalism, many in the new generation of civil rights leaders who emerged in the 1950s considered protesting the police too politically risky. That changed with CORE and SNCC in the 1960s.[17]

To place activism against police violence at the center of our larger narrative of the civil rights struggle is to bring communists and socialists back into the history of the movement. Many in the movement denied this influence for years, hoping to protect themselves from the vicious red-baiting of the Cold War era. Communists forged critical alliances with Black civil rights and labor groups who fought police violence in the 1930s and 1940s—as a number of scholars have skillfully shown—but the alliances that quietly continued in the 1950s and 1960s deserve more attention. In addition to regular protests against physical brutality by police, communists regularly decried political policing in their writings, with frequent criticisms of the "frame-up system" that prosecuted radicals and editorials against police intelligence units as little more than agents provocateurs.[18]

Why did some—but not all—civil rights activists pinpoint police abuses as one of the most significant threats to Black freedom? Generally speaking, those in the movement who devoted considerable energy to fighting police abuses shared two experiences. First, they were open to working with socialists and communists and were shaped by their thinking on police. Second, they had personally witnessed right-wing vigilante attacks on activists made possible by police collusion. For many, this was a formative lesson of the Freedom Rides, when Birmingham and Montgomery police covertly assisted Klan members in carrying out vicious attacks on protesters. Although racist terror lynchings had virtually ceased by 1950, police continued to facilitate mob attacks in the civil rights era, and those activists who endured such attacks were understandably more skeptical of police than their peers who had not.[19]

These differences in experience translated into varying interpretations of police violence among activists. A central question that emerged was whether police violence required a legal remedy or a broader political solution, whether it was merely the doing of individual racist officers who broke the law or, rather, a fundamental expression of an oppressive political ideology. Some of the more radical organizers in SNCC and CORE embraced the view that law enforcement was committed to creating and defending a political order with a wide array of violence. This was not a matter of unkind officers or hardened segregationists; this was baked into the design of the system, they insisted, arguing that anti-Black policing was part and parcel of the larger plague of American racism. Organizers in SNCC and CORE came to view police violence not only as a challenge confronting their movement or a symptom of racial inequality but as an active ingredient of white supremacy. In many ways, their thinking anticipated the theoretical underpinnings of the movement to abolish prisons and police that emerged decades later.

———

In writing this book, I have often felt that I am telling a story that many do not want told. For decades, police and public officials have worked hard to conceal their attacks on the civil rights movement. Most police intelligence work against Black activists remained secret for years—the stuff of lore within the movement but rarely acknowledged by officials or mainstream journalists and almost always denied by police. This changed in the 1970s, when activists in Philadelphia, Los Angeles, Detroit, Chicago, Memphis, and Houston sued local police departments and city governments after uncovering records of sustained surveillance and other invasive counterintelligence measures deployed by red squads. Many of these activists brought their experiences in the civil rights movement from the previous decade to this legal crusade. Today, however, this national movement by organizers against local police repression and surveillance in the 1970s is barely remembered, overshadowed by the revelations of federal intelligence abuses that emerged from the Watergate scandal; the break-in at the Media, Pennsylvania, FBI office; and U.S. Senator Frank Church's Select Committee to Study Governmental Operations with Respect to Intelligence Activities.

No national investigations or hearings were ever held to probe the extensive abuses by local police against activist groups in the 1960s and 1970s, and no federal action was taken. Lawmakers in a handful of states such as Maryland and California convened committees to emulate Church's work, but their impact was minimal. To make matters worse, state legislatures across the country enacted public records laws in subsequent decades that permanently prohibited the release of police personnel and investigative files in perpetuity, as well as the identities of undercover officers—in some cases even after they have passed away. By contrast, the federal Freedom of Information Act allows for the release of personnel and investigative records from the FBI, including hundreds of thousands of pages detailing the Bureau's surveillance of activists. For all that federal law enforcement has withheld, researchers still have far less access to records documenting local political policing of the civil rights movement. Most troubling of all, police departments in New York, Los Angeles, Houston, and numerous other cities shredded and incinerated millions of intelligence documents in the 1970s as activists confronted them with civil suits, deliberately seeking to destroy the primary sources detailing their abuses.

Indeed, police have gone to great lengths to conceal their contemptible record of attacks on the civil rights movement. Each January on Martin Luther King Jr. Day, police departments fall over themselves to celebrate the civil rights leader, all the while glossing over the violence they have perpetrated against racial justice movements, including against King himself. Accounts of the 1960s written by police for their profession's museums and textbooks make virtually no mention of their widespread surveillance or retaliations against the movement, though they often point to FBI abuses. All told, we might conceive of these efforts by police as a remarkable act of unremembering, something much more conscious than mere forgetting—an intentional campaign to erase history.[20]

Using a variety of research strategies, I have reconstructed the historical record on police and civil rights that officials have worked so hard to conceal and destroy. More than sixty years after the civil rights movement, law enforcement agencies have slowly released many of the documents pertaining to the individuals in this book in response to public records requests that I have submitted. I've visited municipal storerooms in dusty basements in Los Angeles and convinced reluctant file clerks in Houston to produce court records believed to be lost for decades, and I've located forgotten police records—including secret surveillance files of civil rights activists—squirreled away in city archives, mayoral papers, and the once-closed files of congressional investigative committees.

Through the Freedom of Information Act, I have obtained thousands of pages of classified FBI records on police investigations of activists, a large share of them held by the National Archives and never before released to researchers. Many of these records are held by the federal government only because the FBI requested that municipal police agencies brief them on local investigations of civil rights organizers. Some of these documents raise new questions about the criminal prosecutions of activists and even whether law enforcement officials themselves may have committed crimes in their investigations of these individuals.

———

Today, many Americans embrace the civil rights movement as the nation's ultimate expression of democracy in action. But anyone serious in that belief must recognize the inverse to be true as well: that police attacks on the civil rights movement were profoundly antidemocratic. In recent years, scholars have advanced the concept of racial authoritarianism to explain the United States' political history. For decades, researchers reserved this term to describe formally segregated states such as apartheid-era South Africa. Increasingly, however, political scientists recognize the corrosive, authoritarian effect represented by formally democratic states' treatment of racial minorities. Of course, African Americans have long been excluded from full participation in the American political system. And it was police, arguably more than any other agents of the state, who employed coercion, violence, and punishment to ensure such disenfranchisement. Police repression of the civil rights movement was nothing less than state action to ward off organized efforts at democratization.[21]

The astonishingly effective work of police against the activists who protested them in the 1960s does much to explain why no national movement against police violence emerged in America for half a century. The sabotage of the civil rights struggle demonstrated just how great the political, legal, and economic risks were for organizers who confronted law enforcement. Local movements against police brutality popped up around the country in the decades that followed, as did organizations devoted to prison abolition that periodically addressed police abuses, such as Critical Resistance. These groups netted meaningful victories along the way. But for fifty years, nothing approached the national significance and visibility of organizers' work against police abuses in the 1960s and early 1970s.

That finally changed in the 2010s, with the emergence of the Movement for Black Lives. Today, we can see the legacy of police antagonism to civil rights in the vilification of Black Lives Matter by law enforcement—and by the political Right more broadly—as they insist that BLM and its allies betray the goals of King, whom they now claim to revere. Many Americans unfortunately believe that activists who attack racist policing do more harm than good, even as the civil rights movement of the 1960s continues to enjoy a reputation as a shining example of American democracy. In the wake of the killing of George Floyd in Minneapolis in 2020, an estimated fifteen to twenty-six million people protested for Black lives and against police violence all over the United States—the largest wave of sustained political protest in American history. And yet, polls three years later suggested that barely half of Americans still supported Black Lives Matter and more than 40 percent opposed it.[22]

Looking back, we can trace the origins of our political paralysis in the face of law enforcement abuses to the war that police waged against the civil rights movement. If we wish to eliminate a culture of policing in which unarmed Black citizens can be killed with impunity, in which law enforcement officers attack racial justice activists with invasive surveillance, legal retribution, and violent force—if we do *not* want this to be our future—then we must confront our past.

1

Political Police

Four thousand people gathered for Glover Davis's funeral at the Mount Zion Baptist Church in Atlanta on Labor Day 1933. Five days earlier, police officer O. W. Allen had shot Davis, claiming that the Black man had threatened him with an ice pick—though he later insisted he had no idea that the man was blind. Now, seventy uniformed officers armed with machine guns and tear gas patrolled the church grounds, and twenty plainclothes police circulated among the mourners. Their assignment was to prevent a protest by the racially mixed crowd, a rarity in Georgia. Officers demanded that the funeral home and Davis's family put away banners reading "End Police Murders." Having ignored official warnings to avoid meetings of Black people, white attendees at the funeral were searched by police, including one who was arrested for distributing leaflets urging "white and colored people to stop the killing of Negroes by policemen." Black attendees meanwhile endured constant "bulldozing and terrorizing" by the officers, as reported by the *Daily Worker*.

In spite of everything, two speakers at the mass funeral were determined to voice their outrage at the killing and call their audience to action. "Lord, give us men who are not afraid to speak against and denounce police brutality, and their slaying of Negroes, shooting them in the back while they flee arrest," the Reverend J. A. Martin beseeched the mourners. A second speaker, twenty-nine-year-old Atlanta native Benjamin Davis, no relation to Glover, was one of the few Black attorneys in Georgia and an official of the International Labor Defense, the leading legal advocacy organization affiliated with the Communist Party. After announcing a mass organizing meeting scheduled for later that day, Davis drew tremendous applause for delivering a message the assembled officers no doubt wished he had not: "The funeral of Glover Davis, whose body lies down there, is the funeral of every Negro in this city unless the murderous brutality of the Atlanta police is stopped!"[1]

Later that week, the Atlanta office of the International Labor Defense was raided by the local solicitor and eight detectives. When Davis protested that they lacked a warrant, the solicitor announced he was preparing a disbarment application for Davis, whose clients included a twenty-year-old Black communist named Angelo Herndon then battling felony insurrection charges for possessing party literature. The detectives proceeded to seize virtually all print materials they could find in the office. The city's police chief, T. O. Sturdivant, proposed even harsher methods for dealing with radicals. "We need machine guns and tear gas guns and bombs to cope with activities of communists in Atlanta," Sturdivant told police officials the same evening that one of his officers shot Glover Davis. "Unless we prepare for it, we may face an emergency and a defiance of authority without being ready."[2]

In early 1934, Davis fled his hometown of Atlanta for the more hospitable political climate of New York City, at the urging of allies who thought that his life and livelihood were in danger. The events of the past half year had made two things apparent to Davis. The first was that Black communities' opposition to racist police killings was so resolute that they would gather en masse to resist it in the most egregious cases—even in the Jim Crow South and even under threat of further violence. Second, Davis noted, police retaliated against Black communities who criticized them, especially when they did so in alliance with multiracial left-wing groups. Perhaps more than any other form of political organizing, protesting police brutality was likely to draw a swift and severe reaction from law enforcement.

And yet, in Atlanta, which prided itself on racial moderation compared with its Southern peers, police figured that mass physical violence against protesters could draw national outrage and embolden local protests. Law enforcement there instead resorted to more respectable means of political policing, punishing their critics with raids, prosecution for supposed insurrectionary acts, and threats of professional excommunication. In Atlanta and cities across the country, these tactics of slow violence would persist as the blueprint for repressing organized movements against police misdeeds for decades to come.[3]

———

The FBI occupies a space in the American imagination as the ultimate political police. But before the Bureau, there was the red squad. In 1904, the New York Police Department (NYPD) established a special unit to investigate political radicals and organized crime syndicates. From its inception, the unit viewed radicalism and criminality as inseparable and understood both to be shaped by race, alternately using the names "Italian squad" and "anarchist squad" to describe itself. Chicago's police followed suit and established their own squad by spring 1908. Only in June 1908—four years after New York launched its antisubversion outfit—did the U.S. Division of Justice form the Federal Bureau of Intelligence. In its early years, the fledgling FBI undertook few investigations of political organizers. Various federal agencies—the Department of Commerce and Labor, the Post Office, the Secret Service—dabbled in investigating radicals and enforcing the Anarchist Exclusion Act passed by Congress in 1903, but none were devoted to combating subversion like New York's and Chicago's squads. It wasn't until America entered World War I in Europe, in fact, that the Department of Justice created an office dedicated to investigating political radicals, the Alien Enemy Bureau, where a young J. Edgar Hoover began his career in July 1917. In short, it was municipal police departments, not the federal government, that pioneered the political intelligence unit in law enforcement.[4]

Other cities formed squads to combat dissent in the immediate aftermath of the Russian Revolution and the war, as an upswell of nationalism and anticommunism fueled a wave of repression by the federal government, culminating in the mass arrests of radicals initiated by Attorney General A. Mitchell Palmer in late 1919 and early 1920. Philadelphia and Seattle established units shortly after the war, and by the early 1930s cities such as Detroit and Boston had as well, as the Great Depression helped drive labor radicalism and the membership rolls of the Communist Party of the United States of America swelled. Antiradical squads operated with almost total impunity in these years. It was not uncommon for their detectives to raid leftist meetings and rallies, breaking them up and arresting organizers on the spot. As they engaged in pitched battle with communists across the country, political intelligence units earned the sobriquet of red squads.[5]

Records were the lifeblood of the red squad. Purloined documents, newspaper clippings, surveillance photographs, vital records, criminal files—all of them provided content for the hallowed dossier. Red squads were, after all, intelligence units. While they might make arrests from time to time, political intelligence units' real power lay in their accumulation of data, much of it mundane but some of it unfavorable or even incriminating. Intelligence was a precious weapon, and red squads wielded it against radicals whenever they could.

The three years leading up to the United States' entry into World War II proved to be a watershed for political intelligence operations. First, in May 1938, Congress established the House Un-American Activities Committee, or HUAC, to investigate subversive activities on both the left and right. Police were eager to collaborate with HUAC, and detectives from Philadelphia, Detroit, Chicago, New York, and Los Angeles—cities where the committee had regional offices—conducted raids of Communist Party offices and testified to the committee about their investigations, often impugning dozens of suspected subversives as communists on the public record in a single hearing. At this time, red squads still had more experience doing on-the-ground political intelligence work than the FBI did.[6]

Only in fall 1939, at the outbreak of World War II, was the FBI finally recognized as the nation's leading domestic intelligence agency. In a public statement, President Franklin Roosevelt directed "all police officers, sheriffs, and other law enforcement officers . . . to turn over to the nearest representative of the Federal Bureau of Investigation any information obtained by them relating to espionage, counterespionage, sabotage, subversive activities and violation of neutrality laws." Roosevelt's statement made public much of what had been semisecret since the early 1920s, that the FBI had vastly expanded the scope of its work to monitor political activists.[7]

More importantly, local police now understood federal expectations, and they rededicated themselves to the gathering of political intelligence. In Houston, for example, the police department assigned five detectives to do political intelligence work in 1941. That June, an FBI agent praised Houston's police for working hard to "gather certain information concerning certain citizens in their communities." Indeed, as the *Houston Chronicle* was happy to report, "special squads from police departments in all sections of the country had been created to spend full time in gathering information for the F.B.I." in the wake of hostilities in Europe.[8]

Once the United States entered World War II, its alliance with the Soviet Union dampened the country's most fervent anticommunist impulses, and law enforcement turned their focus to German and Japanese sympathizers. But in the aftermath of Axis surrender in 1945, as relations between the United States and USSR deteriorated, anticommunist sentiment surged, and police intelligence units experienced a renewed sense of purpose.

True to their name, red squads took a leading role in the assault on communists that so exercised America after the war. In April 1946, just eight months after Japan's surrender, a brief write-up in the *New York Times* advertised the expansive mission of the NYPD intelligence unit, the oddly euphemistic Public Relations Squad. Noting the change of the outfit's name to the more probing Bureau of Special Services and Investigations (alternately BOSS or BOSSI), the *Times* explained that the unit "escorts official guests while they are in the city and watches over meetings throughout the city."[9]

"Watches over meetings"—the phrase conceals as much as it reveals. It was a dodge, maybe the recommended prose of police officials who wanted to downplay the secretive unit's dirty work. But it is as ominous as it is ambiguous, suggesting that wherever groups of people were assembling, BOSS hoped to monitor them.

Police understood subversives as the federal Smith Act of 1940 defined them: anyone who dared to "advocate" or even "teach the duty, necessity, desirability, or propriety of overthrowing or destroying any government in the United States." It was a remarkably broad ban on political expression. Federal authorities had only limited success in convicting people on these grounds—barely more than one hundred individuals were found guilty of violating the law, at a time when the Communist Party's membership numbered as high as 75,000—but the Smith Act's standard of subversive activity provided red squads with an easy rationale for harassing leftists and violating their constitutional rights, demanding their firing from their jobs, and driving them out of public life. Criminal prosecution was far from the only method of inflicting long-term harm on radicals.[10]

———

On October 18, 1947, three New York police officers entered a Harlem candy store owned by Samuel Symonette and accused the forty-two-year-old man of operating an illegal lottery. The officers then proceeded to beat Symonette with pistols and Pepsi bottles. Three days later, the *Daily Worker*, the Communist Party's official newspaper, carried a photograph of a badly bruised Symonette, propped up in bed with an assortment of bandages covering his face. In a report issued to the city's Gamblers and Felony courts, Symonette's doctor disclosed that his patient had possibly suffered skull fractures and internal hemorrhages, to be confirmed pending X-rays. The paper added that it was the "sixth police attack on civilians" in New York in less than two weeks.[11]

Benjamin Davis was troubled. In the decade after he had left Atlanta for New York, Davis had risen in the ranks of the Communist Party, becoming not only the president of its *Daily Worker* newspaper but also a New York city councilman representing Harlem—by far the most important of only a tiny handful of communists ever elected to public office in the United States. In his time on the council, Davis had submitted to the NYPD commissioner no fewer than twenty-six instances of police brutality identified by his office. Three days after Symonette's beating, Davis issued a resolution calling on his colleagues to hold hearings on police brutality as a "serious public issue in the City of New York menacing the peace and order of the community."

"Now for the first time," the councilman declared, "the police are on the defensive. We ought to keep them there." Davis and two hundred allies established a "Citizens Committee to End Police Brutality," while the Communist Party organized protests in Harlem, including in front of Symonette's shop. The following year, Davis pressed further when his office published "Police Brutality: Lynching, Northern Style," a twenty-page pamphlet condemning "a wave of police violence [that] was sweeping the city." Since his time in Atlanta, Davis had maintained a deep commitment to fighting police violence, the rare elected official to make it a signature issue.[12]

As in Atlanta, Davis's activism against police brutality in New York earned the ire of political police. In August 1946, NYPD commissioner Arthur Wallander condemned the councilman's efforts with the communist-affiliated Civil Rights Congress to protest police violence, accusing him of a "campaign of calumny" in which communists attempted to put the city's police into "a similar category with deplorable incidents of lynching or racial prejudice that have transpired in other sections of the country." Unlike in Atlanta, Davis's career would not survive attacks from authorities in New York.[13]

In July 1948, just months after the publication of "Police Brutality," Davis and the ten other members of the Communist Party's national board were indicted under the Smith Act for conspiring to "teach and advocate the overthrow and destruction of the Government of the U.S. by force and violence." Davis and five of the party's top leaders were arrested in New York, forced to do a proverbial "perp walk" on the steps of the federal courthouse at Foley Square before a throng of reporters (see figure 1.1). In what can only be

FIGURE 1.1. Police violence critic and communist New York City councilman Benjamin Davis outside the Foley Square federal courthouse in Manhattan in 1949, where he and ten other Communist Party officials were convicted and imprisoned for violating the Smith Act. LC-USZ62-111434, NYWT&S Collection, Prints and Photographs Division, LOC.

described as a show trial, the federal prosecution was choreographed to maximize the public relations damage to the party. Four hundred NYPD officers were stationed in and around the courthouse for the proceedings. After nine months of trial, all eleven of the indicted communists were convicted of violating the Smith Act in October 1949. Davis was stripped of his seat, a move that many of his colleagues on the council celebrated. After fighting unsuccessfully to overturn his conviction for two years, Davis entered the U.S. Penitentiary in Terre Haute, Indiana, in late 1951 and was imprisoned there until April 1955.[14]

As the campaign against communists raged across the United States, the NYPD's brass were eager to promote their red squad's contribution to the battle. Speaking at a luncheon of the Queens Chamber of Commerce in January 1950—just three months after Davis and his fellow Foley Square defendants had been convicted—NYPD Commissioner William O'Brien lavished praise on BOSS, predicting that its infiltration of the Communist Party would "never be discontinued." No sensible businessperson had reason to worry that radicals could endanger the city, O'Brien assured his audience. "I don't think any subversive movement in this city could get very far."[15]

———

In the wake of Davis's incarceration, the Civil Rights Congress (CRC) accelerated their crusade against police violence. The CRC was a legal defense organization created out of the remains of the National Negro Congress, the International Labor Defense, and the National Federation for Constitutional Liberties, and most of its members were either communists or individuals closely tied to the party. With its founding in 1946, the organization pursued a dual mission of advocating for Black defendants facing dubious, trumped-up criminal charges in the South, while also rushing to the aid of avowed communists facing a barrage of prosecutions as the Red Scare unfolded nationwide. Along the way, they won critical landmark cases that established new precedents for criminal procedure and the rights of defendants.[16]

In late 1951, the CRC produced what was at that time one of the most strident indictments of police violence in American history, *We Charge Genocide*. "Once the classic method of lynching was the rope. Now it is the policeman's bullet," the report's authors declared in their opening pages. "The killing of Negroes has become police policy in the United States."[17] Over more than two hundred pages, the report offered a meticulous, and gruesome, accounting of hundreds and hundreds of acts of state violence against Black Americans since the start of the 1940s, including numerous instances of police assaults and killings, not only in the South but across the entire country. Subtitled *The Historic Petition to the United Nations for Relief from a Crime of the United States Government Against the Negro People*, the report was submitted by the CRC to the United Nations as a formal complaint of genocide—which, as the report's authors emphasized, was not the total annihilation of a people but "any intent to destroy, in whole or in a part, a national, racial, ethnic, or religious group." Dozens of the day's leading Black and white leftists signed the document, including W.E.B. Du Bois, Mary Church Terrell, Stetson Kennedy, Claudia Jones, and Paul and Eslanda Robeson.

CRC leader William Patterson released the report in dramatic fashion by presenting it in person at a meeting of the U.N. General Assembly in Paris. While *We Charge Genocide* garnered considerable attention outside the United States, especially on the left, American media mostly ignored the publication. Federal authorities, meanwhile, punished the CRC for embarrassing the government on the global stage. Patterson had his passport revoked and was sentenced to three months in prison on charges of contempt of Congress due to his refusal to testify on the CRC's funding sources. The NAACP came close to publicly condemning the report as subversive, though it ultimately backed away from such plans. Within several years, the CRC would be broken by the backlash it faced in the wake of *We Charge Genocide* and forced to disband.

As much as police tried to tar all their critics as subversive, Black detractors of police violence were by no means limited to the Communist Party. None other than Jackie Robinson, himself an ardent anticommunist, testified to HUAC in 1949 that policy brutality was a common reality for Black Americans. "Just because communists kick up a big fuss over racial discrimination when it suits their purposes, a lot of people try to pretend that the whole issue is a creation of communist imagination," Robinson explained. But as much as he objected to their ideology, Robinson conceded that communists got some things right: "The fact that because it is a communist who denounces injustice in the courts, police brutality and lynching, when it happens, doesn't change the truth of those charges." And yet, no matter how hard Black leaders tried, by the start of the 1950s they could not dispel the common perception among many whites that police brutality was a trivial rarity, nothing more than a red herring that communists exploited to embarrass America's government.[18]

––––

Jacob Jackson was playing a sidewalk game of dice with his wife and friends in Hell's Kitchen on August 9, 1952, when police officers arrived to disperse the crowd. The thirty-one-year-old Black truck driver replied to the officers that they should mind their own business. The officers responded by beating and almost killing Jackson, sending him to the hospital, where doctors had to perform two brain surgeries to keep him alive. Six months later, Jackson, who earned just $54 most weeks (or roughly $650 in 2025 dollars), was still unable to drive his truck.

To the dismay but not surprise of Black New Yorkers, the officers ended up facing no charges. But many were shocked when Jackson was tried and convicted for assaulting an officer. And the case revealed an even bigger bombshell. The month before police had beaten Jackson, top NYPD officials had met with U.S. Assistant Attorney General James McInerney of the Department of Justice's Criminal Division to propose an extraordinary arrangement between the agencies.

NYPD officials had lobbied McInerney, himself a former FBI agent, to forgo investigating any civil rights complaints against New York officers for police brutality received by the Department of Justice. Such investigations, the NYPD charged, not only were "destroying morale" but were "seized upon by Communist fronts" with the intent "to make the Police Department appear to poor advantage." The FBI, the police officials argued, would be better off returning any accusations of police brutality by NYPD officers to the NYPD's leadership so that they could investigate their own officers.

Without approval from his superiors, McInerney granted the NYPD officials their request. When the agreement was disclosed by the press in February 1953, the president of New York's NAACP chapter, Ella Baker, and NAACP Legal Redress chair Edward Jacko rushed off a telegram to Mayor Vincent Impellitteri condemning the "conspiracy" and urging the mayor "to save the city from further disgrace of this nature by the immediate removal" of Police Commissioner George Monaghan. The NYPD's secret agreement, Baker and Jacko charged, signaled that the department had "acted in bad faith in its investigation of numerous complaints of police brutality brought to its attention."[19]

While Commissioner O'Brien had bragged just three years earlier that his red squad easily curtailed communists' influence, other members of the NYPD now promoted the notion—if not sincerely, at least for their own political advantage—that leftists remained a major threat. "The policemen in New York City are targets of Communists and other radical groups," claimed John Carton, president of the Patrolmen's Benevolent Association, in a telegram rebutting the NAACP's demands sent to Congressman Kenneth B. Keating of the U.S. House Judiciary Committee in early 1953. "The present hue and cry over alleged violations of human rights is in line with communistic propaganda."

The NAACP was far from a communist organization, but its demand that the mayor fire the city's top cop was a bold move— especially coming from a Black woman. Yet if anyone in the NAACP was willing to confront powerful white politicians, it was Ella Baker (see figure 1.2). Born in 1903, Baker was independent and strong-willed, graduating from college first in her class before embarking on a career with the NAACP at the start of the 1930s. She made a name for herself challenging the organization's male leadership and questioning its top-down hierarchy in her role as director of local branches in the 1940s. Baker was not going to be intimidated by the Patrolmen's Benevolent Association, the NYPD, or anyone else. "Police brutality cases are not child's play," she told the *Amsterdam News*. "They represent a fight to the finish."[20]

Two days after news of the NYPD and FBI's agreement broke, Baker helped organize an emergency meeting of major civil rights and labor leaders in New York. Attendees included NAACP executive secretary Walter White and his successor Roy Wilkins, representatives of the American Civil Liberties Union (ACLU) and the Brotherhood of Sleeping Car Porters, and NAACP chief counsel

FIGURE 1.2. Ella Baker led the New York chapter of the NAACP's campaign against police violence in 1953. LC-USZ62-118852, NYWT&S Collection, Prints and Photographs Division, LOC.

Thurgood Marshall, who two months earlier had completed the opening round of oral arguments for *Brown v. Board of Education* before the Supreme Court. Characterizing McInerney as "as bad as anyone who has been in the Department of Justice," Marshall denounced the former FBI agent's civil rights record.

In a press release the following day, the coalition reiterated and expanded upon Baker's initial demand, calling for the firing of the officials responsible for the secret pact and for federal authorities to investigate all police misconduct cases in New York City and to refer any with merit to a federal grand jury. They also urged the creation of a municipal civilian board to review all police misconduct charges.[21]

Baker was convinced that working-class Black people in communities across the country regarded police abuses as a crisis. She had acquired this view through years of work on the ground, while many of the NAACP's middle-class leaders with limited experience in community organizing failed to recognize the severity of the police violence many Black people faced.

In interviews later in her life, Baker recalled the imaginary figure of "John Jones who got drunk on every Saturday night" in Black communities across the country. By the early 1950s, young Black people in these towns had "begun to demand the right to decide whether or not John Jones, who was arrested by the cop and beaten up, whether he was the one they would go down and get out of jail." The more established, respectable Black leaders, Baker recalled, "might have had grave doubts about the virtue of going down and . . . getting him out of jail," especially if Jones "was a drinker and not a church goer." But by 1952, as president of the NAACP's New York chapter, Baker firmly believed that she had a duty to help the John Joneses of her community who endured violence at the hands of police.[22]

The Patrolmen's Benevolent Association wasted little time attacking Baker and the NAACP. "Policemen also have civil rights," John Carton proclaimed, castigating NYPD critics as "pawns" carrying out a campaign "in line with communistic propaganda." But for Baker, the charge that the campaign against police violence amounted to subversion was "pure tommyrot and does not deserve the dignity of an answer." Far from radical, the NAACP faced criticisms from the Left for being too eager to expel members suspected of communist activities, efforts for which J. Edgar Hoover had praised the organization. But here was the NYPD, accusing the organization's New York chapter of trafficking in subversion as they condemned the department for its repeated assaults on Black citizens.[23]

Baker knew all too well the persecution Davis, Patterson, and other prominent Black critics of police violence had endured—but this did not dissuade her from pressing city and federal authorities to intervene against the NYPD's attacks on Black citizens and its secret deal with the FBI. Adam Clayton Powell, newly elected to Congress to represent Harlem, launched extensive hearings to probe the issue. Embarrassed by the bad publicity, the Department of Justice rescinded its agreement to abstain from investigating the NYPD for brutality and transferred McInerney out of its Criminal Division.

Two months after Powell's hearings began, the NYPD established the Civilian Complaint Review Board to vet accusations of officer misconduct. This was a public-facing entity responsible for adjudicating officer complaints long demanded by activists. The board also accelerated the process for handling complaints. Previously, an investigation of an officer for misconduct could not begin if a civil suit was pending against the officer in the courts, and political pressure for accountability often dissolved amid long trial times. Now, departmental investigations of misconduct were to start as soon as a complaint was made.

All in all, however, the culture of racist policing in New York remained intact. Mayor Impellitteri never faltered in his support of the department, and not only did a federal grand jury refuse to bring charges against the officers who beat Jackson, but Jackson's conviction for assaulting an officer was not overturned. The Civilian Complaint Review Board, meanwhile, had no civilian members despite its name. Instead, a board of three NYPD officials processed complaints from the public. One of the members was Deputy Commissioner Frank Fristensky, who had worked closely with Monaghan to secure the original agreement with the FBI. Harlem's city councilman Earl Brown lambasted the board as "the same old system with a new coat of whitewash" as he dismissed a new "human relations" course for officers—essentially racial sensitivity training—as "the current big joke of the Police Department."[24]

If anything, the battle over the NYPD-FBI deal highlighted how much civil rights groups had to lose and how little they had to gain if they challenged police departments. Yes, the NAACP had brought major attention to the festering crisis of police violence against Black New Yorkers, and it had gotten federal authorities to admit that the

NYPD was not up to sorting out its own disciplinary problems. And the Civilian Complaint Review Board, as weak as it was, was better than nothing. But those victories appeared ever more modest as time went on. The NAACP's campaign had expended precious resources and political capital after months of fending off accusations of communist subversion, and both the organization and Jackson had relatively little to show for it. For the rest of the decade, the NAACP's New York branch and national leadership continued to take on civil litigation on behalf of individual victims of police violence—but they would not return to organizing community campaigns against police abuses for many years.[25]

———

At the same time that New York police resisted efforts to stem violence against Black citizens, their colleagues on the West Coast were busy expanding their capacity to deploy surveillance against activists. Of all local law enforcement officials in the country, perhaps none embraced surveillance with more enthusiasm than William Parker, the chief of the Los Angeles Police Department (LAPD). In November 1950, just three months after starting his position, Parker and his newly appointed intelligence chief James Hamilton testified before the U.S. Senate to promote L.A.'s intelligence unit as a model for departments around the country. As Parker explained, the unit's thirty-eight officers and detectives employed a system of "arm's-length surveillance" in which they did "not fraternize with the people they are investigating" but, instead, constantly monitored them. The squad was ostensibly a unit devoted to gathering "information on racketeers" and organized crime. But at the high tide of American anticommunism, the unit prepared "dossiers on all of these people who come to our attention," Parker admitted—without specifying exactly whom he intended to investigate.

Parker and Hamilton believed that police departments across the country were hamstrung in their efforts to share information with each other. Together they called for the creation of a federal clearinghouse of intelligence available to any police department "that really wants to do something about crime." Hamilton rejected the suggestion that the FBI could assume the responsibility, contending that the Bureau kept most files to itself and "so far has not been interested" in supplying local police with intelligence, even though, as Parker pointedly observed, "they are in a good position to assist us." The FBI did not take the criticism lightly, and Hoover, who grew to strongly dislike Parker, saw no need to accede to the Los Angeles chief's demands.[26]

Instead, by 1956, Parker and Hamilton set about establishing their own national surveillance network, the Law Enforcement Intelligence Unit (LEIU). The LAPD officials' basic idea was to create a clearinghouse through which local police departments could share files without relying on the FBI. While the LEIU's stated mission was to share information on organized crime syndicates, behind the scenes it embraced the role of collector of political intelligence as well. The Bureau in turn dismissed the LEIU in internal memos as workaday police officers who "swap information back and forth, have no legal standing, and, in fact, to a degree may be illegally so doing." But the Bureau didn't publicly condemn Parker and Hamilton's pet project, most likely because it wanted to deflect attention from its own political intelligence work. The LEIU prospered as an exchange network for intelligence on both organized crime and political radicals, and by 1962 it had expanded its membership to sixty-three police departments concentrated in the West and Midwest.[27]

The FBI were not the only critics to assail Parker's use of surveillance. In 1951, A. L. Wirin, a lawyer with the Southern California chapter of the ACLU, filed suit against Parker and the LAPD for their practice of planting secret recording devices without warrants. A prominent critic of political policing, Wirin—whose first initials stood for Abraham Lincoln—had arrived in the United States from Russia as an eight-year-old, settling with his family in Boston. In 1920, he became the ACLU's first full-time attorney; eleven years later, the organization's Southern California chapter hired him as their first civil rights lawyer.

By championing the freedoms of a wide range of unpopular groups, Wirin earned the enmity of the LAPD. In January 1934, he was representing striking farmworkers in the Imperial Valley east of

FIGURE 1.3. ACLU attorney and police surveillance critic A. L. Wirin represented accused communists before the House Un-American Activities Committee and was himself called to testify in 1959. *Los Angeles Times* Photographic Archive, Library Special Collections, Charles E. Young Research Library, UCLA.

San Diego when he was kidnapped and beaten by a group of anti-union vigilantes that included Red Hynes, the head of the LAPD's political intelligence unit. Wirin responded by suing his kidnappers and filing a complaint with the U.S. Attorney's Office, triggering an investigation by the Department of Justice. During World War II, Wirin sued the federal government for its internment of Japanese Americans, laying the groundwork for Fred Korematsu's unsuccessful petition to the U.S. Supreme Court to halt Roosevelt's detention program. And though he himself was not a communist, Wirin represented numerous individuals accused of subversion before both HUAC and criminal courts as anticommunism raged after the war (see figure 1.3).[28]

Parker was likely already aware of Wirin when the attorney served the chief with the paperwork for his surveillance suit in 1951. Claiming standing not as a surveillance target but as a taxpayer, Wirin challenged the legality of all funds—no matter the amount—that public officials spent to break into private homes or offices to install recording devices without property owners' consent. But Parker was unfazed by Wirin's constitutional arguments, and he replied to the court in July 1952 that the LAPD had no intention of halting its nonconsensual intrusions onto private property to plant bugs. Three years later, a State Superior judge ruled in Parker's favor, maintaining that the courts had no power to restrain police from such work.

In 1957, Wirin appealed his suit to California's Supreme Court. Two years earlier, in the landmark case *People v. Cahan*, the state's highest court affirmed the exclusionary rule invalidating evidence obtained illegally by police, a decision that enraged Parker and would ultimately provide the basis for the U.S Supreme Court's landmark decision on warrantless searches, *Mapp v. Ohio*. Now, in reviewing Wirin's case, the State Supreme Court ruled 4–1 in favor of the ACLU attorney. The justices enjoined the LAPD from operating warrantless recording devices on private property on the grounds that it violated both the Fourth and Fourteenth Amendments of the U.S. Constitution.

In their decision, the State Supreme Court articulated a concept that was simple enough for any layperson to understand: "Public officials must themselves follow the law." Parker and countless other law enforcement advocates of political intelligence work, however, would continue to reject that argument, especially in the years ahead as a movement for racial equality flourished across the country.[29]

———

At its core, intelligence is information. "About 80% of all information about what is going on in Communist countries," Central Intelligence Agency expert Andrew Tully wrote in his 1962 book, *CIA: The Inside Story*, "is obtained openly." Anthony Bouza, a detective with BOSS in New York, endorsed Tully's dictum as an accurate description of his unit's work as well. But what about the other 20 percent of information political intelligence units got their hands on?[30]

Red squads took full advantage of the constitutional gray area they occupied, as their favored methods of political policing rested on matters of unsettled law. In *Wirin v. Parker*, for instance, the California Supreme Court only invalidated recording microphones installed without a property owner's consent—not all forms of warrantless surveillance. Federal courts had yet to answer the larger questions surrounding electronic surveillance, so law enforcement officials were often free to treat warrants as unnecessary. Police had near free rein to use phone taps as they wished, and they could photograph whomever they pleased, whenever and wherever they wanted. And as to whether police could amass dossiers on private citizens who showed no indication of planning or committing a crime—the courts had said next to nothing. Police believed that they could.

This begged the larger question of what forms of political dissent crossed the line from constitutionally protected speech into the realm of tangible threats against government. After all, the conviction of Benjamin Davis and his ten codefendants had rested on their membership in the Communist Party, not on any concrete plans to foment insurrection. The Supreme Court began to address this matter in 1957 with *Yates v. United States*, ruling 6–1 that the federal government could not ban the expression of any general ideology of "overthrowing organized government by unlawful means"—such as communism—but, rather, the narrower "advocacy of action for the accomplishment of that purpose." Though the ruling suggested that individual state laws against insurrection might be too broad as well, police showed little interest in such matters as they continued to investigate activists for radical affiliations that fell far short of concrete plots to overthrow the government.[31]

The *Yates* decision signaled a cooling of the Red Scare, at a time when communists appeared to be at their lowest point of influence in decades. Writing in 1959, historian David Shannon dismissed the Communist Party as "destined to join a collection of other sects as an exhibit in the museum of American Left Wing politics." In the two years following Soviet Premier Nikita Khrushchev's revelations about Stalin's crimes in 1956, the party's U.S. membership plummeted from twenty thousand to just three thousand, the most sizable decline in its history. American communists, Shannon concluded, were "an impotent party." The "reds" that red squads had so diligently

FIGURE 1.4. Sound truck sponsored by the communist-affiliated Civil Rights Congress condemning police violence as an act of genocide, Brooklyn, 1951. Courtesy of *People's World*.

investigated for decades were now besieged, if not paralyzed, and far from the force they had represented during the Depression and war.[32]

With communists virtually extinguished in America, how could red squads continue to justify their existence? Surely, they would need to identify new targets. As the communist menace began to dissipate, political police envisioned emerging threats on the horizon. For decades, red squads had treated activists for racial justice as nuisances scattered throughout the country, a subset of the larger plague of communists but not a threat that deserved attention equivalent to Marxist radicals. But as the Communist Party hit bottom in the second half of the 1950s, police intelligence units came to realize that a brewing movement against Jim Crow demanded their attention.

2

Jim Crow's Cops

On December 5, 1955, Black leaders in Montgomery, Alabama, held a mass meeting calling for a boycott of the city's buses. Four days earlier, a seamstress and NAACP organizer named Rosa Parks had been arrested by police officers Fletcher Day and Dempsey Mixon for refusing to give up her seat to a white passenger. The officers were carrying out a warrant signed by bus driver James Blake, who was empowered to order arrests of passengers by a Montgomery city ordinance dating back to 1900. This was a cardinal feature of Jim Crow: police could punish you for so-called race mixing, but so could many other whites, some of them legally.[1]

Leading the meeting against Parks's arrest on that December night in 1955 was a virtually unknown minister, the twenty-seven-year-old Martin Luther King Jr. Local Black leaders had chosen King to serve as president of a new organization, the Montgomery Improvement Association. But it was another pastor in attendance that evening, Fred Shuttlesworth of Birmingham—and not King—who would soon emerge as the foremost critic of racist policing in Alabama, if not the entire South.

Shuttlesworth later recalled a harrowing unwritten rule governing Black life in Birmingham in these years: "If the Ku Klux Klan doesn't stop you, the police can; and if the police fail, then the courts will."[2]

In the decade following World War II, a string of bombings against Black homeowners in once all-white neighborhoods in Birmingham went unsolved by authorities, raising suspicions that police were collaborating with terrorists in the hopes of maintaining residential segregation. By 1955, Birmingham was the only major city in the South that still had an all-white police force; many smaller municipalities hired Black officers, but they typically limited their power to arrest whites or patrol in white communities. In a city where the line between the Klan and law enforcement was indistinguishable, Black demands for desegregating the police were about much more than diversifying public employment.[3]

As the thirty-three-year-old pastor of Bethel Baptist Church and membership chairman of Birmingham's NAACP chapter, Shuttlesworth threw himself into a campaign to demand that Birmingham police hire their first Black officers in summer 1955. Calls for Black police officers in Birmingham were nothing new, but that year demands to desegregate the city's force intensified in the wake of the police beating of Charles Patrick, a Black man jailed for arguing with a white woman over a parking spot. Upon hearing of the incident, the woman's husband—who happened to be a police officer—visited Patrick in jail and assaulted him.

Shuttlesworth's campaign against police brutality and the white monopoly on law enforcement in Birmingham had been underway for months when the bus boycott in Montgomery was just getting off the ground in December 1955. Like the boycott, the Birmingham campaign drew on a reservoir of Black activism stretching back decades, part of what historian Jacquelyn Dowd Hall has termed the "long civil rights movement." The anticommunist hysteria of the early postwar years had beaten back most of these efforts in states such as Alabama, however.[4]

As in the campaign for Black police in Birmingham, the NAACP played a critical role in both the Montgomery boycott and the *Brown v. Board* case decided by the Supreme Court the previous year. Shocked by these newfound challenges to segregation, Alabama's attorney general obtained a court order in June 1956 barring the organization from operating in the state on the grounds that it was an unregistered, "foreign" corporation. In Birmingham, Shuttlesworth and his NAACP colleagues acted swiftly, and just four days after the injunction they formed a new organization to work around the law, the Alabama Christian Movement for Human Rights (ACMHR).

Later that year, on December 20, the U.S. Supreme Court sided with the Montgomery boycotters in *Browder v. Gayle*, ruling that laws requiring segregated public transit were unconstitutional. Within days, Shuttlesworth telegrammed the Birmingham City Commission to demand that they desegregate the city's buses, and he vowed that he and other Black residents would defy segregated seating restrictions on city buses as soon as the day after Christmas.[5]

On Christmas Day, as the reverend planned the blitz on the city's bus lines, his home was shaken by a massive explosion. A bundle of dynamite detonated outside the parsonage where the Shuttlesworth family lived and destroyed most of the house. Police officers arrived on the scene in record time, even before the reverend and his family were able to emerge from the rubble. Their unusual timeliness sparked speculation that police had forewarning of the attack. Before long, some fifteen hundred Black residents from the neighborhood had gathered in front of the Shuttlesworth home to see if the family had made it out alive. Many of the bystanders were armed and prepared to defend their community from further attacks, whether they came from police, the Klan, or someone else. But when they tried to rush into the house to help the Shuttlesworths, the police stopped them, intent on slowing down any assistance to the family.

Miraculously, the entire Shuttlesworth family survived. A police officer surveying the destruction showed little interest in catching the perpetrators but, instead, offered a bit of advice. "Reverend, if I were you, I'd get out of town as fast as I could." Without the least bit of interest in the officer's advice, Shuttlesworth snapped back, "You go back and tell your Klan brethren that if God could keep me through this, then I'm here for the duration."[6]

His house in ruins, Shuttlesworth led a contingent downtown to desegregate Birmingham's buses the very next day (see figure 2.1).

FIGURE 2.1. Reverend Fred Shuttlesworth, second from right, on his way to desegregate Birmingham's public bus system the day after he survived a dynamite attack that was likely perpetrated by the Ku Klux Klan with the consent of local police, December 26, 1956. Photo by Robert Adams, *Birmingham News*. Donated by Alabama Media Group. Alabama Department of Archives and History.

The minister sported a broad-brimmed hat and tan coat and flashed a remarkably broad smile for someone who had just survived an attack on his life and been told by law enforcement to leave town. Some 150 Black passengers joined him in riding in the white sections of buses; rather than removing themselves from the transit system, as boycotters in Montgomery had, they put their bodies on the line with the goal of getting arrested. Police responded by jailing Shuttlesworth and twenty riders, before releasing them the next day.[7]

———

When Shuttlesworth denounced the police officer's "Klan brethren," he meant what he said. He was not offering a figurative critique of racist law enforcement but, instead, a concrete claim made by many Black Birminghamians: that the local police force collaborated with the Ku Klux Klan. The string of unsolved bombings that drew close to no concern from police left them little choice but to reach that conclusion. Eyewitness reports of police near the scenes of bombings further fueled this belief. A local minister testified in court that he had seen a police officer parked blocks from a home just minutes after it was bombed, sitting in his car as though nothing had happened, until another police car approached and flashed its lights as if to signal a completed job.[8]

In the Jim Crow South, white supremacy relied on the law. Racial segregation was spelled out in minute detail in state statutes and municipal ordinances. Where one sat on a bus or in a theater, where one attended school, which public library one patronized, if any—these things were established in legislation that local authorities spent considerable time enforcing. Police had the power to punish Black people—and occasionally whites—who defied the laws of white supremacy. They arrested them, or beat them, or in some cases, killed them.

But lawlessness was an essential ingredient of this system of racial oppression as well. Most horrendously, more than four thousand African Americans were lynched between 1877 and 1950. The vast majority of these racial terror killings took place in the South, barred by law but often carried out before large audiences. Police tended to ignore this racist violence as it happened—and in some cases, they took part. Law enforcement might receive advance notice of a lynching and allow it to proceed. Other lynchings they might facilitate with unfortified jails where mobs could kidnap prisoners with ease. In some cases, officers led lynch mobs. Many lynchings—up to half in Georgia, according to one study—were acts of retribution against Black people accused of attacking law enforcement officers. And even in the worst cases of racial violence, local law enforcement enjoyed almost full discretion whether to investigate—and they usually chose not to.[9]

Virtually every Southerner understood this grim reality. For Black people, this was a key to survival: recognizing that officers of the law were no strangers to vigilantism and that they might permit or even assist lawless whites in attacking or killing them if they defied the norms of white supremacy. Most Black Southerners saw it as nothing less than an act of suicide to confront law enforcement officers for their complicity in such vigilantism. But after Fred Shuttlesworth survived the bomb attack on his home on Christmas Day 1956, he saw nothing to gain by avoiding conflicts with the police or any other defenders of white supremacy.

On January 10, 1957, barely two weeks after the bombing, Shuttlesworth joined a group of Black ministers from across the South in Atlanta to consider next moves in the wake of the victory in Montgomery. Although Shuttlesworth and King were not particularly close, the two had emerged as the most activist Black ministers in Birmingham and Montgomery, respectively, and they saw each other as natural allies. At the conference's conclusion on January 11, the roughly sixty clergy and organizers in attendance issued "A Statement to the South and Nation," a press release announcing the establishment of a new organization pushing for racial equality in the South. While the group struggled to settle on a name, they eventually called themselves the Southern Christian Leadership Conference (SCLC).

The attendees couched their calls for equality in terms that embraced lawfulness and rejected vigilantism.

We call upon every white Southerner to realize that the major choice may no longer be segregation or integration, but anarchy or law. We remind them that communities control their destinies only when order prevails. Disorder places all major decisions in the hands of state or federal police. We do not prefer this, for our ultimate aim is to win understanding with our neighbors. In a profound sense, the lawlessness and violence our people face is blood upon the hands of Southern Christians.[10]

Now was the time for the South's police to step forward and protect those demanding equality against deadly violence of the sort Shuttlesworth had experienced on Christmas Day. Every law enforcement official had a professional and moral duty to prevent the slaughter of those organizing against white supremacy in the South. Though they hoped this was possible, the SCLC suspected that local departments might not bear this responsibility. Change would come, with or without the support of police.

———

In June, Birmingham elected a new head of police when Eugene Connor eked out a narrow victory to become the city's commissioner of public safety. Better known by his nickname "Bull," Connor had a long history in the city, having served previously as commissioner for almost twenty years until resigning in 1954 when he was caught having an extramarital affair with a secretary. Under Connor, Birmingham's red squad had distinguished themselves as some of the most vicious political police in the country, raiding properties associated with communists and detaining suspected radicals for days on end without charges. For instances where officers preferred prosecution, their job was made easy by a municipal ordinance against criminal anarchy and another that banned the possession of purported radical literature—not only Marxist publications but even liberal ones such as *The New Republic*. As if these tools were not enough to stymie left-wing activity, Connor penned an additional ordinance passed by the city council in 1950 that essentially banned the Communist Party.

Even in Birmingham, renowned as one of America's most racist cities, Connor had long distinguished himself as a segregationist of almost unmatched determination. This had been the crux of his campaign to get back in office, as he blasted the sitting head of police as insufficiently committed to racial separation. Connor was a short, slight man but ferocious in temperament. Many people assumed that his sobriquet described a man with a large frame, only to learn upon meeting him that "Bull" referred instead to the power of his voice, a nickname he picked up decades earlier as a minor league baseball radio announcer. Connor's aggressive demeanor and a bullheaded self-certainty in all matters—chief among them white supremacy—made the name stick.[11]

The ACMHR knew that the SCLC's hopes of Birmingham police making concessions to their growing desegregation movement were close to nil. But Connor's return to office proved an irresistible provocation for Shuttlesworth. Like the commissioner of public safety, the reverend was not a large man, weighing just over 150 pounds and standing barely five foot, eight inches. And like Connor, he had a fiery disposition and pursued his cause with single-minded devotion and religious zeal—but in his case, it was dismantling white supremacy, not preserving it.

Shuttlesworth's contrasts with King are more intriguing. King was a product of Atlanta's Black elite, the son of a prominent minister, a bookish and worldly pastor with two bachelor's degrees and a doctorate. Shuttlesworth had grown up on a farm, raised by his mother and bootlegger stepfather in semirural Jefferson County outside Birmingham, before becoming the first in his family to graduate from college. If King was a determined and calculating changemaker, patiently prodding more risk-averse ministers into action against discrimination, Shuttlesworth was an unmitigated radical among the SCLC's leadership, calling on his fellow clergy to charge full speed ahead against white supremacy. Time and again, his colleagues tried to talk him out of protest plans, only for Shuttlesworth to brush aside their calls for restraint.[12]

Desegregating Birmingham's police department had remained one of Shuttlesworth's top priorities since his days as local NAACP membership chairman. Shortly after the founding of the ACMHR, in June 1956, Shuttlesworth had convinced two Black men to apply for positions on the force, but they were turned away. One of them, Clyde Jones, was fired from his job at a munitions factory the day after submitting his application.

Almost two years later, in April 1958, Shuttlesworth encouraged the other applicant, George Johnson, to sue local authorities in federal court for denying his bid to join the department. As a U.S. District Court contemplated Johnson's suit, Shuttlesworth and ACMHR supporters appeared at a City Commission meeting in June to confront Connor and demand that Birmingham hire Johnson. In a tense exchange, Connor refused to even consider Shuttlesworth's appeal, prompting the ACMHR contingent to exit the meeting. After they left, Connor made a bizarre accusation in front of the audience and gathered reporters, claiming that Shuttlesworth knew much more than he let on about the explosion at his home on Christmas Day 1956. The minister, he implied, had planted the bomb himself to garner sympathy. Connor challenged the minister to a lie detector test to set the record straight.[13]

In a press release the following day, Shuttlesworth rejected the notion that he had anything to do with the bombing, before turning the tables on the commissioner. Shuttlesworth reported that he was glad to submit to a lie detector, just as long as Connor would do the same and answer questions about his racial attitudes and the string of bombings of Black homes across Birmingham. This, he believed, would not only "clear up a lot of rumors and confusion" but shed light on "the whole fabric of Klannish violence and law enforcement in this city."[14]

It was a remarkably brave claim. Birmingham's police and the Klan, Shuttlesworth suggested, were cut from the same cloth. They were interwoven. With a single word, "fabric," the ACMHR leader had suggested what so many Black leaders were afraid to say in public: Birmingham police had a hand in bombings against Black citizens.

Connor never did sit down for a lie detector test.

———

On June 28, three weeks after Shuttlesworth issued his challenge to Connor, police paid a visit to Bethel Baptist Church. There they found armed guards defending the Shuttlesworths' home and the church, where men from the ACMHR had insisted on standing watch ever since the Christmas Day bombing. The officers confiscated four rifles from the sentries and charged them with illegal firearm possession.

Early the next morning, one of Shuttlesworth's guards discovered a large metal can with a lit fuse outside the church. Thinking fast, he rushed the can out to the middle of the street and then ran to seek cover. The can exploded moments later, leaving a sizable crater. When firefighters and police arrived on the scene, they suggested like Connor had weeks earlier that Shuttlesworth or some of his congregants had set the explosion themselves. But when police asked eight witnesses from Bethel to submit to lie detector tests, all agreed and passed without problem.[15]

None of this fazed Shuttlesworth. If anything, it only emboldened him to step up his attacks on Connor and the police department. In August, the ACMHR president sent a letter—first to Connor, then to the City Commission, and finally to the FBI—in which he condemned the Birmingham police investigation of the bombings and raised the possibility that officers had facilitated the attacks. The letter outlined a string of raids, seizures, and hostile visits by police at Bethel over the previous thirteen months. "The taking of weapons and intimidating of guards are serving to deny us protection and to leave us utterly helpless and at the mercy of bombers," Shuttlesworth charged. "To deliberately or inadvertently allow the property to be bombed again would be a most dastardly act. And the fact that high officials are leading those excursions lead us to believe them the acts of high policy."[16]

Shuttlesworth's hopes that federal authorities might reprimand Connor were unfounded. But the Bethel minister understood the strategic value of documenting police abuses and recounting them directly to Connor, putting the city's head of law enforcement on notice and forcing him to recognize that Shuttlesworth was unafraid to push back against the department's cruel criminality.

As summer turned to fall, the ACMHR continued their efforts to desegregate buses in Birmingham, as city authorities refused to implement the ruling the Supreme Court had issued in *Browder v. Gayle* nearly two years earlier. On October 20, Shuttlesworth and

ACMHR allies boarded city buses and sat in sections reserved for white passengers as news reporters they had alerted about the protest watched. Never one to miss an opportunity to needle the head of police, Shuttlesworth offered a sarcastic rationale for the action: "Mr. Connor asked us good negroes to use our common sense and that is just what we are doing." A group of thirty fanned out onto the buses, but when drivers balked at taking them to their destinations, more than a dozen of them were arrested on the spot. Connor demanded Shuttlesworth's arrest the next day, and within hours the minister surrendered at city hall to avoid being arrested at home after dark.

Police charged the fourteen arrestees with a variety of crimes, including disturbing the peace. As Shuttlesworth languished in jail for nearly a week, his wife, Ruby, received an offer from Dr. King to send a delegation of Montgomery's boycott organizers to strategize with the ACMHR in Birmingham. Solomon Seay, Hillmon Hubbard, and A. W. Wilson—three of Montgomery's leading Black ministers— arrived at the Shuttlesworth home around midday on October 27, where they met with a group of about twenty of Shuttlesworth's allies. Within moments, Birmingham police detectives arrived unannounced. Once the ministers gave their names, the detectives charged them with vagrancy and carted them off to jail, claiming that they lacked adequate identification. "Birmingham does not need outside agitators coming into our city and dabbling in our affairs," Connor announced to the press as Seay, Hubbard, and Wilson were jailed and questioned for more than five hours.

Though the three men were released before the end of the day, their arrest unleashed a firestorm. As an outraged King warned, "If the people of good will, both Negro and white, will not take a stand against these gestapo-like tactics, our southland will be plunged into a state of fascism the likes the world has never known." Within days, the U.S. Justice Department's Civil Rights Division announced that it was launching an investigation. Then, on November 13, U.S. Attorney General William Rogers stated that he would convene a grand jury to look into the matter, explaining that Birmingham police's blanket refusal to discuss the arrests with federal authorities left him no choice. Indeed, months earlier, Connor had announced that his department would not cooperate with any federal investigations, insisting, "We don't need any of the Washington left wing civil rights committee goons snooping around down here."[17]

The ministers' arrest meanwhile raised an unsettling question for Shuttlesworth and ACMHR members. This had been a meeting in a private home in the Black community, unannounced to the public, and police had raided it almost as soon as it started. How had the detectives known when and where it was taking place? As Shuttlesworth and his allies searched for answers, Birmingham police intensified their campaign of repression. Detectives from the department made a habit of attending the ACMHR's meetings, showing up at various churches where the group gathered and sitting down in the audience to take notes.

On November 24, 1958, the ACMHR passed a resolution to prohibit law enforcement officials from attending their meetings. Later that day, the Reverend Charles Billups of New Pilgrim Baptist Church attempted to stop detectives from entering the group's meeting. But the detectives barged their way in, and one of them ran into Billups, his lapel lightly brushing Billups's outstretched hand. The two detectives insisted on staying for the duration of the meeting, threatening to arrest everyone present if they tried to enforce the ban. The following night, two officers came to Billups's home and arrested the minister, claiming that he had laid hands on the detective and interfered with his performance of his duties. Billups was fined $100 and sentenced to sixty days in jail.

Law enforcement utilized ever more disruptive tactics against the ACMHR. In December 1959, the group was meeting at the St. James Baptist Church in north Birmingham when they were surprised to hear a blast of sirens accompanied by red flashing lights. A team of uniformed firefighters armed with axes and escorted by about ten police officers rushed into the church, claiming that they had received reports of a fire. They proceeded to parade through the chapel for almost fifteen minutes, purportedly in search of the fire; in the process, they scared away many of the meeting's attendees.

It was an act of naked intimidation that only confirmed Birmingham police's determination to block Black organizing efforts. One way or another, Connor's department intended to stop their critics in the ACMHR.[18]

———

Two months later, on February 1, 1960, a bewildered police officer in Greensboro, North Carolina, approached Franklin McCain, David Richmond, Joseph McNeil, and Ezell Blair Jr. not long after they sat down to eat. As McCain later recalled, the man gripped

> his club in his hand, just sort of knocking it in his hand, and just looking mean and red and a little bit upset and a little bit disgusted. You had the feeling that he didn't know what the hell to do. You had the feeling that this is the first time that this big bad man with a gun and the club had been pushed in a corner, and he's got absolutely no defense, and the thing that's killing him more than anything else—he doesn't know what he can or what he cannot do. He's defenseless. Usually his defense is offense, and we've provoked him, yes, but we haven't provoked him outwardly enough for him to resort to violence. I think this is just killing him; you can see it all over him.[19]

That day, when McCain, Richmond, McNeil, and Blair politely but firmly demanded to be served at the Woolworth's lunch counter in downtown Greensboro, they caught almost everyone by surprise— the restaurant's employees and customers, elected officials, and, not least of all, law enforcement. The four first-year Agricultural and Technical College of North Carolina students may even have surprised themselves a bit, as it was only the night before, sitting in a dorm room, that they hatched their plan. Woolworth's dining facilities in Greensboro were open to white customers only. Black people simply did not ask to be served there or, for that matter, at almost any other white-owned eating establishment in the South. Not even civil rights groups had expected the sit-ins at Greensboro. The four young men had acted without the backing of any organization. The most prominent such group in Greensboro, the NAACP, withheld its support for the four men's protest at first, as it had in a few other Southern cities in recent years where activists had tried the tactic.[20]

Almost as soon as the four men seated themselves, the Woolworth's manager had rushed to police for advice. Greensboro police informed the Woolworth's employee that he or another manager had to make the request for officers to arrest the demonstrators. But the manager only wanted arrests if violence broke out, and these protests were peaceful so far. Both he and Woolworth's regional office decided that ignoring the protesters would prompt the four men to leave eventually—but Blair, Richmond, McNeil, and McCain showed little sign of giving up.

Neither the police officer nor the restaurant's employees knew what to do. In fact, the students were not breaking a law by asking to be served at the counter. Even though no statute in North Carolina dictated it, white-owned restaurants relegated Black diners to separate sections, restricted them to takeout, or simply turned them away. But as they sat in their suits and overcoats, the four young men did not flinch as they asked to be served, maintaining their composure in the face of repeated denials. They did not run, or even get up, when the officer arrived.[21]

What was at first a singular act of defiance multiplied. Over the course of the subsequent weeks and months, hundreds of other students would join them in protesting segregated lunch counters in Greensboro. Then the protests spread to other cities in North Carolina and across the region. By April, more than seventy thousand protesters in eleven states demanded to be served in whites-only dining sections of restaurants in a set of demonstrations that became known as the "sit-ins." Roughly 3,500 were arrested. Police brought an array of charges against protesters that on their face had nothing to do with racial segregation; vagrancy, disturbing the peace, and trespassing were among the most common. Hoping to further empower law enforcement to stop the protests, every Southern state legislature that met in 1960 following the Greensboro sit-ins passed new laws to restrict demonstrations. But even with mounting arrests, the protests continued. By September 1961, more than one hundred different cities saw restaurants make moves to desegregate in response to the sit-ins.[22]

The officer who arrived at the Greensboro Woolworth's seemed to reflect the mood of many of his fellow Southern police at the start of the 1960s. These men were angry and itching to make arrests, but they were unsure of themselves. They had no idea how to respond to Black defiance on a massive scale, especially when the protesters were calm and nonviolent.

These protests were unlike any boycott. Instead of refusing to patronize a segregated business, as Black residents in Montgomery had done with the local transit company, sit-in protesters did not remove themselves from sites of segregation. Instead, they forced themselves upon them, inserting their bodies into places designated for racial separation, knowing full well that they would be heckled or arrested.

The demonstrations challenged a deep-seated aversion among many Americans toward the idea of political protest. In a public opinion poll conducted in late 1959 and early 1960 before most of the sit-ins erupted, respondents were asked to "suppose several men were trying to influence a government decision" and then to propose the most effective ways to bring that about. The least popular option by far was "organizing a protest demonstration," which only 3 percent of respondents chose. Demonstrating in person against white supremacy simply would not have occurred to most Americans, even for many who wanted to end racial injustice.[23]

Black leaders viewed the sit-ins as a major turning point in the movement against racial inequality. In March 1960, the SCLC announced a "youth leadership meeting" to convene the following month at Shaw University in Raleigh, North Carolina, in an appeal signed by King and the organization's executive director, former New York NAACP chapter head Ella Baker. On Easter weekend, roughly 120 students from more than fifty colleges and high schools across the South who had taken part in the protests of the last two months gathered in Raleigh to build on their momentum. Joining them was a smaller number of older advisers more experienced in antiracist organizing, including both Baker and Shuttlesworth. By the end of the weekend, attendees had come up with a set of nine recommendations for action. The first two were to form a Temporary Student Nonviolent Coordinating Committee and to headquarter it in Atlanta. Another established that "nonviolence is our creed."

But perhaps the most revealing recommendation concerned a tactic whose urgency was emphasized with underlined text: "This conference recognizes the virtue of the movement and endorses the practice of <u>going to jail rather than accepting bail</u>." The fledgling group—which soon dropped "Temporary" from its name to establish what most would refer to simply as SNCC, pronounced "snick"—was announcing a vision for change that required frequent interactions with law enforcement. In so doing, it had determined that the road to freedom and equality ran straight through the police station and the jailhouse.[24]

———

Back in Birmingham, Shuttlesworth escalated his campaign to hold the police accountable in fall 1960. Up to this point, the ACMHR leader had attacked police abuses with protests at City Commission meetings, letters to officials, and press conferences—even by challenging Connor to a lie detector test. None had captured much attention from the national press or prompted intervention by federal authorities. On September 7, Shuttlesworth and Reverend Billups tried a new strategy: they sued the Birmingham Police Department in federal court for denying them their constitutional right to assembly.

The two ministers offered an intriguing analysis of the violence of political policing in their complaint to the court. Representing the pair pro se, Shuttlesworth framed his request for an injunction as an attempt "to secure the rights of the negro people of Birmingham to gather peacefully to plan and protect against the noxious practices of racial segregation so widespread in Birmingham . . . without being subjected to further police intimidation." Unlike the vast majority of cases brought against police departments by the NAACP, Shuttlesworth's suit did not pinpoint a single instance of police brutality or an illegal arrest but, instead, targeted the Birmingham police's long-standing practice of surveilling the ACMHR.

Shuttlesworth and Billups's petition sought to "restrain such practices of intimidation on the grounds that such practices are in violation of the rights of the plaintiff to freedom of assembly and violative of the due process and equal protection clause of the 14th amendment of the U.S. constitution." In addition to requesting that the court enjoin the Birmingham Police Department, the ACMHR leaders were suing for $97,000 in damages, or more than $1,000,000 adjusted for inflation.[25]

Shuttlesworth likely understood that the suit was a long shot. With initial counsel from Len Holt, a radical Black lawyer in Norfolk, Virginia, with experience as a CORE staffer, Shuttlesworth would have grasped the slim odds of a layperson winning a case in court. But as usual, Shuttlesworth was keenly aware of the value of publicity, and he knew that a federal lawsuit brought by Black ministers against Connor and Birmingham chief of police Jamie Moore would guarantee press coverage. On top of that, the suit could give Shuttlesworth his long-awaited chance to question Connor directly, after the public safety commissioner had ejected the minister from meetings, ignored his letters, and spurned his invitation to take a lie detector test.[26]

On November 22, 1960, the U.S. District Court for the Northern District of Alabama heard *Shuttlesworth v. Connor*, Civil Action 9751, with Judge Seybourne Lynne presiding. Appointed to the bench by Harry Truman in 1946, Lynne had ruled in multiple instances against desegregating interstate travel after *Brown v. Board of Education*, including in *Browder v. Gayle*. Plaintiff's attorney Shuttlesworth called ten witnesses to testify in total. In direct examination he asked ACMHR officers to detail the Birmingham police's efforts to monitor their meetings. The first witness, Billups, recounted his arrest in 1958 and the raid by firefighters the following year, explaining that police harassment of the group scared away would-be ACMHR members who supported the group but had no stomach for meetings where detectives took notes and recorded the names of those present.

Billups also offered a possible explanation for the arrest of the three ministers from Montgomery at Shuttlesworth's home in

October 1958. He recalled one ACMHR meeting at a church where an attendee came to him with a discomforting question. "Did you know that the policemen were listening to your meetings on the next block around the corner?" the man asked, adding, "I can hear them just as plain. I just passed there in my car." Billups and the man left the church in pursuit of the officers, and sure enough, they came across a police surveillance team. As Billups explained, "After they seen us standing by they turned it down and the other policemen in the other car had a microphone. Someone must have had a shortwave radio."[27]

The most dramatic moments of the hearing came when Shuttlesworth called Connor to the stand. The ACMHR leader wasted no time challenging the commissioner, asking within the first minute of questioning, "Mr. Connor, do you feel one of the important duties of your office is the maintenance of racial segregation in the city of Birmingham?" For someone who had made a name bragging about his dedication to white supremacy, Connor was surprisingly taciturn in the face of this question. Birmingham's commissioner of safety chose to say nothing, and his attorney quickly objected to the inquiry. Judge Lynne sustained the protest.

Shuttlesworth then turned to the question of police surveillance, asking Connor whether he believed that his officers should attend every ACMHR meeting, a question that the defense attorney also objected to, though in this case he was overruled by Lynne. Forced to answer, Connor conceded that he wanted his officers at every ACMHR meeting to take notes and later share their reports with him, even when they were uninvited and asked to leave. Connor provided a succinct, if misleading, rationale:

> My policy has always been that the Police Department must know what is going on whether it is segregation, integration or anything else. My policy has always been to treat them all alike whether it is the Citizen Council [*sic*] or whatever organization it is or the NAACP. I want to know what is going on.

In Connor's telling, a group using legal means to work toward racial equality such as the NAACP was a dangerous and criminal organization, no better than the Citizens Council, which devoted itself to obstructing racial desegregation. Of course, the commissioner made no mention in his testimony of his close ties to the Citizens Council and his frequent appearances at their meetings throughout the state when he had campaigned for office.[28]

In the end, Billups's and Connor's testimony made little difference. Lynne was never going to give the case a fair hearing. Just three years earlier, he had refused to overturn the conviction of two Black citizens arrested for using a whites-only waiting room at a bus station. "There is no shred of inference which indicates that one of the great constitutional guarantees to protect freedom of speech orders have been violated in any particular," Lynne announced to the courtroom. "There is no evidence that any defendant to this case or anybody working for him has ever restrained any person from attending a meeting or interrupted anything that was said in a meeting. The temporary injunction is denied."[29]

Despite the ruling, Shuttlesworth's suit was significant as perhaps the earliest instance of a civil rights organization suing a police force for infringing on their freedom of speech with surveillance. But in Lynne's view in 1960, Birmingham's police force was free to send as many detectives as it liked to the ACMHR's meetings—or any other meetings organized against racial segregation for that matter. Connor's red squad had a free hand to watch and listen to Shuttlesworth and his allies whenever and wherever they liked, whether in person or covertly. The federal judiciary in Alabama had given Birmingham officials the green light to stifle Black activists with political policing, announcing its approval of unfettered surveillance tactics to law enforcement across the country as they contemplated how to respond to this insurgent movement.

3

Collusion

James Farmer assumed the Congress of Racial Equality's director-
ship on February 1, 1961, one year to the day since the Greensboro
sit-ins. CORE was more than a decade older than both the SCLC
and SNCC, but it toiled in obscurity compared with the younger
organizations. Not long after starting his new position, Farmer
sought to hatch a dramatic campaign that could earn the organization
national headlines. He settled on the idea of Black and white passengers riding side by side on Greyhound and Trailways coaches
for more than one thousand miles from Washington, D.C., to New
Orleans. The previous December, the U.S. Supreme Court had ruled
in *Boynton v. Virginia* that segregated interstate travel violated federal law. Now CORE was set to ensure that the ruling was being
enforced as they launched what they called the Freedom Rides.[1]

On May 4, a group of twelve CORE organizers boarded two
buses in Washington headed for Georgia. The dozen passengers
calling themselves the Freedom Riders received a hero's welcome
more than a week later as they arrived in Atlanta, with sit-in veterans cheering them on as they pulled into the city's bus stations.
On their journey through the Carolinas, two CORE members had
been briefly arrested, and another, John Lewis, a twenty-one-year-
old seminary student from Troy, Alabama, had been assaulted for

entering a whites-only sitting area in a bus station, until local police broke up the attack. These were harrowing experiences, but they raised the Freedom Riders' hopes that any encounters with violent assailants or law enforcement as they approached New Orleans would be fleeting.

In Atlanta, the CORE contingent dined with King, who lavished praise on the group and shook each of their hands. Some of the Riders had hoped that the SCLC president would join them, only to learn that he had no intention of boarding a bus. At one point in the evening, King pulled aside Simeon Booker, a reporter for *Jet* and *Ebony* magazines traveling with the group, to share some disturbing news. King had heard rumors that the Riders were headed into an ambush after they left Georgia, and he warned him, "You will never make it through Alabama." King alerted Farmer as well—but by the night's end everyone in the group was resolved to keep riding.[2]

The next morning, May 14, was Mother's Day. The Riders split into two groups bound for Alabama, one with Greyhound and the other with Trailways. The Greyhound bus was almost empty, with only fourteen passengers, half of whom were Freedom Riders and two others who were reporters. Of the remaining five, two were nondescript white men who sat behind the Riders: Ell Cowling and Harry Sims, two plainclothes Alabama Highway Patrol corporals assigned to record the Freedom Riders with a concealed microphone and report back to their superiors, including Alabama Governor Robert Patterson.

Several hours after leaving Atlanta, the Greyhound bus arrived in Anniston, an Alabama town of some thirty thousand residents. The Freedom Riders were surprised to see desolate streets, but as they arrived at the station, a crowd of almost fifty people surrounded the bus. Armed with chains, pipes, and blades, the screaming mob attacked the vehicle, smashing windows and slashing tires. As several attempted to break into the bus, Cowling and Sims—whose true identities were still unknown to the Freedom Riders—rushed to the front of the bus and managed to lock the door before anyone could force their way in. When the Anniston police arrived, they examined the extensive damage the bus had incurred but saw no reason to make any arrests. Instead, they chatted amiably with members of the mob before sending the bus on its way with a police escort to the town limits.

Shortly after the Riders left Anniston, a series of cars began to trail the bus and box it in from the front, until a flat tire forced the driver to pull over in front of a grocery store. As the bus came to a stop, the driver fled, and yet again a mob rushed the bus. Cowling rushed to the front door with his pistol to prevent anyone from entering. The crowd pummeled the vehicle with their fists as they attempted to turn it over. A pair of uniformed highway patrolmen arrived to watch but did nothing. When someone threw an improvised firebomb through a broken window and set the bus aflame, the crowd ran to block the door and trap the passengers inside. As smoke filled the bus, several Freedom Riders managed to squeeze their way out of windows, before Cowling forced open the door so that the remaining passengers could escape. The crowd beat at least one Rider until two fuel tanks exploded. Finally, a uniformed patrolman who had watched the melee unfold gave a warning shot to clear the area.

Cowling, Sims, and a pair of uniformed patrolmen watched as the bewildered Riders recovered, but none made any arrests. Nor did they collect any evidence or take down license plate numbers from the crowd's cars. This was the best treatment that the Freedom Riders could expect from law enforcement for the rest of their journey, to be protected from death, though not felonious assault or prosecution.

Unaware of what had happened in Anniston, the other half of the Freedom Riders approached Birmingham in a Trailways bus. Not long after their departure from Atlanta, several white men on the bus began to threaten their fellow passengers. By the time the bus reached the Anniston station, they had badly beaten several of the Freedom Riders. "Don't worry about no lawsuits. I ain't seen a thing," a town police officer who observed their injuries told the assailants with a smile.[3]

Matters only got worse once they arrived in Birmingham. There the Freedom Riders discovered more desolate streets surrounding the bus station, but upon disembarking they were greeted by a mob awaiting their arrival. Though they had both been beaten on the bus, CORE members Chuck Person and Jim Peck stuck to their plan of entering the station's whites-only waiting room together. A crowd of men proceeded to swarm the two, savaging them with fists and weapons. Of the five other Freedom Riders, only three managed to escape the crowd. Walter Bergman and Ike Reynolds were less fortunate. They were beaten semiconscious. Then, fifteen minutes after the assaults began, the mob retreated, and as if on cue, the police arrived.

———

As Peck came to, he found the station almost empty. A soldier approached him to ask whether he needed help, but a group of grinning police officers surrounded him before he could answer, feigning concern and giving every sign that they were amused by what had just transpired. Peck declined the officers' questionable offer of assistance. Before long, he and Bergman managed to flag down a Black cabdriver to deliver them to their prearranged resting place for the evening, the Shuttlesworth family home. Later that evening, several officers showed up at the parsonage, threatening to arrest the Freedom Riders for violating segregation laws. Defiant as usual, Fred Shuttlesworth turned the police away, arguing that the Riders needed medical care. When Connor himself called Shuttlesworth demanding that he give up the group, the minister insisted that the city book the Freedom Riders hotel rooms if they could not stay at his house.

Connor relented, likely understanding that arresting the Riders hours after they had almost been killed would attract unfavorable national press. The commissioner may have also been deterred by the armed guards accompanying Shuttlesworth, loyal lieutenants from Bethel Baptist Church who had organized to protect the minister since the Christmas 1956 bombing. Earlier in the day, as reports of the Greyhound attacks reached Birmingham, Shuttlesworth had dispatched an envoy of guards to pick up the Riders in Anniston. Equipped with shotguns, the men from his congregation passed a group of hostile white men in the hospital as they picked up the injured CORE members. As Buck Johnson, one of Bethel's guards, recalled, "Some of them had clubs. There were some deputies too. You couldn't tell the deputies from the Ku Klux."[4]

By the following day, May 15, news coverage of the attacks had created international embarrassment for the United States. Appearing in newspapers around the country was a shocking shot of the mob beating a Black passerby in the station taken by a photographer for the *Birmingham Post-Herald*. After originally discouraging the Freedom Rides, the Kennedy administration was now committed to ensuring that they made it out of Alabama without suffering further violence, and the president assigned his brother, Attorney General Robert Kennedy, to conduct negotiations and maintain constant contact with Shuttlesworth, Governor Patterson, and the Greyhound corporation. After lengthy deliberations, the Riders abandoned their bus journey for a plane ride to New Orleans. Meeting them at the Birmingham airport was a crowd of angry whites, and though they were held back by a reluctantly protective Birmingham police force, a series of bomb threats phoned into the facility delayed the Riders' flight for hours. Shortly before 11 p.m., the Justice Department's chief negotiator in Birmingham, John Seigenthaler, came up with a plan to sneak the Freedom Riders onto a plane for a flash departure. With instructions to the airport to ignore all incoming calls, the plane took off, and an hour later it was in New Orleans. CORE's Freedom Ride had concluded.[5]

———

The Mother's Day attacks on the Freedom Riders raised disturbing questions for the movement, questions that even some whites in Birmingham shared. On May 15, the front page of the *Birmingham News* led with an incredulous headline: "People Are Asking: Where Were the Police?" It was an extraordinary move for the city's leading white newspaper to question police leadership. As the editorial noted, "This newspaper supported Eugene Connor for police commissioner before the first primary, and Mr. Connor swept into office

handily. *The Birmingham News* did so because it believed Eugene
Connor meant what he said when he outlined his policy: that Negro
or white, the city of Birmingham would not tolerate violence, disorder, breaking of law." Of course, the paper had no sympathy for
the Riders, denouncing them as instigators "moving through the
South to create racial trouble to make headlines not only here but
in every city in the United States and in quite a few foreign capitals."
But editors had made a rare critique of white authorities' handling
of the events.

If anything, the *News* seemed concerned that Birmingham's reputation might suffer from public displays of violence, especially attacks
on its own journalists, several of whom the mob had assaulted. "The
business was a 'set up' in a variety of ways," the paper concluded.
"Klansmen or other hoodlums were ready to create trouble. In trying to defend the South they invited every imaginable weapon to
be trained against us. And the police of Birmingham did not stop
the trouble that did develop. The *Birmingham News* wonders why."[6]

The Freedom Riders wondered, too, as they contemplated a series
of unsettling questions about the attacks they had endured. Had the
violent mobs and the police who had done nothing to stop them
coordinated a plan before Mother's Day? What were the undercover
Highway Patrolmen doing on the Greyhound bus, and why didn't
they make any arrests? In a memoir published the following year,
Jim Peck charged Connor with "flagrant incitement" of the attacks,
pointing to the commissioner's total lack of concern as rumors of
imminent mob violence swirled in Birmingham ahead of the Freedom Riders' arrival.

Two days after CORE organizers aborted their journey, a group
of Nashville student activists affiliated with SNCC renewed the
Freedom Rides on May 17. But as they exited a bus in Montgomery
three days later, they, too, were attacked by a vicious mob with no
police in sight. Among those beaten were John Lewis and a white
student from Wisconsin, Jim Zwerg, who was hospitalized. Even
Seigenthaler, serving as the eyes and ears of the Justice Department,
was knocked unconscious. Outraged, Kennedy finally realized that
only the National Guard could ensure the group's safety, and after

protracted wrangling he convinced Patterson on May 24 to deploy almost a thousand Alabama guardsmen to escort them to the state line, where the Mississippi National Guard then accepted responsibility for the group as it continued its journey.

When the bus made it to the state capital of Jackson several hours later, city police arrested the dozen demonstrators. Another bus with Freedom Riders arrived later the same morning, and they, too, were arrested. Forewarned by segregationist U.S. Senator James Eastland, President Kennedy had known that Jackson police would protect the Freedom Riders from vigilante violence, but only by jailing them. At the end of the day, twenty-seven activists had been arrested.

And yet more and more mixed-race groups of bus passengers sponsored by CORE and SNCC continued to make their way to Jackson from across the country, even as they knew they would be jailed. Many refused to pay bail, instead opting to stay behind bars and to keep elected officials and media focused on their protests. Soon their numbers swelled to the point that they put a serious strain on the jails in the state capital. Hoping that harsher conditions would motivate some of the activists to post bond, the sheriff in Jackson coordinated with state officials on June 15 to transfer forty-five Freedom Riders to Parchman Penitentiary, the notorious state prison and labor camp. There, they were segregated from the general population and crammed into overcrowded cells, barred from going outside except for twice a week for mandatory showers. Yet not even the threat of prison dissuaded the Freedom Riders, neither new protesters arriving from out of state nor their jailed comrades who refused bail.[7]

In the coming months, more than 320 Freedom Riders were incarcerated in Mississippi, many of them at Parchman, and additional Freedom Riders were arrested in Georgia, Florida, Arkansas, and Louisiana. It was not until early December, days after the Interstate Commerce Commission implemented a ban on segregated facilities in interstate travel, that the last Freedom Ride took place. Parchman officials only managed to rid themselves of the unwanted Freedom Riders thanks to a Mississippi state law that required anyone convicted of disorderly conduct to post bail within forty days of conviction or otherwise forgo the right to appeal. For this reason, most of the Freedom Riders sentenced to Parchman bonded out after thirty-nine days in the facility.[8]

Many of those in the movement had been arrested before. But it was one thing to sit a night or two in a county jail and another altogether to spend close to six weeks in a Mississippi state prison, crammed a dozen or more into a cell designed for four and denied nearly every physical freedom. "Jail, no bail" may have been the way of the movement, but prison changed the Freedom Riders. Looking back on these events years later, in 1967, SNCC executive secretary James Forman concluded that "it was the Freedom Rides of 1961 which opened the iceberg of Mississippi. Inside that cold monster was poverty, repression, police and civilian brutality—and a population waiting for someone to act."[9]

———

If they had made anything clear, the Freedom Rides showed that white media were eager to report on demonstrations for racial equality if they were marred by violence. Reporting by the country's leading outlets on attacks against protesters recalled war zone coverage and the play-by-play cadence of sports announcing. But few white journalists probed why or how vigilantes attacked protesters with impunity or whether Southern law enforcement had a vested interest in allowing the violence. Those who did raise questions about the police response, such as the *Birmingham News*, suggested negligence, not willful sabotage, as the culprit, and they did so while condemning the Freedom Riders as reckless provocateurs.

Civil rights groups drew different lessons from the Freedom Rides. For CORE and SNCC, it became clear that entering a city to stage a protest with minimal preparation on the ground—as the Freedom Riders attempted to do in Birmingham on May 14—was unlikely to be effective, especially without significant prior coordination with local Black activists. Indeed, aid from Fred Shuttlesworth and the ACMHR may have been the only thing that saved the Riders from worse violence. For SCLC officials, however, the Freedom Rides confirmed their belief that carefully orchestrated, nonviolent protests could bring about change if they inspired the wrath of local whites, in turn generating media attention and embarrassing federal officials on the world stage until they felt compelled to intervene.

This growing divergence in tactics played out in the movement's next major front, Albany. The thriving cotton town in southwest Georgia of more than fifty thousand residents was a regional hub in the state's mostly rural Black Belt, home to an African American community that made up 40 percent of the city's population, as well as Albany State College, a historically Black institution with a politically active student body demanding racial change. By the middle of November, as the Freedom Rides were winding down in Mississippi, the city's established Black leaders formed their own protest organization, the Albany Movement.

On December 10, barely a month since all U.S. interstate travel was to be desegregated on the orders of the Interstate Commerce Commission, SNCC sent its own mixed-race group of organizers into Albany's bus station. Police chief Laurie Pritchett had the group arrested upon their arrival, not for defying a city ordinance mandating segregated transportation but for disorderly conduct, obstructing traffic, and disobeying an officer. Pritchett clung to the technicality that the arrests had nothing to do with enforcing segregation. Unlike police in Montgomery, Greensboro, or Birmingham, the Albany chief weighed both the potential for bad press and the logistical challenge created by mass arrests. Sticking to their "jail, no bail" strategy, organizers were dismayed to learn that Pritchett had arranged for jails outside Albany to take in hundreds more protesters. Two of the counties where they transferred prisoners—derided by Black residents as "Terrible Terrell" and "Bad Baker"—were notorious for racial violence and abusive law enforcement.

By mid-December, Albany police had arrested more than seven hundred protesters, but the desegregation campaign waged by Albany locals and SNCC continued with reinforcements from the SCLC. Anger toward the police intensified in April 1962 after officers shot and killed Walter Harris, a Black man officers accused of wielding a knife as he resisted arrest on moonshine charges. A group of twenty-nine protesters lay on the sidewalk in front of city hall to denounce Harris's killing, staging what the *Atlanta Constitution* dubbed the city's first "lie-down." All were arrested.[10]

Among the hundreds arrested over many months were the SCLC's King and his lieutenant Ralph David Abernathy. When the pair returned to Albany on July 10, they pled guilty to their charges and opted to serve forty-five days in jail instead of paying fines of $178, calculating that they could attract more national support for the Albany Movement from inside a cell. Two days later, on July 12, Pritchett summoned the two men to his office to inform them that they were being released. An unidentified citizen—a "tall, well-dressed negro," Pritchett claimed—had paid the ministers' fines. King pleaded with Pritchett to let them stay. Pritchett's response was blunt. "God knows, Reverend, I don't want you in my jail."[11]

King saw the move for the ruse that it was. "I do not appreciate the subtle and conniving tactics used to get us out of jail," the SCLC leader declared at a press conference. "We had witnessed persons being kicked off lunch counter stools during the sit-ins, ejected from churches during the kneel-ins, and thrown into jail during the Freedom Rides. But for the first time, we witnessed being kicked out of jail," King noted in his diary.[12]

Decades later, Pritchett revealed that he had conspired with James Gray, the segregationist editor of the *Albany Herald* and a friend and college classmate of John Kennedy, to secretly pay King's bond and have him released. Removing the SCLC leader from jail blunted the campaign's momentum by denying King the national spotlight and preempting his claim that he was serving an unjust jail term. Kennedy, who had done nothing to help the hundreds of arrested protesters, had even given his blessing to the plan.[13]

"This is the first time in the history of the Negro non-violent movement that non-violence has been met with non-violence," Pritchett gloated, delighting in co-opting the movement's rhetoric. The chief claimed that he had grasped the "jail, no bail" tactic by studying the history of nonviolent resistance, remarking that "Gandhi had millions of people and when he filled up the jails with them in India, the British had to give in." Based on these lessons, Pritchett had devised a strategy to foil another community of color that was demanding freedom from white rule.[14]

While Pritchett's moves appear transparent in retrospect, credulous white journalists from papers with liberal reputations such as the *New York Herald Tribune* and *Atlanta Constitution* fell for his subterfuge. The *New York Times* may have been the most complimentary, heaping praise on Pritchett in the lede of an unsigned "Man in the News" profile:

> The man charged with preserving the peace in this city of racial crisis believes law enforcement must adapt to the changing times. Probably few other Southern chiefs of police have excelled Laurie Pritchett in making the adaptation. Those who have watched him work consider him an outstanding example of the new breed of Southern policeman—tough, dedicated and intelligent.[15]

Few white reporters admitted, however, that Pritchett had no problem with other law enforcement agencies perpetrating violence, including his colleagues in whose care he had placed arrestees. Albany's sheriff Cull Campbell broke a cane over the head of movement lawyer C. B. King, the first Black attorney in Albany, just paces from Pritchett's office. In another instance, a sheriff's deputy knocked SNCC organizer Charles Sherrod to the ground as he sat in the white section of the local courtroom during his arrest hearing. And in Terrell County, sheriff's deputies beat Albany Movement leader Marion King unconscious. At the time she was seven months pregnant. A month later she delivered her child stillborn.[16]

Movement organizers rejected the view of Pritchett as an enlightened constable, even while Dr. King conceded that Albany authorities were "subtle, tough, smart and determined." But the goals of police in southwest Georgia were not all that different from those in Birmingham. "They are not these rough segregationists you run into in other places, but underneath they are just as determined to preserve segregation," King maintained, contradicting an unsubstantiated claim in the *Times* that he had said he had "never met a finer Southern police chief" than Pritchett.[17]

Realizing that Pritchett and city leaders were dead set on maintaining segregation, the SCLC started to retreat from Albany by the end of summer 1962. The local movement continued to forge ahead, as did SNCC workers stationed in the town and surrounding area, all of them realizing that only slow, stubborn organizing could bring about long-term change. But never again would protests in southwest Georgia capture the nation's attention.

As the pace of protest slowed, some in the movement began to make sense of Pritchett's tactics. Perhaps the most insightful analysis of police's role in the Albany campaign came from a little-known historian by the name of Howard Zinn. Not long after SNCC's founding, the Spelman College professor had accepted the student organization's invitation to join Ella Baker in serving as one of its so-called adult advisers. A year later, in December 1961, Zinn joined the campaign in Albany.[18]

The next year, Zinn penned a scathing report on Albany for the Southern Regional Council, the region's leading white liberal organization to support the civil rights movement. "In Albany sophisticated police work has done the traditional—almost legendary—job of the mob, *i.e.*, the suppression of negro dissent and assertion of rights," Zinn remarked. Any praise of police for preventing brutal attacks reflected a grave misconception of liberty, he argued, as "the standards for freedom in the United States have been pushed to the ground when a police force meets its requirements merely by not torturing or blackjacking its citizens."

The so-called peace kept by Pritchett's department relied on the arrest of some 1,100 protesters on misdemeanor charges for public nuisance and similar offenses. "It was all part of an elaborate judicial game now being played in southern courtrooms, in which everyone pretends that the *race* of the arrested person was the farthest thing from the policeman's mind," in Zinn's view. "Police brutality is evil. Chief Pritchett should be commended for not engaging in it, and also for acting as he has, forthrightly and effectively, to prevent white mobsters from gaining any degree of control. But it is also an evil thing for police to deprive an entire community of human beings of their liberties." Even if police shielded movement organizers from violent harm, if they tried to stifle demonstrations against segregation, they were just as complicit of racial oppression as white leaders were. A. C. Searles, editor of Albany's Black newspaper, the *Southwest Georgian*, went even further in condemning local officials: "The general belief that Albany police have met nonviolence with nonviolence is the biggest hoax ever perpetrated on this nation. Albany is a police state."[19]

———

In a poll released by Gallup in June 1961, 94 percent of respondents shared that they had heard of the "recent outbreaks of racial trouble in Alabama"—but only 22 percent replied that they approved of the Freedom Rides. Most Americans seemed to have accepted the segregationists' view of the activists on the Greyhound and Trailways buses as reckless troublemakers who had it coming. In May 1962, on the one-year anniversary of the Freedom Rides, CORE took aim at that misperception with a probe into the harrowing violence police had perpetrated against the protesters.[20]

That month, CORE announced the Committee of Inquiry into the Administration of Justice in the Freedom Struggle. "Twenty Negro and white civil rights leaders will testify concerning their treatment by police, before courts and in jails," the organization proclaimed as it gave notice of a series of public investigative hearings scheduled for two days over Memorial Day weekend in the nation's capital.

> Witnesses will testify that in a significant number of American cities police have not protected peaceful demonstrators but have acquiesced in violence; that police have used violence; that mass arrests have followed disciplined civil rights actions; that violent whites have almost never been arrested; that courts have brought excessive charges; that prohibitive bond has been set and the normal channels of raising bond blocked—resulting in long incarceration and jail awaiting bond—and that there has been brutality in jails.[21]

In short, CORE was staging a people's tribunal to consider whether police had weaponized the legal system as a tool of political repression and even colluded with vigilantes intent on sabotaging the civil rights movement. If the firsthand accounts of widespread physical and legal police abuses failed to grab Americans' attention, CORE hoped that the prominence of the Committee of Inquiry's membership would (see figure 3.1). First and foremost was Eleanor Roosevelt, the seventy-seven-year-old former First Lady and stalwart civil rights champion who, even as she battled tuberculosis and aplastic anemia, chaired the inquiry. Serving as vice chair was Norman Thomas, the dean of American socialists and five-time presidential nominee on his party's ticket. Among those joining them were Kenneth Clark, the pioneering Black psychologist whose experiments using dolls to reveal young children's racial bias contributed to the NAACP's legal victory in the *Brown* case; Roger Baldwin, the founder and former executive director of the ACLU; and Brigadier General Telford Taylor, chief counsel at the Nuremberg Military Tribunals, whose inclusion suggested that CORE saw the work of prosecuting Nazi criminals as instructive for those demanding accountability from American police.[22]

Over two days, committee members and CORE lawyers convened in the community room of the *Washington Post* to carry out the inquiry modeled on a legislative hearing. As dozens of activists from the movement's front lines shared horror stories of the abuse they received from law enforcement officers, a shorthand reporter transcribed their testimony. Twenty-three-year-old Black longshoreman and New Orleans CORE member Jerome Smith reported being arrested more than a dozen times for protesting since fall 1960, including stints of thirty days in jail for protesting a segregated Woolworth's store and eighty days in Parchman for joining the Freedom Rides. He endured beatings nearly as often, at least a dozen in the same time frame.

Frank Nelson, a twenty-three-year-old white engineer from the Bronx, recounted an incident in New Orleans in which he was having dinner with a Black CORE member and their family when police forced their way into the family's home without a warrant, claiming that there was a disturbance. The officers arrested three white CORE volunteers and, on the way to jail, beat them with blackjacks before

FIGURE 3.1. CORE's Committee of Inquiry into the Administration of Justice in the Freedom Struggle probed Southern police collusion with the Klan and retaliatory prosecution of the Freedom Riders. Committee members included Kenneth Clark, Norman Thomas, and Chairperson Eleanor Roosevelt.

charging them with "no visible means of support," even though they had ample money with them. Not long after their release several days later, Nelson reported the officers to FBI agents in a meeting called by CORE—but nothing came of their so-called investigation.[23]

All told, more than five thousand civil rights protesters had been arrested since the sit-in movement kicked off in February 1960, with an estimated $2,000,000 to $3,000,000 spent on bonds—more than ten times that amount in 2025 dollars. "Some segregationists would be very glad to call off the dogs, call off the violence, call off the arrests, if the civil rights forces would call off direct action. That is not possible now. It will not take place. The new mood is to resist segregation with direct action," CORE Director James Farmer declared. "We ask that the judicial machinery be no longer used as a weapon to crush the civil rights movement. We ask impartiality. We ask that police be impartial."[24]

Albert Bigelow, a U.S. naval commander turned pacifist, had been with the first group of Freedom Riders on the Greyhound outside Anniston as it broke down and was set upon by a mob. As vigilantes attacked the vehicle with pipes and chains, Bigelow saw a police officer on the scene do "absolutely nothing about the vandalism. He seemed to almost collaborate with the mob." Moments later, they set the bus on fire, nearly killing the passengers. "Certainly police had foreknowledge of violence," Bigelow insisted.[25]

Hank Thomas's account may have been the most bizarre. Only nineteen when he joined the original Freedom Ride as a Howard University undergraduate, Thomas was working by early 1962 as a CORE field secretary in Huntsville, Alabama, where, in his words, "police kept a 24-hour tag on me." One day, a few CORE volunteers borrowed Thomas's car but forgot to lock the vehicle after they parked it. As the students returned to pick it up, they were repulsed by a stinging odor inside the car and jumped out immediately. Before long, Thomas arrived to find a few police officers on the scene sniffing the air around his car, but when he asked them to investigate, they refused.

Thomas shrugged off the incident and started driving, but moments later he felt a severe stinging sensation on his backside. Alarmed, he stopped the car and jumped out. The same police officers he had just seen had followed him, but now they refused his pleas to be taken to a doctor. When Thomas finally found a doctor to see him, the physician immediately observed that his patient smelled "just like mustard gas" and deduced that he had been poisoned. Thomas was ordered to burn his clothes and was placed under sedation. Chemists called in from a nearby Army base confirmed that Thomas had indeed inhaled some type of improvised mustard gas. Huntsville police, meanwhile, contended that one of the CORE volunteers must have played a prank—but Thomas was convinced that the police had seen who poisoned him and were covering for the culprit.[26]

The Committee of Inquiry advanced a broad conception of police violence at a time when most commentators defined it strictly in physical terms. Louis Lusky, a leading constitutional lawyer who had worked closely with CORE to raise bonds for the Freedom Riders, testified that "an unlawful arrest is a form of violence." Vigilante mobs had earned the ire of the Freedom Riders' defenders. But Lusky was adamant that law enforcement was every bit as complicit in the attacks. "The fact that the police in Mississippi are avoiding private violence by themselves accomplishing the purpose of the would-be attackers is, to my mind, no distinction at all," he argued.

"I wonder how much of this must be charged to a general failure in the United States to have the administration of justice without cruelty," Norman Thomas noted in the committee's closing comments, taking pains to cast the crimes against the movement as a national dilemma, not simply the work of Southern segregationists. Law enforcement attacks on the movement were nothing less than "widespread police sadism," the septuagenarian socialist charged.[27]

And yet, despite two days of damning testimony on police violence, the overall result was the exact opposite of what CORE had hoped for—the Committee of Inquiry into the Administration of Justice in the Freedom Struggle was virtually ignored by politicians and the press. No fewer than fifteen members of Congress declined Roosevelt's invitation to attend, as documented in the primary archival collection of CORE's papers; those same files do not include confirmation from even one elected official. Meanwhile, media coverage was scant. Brief syndicated pieces on the committee drawn from national wire reports were buried deep inside a few papers, but they failed to mention the Freedom Riders' testimony, instead highlighting a single white CORE volunteer's account that he had been tortured by a Tennessee sheriff after attempting to register African American voters.[28]

While the Black and left-wing press were a bit more attentive, even their stories were skimpy. The most generous coverage came from muckraker I. F. Stone, but the overall takeaway from his newsletter's two-page account of the Committee of Inquiry was that it had been ignored. "Too Few Listen as Freedom Riders and Sit-In'ers Tell Their Dramatic Story," Stone's headline lamented as he described the committee convening in a "sparsely filled small *Washington Post* Community Room last week-end." Stone noted further that the hearings "attested in unintended fashion that degree to which this has been the work of a minority of a minority," adding with dismay that the NAACP did not even send an observer. The *Washington Post* was virtually alone among major newspapers in assigning staff to the hearings, perhaps only because their reporter did not have to leave the office to view them.[29]

The inquiry's gut-wrenching testimonials challenged Roosevelt's faith in American democracy. Writing in *Tomorrow Is Now*, a posthumously published collection of her ruminations on political affairs, she described chairing the committee as "one of the most difficult experiences I have ever been through." She was so disheartened by the lackluster media coverage that she fired off letters to complain to the Associated Press, NBC, ABC, CBS, and the *New York Times*—all of which responded by rejecting her claims that they had overlooked a major national story.

"I found it difficult—and intolerably painful—to accept the fact that things such as I have described could happen here in these United States. This was the kind of thing the Nazis had done to the Jews of Germany," the former First Lady despaired. "How much must be changed was made clear in the repeated pictures of brutality: of policemen directing some of the vandalism, of the police dogs and the tear gas, of the young man who was blackjacked and had to have fifty-seven stitches taken in his head." But Roosevelt—who in Stone's words presided over the committee "not bowed in body but tireless as ever in spirit"—would have little time to open Americans' eyes to the atrocities committed by police against the civil rights movement. On November 7, less than six months after she chaired the committee for CORE, she died of tuberculosis at the age of seventy-eight in her home on the Upper East Side.[30]

The Committee of Inquiry into the Administration of Justice in the Freedom Struggle had detailed a disturbing array of attacks on civil rights organizers by police. As investigators questioned them with lawyerly attention to detail, Freedom Riders shared troubling accounts of officers who had brutalized them in some instances while colluding with vigilante mobs to attack them in others.

But most of white America did not seem to care. They dismissed the revelations as old news of transgressions by a few stray miscreants in law enforcement, not evidence of systematic abuses against civil rights organizers—if they noticed the committee at all. This mass indifference prompted an uncomfortable question. Would white Americans ever be willing to contemplate the violence demonstrators for racial equality suffered at the hands of the nation's police? What, if anything, could bring about a reckoning?

———

As the year came to a close, the movement's future was unclear. Following on the heels of the major victories of the sit-ins in 1960 and the Freedom Rides in 1961, the Albany campaign and CORE's Committee of Inquiry disheartened many organizers in 1962. Both the muted response to the committee and the acclaim Pritchett enjoyed suggested a deep desire among white liberals to believe that most police in the South, while they rejected racial equality, still eschewed brutal force against the movement.

Many activists thought otherwise. But who outside civil rights circles listened to voices like those of Zinn and Searles? Was it true, as a *Washington Post* headline suggested, that the "Albany Anti-Negro Tack May Set South's Course?" If law enforcement in southwest Georgia had deployed "the most sophisticated method so far to resist the increasing demands of Negroes for a life free of discrimination and segregation," as a *Post* reporter suggested, how was the movement to respond? This was a difficult but urgent question to answer.[31]

By outsourcing acts of physical brutality to third parties, political police in Birmingham and Albany had made expert use of slow violence against the movement. Connor had ordered his officers to withhold protection from Freedom Riders, and Pritchett had allowed law enforcement colleagues from other agencies to attack organizers. If SNCC, CORE, and the SCLC realized after the fact that they had been had, credulous white officials and journalists were none the wiser—or in many cases they did not want to admit the truth. Both Connor and Pritchett could claim plausible deniability; when accused of repression, they argued that they were just doing their jobs. For Americans to grasp that these officials were exacting tremendous harm on civil rights activists, they would have to acknowledge the violence perpetrated by police when they colluded in secret with the movement's most virulent enemies.

Police brutality had plagued African American communities for as long as anyone could remember. Through 1962, few in the movement seemed especially surprised by the physical and legal resistance they faced from law enforcement. But was this more than just activists' proverbial cost of doing business? Was police repression more than a symptom of the racist society that the movement was seeking to dismantle—was it also a root cause of oppression? If so, activists needed to develop strategies and analysis with which to attack police abuses. The more radical voices in the movement were inching toward this direction by the end of 1962, many of them organizers who had experienced police violence firsthand on the Freedom Rides. More cautious civil rights leaders—including Roy Wilkins of the NAACP and King—hesitated to address these questions as they remained focused on desegregation. But as 1963 arrived, and brutal attacks by police on the movement intensified, a larger confrontation with police abuses would soon prove inevitable.

4

Freedom Now

Birmingham shocked the world in May 1963. As Black people marched in the streets to demand the desegregation of Alabama's largest city that spring, they were joined by thousands of teenagers, even children younger than ten. In response, Public Safety Commissioner Bull Connor ordered firefighters to point their hoses at the marchers, battering them with fusillades of water powerful enough to remove the bark from trees. Police wielding clubs menaced the protesters, as officers assigned to the department's K-9 units pushed snarling dogs through the crowds, allowing them to maul anyone who got in their way.

The sights and sounds of these police attacks ricocheted across the nation and around the globe. Photographs of Birmingham police attempting to quell the demonstrations with vicious force filled the pages of American newspapers. Most unforgettable was the image of Officer Dick Middleton setting a large German shepherd upon fifteen-year-old Walter Gadsden, which appeared on the front pages of the *New York Times*, the *Los Angeles Times*, and the *Washington Post* on May 4 (see figure 4.1). The United States Information Agency conducted a study of global coverage of the events in Birmingham, concluding that "pictures of police brutality, particularly the use of police dogs, has militated strongly against the U.S. image."

FIGURE 4.1. Bill Hudson's photograph of Birmingham police officer Dick Middleton and his dog attacking Walter Gadsden appeared on front pages around the world in May 1963—catapulting police violence as a cause in the civil rights movement but also reinforcing the misperception that Black protesters endured law enforcement attacks without resisting them. AP Photo / Bill Hudson.

In the Soviet Union, an estimated 20 percent of radio programming was devoted to events in Birmingham in the weeks following the attacks.[1]

The photograph of Middleton and his dog brutalizing Gadsden was more than a snapshot of the Birmingham campaign. It became the ultimate symbol of white backlash against civil rights protesters and an icon of the movement writ large. But many white liberals misunderstood it. As Birmingham chronicler Diane McWhorter wrote decades later in May 1993, "Thirty years ago this Tuesday, America discovered its collective conscience." McWhorter described the photograph of Middleton and his dog attacking Gadsden as "one of those rare cultural artifacts that change history. It nationalized the African American freedom movement and led to the first serious civil rights legislation since Reconstruction."[2]

But in 1963, even those Americans who sympathized with the movement could not agree on the meaning of the Birmingham police attacks. The dominant narrative promoted by white national media and white officials outside the South was that images such as the Gadsden photograph documented oppressive law enforcement in a single city or perhaps region. But they were not, supposedly, indicative of police across the United States. A less common view, but one that resonated with many African Americans, was that the scenes in Birmingham recalled violent and abusive police they had encountered in their own cities and towns, whether they lived in the South or North. Even if the Birmingham police brutalized Black marchers more brazenly than most of their peers would, they disclosed an ugly truth about law enforcement, one that Black people had long known but many whites claimed they did not. The reality was that white officers deployed violence against Black people they believed were defying them, even ones who were peacefully protesting or following the law. This was not Alabama's problem, the protesters in Birmingham were crying. This was America's problem.

The view that Birmingham police were less aberration than archetype resonated among radical civil rights organizers. By spring 1963, these activists were rallying around the cry of "freedom now," an unqualified demand for immediate racial equality, not the gradual change and piecemeal desegregation endorsed by white officials and some cautious Black leaders. In the wake of Birmingham, the more insistent members of the movement sought to fight the scourge of police brutality in communities across the country. And as they attacked a wide variety of law enforcement violence that went beyond street beatings, some spoke of a crisis of "police malpractice."[3]

And yet, other truths about protest and police were left obscured by the press coverage of the Birmingham campaigns. Many observers recognized Black people in Birmingham as little more than victims. That they endured terrible repression was undeniable. But some of them fought back, at times as individuals, in other instances as part of a larger movement strategy that went back decades in Birmingham to communist organizing against police violence in the 1930s and 1940s. Fred Shuttlesworth's legal crusade against Connor's spies and his armed lieutenants' work guarding activists continued that tradition in the late 1950s.[4]

As reporters, white officials, and even some movement leaders focused on the nauseating display of force by the Birmingham police, many failed to connect it to the repressive slow violence that Shuttlesworth and the Alabama Christian Movement for Human Rights had long denounced: false arrests of movement leaders, the sustained monitoring of political organizers, and police who colluded with the Klan and other vigilantes to attack those demanding freedom and equality. It was these more insidious and sophisticated techniques rarely caught on camera that bonded Connor's officers with their peers across the country. No matter how incriminating they were, the images out of Birmingham exposed the police indulging in only their most blatant acts of physical violence. But with their red squads and their expert use of surveillance and incarceration, police in Birmingham and across the South who hoped to crush the movement had much more in common with their Northern counterparts than even many civil rights supporters wanted to admit. In 1963, movement organizers on the ground learned these lessons all too well.

———

King, whose SCLC had organized the protests, recognized just how much the police attacks in Alabama had reshaped popular opinion about the movement. "The sound of the explosion in Birmingham reached all the way to Washington, where the Kennedy administration, which had firmly declared that civil rights legislation would have to be shelved for 1963, hastily reorganized its priorities and placed a strong civil rights bill at the top of the Congressional calendar," the SCLC leader observed in his book *Why We Can't Wait*. As CBS News correspondent Eric Sevareid remarked, the images out of Birmingham were nothing less than unforgettable: "A newspaper or television picture of a snarling police dog set upon a human being is recorded in the permanent photoelectric file of every human brain."[5]

But did Americans see the picture correctly? Photography scholar Martin Berger has argued that many did not, by failing to recognize that Walter Gadsden was actually fighting back against police violence. To many white liberals, the fifteen-year-old Gadsden projected a martyr's devotion to his cause, and his downward gaze, perceived by many as compliance, signaled an almost saintly adherence to nonviolence. Movement leaders did not necessarily want to disavow such interpretations, hoping that violent overreactions by Connor's men would gain sympathy for their cause. SCLC organizers reasoned that it was far preferable for liberal whites to view protesters as powerless victims instead of violent aggressors or any number of other racist stereotypes Black people in the movement routinely confronted.

A closer inspection of the photo and Gadsden's background, however, discredits the prevailing view of the shot. Five months after the image skyrocketed to infamy, the October 10 issue of *Jet* magazine offered its readership a brief profile of the teenager, including a shot of Gadsden proudly displaying a copy of the photo of him and Middleton. A member of the famed Scott family that owned the *Atlanta Daily World* newspaper, Gadsden had ventured out on May 3 to watch the demonstrations, but he had not been protesting. He had not completed the nonviolent training that civil rights organizations offered marchers, as many had falsely assumed. In fact, Gadsden explained, he was not submitting to the officer at all but, instead, had thrown up his right knee to knock the canine in its jaw and prevent it from biting him, a technique for handling large dogs he had learned from his father as a young child. A final detail recast the image's meaning, one that no doubt escaped many readers who saw it reproduced at low resolution in their local newspapers. Few people could overlook Middleton's white fist grabbing Gadsden by his sweater. But much harder to see is Gadsden's darker hand just as tightly gripping Middleton's wrist, as it blends in with a man's sports jacket in the background. Gadsden was, in fact, resisting Middleton, not submitting to him.[6]

Another photograph from May 3 illustrates Black resistance to police repression even more starkly, though it garnered nowhere near as much attention as the Gadsden image (see figure 4.2). A snapshot from freelancer Charles Moore shows a middle-aged white Birmingham police officer uneasily perched on his motorcycle clutching a baton, surrounded by at least two dozen young Black onlookers. Many are pointing at the officer, including a young woman standing just feet from him and yelling. Another young woman appears to be laughing at the man and ridiculing him. And in the middle of the image stands a young Black man, leaning toward the officer and locking eyes with him. The crowd is not at all fearful. Instead, they are defiant—and they display nothing but scorn for the man as they appear to dare him to act.

When *Life* magazine published a spread on Birmingham weeks after the protests, it tucked one of Moore's shots from the encounter at the bottom of the last of eleven pages. Editors cropped out the officer's club, adding a caption that made no mention of the officer's complicity in violence while highlighting the Black protesters' contempt: "JEERING MOB. Waggling their fingers at an officer, youthful Negroes taunt police. Provocation like this, to most whites, is a wide-open invitation to full-scale racial warfare." Here was an admission by white journalists that Black people in Birmingham had, in fact, resisted the police. But *Life* dismissed the crowd's ridicule of the officer as a disservice to the movement, an expression of Black rancor and disorder, not the justifiable resistance against police repression that it was.[7]

Indeed, it was a narrative of Black victimhood, not Black resistance, that became white liberals' preferred means of explaining

FIGURE 4.2. Charles Moore's photograph of defiant Black teenagers jeering a Birmingham police officer appeared in *Life* magazine, but far fewer people saw it compared with Bill Hudson's shot of Walter Gadsden. Charles Moore Photographic Archive, camh-

the protests in Birmingham in May 1963. Most journalists and officials who objected to vicious police attacks on protesters saw non-violent martyrdom—and not fighting back—as the movement's only possible response to law enforcement abuses.

The images of police violence streaming out of Birmingham placed so much political pressure on the city's business leaders that they agreed at last to negotiate with the SCLC. After more than a month of protests, the Senior Citizens Committee, Birmingham's leading organization of business leaders, accepted a truce on May 10. Retailers pledged to desegregate lunch counters and restrooms and to begin hiring Black workers for their downtown stores, and the committee convinced city officials to release all jailed protesters on bond or their own recognizance, in exchange for the SCLC halting demonstrations. There is no way to know whether white leaders would have accepted this agreement without the photographs and news footage exposing Birmingham police's brutal attacks on demonstrators. But one thing was for sure. As the movement's more radical organizers in SNCC and CORE continued to endure police violence over the summer, fewer and fewer of them were willing to accept the role of victim.[8]

———

The police attacks in Birmingham injected a tremendous jolt of energy into the movement. Calling on one hundred of his organization's local chapters to stage protests against the "barbarity in Alabama," NAACP president Roy Wilkins demanded a termination of any federal funds that "help feed the dogs and buy the hoses which are being used against our people by the Bull Connor Storm Troopers." Some argued that Alabama authorities were not the only ones bearing responsibility for the attacks and highlighted the presence of the dogs to sharpen their critiques. As James Baldwin told a rally of predominantly white marchers in Los Angeles, "Those crimes in Birmingham, those dogs and fire hoses, are being committed in your name."[9]

In fact, although many critics condemned the Alabama city's canine unit as a relic of the Old South, it was actually a product of a new America. For many, attacks by police dogs on Black citizens conjured disturbing images from the antebellum era, when bounty hunters pursued escaped enslaved people with bloodhounds. But when Birmingham officers brutalized protesters in spring 1963, their dog squad had existed for not even three years. It was established in June 1960, just months after the sit-in movement erupted that spring. Though a handful of U.S. police forces had experimented with dogs before, none had sustained a squad for more than a few years before Baltimore police established its unit in 1956. Baltimore's department embraced the role of pioneer, promoting its dogs with an almost evangelical zeal and inviting police from across the country and around the world to visit their department to study their new crime-fighting division. Among their disciples was Sergeant M. W. McBride of Birmingham, who completed a three-month course on dog handling in Baltimore in 1960. Upon returning to Alabama, McBride launched Birmingham's canine squad with a dog whose name reflected the department's Confederate sympathies: Rebel.[10]

Birmingham's attack dogs outraged civil rights supporters across America. In Philadelphia, as nearly one hundred uniformed and plainclothes police officers looked on, two thousand marchers joined the local NAACP chapter in denouncing discriminatory unions hired by the city, with signs proclaiming "No More Dog Government in Alabama" and "We Want Rights, Not Bites" (see figure 4.3). In Boston, some ten thousand demonstrators gathered on the Common to signal their solidarity with the movement in Alabama. "We've got a stack of membership applications at least six inches high, but we haven't been out recruiting," a CORE organizer in Los Angeles told a reporter. What explained the huge spike in interest? "Birmingham has done the recruiting for us."[11]

And in New York City, on May 17, some 1,500 demonstrators gathered in front of city hall to express their outrage at the Birmingham police and to call on Mayor Robert Wagner to urge President Kennedy to send troops to Alabama to protect marchers. "Call off the dogs" signs in the crowd demanded as attendees heard from NAACP leaders, Jackie Robinson, and the mayor himself. Both the rally's organizers and Wagner emphasized that they were speaking out against a problem in the South, not the entire country. An

FIGURE 4.3. In the wake of the Birmingham police attacks, protests broke out across America, including in Philadelphia, where NAACP demonstrators demanded "rights not bites." Image courtesy of the African American Museum in Philadelphia.

NAACP flyer for the rally condemned the region's injustices no fewer than five times, demanding "an end to police brutality against Negroes who seek the constitutional right to vote in the deep South." Wagner's speech took a similar tack, decrying "the outrages of Birmingham" and the "defiance of Constitutional law by the officials of Birmingham and of Alabama." The mayor went as far as to claim, "Practically the entire eight million people of New York have been, in their hearts, marching with you." Almost as an afterthought, the mayor conceded near the end of his speech that New York might be less than perfect, and he urged his audience to "make as sure as we can that none of the blindness or the stupidity or the brutality that has been shown by the officials and the police of Birmingham is going to be tolerated in this city of ours."

And yet, at the very moment Wagner was declaring his solidarity with marchers in Birmingham and calling for equality in New York, the city's police were monitoring the crowd. A surveillance report authored by detectives from the Bureau of Special Services described the protests as an attempt to "urge Mayor Wagner to use his influence to have Pres. Kennedy exert the power of his office to stop the brutality" in Birmingham, with a handwritten notation adding the word "alleged" right before "brutality." The report mentioned nearly twenty attendees by name, including CORE Freedom Rider Jim Peck and one Joseph Matthews of Goldsboro, North Carolina, who was briefly detained after he "attempted to answer some of the statements made by the Mayor." Detectives also noted the license plate number of an attendee who had transported literature to the rally in her late-model Volkswagen.[12]

Directing the surveillance operation at the rally was William DeFossett, among the NYPD's most celebrated Black officers. DeFossett had joined the force in 1946; four years later he secured a coveted promotion to detective and was assigned to BOSS. He was only the third ever Black detective on the intelligence squad; the first, Joseph Carrington, had joined the unit just a few years before in the early 1940s.[13]

DeFossett made himself available to activist groups in Harlem as a liaison to the department and maintained cordial relations with their leaders. In 1956, as the president of the 369th Veterans Association, a Black veterans group based in Harlem, he was awarded a commendation by the NAACP's Thurgood Marshall in a public ceremony at the regiment's armory. The pages of the Black-owned *Amsterdam News*, meanwhile, made regular mention of DeFossett as an NYPD officer and community pillar.[14]

Yet, by 1957, DeFossett was reporting to BOSS about the activities of Black activist groups on a regular basis. That May, DeFossett was assigned to monitor the Nation of Islam, just weeks after Malcolm X led members of Temple #7 in a protest of the beating and arrest of Johnson X Hinton outside a Harlem police precinct. Within hours, the phalanx of protestors won Hinton's transfer from jail to a hospital, a scene immortalized in Malcolm's autobiography and Spike Lee's biopic. Over the course of the next few years, DeFossett attended numerous Nation of Islam events and authored at least two dozen memos on the temple's activities for his BOSS superiors.[15]

DeFossett also monitored the NAACP, an organization in which he was an active member. From April 1961 to May 1963, DeFossett authored no fewer than sixteen reports on the activities of the organization's New York chapter. Some of the memos detailed public events, such as membership drives and rallies, including several where audience members' names and even license plate numbers were noted. Other were closed-door Executive Committee meetings on sensitive topics ranging from ongoing conflicts with Black nationalist groups to an NAACP member's plans to file a lawsuit against city schools for racial discrimination. DeFossett's colleagues in the organization seemingly had no inkling of his double-dealing. In early 1961, lawyer Percy Sutton was elected chapter president of the New York NAACP and nominated DeFossett to join his leadership team, both as chair of the chapter's committee on veterans and as a member of its Executive Committee.[16]

This was the same NAACP chapter that had sought to combat police violence against Black citizens in New York a decade earlier under Ella Baker's leadership. At that time, the chapter had railed against the department's secret agreement with the FBI to quash investigations into police brutality. A decade later, they welcomed a police officer into their leadership, failing to realize that he was monitoring their work and reporting back to his superiors in the NYPD's intelligence unit.

———

Len Holt was terrified as he walked through the Danville, Virginia, airport on the morning of June 24, 1963. "Every policeman, state trooper, and prison farm guard knew me and hated me as 'that smart n____r bastard who tried to make fools of white folks,'" he thought to himself after stepping off a plane from New York.[17]

Holt was one of about just eighty Black lawyers in the entire South who took on civil rights cases and one of only fifty licensed Black attorneys in the state of Virginia. Working as a field secretary for CORE, he had attended the inaugural SNCC conference in April 1960, and he counseled Fred Shuttlesworth on his unsuccessful suit against Bull Connor later that fall. He had also felt the brunt of state repression. In September 1961, Holt and his law partners' office in Norfolk was visited by sheriff's deputies and state officials demanding that they turn over all records from their desegregation casework. The attorneys refused.

Holt's personal experiences as an organizer and a target of political policing informed the daring legal strategies he deployed in representing movement activists. Not long after fending off law enforcement intent on seizing his firm's papers, Holt appealed to the nearly all-white National Lawyers Guild regarding the rising wave of legal persecution facing civil rights organizers and their attorneys. In 1962, the Guild established the Committee to Assist Southern Lawyers, selecting Holt as one of its two chairs. Holt enjoyed a status as one of civil rights workers' favorite attorneys. "Local lawyers have not always acted in the best interests of their clients," SNCC communications director Julian Bond lamented in a letter to National Lawyers Guild president Ernest Goodman. "We really need about 300 Len Holts."[18]

A trim thirty-five-year-old with glasses and a fondness for bowties and cigars, Holt would have been easy to pick out at Danville's small airport. The FBI agents who followed him from a close distance as he exited the facility had no problem spotting him. But Holt was not worried about federal agents. Instead, he offered himself a grim reminder as he rushed to surrender to Danville's police. "Legally my status was that of an indicted felon-at-large. 'Resisting arrest' or 'escaping arrest' were the magical phrases that officers could use if any explanation became necessary as to why I had been shot."[19]

Not for nothing, Holt feared the police more than even most Black lawyers who challenged segregation. Two days before his arrival

Name: HOLT, LEONARD W., N/M
DOB Age 45 years, 5'11", 185 lbs., brown
eyes, black hair.
Address: 1962-Norfolk, Virginia
Occ.: Attorney
Arrest:
Organization: National Lawyers Guild. On
Editoral Board of the Liberator, a radical
publication by the Afro-American Research
Institute, Inc. This publication represents
the radical Black Nationalist Movement in
the United States
Associates: Carl Braden, Ervin Rosenfield,
Victor Rabinowitz, and Benjamin E. Smith.

FIGURE 4.4. Radical movement attorney and outspoken political policing critic Len Holt appeared in *Individuals Active in Civil Disturbances*, a catalog of more than 350 activists distributed to law enforcement by the Alabama Department of Public Safety. Alabama Department of Archives and History.

in Danville, he learned that a local grand jury had brought felony charges against him and thirteen other individuals associated with SNCC and the SCLC on account of their political organizing. The charges: violating an 1832 statute passed in the wake of Nat Turner's rebellion that prohibited "riots, routs, unlawful assemblies, trespasses and seditious speeches, by free negroes or mulattoes." This was the same law that state officials had used in 1859 to convict and execute the armed abolitionists led by John Brown when they seized control of a federal armory in Harper's Ferry in a failed bid to liberate enslaved people across Virginia and the South.[20]

As Holt exited the airport on that day in June 1963, and as the misdeeds of Birmingham police remained fresh in the minds of organizers, he of all people understood the particular dangers of a town such as Danville, where law enforcement was determined to halt local organizing. Holt knew that he would probably be fine if he could make his way to authorities to surrender, hands raised and defenseless, before they came looking for him. But in this Virginia city that escaped the notice of most reporters and federal officials, where Black protesters had endured weeks of heinous physical and legal violence, there was no telling what police might do to a Black attorney representing a group of insurrectionists against Jim Crow.

––––

Danville was a small city of more than 46,000 in south-central Virginia, just a few miles north of the North Carolina border, and home to the Dan River Mills, said to be the largest single-unit textile production facility in the world. In the early 1960s, the site employed 12,000 people. Though the town was almost one-third African American, barely more than a thousand of the mill's employees were Black, and they were limited to working in the lowest rungs of the facility, scratching out just $75–80 a week. Participation in political life was almost entirely shut off to Black residents, barely 6 percent of whom had overcome stifling white resistance to register to vote.[21]

On the last day of May 1963, the Danville Christian Progressive Association launched local sit-in protests in conjunction with SNCC and the SCLC, emboldened by the movement's victory in Birmingham just weeks earlier. A local affiliate of the SCLC led by a pair of Black ministers, Lawrence Campbell and Alexander Dunlap, the association began by staging marches to demand that Danville's public facilities and municipal hiring be desegregated. When they tried to see the mayor one day in early June, police rushed the protesters and choked a Black teenage girl, prompting her to swing her purse at the officer. The young woman was arrested along with Campbell and Dunlap, who were charged with "encouraging a minor to commit a misdemeanor" and "inciting a riot." Bond was set at $5,000, equivalent to more than $50,000 in 2025 dollars. The following day, Judge Thomas Aiken issued an ironclad thirty-day injunction barring all "unlawfully assembling in an unauthorized manner on the public streets," as well as any interference with private businesses or foot traffic.[22]

At Campbell's request, SNCC dispatched the first of fifteen field secretaries to the city. Two days later, on the afternoon of June 10, a group of SNCC organizers and local Black residents marched to city hall to resume their protests. When the marchers refused to heed law enforcement's demands to leave, police beat them with clubs and, as in Birmingham, firefighters blasted them with high-powered fire hoses.

That evening, sixty-five Black marchers and one white person—SNCC staffer Dorothy "Dot" Miller—marched to the town jail to support their incarcerated comrades. As they sang spirituals and made a second loop around the jail, police chief E. G. McCain yelled to his men, "Let 'em have it!" Firefighters turned their hoses on, and police set upon the crowd with nightsticks, assisted by armed garbage collectors they had deputized. The police response was even more brutal than earlier that afternoon. Some marchers were washed under cars; others were beaten. Forty demonstrators were injured. "Bodies lay on the street, drenched and bloody," Miller recalled later.

After learning of the police's retaliation earlier in the afternoon, SNCC executive secretary James Forman departed the group's head-quarters in Atlanta for Danville, bringing with him Danny Lyon, a photographer he had just that day hired as a full-time staffer. The pair arrived shortly after the evening's attacks. When they located Miller, they found her carrying out her staff duties even though she was nursing an open head wound, having been beaten and hosed. She had been the first person to call SNCC's national office in Atlanta to report the attacks, and when a staffer answered the phone, Miller broke down in tears—despite the expectation, as she later told Lyon, that "you were supposed to be so brave you weren't supposed to cry."[23]

Forman directed Lyon to document evidence of police misdeeds in Danville. While he would have known that there was no chance of obtaining redress for the beatings in local courts, Forman seemed to be planning how SNCC could otherwise share evidence of the violence with the world.

That evening, Forman, Lyon, and Miller found a gruesome scene at the town's only Black hospital. "People with lacerations and fractures were lying on stretchers waiting to be stitched up," Lyon recounted.

Forman kept telling me to take close-ups of the wounds. Later I photographed a man whose shirt front was completely covered with his own dried blood. His broken arm was in a sling. Next to him stood his friend, one eye swollen and closed, his head split open in two places; sutured closed, the swelling rose about two inches above his scalp. These people had been kneeling and praying at city hall.[24]

———

Through early June, Danville police reacted to the movement not all that differently than officers in Birmingham had earlier that spring. In both cities, officers subjected marchers to tremendous violence. In both cities, police enlisted the fire department to weaponize their hoses against demonstrators. And in both cities, police arrested large numbers of protesters—hundreds in Danville and thousands in Birmingham.

But starting in the middle of June, authorities in Danville diverged from their Birmingham colleagues with a set of legal and psychological tactics that brought the local movement to all but a complete halt. National guardsmen were deployed to Danville, bringing with them a tank, and police erected sandbags around their station, as if defending against an invading force. After organizers and locals held a mass meeting at a church one night, police armed with submachine guns stopped several carloads of SNCC staffers at roadblocks and searched them. Although police let the civil rights workers go, their act of intimidation against the backdrop of a tank with mounted guns made it clear that this was war.

Armed with Judge Aiken's injunction, police had already arrested more than one hundred individuals. Their first required appearance in court was June 17. As SNCC counsel, Holt had requested that Aiken provide a jury trial for Ezell Barksdale, the first defendant and a seventeen-year-old high school senior. Aiken rebuffed the request and, without disclosing which of the dozen clauses of the injunction Barksdale had violated, convicted the teenager and sentenced him to ninety days in jail. Aiken then ordered the more than one hundred remaining defendants to attend court every day until the entire group's cases were completed. It was a near certainty that all would serve similar jail terms. Holt later pointed out that he had "been in hundreds of southern courts and seen a lot done in the name of 'justice.' None of those experiences had prepared me for this day, and this event."

Still more draconian prosecutions awaited SNCC's most active organizers, and on June 21, a grand jury in Danville indicted fourteen organizers for felony insurrection, with each defendant facing five to ten years in prison. Among those indicted were Holt himself, who had gotten advance warning of the charges and sought refuge in New York for several days before opting to return to Danville to surrender. Other civil rights attorneys had faced harassment in the form of brief jail stints or having their law licenses rejected by Southern courts. But few if any had faced felony charges for insurrection.

Several indicted SNCC staffers chose to hole up at High Street Baptist Church, where Lendell Chase, one of the Danville Christian Progressive Association's leaders, ministered. Before long, Danville police raided the church, prying open its front door and then kicking down another door to a locked office. There, the officers arrested SNCC field secretaries Bob Zellner, Avon Rollins, and Daniel Foss. Police claimed that they had broken into the room because they had seen, through a window, Rollins pointing a pistol at the door and waiting to shoot the officers.[25]

Two weeks later, on July 11, Dr. King heeded the call of local organizers and came to town to headline a rally. King did not mince words as he condemned the abuses of the last month. "Very seldom if ever have I heard of a police force being as brutal and vicious as the police force here in Danville, Virginia. And you have stood up amid this with great courage." The local struggle in this Virginia textile town, King declared, was a barometer for Black people's struggle nationwide. "As long as the negro is not free in Danville, Virginia, the negro is not free anywhere in the United States of America." Inspired by King's speech, sixty Black residents marched on city hall and were promptly arrested. But the following day King was already gone, off to New York to throw himself into preparations for the next month's March on Washington for Jobs and Freedom.[26]

Arrested protesters who could not make bail remained in jail as federal courts vowed to assess the legality of Aiken's temporary injunction, but not until September. SNCC's organizers who had made bail felt that with felony indictments hanging over them they had no choice but to leave town, placing the movement back in local hands. The following day, Judge Aiken made his injunction against protesting permanent.

Then, in early August, after seeking the advice of Albany's Laurie Pritchett, Danville's Chief McClain transferred forty jailed protesters to counties outside the town, some of them as far as 250 miles away. The defendants now faced the prospect of drawn-out cases in even more conservative rural jurisdictions, with their overburdened attorneys looking at hours of driving time to travel from Danville to their clients' newly designated courts.

By late summer, national media's meager coverage of the Danville campaign accepted, if not applauded, local police tactics as a preferable alternative to Bull Connor's naked repression. A chief example appeared deep inside the *New York Times* August 11 edition by reporter Ben A. Franklin. "Danville, Va., the last capital of the Confederacy, now a drab textile and tobacco town of 50,000, is widely regarded as an example of successful resistance to Negro demonstrations demanding equality," the piece opened. Franklin told of police who combated protesters with "a defense strategy that is among the most unyielding, ingenious, legalistic and effective of any city in the South," drawing admiring observers to Danville from police departments across Virginia. Even in describing the police's most flagrant acts of abuse—assaulting nearly fifty Black protesters on June 10 or arresting Reverend Chase at his home one morning at 4 a.m. for allowing his children to protest—Franklin acknowledged their effectiveness without passing any judgment on Danville officials.[27]

Len Holt was less sanguine in his assessment. "Mass brutality was abandoned by Danville, thereby minimizing the possibility of FBI investigation and the presence of outside reporters. Less dramatic and more corrosive tactics were adopted," Holt recalled in his 1964 account of the Danville campaign, *An Act of Conscience*. Instead, McClain's officers engaged in "constant surveillance of the movement headquarters located in a storefront at 226 Union Street, constant trailing of movement people by police cruisers, a flurry of traffic arrests, midnight raids on the homes of persons known to be housing 'outside agitators,' massive policy scrutiny of the nightly public meetings." Local residents charged with demonstrating had their unemployment insurance withheld and were ejected from public housing, while repeated court appearances had them missing work, in turn getting them fired from jobs. As one organizer told Holt, "This court is but a different kind of policeman's club."[28]

In Danville, officials had deployed the sophisticated weapons of political policing to near perfection, mostly eschewing naked physical brutality by late summer. The consequence was that demonstrators for racial equality in the southern Virginia town received far less press attention than their colleagues in Alabama had. The power of the journalistic dictum "if it bleeds, it leads" was rarely more apparent. Civil rights reporters were eager to chase stories of fast battle between Southern officials and organizers—but not so much the slow violence favored by Danville and Albany.

———

The media were not the only ones to treat police in Birmingham and Danville differently—two of the movement's leading organizations did as well. In the SCLC's eyes, Birmingham had been close to a total victory, and the organization attributed that in no small part to what they saw as Connor and the police's tactical missteps. Wyatt Walker, the organization's executive director, remembered Connor as a dupe whose vitriol repulsed moderate whites across the country, ensuring the movement's victory. In one interview, he remarked that the Birmingham police chief was a villain who had "served our purposes well." In another, he candidly admitted, "We knew that when we came to Birmingham that if Bull Connor was still in control, he would do something to benefit our movement. We didn't want to march after Bull was gone."[29]

SNCC's Forman blasted the attitude of Walker and the SCLC toward police violence as callous, if not exploitative. Forman recalled in his memoirs encountering Walker and his colleague Dorothy Cotton in the SCLC's Birmingham headquarters hours after police had attacked protesters with German shepherds. In Forman's telling, the two SCLC staffers were "jumping up and down, elated. They said over and over again, 'We've got a movement. We've got a movement. We had some police brutality. They brought out the dogs. They brought out the dogs. We've got a movement!'" The SNCC leader was appalled. "It was a disgusting moment to me, for it seemed very cold, cruel, and calculating to be happy about police brutality coming down on innocent people, bystanders, no matter what purpose it served."[30]

If Walker and Cotton understood the violence by Birmingham police as a blunder that sympathetic white media could help them capitalize upon, Forman and SNCC treated police abuses in Danville as calculated oppression they had no choice but to confront. For the SCLC, a primary objective was to get news crews to share disturbing images of police violence as widely as possible. But if police violence was one of the inevitable costs of protesting in Birmingham, it was not an issue that the SCLC hoped to focus on, even if they saw it as a collateral evil of segregation.

Instead of relying on national reporters to publicize police attacks, SNCC created its own media to expose law enforcement abuses. Shortly after fleeing town, Miller and Lyon issued a grim account of their experiences for SNCC titled simply "Danville, Virginia" (see figure 4.5) In contrast to the superficial blow-by-blow accounts of police brutality favored by white media outlets, SNCC staffers articulated a probing political critique of the violence they had endured. The cover of the sixteen-page pamphlet features a haunting photograph of a single police officer in dark sunglasses patrolling on a motorcycle through the town's Black community. A crowd of onlookers watches the officer pass, appearing restless but reluctant to engage him. An American flag flies overhead in the background, small and distant, suggesting the acknowledged but secondary authority of the federal government. This is a place where Black residents instinctively fear law enforcement, a place where local police exercise the ultimate power.

FIGURE 4.5. SNCC's pamphlet "Danville, Virginia" documented police attacks on the organization's staffers in the city in 1963. Courtesy of the SNCC Legacy Project.

The booklet's first page displays a list of fifteen marchers assaulted by officers and a summary of their injuries under the heading "Official Record of Hospitalized Demonstrators." Below the inventory of injuries appears a photo spanning the width of the page, a pair of police officer's hands clutching a club. The next page features photographs of head injuries endured by several protesters, one of them a close-up.

Lyon's pictures leave a very different impression than the more famous images of police violence in Birmingham earlier that year. These are close-ups of bloody wounds and disfigured body parts, of broken bones and scalps with the skin beaten off. They are graphic, disturbing images, an unblinking record of the bodily harm Black people in Danville endured at the hands of police. Unlike news photographs from Birmingham, Lyon's shots portray the violence endured by protesters not as the result of pitched battle between adversaries but as the rotten fruits of political repression.

"A young Negro woman who will bear the scars of a police billy stick on her face for the rest of her life—she questions Danville as a 'fine place to live and work,'" Miller's text opens, in reference to the local Chamber of Commerce's boosterish slogan. "A Negro man who was beaten so savagely by police that he almost lost an eye, and was refused medical attention in jail for three days—he has questions also." The publication reads as equal parts indictment of Southern white hypocrisy and forensic report of police violence in Danville. SNCC's account recalled the Civil Rights Congress's *We Charge Genocide* and CORE's Committee of Inquiry on the Freedom Rides, grim inventories of racial violence by law enforcement. Miller had had her head broken open and her shoes torn off by fire hoses, and now she was telling the story of SNCC and Danville's Black community to anyone who would listen.[31]

More than anywhere else, Danville made police violence an abiding focus for SNCC in 1963. "We have encountered some of the greatest resistance of the demands of the twentieth century," SNCC chairman John Lewis proclaimed, denouncing Danville for "examples of the worst police brutality in any Southern city, including Birmingham." For James Forman, police violence had emerged as one of SNCC's most pressing challenges. "What are the main dangers that your members face when they're actually in the field?" Kenneth Clark, the famed Black psychologist who sat on CORE's Committee of Inquiry, asked Forman on a National Education Television special the same month the Danville pamphlet was published. SNCC's executive director replied without hesitation: "Police brutality is the number one problem in the South."[32]

Law enforcement from around the country drew different lessons from Danville, of course. In their final analysis, police in the Virginia town had defeated the local movement not with clubs and fire hoses but with mass arrests, felony indictments, and unrelenting surveillance. As in Albany, police in Danville avoided Bull Connor's habit of bragging about enforcing segregation laws. Instead, they claimed that they were forced to defend themselves against violent protesters as they sought to implement Aiken's injunction. These were the stifling tools of slow violence.

This more sophisticated and strategic approach, not Birmingham's, was the future of political policing against the movement. For all their differences, police in Danville and in Northern cities such as New York shared more in common in their approach to civil rights activists than most knew or admitted at the time. Convinced of his tactics' value for police across the country, Danville's chief of detectives would soon write a guide to suppressing civil rights protests for a leading publisher of law enforcement manuals.[33]

Compared with Birmingham, the Danville campaign appeared to be a loss for organizers. City officials had refused to negotiate with protesters, and both the SCLC and SNCC had reduced their presence in town to almost nothing by the end of summer, as more than one hundred marchers awaited trial across Virginia, including the fourteen organizers with felony insurrection charges still pending— charges that were only dropped close to a decade later. Although local organizers persisted with scattered protests into fall 1963, by the end of the year they had made only modest gains in desegregating public facilities and local jobs.[34]

As the frustrations mounted, organizers in Danville could point to at least one victory. In November, the city council became the first in the South to pass an antidiscrimination ordinance for municipal employment. Danville's local government hired three Black residents as city employees: two as social workers and, joining Chief McClain's men who had assaulted marchers just months earlier, one police officer. But as organizers would learn the hard way in the years ahead, not even Black police officers could always be counted on to protect the growing movement for racial justice.[35]

5

Up North

By spring 1963, the limits of the federal government's willingness to stem police violence were becoming painfully apparent to many in the movement. Federal authorities responded only to the most egregious instances of repression against protesters, and they did so with reluctance. The SCLC considered the Kennedy administration's intervention in Birmingham a victory, but it came only after Connor's officers had perpetrated an unrelenting wave of mass violence against Black protesters in front of national media. But years of Birmingham police spying on the movement and likely collaborating with the Klan to murder its leaders had drawn no response from Washington. And, of course, federal action in Birmingham only slowed police abuses in a single city. If many liberals were heartened by the White House's support of the negotiations to end segregation in the Alabama city, the repression the movement had endured in the first half of 1963 had convinced many organizers that they had to do more to combat it.

Of the leading civil rights organizations, CORE was the best positioned to confront police violence. The group had grappled with the issue as far back as May 1962, when its Committee of Inquiry had probed police attacks on the Freedom Riders. Two months later, the organization's national convention passed a resolution decrying the "broad pattern of police harassment of Negroes, particularly those demonstrating in support of civil rights. If this continues it will produce a cycle of growing alienation, disaffection and retaliatory violence." By year's end, Earl Walter, the African American chair of CORE's Los Angeles chapter, argued that police brutality was "an issue that is very important in the Negro community and one that can be used to bring CORE closer to the Negro community."

CORE's growing interest in police violence was due in no small measure to its national network of member chapters focused on direct action protest. Unlike SNCC and the SCLC, which were limited to paid staff working in the South, CORE had a thriving membership not only in the former Confederacy but also in the cities of the North and West. This was an important distinction at a time when many Southern Black communities were consumed with the fight to end legal segregation and gain access to the ballot. SNCC in particular sent staff into some of the region's most treacherous counties, where it was just too dangerous for organizers to protest law enforcement. And unlike the NAACP, which still favored a more cautious legalistic approach over street protests and sit-ins, CORE's members were among the most daring and insistent volunteers outside the South. Since at least the days of Ella Baker's tenure at its New York chapter, the largely middle-class NAACP had favored a legalistic approach of addressing police violence in civil courts over fighting it with direct protest. CORE's members operated closer to the ground, so to speak, and were more attuned to growing demands from Black working-class people to halt police brutality. As CORE director James Farmer told the group's National Action Council at the end of 1962, police violence was "an important fourth to employment, housing and schools as an area of concern in the north."[1]

In June 1963, just one month after the Birmingham attacks, CORE distributed recommendations for fighting police brutality to members of its nearly seventy chapters scattered across the country. The memo's author, Alan Gartner, chaired the organization's Boston chapter and was one of a handful of white people to serve on CORE's seventeen-member National Action Council. Gartner's definition of police abuses extended far beyond physical violence.

"Police brutality has long been with us. However, police malpractice takes other forms as well," he explained. These forms of malpractice included illegal arrests, searches, and detentions, often without warrants or even formal charges. They represented a nationwide scourge of harassment, Gartner noted, and law enforcement in the South prized them as weapons for enforcing discrimination. As Gartner saw it, "These practices affect white and Negro. They most affect the poor, the illiterate, and the disadvantaged. We in CORE must carry on our opposition to police malpractice within the framework of our desire to 1) enforce the law impartially, and 2) maintain a public atmosphere encouraging the free exercise of constitutional rights."

Gartner recommended several tactics to CORE chapters for addressing police malpractice. First, documenting abuses was critical, ideally in the form of affidavits. Organizers could use eyewitness statements to pressure city leaders and police officials into meeting in closed-door sessions, where they could present them with the affidavits and demands for concrete changes in their departments. Most importantly, CORE members were to demand the creation of civilian boards to review complaints against officers, as well as increased hiring of Black officers and improved training for police in "human relations," a popular catchall of the era for training in intercultural communication and racial sensitivity. If such demands failed to move officials, Gartner explained, "large scale direct action" would be necessary. CORE activists were advised to launch publicity campaigns apprising their allies and the press of incidents of police violence before besieging police headquarters and mayor's offices with pickets and sit-ins.[2]

Gartner expanded upon these ideas in a detailed seventy-eight-page report on police malpractice he authored as a researcher at Brandeis University, *The Police and the Community: Police Practices and Minority Groups*. A case study of Boston, it was an early acknowledgment that police violence against Black people in Northern cities may have been more subtle than in the South but was every bit as oppressive. The report offers a lengthy list of abuses, including illegal searches and seizures, unconstitutional arrests after dark for "abroad at the nighttime" violations, frequent harassment of interracial groups, the mass accumulation of photographs and fingerprints of uncharged individuals, and having arrestees sign forms indemnifying police as a requirement of their release from jail. In addition to creating review boards, Gartner urged police departments to mandate psychological screening for all applicants and to offer all at least one week of race relations training.[3]

In retrospect, Gartner overestimated the power of his proposals to right police wrongs. Still, CORE was envisioning remedies that far exceeded the near total lack of redress available to victims of police abuse in the early 1960s. Aside from New York and Florida, every state recognized "sovereign immunity," a centuries-old legal theory that denied citizens the right to sue law enforcement and other public officials for misconduct. At the time, only two cities in the country—Philadelphia and Rochester—had civilian boards that reviewed complaints against officers, and they could only suggest punishments, not order them. Even a week of racial sensitivity training represented an ambitious improvement at Northern police departments, where a single day or a few hours of "human relations" was the norm for cadets, if any was offered at all. And with African Americans making up on average around just 5 percent of major cities' police departments, many more Black officers would need to be hired if their numbers were to mirror the demographics of the communities where they worked.[4]

Most important of all, CORE was advocating direct action strategies that other civil rights organizations had not utilized against law enforcement agencies. Neither the NAACP nor the SCLC nor even SNCC had developed national programs to address police abuses. These organizations tended to appeal to federal authorities in the courts or the Department of Justice on a case-by-case basis in the hopes of securing long-shot interventions against individual police agencies that brutalized movement organizers. CORE was trying to do something much bigger: to wage war on police malpractice in all its manifestations and to do so across the country, not just in one or two local campaigns. The organization set about deploying the very same tactics of civil disobedience used against segregated restaurants and voter disenfranchisement to demand an end to police violence.

———

These appeals by CORE's leadership to its chapters began to bear fruit before long. In Gadsden, Alabama, an industrial town of some 58,000 inhabitants, hundreds of Black residents involved in a CORE campaign staged protests at police headquarters and the local court-house in summer 1963, only to be turned away by state troopers with clubs and cattle prods. In Plaquemine, Louisiana, a town of just 6,700, three hundred youth marched on a sheriff's private home after his deputies used tear gas to break up a march led by James Farmer and jailed hundreds of protesters. In response, the deputies tear-gassed the crowd outside their boss's house and attacked them with clubs and cattle prods before launching a manhunt for Farmer in private homes in the Black community. As part of the search, police staged yet another tear gas attack, this time on a church where they broke many of the chapel's windows, and CORE's national director was forced to sneak out of town in a hearse.[5]

But it was in the cities of the North and West where CORE's campaign against police violence thrived. In San Francisco, hundreds marched on city hall in October 1963 after fourteen officers chased a fleeing Black teenager into his home and proceeded to beat the boy, his two sisters, and his aunt after they resisted the forced warrantless entry. In Syracuse, more than two hundred people joined a CORE protest at police headquarters in March 1964. In Cleveland, CORE volunteers organized a monthslong campaign against police violence throughout 1964, with protests at city hall and department headquarters. And in New York, a battery of the organization's chapters—including Downtown CORE, East River CORE, Brooklyn CORE, and Bronx CORE—staged a monthslong demonstration campaign against police violence starting in late 1963 and extending deep into 1964.[6]

"We now find ourselves in the most crucial critical era of modern American history. The civil rights and racial problems are nationwide and extremely explosive," San Francisco's Chief Thomas Cahill warned in a seminar called "Police Training for Inter-racial Problems" at the annual meeting of the International Association of Chiefs of Police in October 1963, weeks before CORE marched on city hall in his hometown. Cahill had established a so-called community relations unit in his department the year before in response to what he called "racial troubles," and he urged his colleagues to do the same. "We have to go far beyond the concepts of law enforcement," Cahill instructed his audience as he bragged of the fourteen hours of training in race relations that his cadets had to complete. "We now find ourselves reaching away out into the social service sphere."[7]

But Cahill's reaction to CORE's protest later that month revealed another rationale for community dialogue. "You people, by marching like this, are building tension up again," Cahill charged. "I don't want anyone to get the idea that you have to put on a demonstration in order to get an audience with me." Cahill pled with the protesters not to picket but to take their complaints to a meeting of his department's community relations unit instead. As he told his International Association of Chiefs of Police colleagues, maintaining constant communications with civil rights groups was a means of maintaining peace and order, because "demonstrations must be anticipated. The leaders of the participants must be sought out and conferred with. When the demonstration is carefully planned and organized through complete cooperation between the leaders and the police, the policeman's task is much easier." According to Cahill, a critical component of handling protests was close collaboration between a department's community relations unit and its intelligence unit. What both shared was a need to know as much as possible about civil rights groups and their activities, even if they used different means of obtaining that information.[8]

But how different were community relations and intelligence work, really? While police promoted dialogue with activists as a recipe for improved relations, those communications also lay at the heart of efforts to collect intelligence on the movement. Indeed, sometimes community relations doubled as surveillance, as was the case in BOSS detective William DeFossett's activities with the NAACP. Police in Philadelphia almost entirely blurred the distinction between the two as well. In early 1963, Commissioner Howard Leary created the Civil Disobedience Unit (CDU) in the aftermath of protests by the city's NAACP chapter against construction companies that refused to hire Black workers. From its inception, the CDU's leadership conceived of it as an intelligence squad that would minimize civil rights groups' effectiveness with two contradictory methods.

Philadelphia's unit employed surveillance methods long utilized by political police, including regular collaboration with informers and dossiers filled with news clippings, photographs, and recordings from protests. Among other responsibilities, the CDU was tasked with creating a file card for every demonstrator it could identify at protests in Philadelphia. But unlike most red squads before it, the unit claimed to enjoy cordial relations with organizers and movement leaders. "We always attempt to establish really good relationships and rapport with demonstrating groups. We try to show them we are not their adversaries or opponents, that we recognize their right to assemble and demonstrate," Millard Meers, the inspector leading the CDU, told the *Greater Philadelphia Magazine* for a glowing profile of the unit. Reflecting this posture, the CDU was housed in the Philadelphia department's Community Relations Division.[9]

Harry Fox, chief inspector of the Philadelphia police and head of its Community Relations Division, described to the International Association of Chiefs of Police's *Police Chief* magazine how his officers used diplomacy and tact to keep tabs on protest groups.

> Members of a good Civil Disobedience Squad should have daily contact with the various leaders, planners and rank and file of these groups. They get to know them by name, sight and action. The CD officer talks to them, establishing rapport. He develops intelligence about their connections, background, personal life and ambitions. He influences them to give him a phone call prior to demonstrations or meetings. He points out that police protection is essential to the safety of the civil rights group.[10]

In Fox's eyes, effective intelligence units did not rely on subterfuge and covert action alone. They had little to gain by treating civil rights groups as unmitigated antagonists, as Birmingham's intelligence unit had. The objective, as Fox defined it, was to reduce the chance of violence and minimize the burden that protests placed on the rest of the department.

Intelligence police had to be better than rank-and-file beat cops, many of whom Fox believed resented protesters to the point of wishing physical harm on them. As a longtime victim of harassment and false charges of brutality by protesters, "the average policeman doesn't enjoy guarding a picket line or protecting and preventing demonstrators from being attacked." While Fox sympathized with these beat officers, he sought intelligence police who wanted to immerse themselves in the movement, to converse with its leaders and study their writings. Just as Laurie Pritchett read up on Gandhian nonviolence before King came to Albany, Philadelphia's intelligence squad dissected *A Manual for Direct Action*, a guide to protest methods written by two members of Philadelphia CORE.[11]

Fox hoped that each CDU member would be "intelligent, verbal, poised and courteous," not to mention "a self-disciplined enforcer of the law." Perhaps just as importantly, the intelligence officer should be "unprejudiced with the firm belief in the equality of man," or, in Fox's words, "'color blind' when dealing with racial groups." The intelligence officer, in other words, was not supposed to be racist. The fact that Fox even had to spell this out speaks to how widespread anti-Black attitudes were in his department, as though the absence of racial animus distinguished an intelligence squad as a skilled elite unit.[12]

While Philadelphia media and the national police press praised the CDU, not everyone was impressed. Chief among its detractors was Spencer Coxe, executive director of the Philadelphia chapter of the American Civil Liberties Union and a longtime critic of police abuses. Coxe objected in the strongest terms to the intelligence unit's propensity to photograph and record demonstrations, charging that "its purpose was to give the demonstrators a sense of being watched." In effect, Coxe accused the CDU of subjecting organizers to a "chilling effect," a term first employed by the Supreme Court in 1952 to describe any action that discouraged citizens from exercising their constitutional right to protected political speech.

No one in the movement had yet succeeded in challenging police's right to surveil activists, including Fred Shuttlesworth in his audacious pro se suit against Bull Connor. Not yet at least. But Coxe was already articulating legal arguments that activists would wield against intelligence squads to great effect in the years to come.[13]

———

As protests condemning the Birmingham police attacks broke out across the country, leading civil rights organizations coalesced around the idea of staging a unified march in the nation's capital. On May 7, the SCLC, CORE, SNCC, and the Negro American Labor Council issued a joint "Call for the Emancipation March on Washington for Jobs." Seventy-three-year-old Negro American Labor Council director A. Philip Randolph had proposed such a march by Black organizers as far back as 1941, as the head of the International Brotherhood of Sleeping Car Porters. The mere threat of such a protest had convinced Franklin Roosevelt to issue an executive order banning discrimination in federal defense jobs. Randolph's organization had begun to revive the idea of marching on Washington in spring 1963, and as the Birmingham campaign reached a climax in early May, they convinced their peer organizations to join them.

In a week when images of children of being attacked by German shepherds and fire hoses sparked protests all over the nation, the call for the Washington march made no mention of police brutality, instead pinpointing employment discrimination as the defining crisis of Black America. Only an accompanying statement individually authored by Randolph and not his organization addressed the recent attacks, as the elder labor leader denounced Connor's assault on protesters as "a spectacle of incredible barbarism and racial sadism which has precipitated a grave crisis of confidence between the races, not only in backward Alabama but in all America."[14]

As public support for federal civil rights legislation swelled in the summer, organizers settled on the name of the March on Washington for Jobs and Freedom. On July 2, the official proposed plans for the demonstration were accompanied by a revised call for a march at the end of August to demand a federal civil rights bill to address the country's "twin evils—racial discrimination and economic deprivation." But that proposal also ignored police abuses.[15]

Police, however, were not ignoring the planned march. That July, the all-white Prince George's County Police Department in Maryland hired psychologists from the National Institute of Mental Health (NIMH) to train their newly formed Civil Disturbance Unit. Fearing that nearby events later in the summer could spark mass protests or even riots in their own backyard, the department's leadership was eager for advice on reducing the likelihood of violence. The NIMH team responded to a charge "to prepare a group of police officers for mediating contemplated interracial conflict in the public streets" with a series of lectures and discussions designed to educate officers on the mindset of those who demonstrated against racial inequality. The psychologists soon found their assignment more difficult than they had anticipated.

A majority of officers in Prince George's Civil Disturbance Unit rejected the idea that Black Americans had reason to march. In their portion of the training, intelligence officers screened *Operation Abolition*, a 1960 propaganda film produced by HUAC that denounces left-wing political protest as the work of communist subversives intent on fomenting riots. The NIMH team reported hearing several officers share "fantasies regarding what battle would be like with large crowds of Negroes and whites under riot conditions." Taken aback, the researchers were struck by the talk of retaliation as a "disturbing reminder that, as a group, these policemen relished violence and were quite at home in it." But the NIMH team also detected a palpable anxiety among the officers as they contemplated the insurgent movement, noting that "there was no doubt that the highly charged topic touched upon the fears and apprehensions of these southern white policemen. This was new, unfamiliar, and unexpected behavior on the part of Negroes." Some officers went as far as to accuse the psychologists not only of sympathizing with the movement but of promoting interracial marriage—a recurring canard invoked by segregationists against civil rights organizers.

One of the federal psychologists later admitted that his team left the training feeling "slightly defeated, exhausted, and uneasy about how the officers would behave when confronted with a live challenge in the street." But as it turned out, contrary to the officers' fears, the March on Washington provoked no mass disturbances or violence, either in the nation's capital or in neighboring Prince George's County, where the NIMH psychologists noted "a strange quiet even on the crime front for two days following the demonstrations." Indeed, police officers and intelligence units across the country had anticipated the mass gathering on the National Mall with a mix of suspicion, dread, and contempt, but the March—one of the largest demonstrations in the country's history up to that point—was pulled off without any reported instance of violence.[16]

———

When John Lewis stepped up to the podium on the National Mall on August 28, 1963, he was just twenty-three years old. Tentative, if not nervous, he was by far the youngest speaker at the March on Washington. Lewis is better remembered for what he did not say that day, instead of what he did. The night before his speech, movement leaders had reviewed Lewis's draft and demanded that he remove several sentences they deemed too incendiary for public expression. Their fear was that Lewis's words were so radical they might scuttle progress on a federal civil rights bill. As march organizers met to debate Lewis's draft, Fred Shuttlesworth was the only older leader present who supported Lewis and the SNCC contingent. As usual, the Birmingham minister pushed a more radical line than most of his peers.

Chief among the prescribed excisions was Lewis's pledge, "We will march through the South, through the heart of Dixie, the way Sherman did. We shall pursue our own scorched earth policy and burn Jim Crow to the ground—nonviolently." Lewis also removed what would have been just the fourth sentence of his speech, an explanation that he could only offer lukewarm support for President Kennedy's proposed civil rights legislation because "there's not one thing in the bill that will protect our people from police brutality."[17]

Lewis reluctantly complied with the older leaders' editorial directives, and today his speech is remembered as the ultimate moment of censorship in the movement. But despite these redactions, Lewis still offered a searing critique of police violence in his delivered speech. "We are tired of being beat by policemen," Lewis declared. Kennedy's proposed civil rights bill did "nothing to protect the young children and old women who must face police dogs and fire hoses in the South." The charge prompted loud cheers from the crowd, the first of more than a dozen times that applause brought his address to a pause (see figure 5.1). Lewis went on to blast the proposed legislation for failing to protect "thousands of people that have been arrested on trumped up charges," the many protesters bludgeoned by mass arrests and felony insurrection charges. Lewis insisted that the bill would do little to change Danville, Virginia, where Black citizens "live in constant fear of a police state," invoking a term Americans generally reserved for foreign dictatorships dominated by secret security agents. Lewis was articulating a critique of police violence against the movement as something far more insidious than just physical attacks on marchers.

That day, before 250,000 people gathered on the Mall and the cameras of all three major television networks broadcasting to millions, John Lewis voiced what was up to that point the movement's most prominent denunciation of police violence not just in one town or city but across the South. The March's official program made no mention of police brutality in its outline of demands. But Lewis's young comrades in SNCC and their counterparts in CORE were done accepting police repression as the cost of doing business in the movement. As Lewis neared the end of his speech, he addressed those who might question the forcefulness of his message, those who might plead with him to slow down and ask for less. "We are tired of seeing our people locked up in jail over and over again, and then you holler 'Be patient.' How long can we be patient? We want our freedom and we want it now." If older leaders such as King, Randolph, and the NAACP's Roy Wilkins maintained a single-minded focus on the passage of federal legislation, the young radicals of the movement had found common cause under a more ambitious rallying

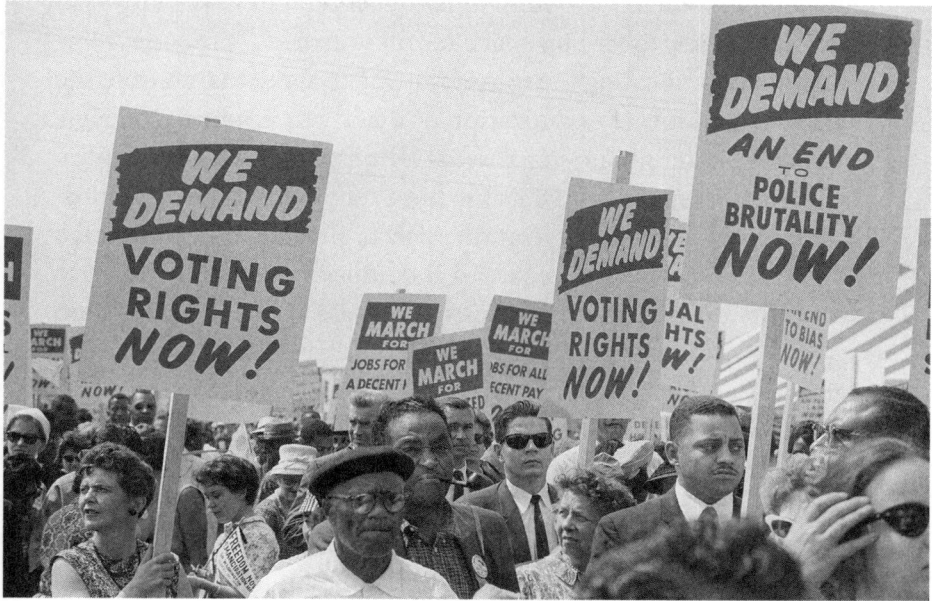

FIGURE 5.1. Placards reading "WE DEMAND AN END TO POLICE BRUTALITY NOW" were outnumbered by other signs at the March on Washington, but John Lewis's speech denouncing police violence was brought to a pause more than a dozen times that day by cheers from the audience. LC-U9-10344-16, Prints and Photographs Division, *U.S. News & World Report* Collection, LOC.

cry, and one that demanded an end to police violence: "Freedom Now!"[18]

And yet, just as Lewis condemned the wave of police repression the movement had endured that year, he and his fellow marchers were surrounded by police. No fewer than 1,900 of Washington's officers—nearly two-thirds of the city's entire force—were assigned to work at the March. They were assisted by an assortment of four hundred additional military police, police reservists, and park police, bringing the total to 2,300 officers. Law enforcement at the March far outnumbered the 1,800 police who had guarded President Kennedy's inauguration in January 1961, when an estimated one million people turned out. In anticipation of mass violence, D.C. police banned the sale of alcohol across the city for more than twenty-four hours and transferred 350 individuals incarcerated in the city's jail to other facilities, to free up space for mass arrests.[19]

Further complicating the role of the police at the March were the Guardians, a fraternal organization of Black officers from the New York and Philadelphia departments who traveled to Washington to serve as volunteer marshals for the event. Nearly 1,500 Guardians took up the call to serve at the March. Bedecked in white caps and gold arm bands, they regarded their duties not as a mandate to prevent the disaster that many of their white colleagues expected but, rather, as the opportunity of a lifetime, a chance to serve the movement and be a part of history. Several of them appeared on national television, standing just one row behind the podium as the day's speakers addressed the crowd.[20]

Yet these were just the police who *openly* watched the March on Washington. Back in New York, where the March on Washington movement was headquartered, BOSS had compiled inventories of the more than four hundred buses and one hundred trains to travel from New York for the March in the days leading up to August 28. Intelligence officers tracked the travel plans of established civil rights groups such as the NAACP and local chapters of CORE from Brooklyn and the Bronx. But they also took note of other groups arranging travel to the March: churches and unions, a local chapter of the Alpha Phi Alpha fraternity, and small businesses with less-than-subversive names like Whimpey's Restaurant and Harlem Steak House. Intelligence officers stationed at Penn Station and various departure points on the morning of August 28 took notes on thousands of marchers as they filed onto trains and buses, choosing to photograph some as well. BOSS filed the images away in its massive dossiers before sharing them with D.C.'s Metropolitan Police Department.[21]

Intelligence detectives in Chicago also monitored locals participating in the March, obtaining lists of residents planning to attend and surveilling Grand Central Station to record the names of individuals leaving for Washington by train on August 27 for the following day's events. Birmingham's all-white police department assigned at least one officer to the March as well, sending him more than seven hundred miles beyond their city limits to Washington,

FIGURE 5.2. Birmingham police surveillance photograph of the March on Washington. Birmingham, Ala. Public Library Archives.

as documented in a cache of twenty surveillance photographs from the March, one close-up after another in which the subjects betray no sign of recognition that their picture is being taken (see figure 5.2).[22]

And in Philadelphia, Commissioner Howard Leary assigned James Reaves, a Black inspector heading the Police Community Relations Division, to travel to D.C. to attend the March in plain clothes and issue a written report of what he saw there. Reaves already had a long record of collaborating with Inspector George Fencl, the head of Philadelphia's intelligence squad. Reaves recalled in his memoirs that he had at first been "hesitant to attend for fear of trouble" at the March. Law enforcement had good reason to expect violence, Reaves contended, because "riots and demonstrations were the order of the day in many urban communities, and the expression 'long hot summer' was well understood. Therefore any information on the subject was anxiously sought." When Reaves returned to Philadelphia after the March, his report to Leary highlighted how peaceful the event had been, in his estimation largely due to the security provided by the Guardians. But Leary "seemed more interested in who was there, who spoke, and the attitude of the speakers as well as the crowd. He was so impressed that he had me give a verbal report at the following inspectors meeting in his office."[23]

Today, the March has come to be regarded as an almost holy day of American nonviolent protest, with many lionizing it as the movement's zenith, a virtuous expression of multiracial unity and a defining moment in American democracy. Conservatives in particular praise King's speech as the ultimate endorsement of color-blind meritocracy. That so many police departments monitored the March suggests just how much they mistrusted the movement and how dismayed they were to witness its gains in 1963, as mass protests erupted across the country in the months since Birmingham police had attacked marchers while the world watched. After all, if organizers could pull off the March, they would have no problem staging smaller demonstrations back home. At the root of police's spying that day was a fear that the rally would radicalize its attendees, inciting those on the Mall to put together their own local marches and protests when they returned home.

———

"This has been the year of the picket," a report in the *New York Times* opened two months later, on the final day of October. "According to the Police Department, there have been more demonstrations in New York City in the last 10 months than in any other year in the department's memory." Deputy Commissioner Walter Arm, the department's lead official for community relations, complained that protest activity in 1963 had "resulted in the loss of hundreds of thousands of man-hours." Among the many demonstrations tying up the department were a series of protests in July by local CORE chapters at tax-funded building sites where construction companies refused to hire Black people. At these protests alone, Arm told reporter Philip Benjamin, "there were 800 arrests but very little violence or charges of police brutality."[24]

Indeed, the city's leadership swore that New York police abstained from violence against protesters. In May, before the rally of 1,500 advertised as a protest against "dog government" in Birmingham, Mayor Robert Wagner declared that "something—not only something but everything possible—must be done to bring an end to the defiance of constitutional law by officials of Birmingham and Alabama," as he took pains to praise the "heroism of the people, the young people and the children" protesting there. Two years earlier, Wagner had proclaimed a citywide Freedom Riders Week in 1961.[25]

And yet, New York officials did not greet protests against racial discrimination within their city limits with quite as much enthusiasm. "Whenever picketing appears to be political in nature, as against the more conventional picketing in labor disputes, the Police Department puts men from its Bureau of Special Services on the scene," Benjamin disclosed in his *Times* report on the city's handling of protests. "The bureau, which is the department's secret, or undercover, arm, keeps tabs on demonstrators, takes photographs of them, tries to learn their names." Here was an unusually candid description of BOSS's activities right on page 29 of the Thursday edition of New York's paper of record.[26]

The *Times* continued its fawning coverage of the NYPD with a November 7 story informing readers that police violence against unarmed citizens was on its way out in New York. "Police brutality is waning in city" the headline read. Anthony Marra, a criminal defense attorney for Legal Aid, happily reported that the NYPD had all but abandoned the violent techniques it once used against unarmed citizens. In fact, it had been more than three years since Marra had submitted a complaint to the district attorney regarding physical brutality by an officer. "It is a wonderful thing," the attorney exclaimed. "The days of the so called third degree, where a man was beaten severely appear to be gone." Marra credited the change to the "higher morality and tone of leadership" of the NYPD as well as the fact that "the patrolman and detective of today are more intelligent and have a higher caliber than those of years ago."

Commissioner Michael Murphy concurred, describing attempts by his officers to beat confessions out of criminal suspects as "passé as the nickel subway ride," in reference to the five-cent fares that New York's transit system had eliminated more than a decade earlier. Police now relied on psychological manipulation—particularly the good cop, bad cop routine—to get arrestees to talk. Sometimes they even threatened a suspect with "immediate electrocution" or the "tossing of his body out a window," the *Times* conceded, before expressing approval that officers stopped short of exacting those punishments.[27]

By sheer coincidence, two events on the very same day the *Times* story was published gave lie to its glowing profile of a nonviolent New York Police Department. Starting on the evening of November 6 and continuing into the early-morning hours of the next day, more than one hundred members of CORE gathered outside the ABC studios on the Upper West Side to protest an appearance on a local late-night television show by Alabama governor and arch-segregationist George Wallace.[28]

As they waited for hours in heavy rain, the CORE picketers barely noticed as a car pulled into the studio's driveway and Wallace scurried out, somehow evading the crowd before making his way into the studio. By 1:00 in the morning, the CORE cohort had grown restless, and demonstrators broke through a barricade to block traffic on West 66th Street. After a dozen officers failed to disperse the crowd, they were joined by more than twenty mounted police on horseback.[29]

While protesters sang "We Shall Not Be Moved," the officers surrounded them and attacked. One CORE member, Joseph Sweeny, recounted being "savagely clubbed and kicked on the head" before almost losing sight in his left eye. Another protester, Auttamese Boatswain, was eight months pregnant, but the cops did not seem to care. "I'll never forget the face of the policeman who struck me in the stomach with his nightstick," Boatswain recounted to the *Amsterdam News*.[30]

That same evening, more than one hundred blocks to the north in the Bronx, a Black auto mechanic named Jesse Roberts walked into the 48th Police Precinct Station to report his car stolen. As Roberts considered pressing charges against a teenager already in custody, two detectives snuck out of the station with the suspect. Roberts returned to his shop shortly afterward to find that the detectives and the boy had let themselves in for the stated purpose of finding the missing car's keys. To Roberts's great surprise, the officers then produced a bag of marijuana they claimed to have found in his shop. The detectives arrested the mechanic and took him back to the station. There they stripped him down to his waist and had him step on a pile of books, cuffing him to a light fixture in a crucifix pose. The men then kicked out the books from underneath Roberts and left him suspended in midair.

The violence that followed was grotesque. An officer entered wearing an improvised white sheet intended to evoke a Klansman's garb. He and his colleagues blindfolded Roberts and proceeded to throw hot coffee on him and beat him. The officers then forced Roberts to clean up the mess before booking him on narcotics charges and sending him home with two cracked ribs and a broken tailbone.

Roberts's case went virtually unnoticed in New York at first. Neither the *Times*, nor the *Daily News*, nor the Black-owned *Amsterdam News* wrote a single story about the incident in 1963. It would be months before the story received any significant attention, and then only because of efforts by CORE to publicize it.

———

Undaunted by their casualties at the Wallace protest on November 7, many of the same CORE members made their way two evenings later to the Hilton Hotel in Midtown to protest another elected official: John Kennedy. Months earlier, the president had welcomed movement leaders—including CORE official Floyd McKissick—to the White House following the March on Washington on August 28 to discuss a desegregation bill. By early November, the bill was stalled in committee, a development that some in the movement attributed to a deficit of enthusiasm on the president's part.

Now, as Kennedy visited the city to receive an award from the Protestant Council of New York, CORE members sought to convey their displeasure with what they saw as the president's "lack of a strong pro–civil rights stand against Dixiecrat Congressmen." Granted, CORE's chapters in New York were more assertive than the national organization. But the fact that they were demonstrating against the president just months after he had welcomed their national chairman into his office spoke to how quickly some in the movement were radicalizing in the wake of Birmingham and the March on Washington.

As protesters sat on the sidewalk outside the Hilton during Kennedy's reception, police rushed in to disperse the crowd. An account by CORE members described officers "pushing and punching with their hands, prodding and clubbing with night sticks," while mounted police on horseback sought to "intimidate and to terrorize the peaceful demonstrators." Six CORE members were hospitalized by the end of the evening.

For CORE's East River chapter, the attacks at the Wallace and Kennedy protests represented more than just a few officers losing their cool. A letter by members of the chapter's coordinating committing—a copy of which BOSS retained for its files—described the incidents as ideological assaults with a "definite political, rather than purely emotional cause." The violence was "not due to isolated cases of loss of temper on the part of the patrolmen." The letter accused NYPD officers of aligning themselves with a growing white backlash against the push for racial equality. As the East River chapter noted, the overzealous officers they encountered stood in sharp contrast to other police who had watched and done nothing as a far-right demonstrator struck Supreme Court Chief Justice Earl Warren with a picket at a protest in New York several weeks earlier.[31]

Then, on November 19, eighty CORE members held a midday protest outside NYPD headquarters at 240 Centre Street. "Protect Us—Not Attack Us" and "End Police Brutality," two placards demanded, while another called for "No Protest Horses, Dogs, Cattle Prods." Echoing the claims of a formal complaint that protesters had submitted to Commissioner Murphy after the November 6–7 incidents, CORE members declared their plan in an announcement for the picket to "expose and punish those law enforcement officers responsible for the planned brutal treatment meted out to CORE demonstrators." CORE was posing a direct challenge to the New York Police Department at its very doorstep.

As part of a three-page report on the demonstration, BOSS detectives listed every individual they could identify at the protest, mostly obscure names except for two: Mickey and Rita Schwerner (see figure 5.3). The young couple were active members of the Downtown CORE chapter but otherwise unknown outside New York's movement circles. Seven months later, Mickey would make headlines around the world for a very different encounter with law enforcement officials, one with far more dire consequences.[32]

———

On November 20, just shy of two weeks after officers assaulted CORE members at their protest against George Wallace, the NYPD devised two responses to the brewing controversy, one overt and one covert. In public, the department took the rare step of trying to convey that it took charges of police brutality seriously. In the face of mounting political pressure, the department's 24th Precinct staged a lineup of 130 of their own officers outside their station that evening. Invited to identify any they believed had beaten them, CORE members pointed to at least two officers as their assailants. Those officers remained on the force, however, and received no publicly disclosed discipline. The lineup had been largely for show. But it was a grudging admission on the police's part that accusations of violence against civilians substantiated by multiple witnesses could not always be dismissed or ignored.[33]

Outside public view, however, the NYPD adopted a much less conciliatory stance toward CORE. On November 20, the department escalated its surveillance of the leading civil rights organization in New York. In a blind memo lacking a signature or identifying marks, an NYPD official ordered BOSS lieutenant Bernard Mulligan to investigate CORE for communist members and "potential trouble makers." The directive further instructed detectives to determine whether there was "a faction within C.O.R.E. which advocates dropping the 'non-violent' approach and adopting instead 'an eye for an eye–a tooth for a tooth' approach."

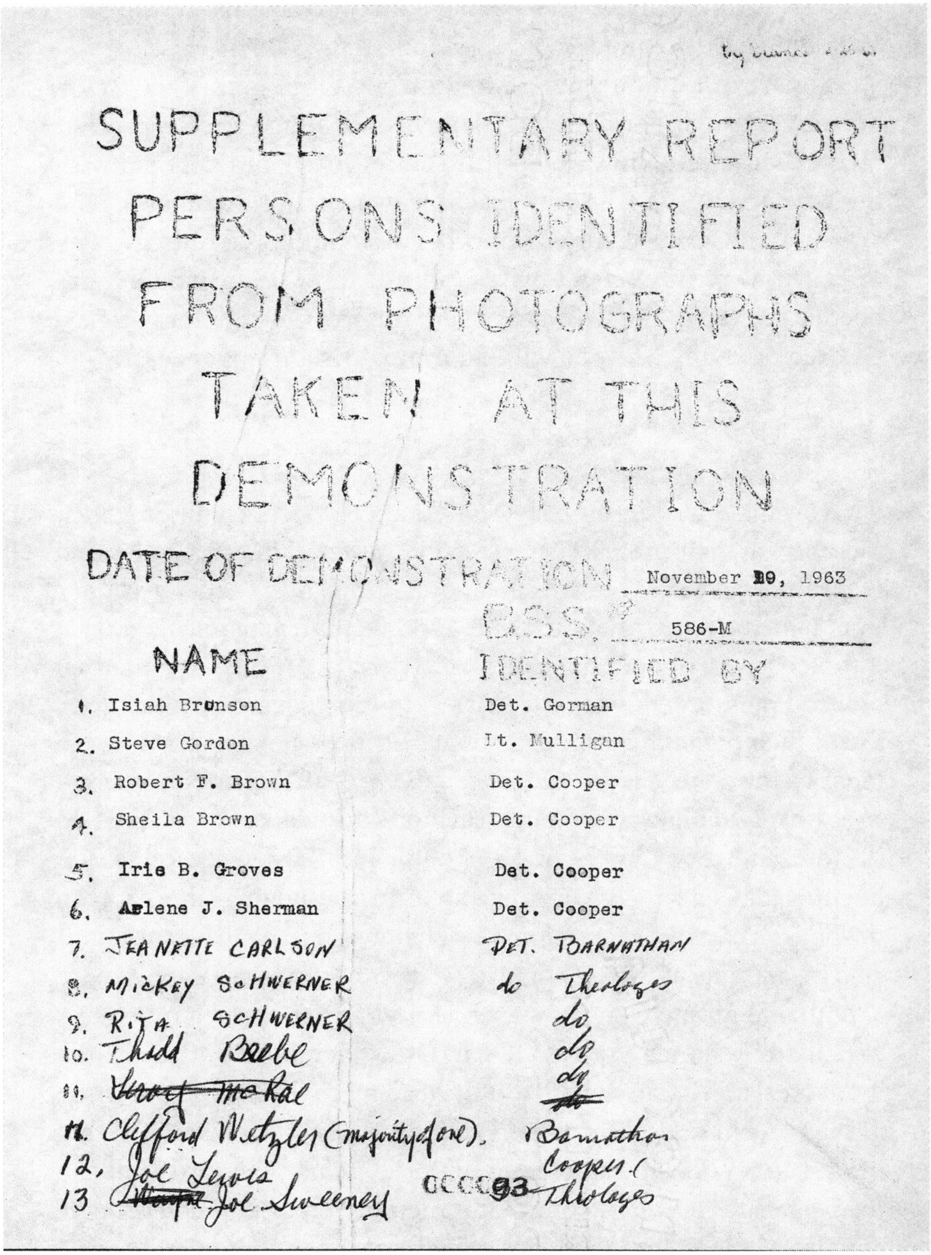

SUPPLEMENTARY REPORT
PERSONS IDENTIFIED
FROM PHOTOGRAPHS
TAKEN AT THIS
DEMONSTRATION

DATE OF DEMONSTRATION   November 19, 1963

B.S.S.   586-M

NAME	IDENTIFIED BY
1. Isiah Brunson	Det. Gorman
2. Steve Gordon	Lt. Mulligan
3. Robert F. Brown	Det. Cooper
4. Sheila Brown	Det. Cooper
5. Irie B. Groves	Det. Cooper
6. Arlene J. Sherman	Det. Cooper
7. JEANETTE CARLSON	DET. BARNATHAN
8. MICKEY SCHWERNER	do Theologes
9. RITA SCHWERNER	do
10. Thdd Beebe	do
11. ~~Verod the hal~~	do
11. Clifford Wetzler (majority of one).	Barnathan
12. Joe Lewis	Cooper (
13. ~~Harry~~ Joe Sweeney CCCC93	Theologes

FIGURE 5.3. CORE member Michael Schwerner was among those photographed by detectives at a protest against police violence outside NYPD headquarters on November 19, 1963—seven months before Mississippi police orchestrated his murder. NYPD Intelligence Records, NYCMA.

BOSS for its part failed to comprehend CORE's membership or ideological orientation, as suggested by marginalia on the memo erroneously identifying the March on Washington organizer Bayard Rustin as the strategist behind CORE's "militant group." Though Rustin had been active in the organization years earlier, he was now at best an honorary member on the fringes of its leadership, not to mention a moderate compared with the group's radicals.

And yet, no matter how little the NYPD understood CORE, by the end of 1963 BOSS had begun to hatch plans for derailing the organization's New York chapters. CORE's members had no idea what they were facing in the year ahead.[34]

6

Undercover

The NYPD's Holy Name Society held its forty-sixth annual Easter Communion breakfast on the morning of March 15, 1964. Holy Name was a brotherhood of Catholic police in a department where Irish cops dominated the leadership and made up the largest share of officers. Their Communion breakfast was a cherished event where members could let their guard down and celebrate off the clock—less an act of religious observance than a fraternal roast with red-meat conservative pronouncements and jokes about police abuses.

At the 1954 event, the society's guest of honor, Senator Joseph McCarthy, enjoyed boisterous ovations from officers as he attacked "Pentagon politicians" and "bleeding hearts." Six years later, the audience howled with laughter as the state's lieutenant governor (and later governor) Malcolm Wilson regaled them with a tale about his uncle, an officer who retired on proceeds from traffic ticket graft—some $60,000, or more than $600,000 in today's dollars.[1]

As was customary, officers began the 1964 event with Communion at St. Patrick's Cathedral on Fifth Avenue. Many attended in full uniform: double-breasted navy peacoats with brass buttons and matching slacks, topped with peaked caps featuring brass NYPD police shields. From St. Patrick's, more than six thousand officers marched in stern formation to the Midtown Hilton, a sparkling modernist showpiece that had opened to great fanfare the previous June, where they squeezed into three ballrooms—the biggest gathering to date at the city's largest hotel.

Four months earlier, in November, police had assaulted picketing CORE members outside the hotel, sending six of them to the hospital. But police commissioner Michael Murphy mentioned none of that as he addressed his officers at the breakfast. Murphy was a career policeman—fifty years old, Irish, and born and raised in Queens, where he lived with his wife and four children. He was only the eighth man in NYPD history to work his way up from the bottom of the department to its top position. "A big, bull-necked man, 6 feet tall and 210 pounds," in the words of the *New York Times*, Murphy was "impassive, cautious, perhaps a little suspicious with outsiders, relaxed and hearty with intimates."[2]

This morning Murphy was among intimates. As he looked out at the crowd, he laid his eyes on a sea of white men. At the time, less than 5 percent of the NYPD's ranks were Black. Women made up a mere 2 percent of the force. After commending his officers for expressing "publicly and proudly their belief in God," Murphy shifted to the focus of his talk: New York City's burgeoning civil rights movement. The commissioner acknowledged that some of the movement's leaders were "men of intelligence, stature, and good judgement." But a new wave of Black radicals betrayed their cause with "sinister motives" and "no real concern for the fight for equality." Activists' recent charges of police brutality against NYPD officers amounted to "an organized campaign to besmirch this department and increase disrespect for law and authority."

For his own officers Murphy had nothing but praise. "I cannot tell you how proud I am of how you have withstood the baiting, the insults, the unreasonable demands and the premeditated efforts to discredit your work." But he was unsparing in his message for civil rights troublemakers. "We will not be intimidated. We reject your lies and so do the people of this city."

Murphy singled out three of the worst offenders. The first was Jesse Gray, a rent strike leader in Harlem, whom Murphy blasted for seeking to "destroy the image that the New York police are democratic and not on the 'side of the slumlords.'" Another was "self-proclaimed leader" Malcolm X, a man who "advocates violence, bloodshed and armed revolt, and sneers at the sincere efforts of reasonable men to resolve the problem of equal rights."

But Murphy got the biggest response from his audience as he turned to a civil rights organizer who "presented a series of demands to this department and set a deadline for answer under threat of further 'direct action.'" Denouncing him as a reckless agitator, the commissioner bellowed, "We reject his demands and serve notice we will not be dictated to nor will we bargain or compromise with pressure groups."

The crowd of six thousand uniformed men erupted in applause. Murphy had not named the individual. But everyone knew he was describing Herb Callender.[3]

———

Thirty years old, Callender stood six feet, two inches, a handsome man with a dark brown complexion and a round face sporting a pencil moustache. The son of immigrants from the British West Indies, Callender struggled after his mother's death when he was just nine years old. Arrested twice before his sixteenth birthday, he dropped out of high school after just three semesters. At seventeen, Callender enlisted in the U.S. Army, where he served four years, including in the war in Korea.[4]

After returning to New York, Callender secured a position on the assembly line at Ford Motor Company in Mahway, New Jersey. There he joined the United Auto Workers, where he would go on to become the plant's first ever Black foreman and his union local's representative in the body shop. It was through the union that Callender was recruited by CORE to join one of the Freedom Rides in 1961, the twenty-first that year. Five days after volunteering, on June 13, Callender was sitting with thirteen other Black and white New Yorkers on a bus leaving the Washington, D.C., Greyhound terminal station for Florida.[5]

On the fourth day of the journey, as the bus stopped in the small town of Ocala, Florida, Callender and two other members of the

New York contingent asked to be served at a segregated restaurant in the station. Local sheriff's deputies arrested the trio, and Callender was given a six-month jail sentence, though he returned home on appeal before having to serve it. But back at home, Callender and the Freedom Riders were heroes. New York officials celebrated the daring integrationists, and Manhattan Borough president Edward Dudley declared July 7, 1961, to be Freedom Riders Day. Heralded as an unblinking commitment to fighting oppression, completing a Freedom Ride was regarded as a badge of honor in left-wing circles.[6]

Callender's ongoing legal struggles in Florida and the prospect of half a year in a jail did little to dampen his resolve to fight for racial justice. If anything, they whetted his appetite to resume his protest activities in New York. The following year, Callender and a self-described "handful of Bronx militants" organized the borough's first CORE chapter. Though the organization had nearly seventy chapters spread across the country, no other city had close to as many active members as New York. CORE members formed chapters in Brooklyn, Harlem, East Harlem, Downtown, and Queens, as well as on the Lower East Side and Staten Island.[7]

While New York City officials had applauded Callender's efforts to combat racial discrimination in the South, they were much less supportive when he brought his efforts home. Murphy's attack at the Holy Name breakfast was both political and personal. At its heart, it countered CORE's accusation that officers used unjustified force against defenseless Black and Latino citizens and even planted evidence and filed false charges against them. The charge outraged the NYPD's rank and file, yet CORE was adamant: these were crooked cops.

———

On January 17, Jesse Roberts had been convicted by the Bronx Criminal Court on narcotics charges and given a three-year suspended sentence. Two months earlier, when Roberts had reported a stolen car to the police department's 48th Precinct, he returned to his mechanic shop to discover officers inside without a warrant, holding a bag of weed they claimed they had found on the premises.

Worse yet, the brutal assault Roberts endured from officers later that evening went unpunished, with a grand jury opting to forgo charges despite testimony from a doctor that Roberts's injuries had resulted from a beating. Remarkably, Roberts's plight had triggered almost no community response—until CORE set about changing that.

"Dear Sir: On behalf of the victim of the brutal and inhuman experience described in the enclosed factsheet, Bronx CORE will wage a nonviolent protest in front of the 48th Precinct." So began Herb Callender's February 13 letter to NYPD Commissioner Murphy, Mayor Wagner, and Governor Nelson Rockefeller, with copies sent to the U.S. Justice Department and the United Nations Commission on Human Rights for good measure. "Our protest is aimed at the police brutality in this case and we are demanding an end to the cruel treatment of citizens by law enforcement officers from Birmingham to the Bronx." On February 14 and 15, roughly one hundred members of the Bronx CORE chapter followed through by picketing outside the Bathgate Avenue police station.[8]

It was a bold statement. New York City police had the largest department in the country and celebrated themselves as a national model of fairness and justice for law enforcement. But in the eyes of Bronx CORE, their officers were no better than Birmingham's notorious segregationist cops, who brutalized Black marchers with billy clubs, German shepherds, and fire hoses on national television.

Weeks later, Callender demanded to meet with Murphy in person. The commissioner pawned off the CORE organizer to Deputy Inspector Arthur Savitt, the department's top official for reviewing civilian complaints, and on March 6, Callender led a small group of CORE members to visit Savitt in his office at NYPD headquarters. The building was an imposing citadel of granite, constructed in the Second Empire style at the turn of the century and occupying a small city block on Centre Street just west of the Bowery and north of Canal. The "old, dirty gray building," one detective recalled in his memoirs, was "dark inside" and "didn't seem like a very pleasant place to work."[9]

Savitt heard out the CORE contingent as they recounted the ugly details of Roberts's case. Callender's group hoped to force a larger conversation about police brutality against Black and Latino New Yorkers. But after just half an hour, Savitt sent them on their way.

Leaving Savitt's office, Callender and his colleagues Howie Quander and Isiah Brunson pulled out handcuffs and locked themselves to an ornamental iron grill outside the commissioner's office. Two more CORE members and a pair of organizers from Progress for the Youth of Puerto Rico sat down in the hallway and linked arms with the handcuffed men. The group of seven demanded to speak with Murphy, only to learn that he was out of the office.

"Please leave," Savitt begged the demonstrators. "This is a public place for public business. You have made your complaints." The protesters refused to budge. Moments later, officers arrived with bolt cutters, snipping the trio's cuffs and moving the entire group into a police wagon to transport them to a precinct station, where they were booked for trespassing, disorderly conduct, and resisting arrest (see figure 6.1).[10]

———

The sit-in was a shock to the NYPD, announcing itself to department leadership as the opening salvo in a street-level organizing campaign, the first against New York police in more than a decade. By the middle of the 1950s, as anticommunist hysteria crested, city officials had succeeded in branding all criticism of law enforcement as communist subversion. This public relations campaign was so effective that protests against the police close to disappeared in New York—even as police violence against Black and Latino citizens continued unabated. In Harlem, "police brutality is an accepted fact of life," Black journalist Louis Lomax lamented in 1962. "Without such cases to report, Negro newspapers would have considerable blank space."[11]

Since the 1950s and early 1960s, the NAACP had sued the NYPD from time to time or sponsored rallies to denounce its most egregious acts of violence. At the same time, the Nation of Islam had organized small, brief protests outside courthouses and police stations in New York against police attacks on their members. But for CORE to deploy civil disobedience tactics used at segregated Southern lunch counters

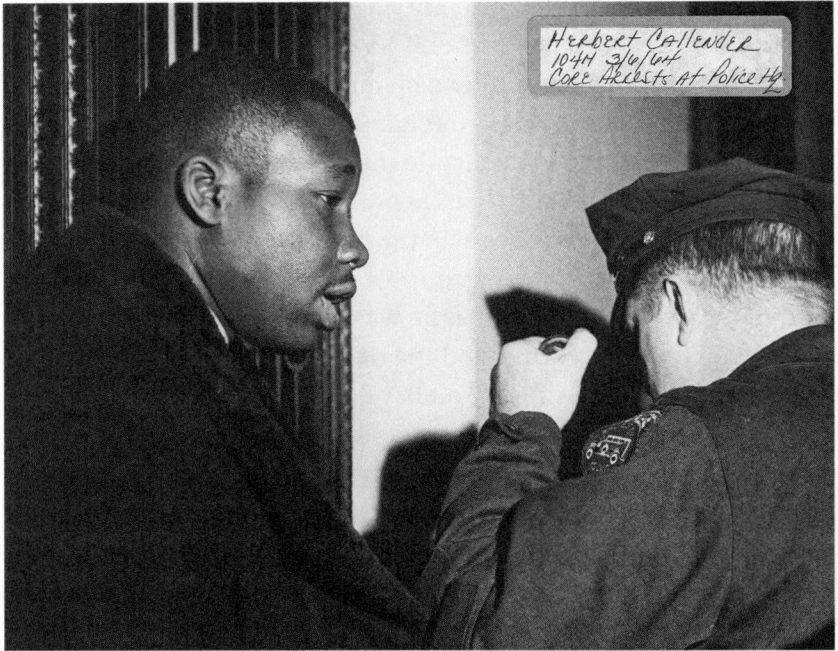

FIGURE 6.1. Officer cutting Herb Callender loose after he handcuffed himself to an iron grill at a protest inside NYPD headquarters, March 6, 1964. BSS 104-M, NYPD Intelligence Records, NYCMA.

and bus stations against the NYPD in its own headquarters—that was a daring move with virtually no precedent.[12]

To top it off, the March 6 precinct sit-in was just the start of CORE's day. Later that afternoon, members of the organization's East River chapter sat down linking arms across the Triborough Bridge and brought the entire flow of Bronx- and Queens-bound traffic to a standstill for almost half an hour as they protested East Harlem's underfunded city schools.

"CORE SITTERS SNARL COP HQ," read the *Daily News* headline the next morning. To reporters' disbelief, Callender and his colleagues had "audaciously conducted a sit-in demonstration in Police Headquarters itself—the first in city history." Arnie Goldwag, a staffer with Brooklyn CORE, told the newspaper that police could expect more sit-ins in their stations. Commissioner Murphy meanwhile declared that "no group can be permitted to disrupt police functions and thus endanger the well-being of the city."

"We are just going to have to get more and more, larger and bigger demonstrations," Callender told the *Amsterdam News*. "We'll have to shock officials and the public to get the city to face up to the realities of the day."[13]

Commissioner Murphy vowed that his department would "not submit to rule by pressure or mob." He ordered the addition of security checkpoints to the Centre Street headquarters and assigned four hundred office employees to start wearing uniforms in the building. Deputy Commissioner Walter Arm compared the measures to those following the Japanese bombing of Pearl Harbor and the Cuban Missile Crisis. CORE's demonstration inside police headquarters had so violated the department's honor that it merited the same response as a military attack.

Murphy's Holy Name harangue came nine days after the sit-in. His declaration of war netted Callender a new level of prominence, including a front-page mention in the *Times*. Bronx CORE was unfazed. Less than a week after the commissioner's speech, their chapter took their pickets to his own doorstep, crossing the East River to Murphy's home in Queens. Protesters carried signs reading "Get the Sadists Out of the Police Dept" and, in a double entendre that referenced Birmingham's public safety director, "No More Bull Murphy." With the past month's protests, CORE's Bronx, Brooklyn, and Harlem contingents—what one activist dubbed the "ghetto CORE chapters"—had established their credentials as one of the civil rights movement's most radical cohorts.[14]

Ray Woodall walked into CORE's office at 1301 Boston Road in the South Bronx on April 18, a month after the pickets at Murphy's home. Woodall explained to the chapter that he had worked with one of the borough's reform-oriented Democratic clubs but had tired of their moderation on civil rights. Though he lacked community organizing experience, he was eager to get involved.

The newcomer quickly made a positive impression. One CORE member remembered him as "a tall, good-looking Negro," an attractive man with a light brown complexion, a sharp dresser who stood over six feet. Woodall was soft-spoken and educated, a graduate of Manhattan College currently studying law at Fordham University. Perhaps because he so impressed them, or just because they were desperate for active volunteers, Bronx CORE's leadership waived the typical probationary requirements for Woodall, granting him immediate official membership.[15]

But Woodall was not quite who he seemed. His real name was Raymond Wood. Born in 1933, Wood bounced as a child between an aunt in Harlem and a foster parent in Chester, South Carolina, where he attended the town's Black high school and played on the football team. Family remember him as a "hotheaded" teenager who got into trouble on more than a few occasions. Shortly before he would have graduated, Wood left school and enlisted in the Air Force. He served four years, most of them as a communications specialist in West Germany. But his transition back to civilian life in New York was difficult. As Wood drifted from job to job and even contended with bouts of homelessness, he remained single and developed few friendships or connections in the city.[16]

By summer 1963, Wood was thirty years old, working part-time as a teletype operator for the phone company, and living in the Bronx. Striving to better himself, he took business coursework at Fordham University—his third attempt at college. When he inquired about a subscription to Encyclopedia Britannica's Great Books of the Western World series, a visiting salesman determined he could not afford the monthly payments.

The following spring, Wood joined the New York Police Department—a Black man on a force that was about 95 percent white. But Wood did not receive a badge or a uniform. He had been assigned to work for BOSS. His direct supervisor was Anthony Ulasewicz, a forty-five-year-old department veteran who had been selected earlier that year to revive the NYPD's infiltration of political groups, under new BOSS chief John Kinsella.

"In Harlem and elsewhere in America, demonstrators weren't just marching, busing, sitting in, or going limp; they were also arming themselves," Ulasewicz contended, as he later rationalized resurrecting undercover operations at BOSS. "America was living on the appearance that all was right with the world; it wasn't. The 1960s, when protest replaced patriotism, changed all that. Nothing's wrong with protest except when bombs and bullets are used as its symbols and innocent people are killed or maimed as a result."

Wood's supervisors thought the less he knew, the better. To maximize secrecy, BOSS interviewed candidates for undercover positions who had not yet entered the academy. No one outside a small leadership circle was to know who the red squads' spies were, and those spies were believed to be more convincing in the field if they had not been trained by the academy. BOSS trained its agents internally, in buildings separate from the academy and headquarters.

After Wood's initial interview, several BOSS officials expressed concern that he looked too much like a police officer. Ulasewicz disagreed, countering that Wood "could appear to be all things to all people," especially if they "put a big-brimmed hat on his head and a diamond on his pinky and stuck him up in Harlem." Wood, he argued, "could talk the talk, take care of business, act like a numbers man, a pimp, a big drug connection, an after-hours crap dealer, or a successful businessman tired of the white man's jive." Though Ulasewicz's assessment relied on racial stereotypes and the imagined appearances of various criminals, he was ultimately taken by Wood's powers of persuasion.

It is unclear whether Wood understood what he was getting into. He must have known he would be earning an annual salary of $6,235, or more than $64,000 in 2025 dollars. But did he understand that he would be sent into subversive organizations that, in Ulasewicz's words, "pose a threat to life and property?" And did he know that his first assignment would be CORE? Did he even know what CORE was? In Ulasewicz's recollection, candidates for undercover work were told "what they would be doing was important for the safety and security of the City of New York." But did Wood realize that he would be impersonating a civil rights organizer? Either way, Ulase-wicz was sure of his decision. "Without doubt he was the man for the job."[17]

———

Wood walked countless picket lines throughout spring and summer 1964. He "went along with whatever things we were planning to do," remembered CORE organizer Sol Herbert, and he was never "shy or afraid to speak up." With Callender's approval, Wood became the Bronx chapter's housing committee chairperson within two months of joining, and soon he was tasked with leading its voter registration efforts as well. More than anything, Wood made himself available.[18]

By the end of spring, Wood was communicating with the press on Bronx CORE's behalf. On May 30, the *Amsterdam News* reported that he and his colleagues were issuing court summonses to Mayor Wagner, City Comptroller Abe Beame, and State Comptroller Arthur Leavitt. Drawing on his purported expertise as a law student, Wood explained that public officials were violating New York's antidiscrimination statutes by employing contractors who refused to hire Black workers. On June 12, a judge in the Bronx Criminal Court dismissed the summonses as null and void.

Several days later, BOSS reported to the department's chief of detectives that, according to "a highly sensitive source," Bronx CORE had escalated their tactics, planning a citizen's arrest of Wagner, Beame, and Governor Nelson Rockefeller. Of course, CORE members had no idea that the NYPD knew about their plans. But if they had, they might have asked more questions about one of their newest and most enthusiastic organizers.[19]

———

On the evening of June 22, CORE was shaken with the news that three of its field-workers stationed in Meridian, Mississippi—Mickey Schwerner and Andrew Goodman, a pair of white New Yorkers, and James Chaney, a Black Mississippi native—had gone missing. The men had been working on the Freedom Summer voter registration project when they were pulled over in rural Neshoba County by a sheriff's deputy who arrested and jailed them. Local sheriff Lawrence Rainey and his deputies were the last people to admit having seen Chaney, Goodman, and Schwerner on June 21. Although their jail released the trio several hours before midnight, by early morning the men had still not returned to CORE's field office. A badly burned car with plates matching an automobile registered to CORE was pulled out of a swamp the following afternoon. But Rainey was not the least bit concerned about their whereabouts. "If they're missing, they just hid somewhere, trying to get a lot of publicity out of it," Rainey speculated to reporters.[20]

On June 24, New York's CORE chapters launched an overnight vigil in front of the U.S. Courthouse at Foley Square, and dozens of organizers vowed to "sleep-in" until federal authorities located the three men. "Demand F.B.I. Protect Lives of Civil Rights Workers," one placard at the encampment read. "Is the South in South Africa?" asked another.[21]

James Farmer made a predawn appearance at the vigil on June 27. Speaking to more than 150 protesters who had camped in the square for three days, the CORE national director accused Rainey and his deputies of having a direct hand in the three men's disappearance. This was not just a crime, Farmer insisted, but part of a larger pattern of law enforcement perpetrating a "reign of terror which grips Mississippi." At first glance, Farmer was condemning police violence in a single Southern state. But he was also addressing the trauma many New York CORE members had experienced the previous November when they had been attacked by the city's officers.[22]

In the wake of those attacks, Schwerner and his wife, Rita, had joined CORE pickets against police violence outside NYPD headquarters in November, as recorded in BOSS surveillance files. Granted, they were protesting an instance in which police had beaten, not killed, activists. But did the NYPD's acts of aggression share a kinship with worse violence? As CORE members saw it, police assaults on their organizers were not just a matter of officers losing their tempers but, in fact, were direct ideological attacks against the movement. From that perspective, New York officers and the segregationist sheriffs of Neshoba County might have much more in common than most wished to admit.[23]

As the Foley Square encampment continued, some CORE members contemplated more radical measures to awaken white New Yorkers to the racism that plagued their city. One of the demonstrators, a young woman named Barbara Loeb, recalled Wood proposing a bizarre idea for a protest. "We should bomb the sewers in New York City so that the rats would run throughout the white neighborhoods," he had suggested, without betraying a smile or hint of sarcasm. That way, white people "would know what it's like, just like we have rats in Harlem." Wood was not recommending that CORE necessarily hurt anyone—but it was still a dangerous idea, and one at odds with CORE's long-standing devotion to nonviolence. Loeb did not quite know what to make of the conversation—but it stuck with her.[24]

———

Herb Callender had come to trust Ray Wood. The two men were born within six months of each other, and both had finally figured out in their early thirties how to make their mark on the world. Both had lost their mothers at an early age and had been raised by their fathers; both were rebellious teenagers who left school before graduating; both had served in the military and then struggled professionally when they returned to civilian life; both were handsome, charismatic Black men and gifted leaders.

Callender's work was taxing, and he needed all the help he could get from Wood. The Bronx chairman remained a top target of law enforcement, and in the first half of 1964 the NYPD arrested him on five different occasions. As CORE's national convention in Kansas City in July approached, Callender chose Wood to represent the radical New York chapters in their ongoing disputes with national leadership over strategy. Meanwhile, Wood's cover was so complete that BOSS's own internal files described him as an officer in the organization's Bronx chapter, not as one of their agents.[25]

On July 1, Bronx CORE pushed ahead with their plan to place the mayor, comptroller, and governor under citizen's arrest for labor discrimination. The activists had informed the officials of their intentions by telegram and even written to Commissioner Murphy and the superintendent of state police "enlisting their cooperation" with the arrests, in a move clearly intended to goad them. Moments after releasing their statement, Callender and his colleagues walked into the New York County Criminal Court for a hearing on their trespassing convictions from their sit-in at the NYPD headquarters in March. "The sentences that have been handed out in New York City are harsher than those given Civil Rights demonstrators, even in Mississippi," the CORE members contended. "We hope we don't face 'Mississippi justice' in this court house."[26]

The three CORE workers Chaney, Goodman, and Schwerner—still missing after ten days—were fresh on everyone's minds, as were the local law enforcement officials who denied any involvement in their disappearance. "The events of the past week show the fallacy of a corrupt agency investigating itself," the CORE statement continued. Because "those who administer the law are not above the law," Bronx CORE was demanding the creation of a civilian review board to oversee complaints against the NYPD.[27]

In retrospect, it is difficult to understand why experienced civil rights organizers would attempt to arrest New York's mayor and governor, much less announce their plans in advance. But Bronx CORE's actions were based on a sound reading of the law. New York State's criminal code did allow for "arrest by a private person," if a citizen informed the arrestee of the charges and delivered them immediately to a magistrate or officer of the law. The activists' telegram appears to have been conceived to fulfill this requirement.

But the law also stipulated that citizens making an arrest must have witnessed the lawbreaker committing the crime. This was the most questionable aspect of the plan, though CORE could argue that the mayor was knowingly violating New York's prohibition on discriminatory hiring by providing public funds to an employer that refused to hire Black workers. Lawyers for the city did not see things this way, however, and in confidential memos to Wagner and the police department they advised that any private citizens attempting to arrest the mayor be apprehended.[28]

The scheme also grew out of a keen understanding of the media. Conflict with law enforcement—be it in the form of arrests or violence—brought coverage, and that, in turn, allowed protesters to circulate their message. Except for the Black-owned *Amsterdam News*, the city's reporters displayed a strong preference for covering civil rights stories in the South instead of in their own backyard. To get the press and the public to pay attention to racial injustice in New York, Callender understood that Bronx CORE had to be more confrontational than organizers in other parts of the country. The sit-ins at police headquarters and city hall in March and now an attempt to arrest the mayor—they all pointed to a larger strategy. But the far-fetched plan to arrest New York's mayor still raises a difficult question: How much was it the brainchild of an undercover police operative hoping to ensnare unwitting activists in legal trouble?

———

On the morning of July 15, Callender, Wood, and John Valentine, Bronx CORE's new housing chairman, arrived at City Hall Plaza. Callender wore his signature dark suit, white shirt, and skinny black tie, while Wood sported a white seersucker jacket, black bowtie, and dark sunglasses (see figure 6.2). Callender and Wood looked every part the young civil rights leaders of 1964. The long hair and bare feet that appeared at protests later in the decade were still a long way away.

Virtually as soon as the three CORE members showed up at city hall, they were surrounded by reporters questioning them about their plans. Distracted, the trio failed to notice Wagner's limousine pull up. The mayor made it into the building with his deputy and two detectives, as Wood, Callender, and Valentine were late to follow. As they tried to enter the building, Callender asked a police officer in civilian clothes to assist in the arrest. "I am not going to make any arrest—and neither are you," Inspector Henry Yack snapped back.[29]

FIGURE 6.2. NYPD Bureau of Special Services agent Ray Wood, masquerading as a CORE activist on the day he prodded Herb Callender into a failed attempt to arrest Mayor Robert Wagner. LC-DIG-ds-17340, NYWT&S Collection, Prints and Photographs Division, LOC.

Blowing past Yack, the CORE men made it to the entrance to the mayor's office, where Sergeant Dennis Burke stopped them to explain that they would be breaking the law by attempting to arrest the mayor. A photograph of the scene shows Callender facing off against Burke just inches from the detective's face. The men are surrounded by a scrum of at least thirty onlookers, including four reporters holding microphones. Wood appears in the middle of the shot, standing right behind Callender. Even through the lenses of his dark sunglasses, we can make out the sharp glare he is giving to the photographer.

A silent NYPD surveillance film shows a similar scene of a crowd jostling around Callender as he gives what looks to be an

FIGURE 6.3. Plainclothes officer arresting Herb Callender after he attempted a citizen's arrest of New York mayor Robert Wagner, a scheme encouraged by undercover police spy Ray Wood that landed Callender in the psychiatric ward of Bellevue Hospital. AP Photo.

impassioned explanation of the attempted arrest. Callender's body language registers a mix of assuredness and agitation. Moments later, we see Burke whisking Callender away outside city hall as a crowd of reporters race to keep up.[30]

Callender, Valentine, and Wood soon found themselves standing before Judge Edward Caiazzo in the Criminal Court. Just two days earlier, Callender had gotten off with a thirty-day suspended sentence from the same judge for the March sit-in at NYPD headquarters. But

Caiazzo was now in a less forgiving mood. "You are not in the South," the judge declared, as he excoriated Callender for his newest arrest. "If any place has treated a minority well, it is the City of New York." Without providing any evidence, Caiazzo was characterizing the city as a bastion of racial equality and accusing Callender of slandering the mayor.

It would have been difficult to find a judge more eager to reprimand the three defendants. Caiazzo was a strict disciplinarian and enthusiastic enforcer of judicial decorum, the city's only judge to commence each courtroom session by requesting everyone in attendance join him in reciting the Pledge of Allegiance. Once, he ejected a woman who had worn slacks to a traffic court hearing and ordered her to return the next day wearing a dress. "You come here looking like a man," Caiazzo admonished Lois Rabinowitz of Jamaica, Queens. "The court is entitled to respect and dignity."[31]

Callender might have expected jail time from Caiazzo, having been arrested just two days into his suspended sentence on a previous charge. But the judge had something different in mind. "Our government is not run by people who take the law into their own hands," he lectured, dismissing those "who wish to go off half-cocked." Instead of an extended stay in the Tombs, the judge ordered that Callender be committed to the notorious psychiatric ward of the city's Bellevue Hospital. "I think he needs a little attention," the judge concluded.[32]

Callender for his part was defiant. "I'm not crazy," he insisted. "I'm black."[33]

———

The attempted arrest of Wagner was the latest development in months of carefully orchestrated protests against the NYPD. But the very next day after Wood, Callender, and Valentine charged into city hall, an unplanned conflagration of resistance against police violence exploded in New York, totally eclipsing CORE's campaign. On July 16, Patrick Lynch, a white building supervisor in the Yorkville neighborhood on the Upper East Side hurled racial slurs at a group of Black junior high students and sprayed them with a hose after they refused to move from his stoop. As the teenagers began to throw bottles and trash at Lynch, off-duty police lieutenant Thomas Gilligan rushed out of a nearby business. Within moments, the officer encountered fifteen-year-old James Powell exiting Lynch's building after the supervisor had chased after him. Gilligan—who had twice previously shot and injured individuals—claimed that Powell was holding a knife. The officer later insisted that he flashed his badge and fired a warning shot before Powell lunged at him, leaving him no choice but to shoot the teenager, killing him instantly.

Students rushed to the scene to view Powell's body. Outraged at the killing of their classmate, roughly three hundred teenagers joined in throwing rocks and bottles as they were confronted by seventy-five police officers, while Gilligan was whisked away. Miraculously, the day ended without any further injuries or arrests—but the protests were far from over.[34]

Within hours, CORE had seized upon Powell's death as a rallying cry. That afternoon, representatives from the organization's East River chapter and its national office held a press conference on the corner of Lexington and 77th, just two blocks from the scene of Powell's death, renewing calls for a civilian board to review officer misconduct. The following day, a protest organized by CORE drew some two hundred students who marched from Wagner Junior High to the nearby 19th Precinct of the NYPD, carrying signs reading "Stop Killer Cops" and "Save Us From Our Protectors" as they chanted, "Freedom Now."[35]

A day later, CORE organized a street rally in Harlem at 125th Street and Seventh Avenue. Among the speakers was Judith Howell, a seventeen-year-old colleague of Callender and Wood in the Bronx CORE chapter. "James Powell was shot because he was Black," Howell told the crowd. Following several other speakers, the Reverend Nelson Dukes urged attendees to follow him and march on the nearby 28th Precinct (see figure 6.4). Outside the station, a crowd of about one hundred people joined Dukes, shouting, "Murphy must be removed," and, "Killers, murderers, Murphy's rats." As a few stray bottles and garbage can lids were thrown—by whom

FIGURE 6.4. Junior high students affiliated with CORE on their way to an NYPD precinct station to protest the police killing of fifteen-year-old James Powell, July 18, 1964. LC-DIG-ds-17338, NYWT&S Collection, Prints and Photographs Division, LOC.

it was not clear—a contingent led by Dukes and a CORE organizer approached Inspector Thomas Pendergast to inform him that they would not leave until Commissioner Murphy made an appearance in Harlem and Gilligan was suspended.

After police erected barricades on the street outside the station, sixteen protesters sat down on the sidewalk and assumed the non-violent poses taught by CORE in its trainings, tucking their knees to their chests. Other protesters were dragged into the station by police. As those standing in the crowd showered projectiles onto the police, dozens of officers spilled out of the station, and before long they were joined by nearly fifty members of the Tactical Patrol Force, a forerunner of the SWAT teams that later proliferated in America. By now, nearly five hundred protesters had gathered and were starting to spread to nearby blocks. Officers charged into the crowd, swinging their clubs wildly and beating anyone who stood in the way. In the hours that followed, some stores in Harlem were ransacked as isolated fires were set. Gunfire echoed throughout the community, much of it courtesy of service weapons.

Though police quelled the evening's disturbance by daybreak, the pause was temporary. The Harlem uprising was well underway. Over the next four days, fires, looting, and clashes with police consumed Uptown and spread to Bedford-Stuyvesant in Brooklyn. By the time they had finally concluded on July 22, more than 120 people had been injured, 465 had been arrested, and one had died. Though they would soon be overshadowed by far more violent and deadly uprisings in Watts, Newark, and Detroit, the riots in New York were significant in two critical but overlooked respects.

First, though media characterized it as an uncontrolled explosion of violence, the Harlem uprising was just as much a series of organized protests by groups committed to fighting police violence in New York. Chief among those groups was CORE, which coordinated or participated in no fewer than seven of the thirteen rallies, public meetings, and pickets against police violence in the week of the uprising. Joining CORE in challenging police abuses this week were an array of leftist groups including the Progressive Labor Movement, Youth Against War and Fascism, and the Socialist Workers Party. Though this did not quite amount to an alliance, Powell's killing had jolted the normally discordant groups into a short-lived united front against the violent misdeeds of the NYPD.

Second, as the most visible organization to face off against police during the riots, CORE was blamed for instigating the uprising. In a five-page timeline in BOSS files titled "<u>EVENTS LEADING TO RIOTS</u>," the red squad argued that the primary culprit of the events of July 16–22 was the city's foremost civil rights organization—not decades of violence against Black New Yorkers, or the city's deep-seated racial inequality, or even Gilligan's killing of fifteen-year-old James Powell. Virtually every single one of the more than twenty events detailed in the document was a demonstration or meeting organized by left-wing groups to oppose police violence. The intelligence unit had determined that activist groups—most of all CORE—had triggered the uprising, inciting an otherwise content Black community into violent attacks on the police. Far short of prompting any meaningful reflection by law enforcement, the events of July 1964 only reinforced BOSS's perception that surveillance and infiltration were necessary responses to CORE and any other group that questioned the NYPD.[36]

———

Police violence against the movement persisted as a national story for the rest of the summer. On August 4, FBI agents discovered the bodies of James Chaney, Andrew Goodman, and Michael Schwerner in an earthen dam in Neshoba County. Rumors swirled about the culpability of Sheriff Lawrence Rainey and his deputy Cecil Price, who had arrested the men and released them from jail hours before their disappearance, and the two officers were questioned repeatedly by federal investigators. In July, two family members of the missing men, Fannie Lee Chaney and Rita Schwerner, had brought an unsuccessful federal suit against Rainey, Price, and every law enforcement officer in Mississippi, accusing them of denying civil rights workers protection and demanding that a federal monitor be placed in each sheriff's office in the state. Investigative journalist William Bradford Huie later claimed that in researching for his 1965 book *Three Lives for Mississippi*, "if there was a state police officer who doubted Deputy Price had been party to the murderers, I didn't meet him." That year, federal prosecutors indicted sixteen men on charges of conspiring to violate the murdered trio's civil rights. Price, one of seven convicted, ended up serving four and a half years in federal prison.[37]

Through the Freedom Summer project of 1964, CORE staff like Chaney, Goodman, and Schwerner had worked with Black Mississippians to secure voting rights and establish schools and community centers. That August, on the largest platform ever provided the project, one of Freedom Summer's fiercest advocates bravely explained to America how police violence remained among the most formidable barriers to achieving those goals. Earlier that year, the Council of Federated Organizations, a coalition of the state's civil rights groups, had established the Mississippi Freedom Democratic Party (MFDP) with the goal of displacing the state's all-white Democratic Party and challenging its seating at the Democratic National Convention in late August.

On August 22, two days before the start of the convention, members of the insurgent group took their fight to the Democratic Party's Credentials Committee in Atlantic City, with one MFDP member after another testifying on the stifling discrimination they were subjected to by state Democratic Party officials. Among those to speak before NBC's national camera crew were Mississippi State NAACP head Aaron Henry, Martin Luther King Jr., and Rita Schwerner, now a field secretary for CORE.[38]

But it was Fannie Lou Hamer, the MFDP's vice-chair, who electrified the Credentials Committee (see figure 6.5). In just over eight minutes of testimony, the forty-six-year-old former sharecropper delivered a gut-wrenching testimony that laid bare the gruesome violence perpetrated by law enforcement officials against Black Mississippians as they attempted to exercise the franchise. Hamer's speech centered on an incident from June 1963 when she and four of her comrades were arrested after a voter registration workshop by local police and the State Highway Patrol for trying to use a restroom in a white-owned restaurant in the town of Winona.

"We are going to make you wish you was dead," a patrolman told Hamer in jail. In a ritual of torture that recalled the cruelties of slavery, two Black prisoners were then ordered to beat Hamer with a blackjack. "I began to scream and one white man got up and began to beat me in my head and told me to hush," Hamer recounted. "One white man—my dress had worked up high—he walked over and pulled my dress. I pulled my dress down—and he pulled my dress back."

The Credentials Committee and the audience sat there stunned, absorbing Hamer's impassioned retelling of the terrible physical and sexual abuse she had endured at the hands of police. "All of this is

FIGURE 6.5. On August 22, 1964, Fannie Lou Hamer testified to the Credentials Committee of the Democratic National Convention on her physical and sexual assault at the hands of law enforcement officers, exposing a national audience to a brutal variety of political policing. LC-U9-12470B-17, *U.S. News & World Report* Collection, Prints and Photographs Division, LOC.

on account of we want to register, to become first-class citizens," Hamer concluded.

> If the freedom Democratic Party is not seated now, I question America. Is this America, the land of the free and the home of the brave where we have to sleep with our telephones off of the hooks because our lives be threatened daily, because we want to live as decent human beings, in America?[39]

As many people in the room wept, Hamer received a standing ovation. The MFDP organizer had transformed law enforcement's attempt to humiliate and dehumanize her into a clarion call for justice.

Only after returning to her motel did Hamer learn that NBC had cut its live feed of the Credentials Committee three minutes and forty-one seconds into her testimony, just moments before she started to describe her arrest and beating in Winona. President Johnson had informed the network that he had an important announcement to make and, believing that he was about to reveal his running mate, NBC switched to a live feed from the White House—only to learn that the president was commenting on the less-than-newsworthy nine-month anniversary of Kennedy's assassination.

And yet, the president's attempt to censor Hamer failed. In light of her extraordinary statement, NBC made certain to re-televise her testimony in its entirety later that evening. If anything, taking Hamer off the air had made her a much bigger story. Though she and her colleagues failed to convince the committee to replace the segregated delegation with the MFDP, Johnson's attempt at censorship guaranteed that millions of households would hear Hamer's vivid description of her horrific treatment by law enforcement.

It is worth speculating why Johnson chose to preempt Hamer of all speakers and why he waited more than three minutes into her testimony to do so. Without a doubt, she was a powerful speaker with a bracing story of trauma that put Mississippi's white delegation in a terrible light. And yet, Johnson did not attempt to preempt King, to name another powerful speaker who testified, nor did he preclude Hamer's entire testimony.[40]

One intriguing possibility is that Johnson or someone on his staff knew that Hamer was moments away from sharing a story of disturbing police violence and sexual abuse. In the month leading up to the convention, Hamer had keynoted a tour of Freedom Rallies with stops along the East Coast. As the *New York Amsterdam News* reported, the gatherings targeted "the racist police state of Mississippi, of what it is and how it effects the rights and liberties of all Americans, especially in the Negro ghettoes of the North."[41]

The very day before the MFDP's testimony to the Credentials Committee, the *New York Times* ran a nearly four hundred-word piece in its front section under the headline "Mississippi Negro Tells of Beating," with the first three paragraphs describing Hamer's story of her beating by Winona law enforcement. With echoes of CORE's Committee of Inquiry on police violence two years earlier, a committee including former Kennedy administration staffer Arthur Schlesinger Jr. and fellow historian C. Vann Woodward questioned those testifying, in a trial run of what they could expect in Atlantic City.[42]

Johnson and his staff, if they had read the *Times* the day before the Credentials Committee, could have known exactly where Hamer was going with her speech. While it cannot be known for sure, it may well have been Hamer's account of physical and sexual violence by police that the president of the United States decided could not be aired on national television on the cusp of his nomination. The country, Johnson might have reasoned, simply could not stomach such hard truths.

———

Back in New York, Herbert Callender was readjusting to life after his five-day stay in Bellevue Hospital's psychiatric ward ordered by Judge Caiazzo. Only as the Harlem uprising was petering out on July 20 had authorities released him from what could be presumed to have been an effort to sideline the CORE leader at the height of the protests. The American Civil Liberties Union's New York chapter blasted the institutionalization as an "outrage," nothing more than an attempt to humiliate Callender. "I don't think it is fair to treat a

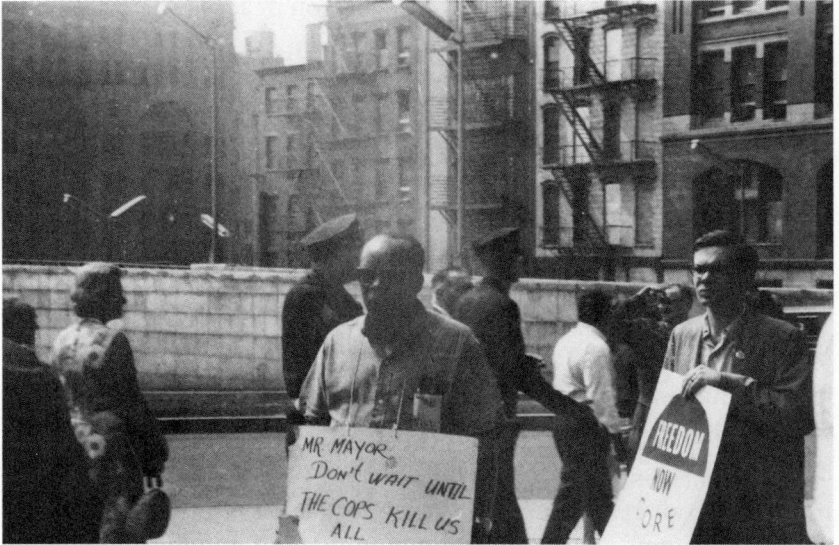

FIGURE 6.6. NYPD surveillance photograph of protesters denouncing police violence and demanding a civilian review board, June 29, 1965. #44198, PUM Series, NYPD Photo Unit Collection, NYCMA.

peaceful civil rights demonstrator as if he were an insane person," the Bronx CORE leader remarked upon his release.

Records from Callender's commitment remain closed to the public to this day, per New York State's health records law, so one can only guess what he experienced there. But his punishment did not stop at Bellevue, as Callender was also sentenced to sixty days in jail for disorderly conduct. Wood was spared any punishment, however, and according to BOSS official Ulasewicz, Caiazzo was "discreetly asked not to impose a jail term" on the undercover officer.[43]

Three years later, the Black Arts Movement poet David Henderson memorialized Callender and his colleagues for their daring in "Boston Road Blues," an ode to the neighborhood where their CORE chapter was headquartered.

> 1501 Boston Road is Bronx C.O.R.E.
> (stompers have risen to politics)
> Herb Callender Isiah Brunson knife riding
> shit talking genius pacifist.[44]

Wood's role in the audacious scheme burnished his radical credentials as well, and many local activists were impressed by a picture of him published in the *Times,* looking chic and unperturbed in his jacket and dark sunglasses behind Callender as Detective Burke led him away. But Wood was not entirely pleased, later complaining that CORE had left him to pay his own bail, even though that payment had not come out of his own pocket. His employer had covered it, after all.[45]

Wood's employers were not satisfied yet either. From their vantage point, the attempted arrest of Wagner had temporarily sidelined Callender and exposed how unhinged CORE had become, but it had failed to capsize the organization. According to Ulasewicz, the attempted arrest "was regarded as a joke and an embarrassment by angry Blacks who wanted real action from CORE, not just symbolic action doomed to failure." Whether that was true or not, BOSS officials believed that dissension among activists over the attempted citizen's arrest was a vulnerability they could exploit.[46]

Wood's supervisors considered his work unfinished. Dangerous militants were on the move in New York, those eager to spark destructive riots and massive destruction, radicals who would not stop at arresting a mayor. It was these so-called angry Blacks denounced by Ulasewicz that BOSS hoped their man on the inside could sabotage.

7

Infiltration

Assistant U.S. Attorney Stephen Kaufman rose to address Judge William Herlands. Three days earlier, on June 14, 1965, jurors in the federal courthouse at Foley Square in Manhattan had convicted Robert Collier, Walter Bowe, and Khaleel Sayyed of conspiring to destroy the Statue of Liberty, the Liberty Bell, and the Washington Monument with thirty sticks of dynamite. Herlands was now deliberating on sentencing for the three Black activists.

The defendants had sought to justify their actions with claims of drawing "attention to the problems facing Negroes in the United States, with particular focus on the civil rights movement," Kaufman contended. "Your honor, it is beyond doubt that every decent American wants to join with the Negro community in achieving progress in civil rights. It is a problem that must be solved and it receives the daily effort and attention of the government and all decent citizens."[1]

But now, Kaufman explained, a clique of dangerous militants had hatched a plot that threatened to erase the movement's gains.

If people had been killed or national monuments destroyed these defendants would have caused irreparable harm to the civil rights movement and risked arousing unwarranted indignation towards responsible and legitimately concerned members of the Negro community. They are, if your honor please, these defendants, enemies of the Negro community. They are subversive fanatics and are traitors to the civil rights movement.

Thankfully, this cabal had been stopped at the last possible moment by the NYPD's Bureau of Special Services, most of all second-grade detective Raymond Wood, who had infiltrated the would-be bombers' circle and alerted authorities to their plans.

The defense saw things differently, of course. Mark Lane, one of Collier's attorneys, had himself been imprisoned as a Freedom Rider in Mississippi in 1961, so he was all too familiar with the repressive measures white authorities took against activists for racial equality. Lane proceeded to turn the spotlight onto the prosecution.

> Since Mr. Kaufman has raised the question of determining—taking it upon himself to determine—who are the friends of the civil rights movement and who are the enemies of the civil rights movement—I think one must address oneself to the Police Department which he has lauded for its role in this case and to the fact that the Police Department sent into the Congress of Racial Equality, a legitimate civil rights organization in the city of New York, an agent provocateur, a spy.

Lane rejected the notion that anyone involved in civil rights activities would blow up the Statue of Liberty. Anyone except law enforcement, that is. Ray Wood had entrapped the three defendants, Lane insisted. "The civil rights movement and the terror in those who participate in the civil rights movement was skillfully utilized by Mr. Wood." The undercover officer had seized on the fears and anger triggered by racist violence against the movement and offered his own destructive plan as an opportunity for retribution. "How would you like it if your daughter was blown up as were those four children and church in Birmingham, Alabama?" Bowe recounted Wood asking as he suggested his plot to the three codefendants.

Jurors had already found this explanation unconvincing. But Lane could not resist bringing up his theory again. It was Wood, not the defendants, who had dreamed up the scheme to destroy a trio of the nation's most beloved monuments. He had pushed it along, transforming it from a joke into a concrete plan. Law enforcement's duty, Lane reminded the courtroom, was "to prevent the occurrence of crime; not to encourage it, not incite it, not to suggest it. And there is no question but that in this case there was encouragement."[2]

Ray Wood's undercover work offers us what may be the best-documented case of police infiltration of the civil rights movement. Few if any red squad officers who masqueraded as activists left behind a comparable paper trail. Indeed, it stands to reason that many such undercover missions were never disclosed, if one considers how few red squads unmasked their own agents or left behind records of any of their activities. In spring 1965, as Congress and a newly elected president threw their support behind landmark civil rights legislation, the prosecution of Bowe, Sayyed, and Collier made it clear that the movement's political gains would not slow police machinations against Black activists. If anything, they would accelerate them. As the three so-called State of Liberty plotters and their supporters learned the hard way, police spies like Ray Wood would engage in all manner of unethical, dangerous, and illegal behavior if it produced the arrests that their commanding officers so desperately craved.

———

In the wake of the Harlem uprising of July 1964, the NYPD embraced the idea that protest groups in New York were instigating a war on law enforcement. The NYPD simply could not believe that Harlemites would erupt in anger as they had after the police killing of James Powell without guidance from activists, and the department refused to recognize any distinction between legal protests and illegal acts of violence. Exemplifying this idea that civil rights groups had fomented the riots was an unsigned seven-page internal report by BOSS titled "C.O.R.E. Participation in N.Y.–Harlem–Bedford-Stuyvesant Riots, 1964."

CORE members had created the riots by charging police with violence against Black citizens, BOSS claimed. "The 'police-brutality' theme" was nothing more than "a long-term expression of communist groups in America in their journals, newspapers and speeches," the memo's authors insisted. "The expression 'police-brutality' is designed, primarily, to inflame the public anger against police arrest tactics or mob control and cause a breakdown in relationships between the police force and the community. Statistics are readily available which prove that the overwhelming majority of 'police brutality' charges are either patently false or grossly exaggerated."[3]

The press and elected officials had been duped by CORE's claims of fighting racial discrimination. In fact, BOSS officials insisted, a "great part of the responsibility for the riots must be attributed to the activities of the national CORE headquarters and its several New York chapters," due to their "exploitation of hostile feelings against the white society in general and white policemen in particular." BOSS further alleged that CORE members had encouraged violent attacks on the police in speeches they gave.[4]

Behind closed doors, as police accused the civil rights group of criminal liability in the riots, Ray Wood assumed a leading role in one of its most radical chapters. While events in Harlem spiraled that July, he was in the streets marching with Bronx CORE, at times even protesting the police in front of their headquarters. But Wood never produced any evidence that CORE members had organized the uprising. Coming up empty-handed by the end of summer 1964, the undercover officer drifted out of CORE in search of more radical groups, ones he hoped might employ violence in the name of racial justice.

———

Wood set about on a fishing expedition for revolutionaries. Just days after uprisings had rocked New York in July, the BOSS agent attended a "Rally to Protest Police Terror in Harlem" organized by the Militant Labor Forum. Sponsored by the Socialist Workers Party, the forum speaker series was a key meeting place for radicals in New York; Malcolm X had delivered two lectures there since April of that year.[5]

Wood was likely drawn to the Militant Labor Forum because of Paul Boutelle. Boutelle was a leading Socialist Workers Party official who happened to also work as a salesman for the Great Books of the Western World series. In summer 1963, Wood mailed a postcard to the company requesting information on the books, as part of a personal self-education effort that appears to have had nothing to do with police work. Boutelle was dispatched to his apartment to make the sale. After it became clear that Wood could not afford the books, Boutelle changed the subject to politics. As Wood recalled, Boutelle "was trying to ask me what I was doing in regard to the Black question." Wood had little interest in the topic, but the two men exchanged contact information before Boutelle left.

A year later, Wood attended the Militant Labor Forum on police violence. After the program, Wood approached Boutelle and reminded him of their previous meeting. But this time Wood introduced himself by his newly adopted name, Woodall. He related that he had been working with CORE but had grown disillusioned with what he saw as their moderate approach. Boutelle was pleased to meet again, and he updated Wood's name in his address book.[6]

By this time Boutelle had also gone to work for the Freedom Now Party, an all-Black political group launched by activists on the leftmost wing of the civil rights movement. Among its founders were journalist William Worthy and attorney Conrad Lynn, committed radicals who had participated in the Committee to Aid the Monroe Defendants, a support group for NAACP dissident and self-defense advocate Robert Williams, who had fled his hometown of Monroe, North Carolina, for Harlem and then Cuba after police falsely charged him with kidnapping a white couple in August 1961. In its call for an all-Black party, Freedom Now rejected the Democratic Party's tolerance of police violence, asking in a manifesto they distributed at the March on Washington, "What sense does it make to go on supporting the party of Eugene (Bull) Connor?"[7]

Tony Ulasewicz later recalled that he had assigned Wood to focus on subversive groups posing "a threat to life and property." In light of that directive, Wood's departure from CORE suggests that he gave up on the idea that the group was dangerous. Now, in fall 1964, he inserted himself into the Freedom Now Party to see how far they would go to achieve their goals.[8]

BOSS provided Wood the funds for his membership dues. As he had at CORE, he wasted little time working his way into the leadership of the party's New York chapter, a reflection of how valuable his enthusiasm was to a small political group. By October, Wood accepted Boutelle's invitation to join him as co-treasurer of the party chapter, and the two opened a joint checking account in the chapter's name. But once again, Wood came to realize that the group he had infiltrated was not filled with violent extremists.[9]

If Wood's superiors were surprised, or even disappointed, to learn that the Freedom Now Party was not hatching violent plots, they still recognized the value of Boutelle's connections. On December 14, Wood and Boutelle attended a rally sponsored by the May 2nd Movement, a student group launched by Progressive Labor, a Marxist-Leninist party that was the first U.S. organization to oppose an American war in Vietnam. There Boutelle introduced Wood to Robert Collier. A thirty-year-old activist with ties to the Freedom Now Party, Collier had returned earlier that summer with more than eighty people from a trip organized by the Student Committee for Travel to Cuba. A political education program of Progressive Labor, the group openly advertised its defiance of the U.S. ban on travel to the socialist redoubt ninety miles south of Florida. Upon their return from Havana to Kennedy Airport, they hosted a press conference where they were awaited by reporters, as well as several BOSS detectives and FBI agents. Though no arrests were made, the travelers had their passports revoked on-site.[10]

On the trip to Cuba, Collier and several other activists had established the Black Liberation Front (BLF), a caucus within the travel party that did little more than pose for pictures with a banner featuring the group's name. Though the BLF comprised no more than a couple dozen members, it caught the attention of law enforcement officials. In July 1964, the FBI opened a file on Collier containing an eight-page outline detailing his employment record, addresses, and political beliefs, based on interviews with his acquaintances.[11]

Later, when Wood recalled his first encounter with Collier at the Freedom Now rally, he claimed that it was only by chance, not on orders from superiors. Boutelle purportedly had described Collier to Wood as "someone very important I want you to meet." The day after the rally, Wood again saw Collier at a Progressive Labor meeting. Collier, as Wood recounted, related that he had recently gone to a party attended by the Cuban guerilla leader Che Guevara, who was in town for a meeting at the United Nations. Guevara had asked Collier if he could find scientific books to ship to Cuba—and now Collier was asking Wood, whom he had just met, if he might help him with the project, which violated the United States' embargo on the importation of goods into Cuba. As it turned out, Wood knew of a large collection of books that Downtown CORE needed to dispose of as they prepared to be evicted from their office.[12]

The next day, Wood picked up Collier in a car rented by BOSS, and the two men headed to the CORE office on Delancey Street. There they found a large collection of books and clothes set aside to be shipped to Black communities in Mississippi for a relief drive. The two men filled up sixteen boxes with some two hundred books to send to Cuba instead. Wood noted in a report that Collier also took some garments for his own personal use. The implication was clear: Collier was willing to pilfer supplies intended for the Southern movement. He was not fighting for Black people in America but, rather, was out for himself and a traitor to his country.[13]

Wood later reasoned that offering up the books had put Collier at ease, prompting him to open up about far more sensitive plans. According to the BOSS agent, Collier revealed the true purpose of his trip to Cuba. It had not been for student travel or even for Marxist indoctrination; it was to obtain training in "guerilla warfare" and instruction in karate and bomb-making. Now that he was back in the States, Collier intended to enlist his own militia of Black men across the country to wage war against the American government, with the Freedom Now Party providing the facade of a legitimate organization. To boost the BLF's paltry numbers, Collier planned to recruit teenagers for the guerilla campaign and take them on paramilitary training trips where they would hike long distances with nothing to eat other than a few beans and kernels of rice paired with strips of raw bacon. These teenagers would form revolutionary cells across the country, and after several years of preparations, they would carry out bombings on New York City police stations, the White House, and the U.S. Capitol.

Any such scheme to organize underaged novices into overthrowing one of the most powerful governments in the world likely would have struck even the most militant advocates of violent revolution as far-fetched and ill-conceived. Collier after all had severe logistical limitations, with little money and neither a car nor a phone to his name. One would expect any serious person to think Collier delusional, if he had in fact said these things. But Wood later testified that he took Collier at his word. The little resistance Wood offered was to encourage Collier to consider less ambitious ideas, telling him his plan for nationwide revolution "sounds great, but I wish we could get to those damned cops in Harlem."[14]

It strains credulity to think that Collier would divulge his plan for armed rebellion to a man he had just met. Perhaps Wood had earned his trust by coming up with the idea to ship books to Cuba. Though Wood claimed it had been Collier's suggestion, maybe the undercover agent had proposed it in the hopes of impressing his new target. Either way, the result was the same. Wood charmed Collier by sharing three things that were in scarce supply in New York's activist circles: material resources and almost unlimited time and energy to assist in any project.

———

Over the next several weeks, the two men grew closer as the end of the year gave way to 1965. On January 10, Wood and Collier invited seventeen teenagers to join them at Boutelle's Upper West Side apartment to discuss their plans for insurrection. The meeting went poorly, however, with Boutelle accusing Collier of scaring off the group with overheated talk of revolution.[15]

Wood remained committed to helping his new friend carry out whatever plans they could concoct. One day, he surprised Collier with a gift: a copy of *Explosives and Demolitions*, the U.S. Army's guide to bomb-making. Collier had not asked for the book, but Wood thought that it would interest him. Then, on January 19, Wood arrived at Collier's Lower East Side apartment bearing more gifts, all purchased with NYPD funds: cotton balls, empty glass bottles, and three gallons of gasoline. The items represented the basic ingredients needed for manufacturing Molotov cocktails.[16]

That evening, Collier introduced Wood to Khaleel Sayyed and Walter Bowe, a pair of friends with backgrounds in civil rights work. As a Howard University undergraduate, Sayyed had joined the Nonviolent Action Group, a campus organization affiliated with SNCC through which he met several of that group's future leaders, including Stokely Carmichael and Courtland Cox. With the Nonviolent Action Group and SNCC he joined protests in Cambridge, Maryland, including one in May 1964 where he was arrested for disorderly conduct while protesting Alabama governor George Wallace.[17]

Bowe, who at thirty-two was ten years Sayyed's senior, was a full-time youth counselor at the Henry Street Settlement House, a husband, and a father. He was also a karate enthusiast and an accomplished jazz trumpeter and had once led a band he half-jokingly called Walter Bowe and His Angry Young Men. If Bowe now identified as a musician and family man, he had until recently considered himself part of what he called the "sit-in generation." As CORE and SNCC's Freedom Riders wound their way through the South in May 1961, Bowe had helped to organize the Washington Freedom Riders Committee, a group of around 150 leftists from New York and Philadelphia who traveled to the nation's capital to demonstrate in front of the White House and demand that the Kennedy administration protect the bus integrationists with federal troops. Then, in 1964, Bowe and his wife collaborated with Malcolm X to establish the Organization of Afro-American Unity, in which Sayyed served as one of Malcolm's bodyguards.[18]

Wood later testified that on the evening he met Bowe and Sayyed, the pair debated how they could best dramatize their anger over America's oppression of its Black citizens. In Wood's retelling, Bowe was quick to chime in with an idea. "I used to look at that old girl out there in the harbor," referring to the Statue of Liberty. "If we can make that girl blow her top, we would really put a hurt on that damn old bitch."

Wood was enthusiastic. "Man, we can place some primer cord around her neck and blow her head sky high." If the men really wanted to make a statement, Wood claimed Bowe suggested, they could destroy multiple targets simultaneously—not only the Statue of Liberty but also the Liberty Bell and the Washington Monument. Wood testified that he even encouraged the men to "go out to those Nazi storm troopers down in Virginia," in reference to the American Nazi Party. "I think we should blow up that damn headquarters of theirs." Reminding the group of the four girls killed in the Birmingham church bombing, Wood urged the men, as Bowe recalled, "to get down to the business of doing what men are supposed to do in these instances, and that in his estimation was seeking vengeance."[19]

"I think we should get to know each other better before we pull a job of this size," Sayyed demurred. "I don't even know Ray." The twenty-two-year-old proposed instead that they rob a few stores in Harlem. As Wood recalled, he, Bowe, and Collier overruled Sayyed, and each resolved to visit the Statue of Liberty in the coming days to case its security. When the four men gathered a week later to share their findings, they agreed that it would be easy to sneak explosives into the statue's head.[20]

But how would they procure the explosives? Collier came up with an idea. In Cuba he had befriended Michele Saunier, a French-Canadian woman with links to the Front du Libération du Québec, a paramilitary organization that had carried out a series of bombings in the name of Québécois independence. Collier believed that she might be able to get her hands on some dynamite. The only problem was that the men would have to travel to Montreal to procure explosives from Saunier and her associates. The trip was too risky to make by plane or train, and Collier did not have access to a car.[21]

Yet again, Wood came through. With funds from BOSS, he rented a car for him and Collier. The men were unconcerned that the round trip required twice crossing an international border, according to Wood, who quoted Collier as improbably vowing to "waste the cats right on the scene" if Border Patrol agents gave them any problems on their way back into the United States.[22]

If the trip raised questions for Wood about the legality of operating outside New York City—or the country for that matter—he never admitted it. What did concern him was the prospect of being discovered as a spy far from his colleagues. Wood later maintained that he took the international trip without notifying anyone in the department. But FBI documents contradict that claim, as did Ulasewicz, who recalled in his memoirs that BOSS officials had agonized over letting an undercover operator travel abroad, as they believed that it was "extremely dangerous."

Wood's trip convinced BOSS's leadership to disclose their unit's deep cover operations initiated in 1963 to the FBI almost two years after they had been launched. Whether due to mistrust of the Bureau, competitiveness, or simply a desire for secrecy, BOSS officials had until then concealed Wood's work in CORE and the Freedom Now Party—as well as that of undercovers Abe Hart in Progressive Labor and Gene Roberts in the Organization of Afro-American Unity—even as FBI agents conducted extensive surveillance on all four groups. The red squad's reluctance to reveal this work suggests that it believed it needed no help from the Bureau with political policing. But the geopolitical stakes of dispatching an officer abroad without notifying federal authorities were too great. As Wood and Collier prepared to leave for Canada, FBI agents established surveillance of border crossings in Upstate New York where the two men might return with explosives.[23]

In Montreal, Collier and Wood stayed with one of Saunier's comrades, Michele Duclos, a television reporter. The two women were surprised that Collier and Wood had driven nearly eight hours for the explosives, noting that Québécois separatists got most of their dynamite from New York. Indeed, BOSS officials were well acquainted with the domestic market for dynamite, having just that month identified five local retailers in New York who sold large quantities of plastique. But the red squad's leadership may well have hoped that they would crack a bigger case if they dispatched an officer to obtain explosives from separatist radicals and Cuban sympathizers in Canada, instead of black market munitions dealers based in their own jurisdiction.[24]

Wood played a decisive role in advancing the plot. Collier had nowhere near the money needed for the dynamite, so his undercover companion used $112 of the department's funds—equivalent to more than $1,100 in 2025 dollars—to cover the rental car, explosives, and assorted travel costs. After several days in Montreal, Wood and Collier returned empty-handed on February 1, with a plan to wait another two weeks in New York for Duclos to deliver the materiel to them once she could procure it.

Upon returning home, Wood set about ensuring that the plan would come to fruition. When Wood met with BOSS officials to debrief them on the successful payment for the dynamite, he characterized Collier, Bowe, and Sayyed as cruel conspirators unconcerned with whether people died due to the plot. The men had "no remorse, none whatsoever, in terms of loss of life." And yet, Wood himself did not express any concerns that dynamite might kill people if it somehow detonated during Duclos's delivery. It was as though he considered his participation in furthering a dangerous plot inconsequential.[25]

The only concern that Wood expressed to Collier, Bowe, and Sayyed was that their plot might have come under surveillance. Though the undercover officer was trying to camouflage his own deceptions, his three targets did have reason to worry. Collier's neighbor had reported, for instance, that he had overheard men in their building hallway discussing how to run a wire into Collier's apartment while he and Wood were on their Canadian road trip. When the neighbor approached the men, they claimed that they were with the phone company but agreed with his suggestion to return when Collier was back in town. Hours later, the neighbor caught another man who purported to work for the phone company as he attempted to enter Collier's apartment. But Collier did not even own a phone.[26]

As for Bowe, the previous weekend he had also encountered a man claiming to work for the phone company in the basement of his apartment building. The building's superintendent later shared that a white man had approached him with a picture of Bowe and asked a series of questions. That evening, Bowe picked up his phone and was surprised to hear music coming out of the receiver, a strong indication that his line had been compromised.

"Why in the hell are we all of a sudden being treated like we are dangerous criminals?" Wood reported Collier asking. Perhaps his own phone was tapped too, Wood suggested, and he instructed the group to stop calling him at home. The men were convinced that they needed to be more careful about what they said and where they said it. Bowe recalled recommending that they drop the plan—but Wood was having none of it.

"He called us Uncle Toms, I think he called us deserters, and I think he said that we had grown callous to the needs of our people," Bowe recounted. If they really wanted to fight racial oppression, Wood insisted, they would follow through with bombing the Statue of Liberty. In a claim that beggars belief, Wood later reported that Bowe responded to the insults by recommitting to the dynamite plot then and there, in an apartment the men had just speculated might be under surveillance.[27]

––––

The FBI became much more interested in Wood and Collier once they returned from Canada. What had begun as an undercover investigation operated by the NYPD transformed into a joint investigation by city and federal authorities. The two agencies had something of an arranged marriage, as FBI special agent Gus Micek maintained an office within NYPD headquarters, in a rare level of coordination between the Bureau and a local police department. Still, neither agency seemed to trust the other entirely as the Statue of Liberty investigation unfolded.

In February, after questioning the NYPD on "discrepancies" in information provided by Wood, the FBI insisted on speaking to the undercover officer. NYPD officials invited Wood to a secure room at the Waldorf-Astoria to meet with four representatives of the FBI, among them the New York office's special agent in charge, and a group of five NYPD officials that included the chief of detectives and the chief inspector, the department's third-highest official. The investigation had become a top priority for both agencies.

After questioning Wood for more than three hours, FBI officials were satisfied that his account was "substantially identical to data previously furnished," blaming any previous discrepancies on Wood's purported tendency to mix up dates. Most importantly, FBI officials were convinced by Wood himself, noting that he "made an excellent impression on NYO representatives as intelligent, clean-cut, competent, lucid individual, and appears to be sincere and conscientious." Their initial expectations for Wood had been low, as reflected in their racist surprise at a Black officer's professionalism and skill. These were officials, after all, who may have never even worked with African Americans before, coming from a Bureau in which less than half of 1 percent of agents were Black—a proportion far lower than even overwhelmingly white police forces such as the NYPD could claim.[28]

Three days later, on February 15, Michele Duclos left Montreal with two friends in a Rambler American convertible carrying more than two dozen sticks of dynamite concealed in the trunk. The group made it through customs without a hitch, but as their car approached Manhattan, FBI agents began to follow them. Intercepting the explosives before they reached America's most populous city was less important than catching certain people with the dynamite—namely, the Black organizers Wood had targeted.[29]

Shortly after dropping off her friends, Duclos noticed that she was being followed. Breaking away from her pursuers, she pulled off into the Riverdale section of the Bronx, where she buried the dynamite in a shallow hole in a garden next to a parking lot surrounded by apartment buildings. She then drove to a Manhattan hotel and called Wood at home. Fearful of saying much over the phone, Duclos insisted that Wood come meet her right away. When he arrived, Duclos was in a state of near panic as she explained where she had left the dynamite.

Wood headed straight to the parking lot in the Bronx, where he found the explosives just as Duclos had described them. Despite the grave danger they posed to the residential neighborhood, Wood left the explosives barely hidden by a pile of soil and a rock. He needed Collier to take possession of the dynamite. Wood had not come this far, impersonating an activist with a fake name for ten months, only to nab a small-time Canadian television reporter.

Though it was the middle of the night, Wood called his superiors to rent him another car. Wood was soon driving to the Lower East Side to pick up Collier. In Wood's retelling, Collier could barely contain himself as the two sped back to the Bronx. "Man, this Black Liberation Front is a real bitch," Collier supposedly gloated. "Nobody knows anything about our operation. I mean we've been so cool so far that we've been able to keep everything just within the group of us."[30]

When the pair arrived at the parking lot, Wood pretended to be unsure of the dynamite's location, allowing Collier to unearth a Moore Paint box containing the explosives and a set of blasting caps. Just as Collier carried the box to the rental car, a loud voice from behind the two men called out, "Hold it. New York City Police. Hold it."[31]

———

"4 Held in Plot to Blast Statue of Liberty, Liberty Bell and Washington Monument—A Rookie Policeman Here Infiltrated Group of Negro Extremists." So read the top headline of the *New York Times* on the morning of February 17. A detailed account of the investigation followed, accompanied by individual headshots of Collier, Bowe, Sayyed, and Duclos, whom authorities had arrested separately over the course of the previous day (see figure 7.1). Veteran war correspondent Homer Bigart credulously paraphrased the police explanation of the group's "bizarre motive," contending that Collier sought to "maim these symbols of American democracy to dramatize the plight of the Negro."[32]

The *Daily News* front-page headline was concise but no less dramatic: *"HERO COP FOILS BOMB PLOT—Liberty Target; Girl & 3 Seized."* Coverage in New York's self-proclaimed "Picture Newspaper" took up nearly four of the first five pages of that day's tabloid, with a profile of Wood, the man of the hour, as well as photos of the

FIGURE 7.1. Activists Walter Bowe, Khaleel Sayyed, and Robert Collier were arrested in February 1965 and ultimately imprisoned for an alleged plot to dynamite the Statue of Liberty, a scheme for which NYPD undercover officer Ray Wood provided material and logistical support. AP Photo.

four arrestees and a close-up shot of Bowe's wife and sixteen-month-old child as Bowe was processed for arrest. The *Washington Post, Boston Globe, Chicago Defender,* and *Irish Times* placed the story on their front pages as well, with magazine pieces appearing in *Newsweek, Life,* and *Time.*[33]

News publications impugned the arrestees before they were even tried in court, repeating law enforcement's account of the arrests almost verbatim. As readers learned, Bowe was a Castro supporter and a member of the Fair Play for Cuba organization that Lee Harvey Oswald had joined. Collier had received a dishonorable discharge years earlier for a knife fight in the Air Force; more recently he had visited Cuba. And Sayyed had been charged with assaulting a police officer in recent months—though no article mentioned that the arrest had failed to result in a conviction. Taken almost word for word from a press statement released hours after the arrests by U.S. Attorney Robert Morgenthau, these details rendered the three men as violent subversives. The *Times* and *Daily News* even printed the suspects' home addresses, family details, and alma maters, all culled from Morgenthau's press statement. This was a routine act of slow violence perpetrated by authorities, what ACLU attorney and political policing expert Frank Donner dubbed the "exposure system," a means of public shaming that HUAC and other communist hunters had used to great advantage against alleged radicals.[34]

The hero of the day was Wood. The undercover officer's colleagues had arrested him with Collier, unaware of his identity until they took the pair to a precinct station and a superior officer ordered, "Open the handcuffs—he's one of us." From there, Wood was spirited off to a press conference assembled in his honor at police headquarters downtown. When he arrived, he found nearly one hundred reporters and Commissioner Murphy awaiting him. "I have a surprise for you," Murphy informed Wood in front of the gathered press. The commissioner then presented the undercover officer with a second-grade detective's shield, although he had not even completed the academy. He was promoting Wood on the spot and awarding him a 28 percent annual raise, from $6,325 to $8,126, for a salary equivalent to more than $82,000 at the time of writing. "You certainly deserve it," Murphy told Wood.

"Gold Badge of Courage for Cop; Dynamite Outplayed," the *Daily News* headline announced following the press conference, in a fawning piece that insisted Wood had been assigned "to live for months with terror, death no further away than one wrong word out of his mouth." The paper quoted police claims that Wood was "taken to Quebec with the plotters to buy dynamite," put in such grave danger on the international road trip that "he couldn't risk contacting us. If he had been killed, we would not have known it. He was completely on his own with the most fanatic inner circle of the conspiracy mob." The NYPD and federal authorities were doing their best to deny that they had sanctioned the undercover foray out of the country. Accompanying the *Daily News* article was the single photograph of Wood permitted by the department, a shot of the newly minted detective in a blazer, back to the camera with head bowed, as he received his gold shield from Murphy (see figure 7.2). Wood looked downward to prevent his face from appearing in the photograph— but perhaps he also felt a tinge of shame for his actions and, almost as if praying, was silently asking for forgiveness.[35]

———

The Statue of Liberty defendants' federal trial began in the U.S. Courthouse on May 17. In the three months since their arrest, Michele Duclos had turned state's witness and agreed to testify against the others in the hopes of bypassing prison and returning to Canada. All four sat in jail, unable to pay their bail—$50,000 for Bowe and Sayyed and $100,000 for Collier and Duclos, the latter amount equivalent to more than $1,000,000 in 2025. After receiving the devastating news that their friend and comrade Malcolm X had been murdered just five days after their arrest, Bowe and Sayyed were both denied permission to attend his February 27 funeral.[36]

Bowe, Sayyed, and Collier's charges contradicted white liberals' assumptions about a civil rights movement with a saintlike devotion to nonviolence. Headlines about "Negro extremists" scheming to destroy the country's memorials to liberty did the movement no favors, and most civil rights organizations wanted little if anything to do with the men. CORE, which had fallen prey to Wood's masquerade just one year earlier, kept its distance.

And yet, the involvement of leading civil rights lawyers in the men's defense made it clear that the movement had not given up on them entirely. Of the four defense attorneys working the case, only Sayyed's lawyer was not connected to the movement. Representing Collier were Mark Lane, who had joined CORE members on Freedom Rides and picket lines, and SNCC lawyer Len Holt. Bowe retained Ernst Rosenberger, who had defended Freedom Riders and other civil rights workers on behalf of the ACLU.[37]

FIGURE 7.2. NYPD commissioner Michael Murphy promoted Ray Wood to second-grade detective before an audience of gathered reporters, a reward for his role in the arrest of the purported Statue of Liberty dynamite plotters. LC-DIG-ds-17339, NYWT&S Collection, Prints and Photographs Division, LOC.

From the start, the defense questioned the constitutionality of the case against their clients, first by zeroing in on the jury. Though Manhattan's population was nearly one-quarter African American, only one of ninety people in the trial's jury pool was Black, and once he was struck, the jury was left entirely white. To make matters more dire for the defendants, two of the first twelve jurors selected were former police officers. But the defense's motion to dismiss jurors before the trial was rejected by Judge William Herlands without much deliberation.[38]

Lane and Holt also hoped to put Wood and BOSS on the defense for their legally questionable tactics. But discrediting the prosecution's star witness proved much harder than anticipated. Assistant U.S. Attorney Stephen Kaufman succeeded in convincing Herlands to exclude almost any evidence or testimony that raised doubts about the legality of BOSS's work or cast Wood in an unflattering light. Among the many questions that Herlands blocked Wood from answering were "Did the New York City Police Department send you into Bronx CORE as an agent of the Police Department?"; "As a member of the CORE leadership, you did make suggestions, didn't you?"; "Did you receive advice and orders in terms of what your activities should be in these organizations?"; "Did you ever carry a tape recorder on your person?"; and even "Do you know what a tape recorder is?" Herlands sustained objections to every one of these questions and dozens more, admonishing Lane that Wood's "intent, purpose and motive is by itself immaterial and irrelevant."[39]

Herlands preempted virtually any scrutiny of BOSS's operations, as though Wood alone bore responsibility for the undercover sting. "You are not entitled to know who gave him the orders," the judge lectured Lane in response to his continued questions about Wood's superiors. Here was a Black officer, in a department that was 5 percent African American, being forced to account for the actions of the entire NYPD's political intelligence unit. BOSS itself was virtually all white, except for officers assigned to the "Black Desk," the subunit that investigated African American activists. By blocking the naming of almost any additional members of BOSS, the prosecution prevented larger questions about the legality of the unit's clandestine operations. Wood's white superiors avoided testifying, both BOSS chief John Kinsella and unnamed supervisors like Ulasewicz.

And yet, Wood admitted that he was conflicted about his work, at least to those he spied on. Not long after he surfaced, he told a former CORE colleague, "I did the right thing. I joined CORE because I believe in the principles of CORE. I did not join CORE at the request of the Police Department, because I was in CORE before I was a police officer." It was a dishonest version of his timeline but nonetheless revealing. Even after he was hailed as a hero for foiling a purported dynamite plot, Wood still wanted to be viewed as someone who had joined the movement with sincere intentions.[40]

Additional inconsistencies plagued Wood's account. Chief among them were the two versions of Wood's report on December 16, the day that Collier supposedly disclosed his plans for violent revolution. In Wood's telling, he first composed notes by hand on December 17 and then dictated them to a typist about a month later. But there were glaring differences in the two reports. Wood's handwritten notes made no mention of Collier's vow to organize a militia of Black guerillas to attack police stations, the White House, and the U.S. Capitol. The subsequent typed reports, however, described the violent conspiracy in lurid detail. "I doubt if I would have carried a diary around with me for fear of my life," Wood claimed, chalking up the discrepancy to the danger of keeping notes while undercover.[41]

The defense team seized upon one detail as a possible explanation for the difference in the accounts. The typed version displayed the letters "TT" and "FM," while the handwritten notes did not. Wood first claimed under oath that he had typed the entire report, initials and all. Then, moments later, he conceded that he was unsure whether he had—and admitted that he was acquainted with BOSS official Teddy Theologes and a police stenographer named Frances Molino. Ultimately, the prosecution agreed to the defense's demand to affix an addendum to the trial record: Molino had typed the notes by taking dictation of Theologes's verbal account of a phone conversation with Wood in which the undercover officer summarized his original handwritten notes. Taken altogether, it seems most likely that either Theologes or Wood fabricated the whole story of the revolutionary plot in order to establish that Collier—and not Wood—had devised the plan to blow up the Statue of Liberty.[42]

Though Wood recalled most of his two months of undercover work with the BLF with laser-like precision, his memories faltered in the face of sensitive questions. When Lane inquired whether the newly minted detective could "recall ever telling Mr. Collier that you did not give a damn whether white people were killed," the best he could muster was, "Not to my recollection, no, sir. I don't remember making any statement like that." Pressed as to whether he had urged Herb Callender to attempt the ill-fated citizen's arrest at city hall, Wood replied uncertainly, "To the best of my recollection, sir, I made no such suggestion to Herb Callender that he should arrest Mayor Wagner." And when asked whether he had kissed Michele Duclos—a *Village Voice* article published during the trial reported that Wood had seduced numerous CORE women to extract information from them—even then Wood waffled, replying, "To the best of my knowledge, I did not kiss her."[43]

Lane and Holt also tried to determine whether BOSS had violated the law by surveilling the defendants and breaking into Bowe's and Collier's apartments without warrants. But Herlands prohibited defense attorneys from questioning Wood or any other NYPD official on the matter of surveillance. This was despite two recent Supreme Court rulings—*Mapp v. Ohio*, which invalidated evidence obtained from warrantless searches, and *Silverman v. United States*, which barred electronic surveillance resulting from illegal entry into private property—that both suggested that recording devices in Collier's and Bowe's homes would have been illegal. And in Wood's own notes—which surfaced years later in BOSS's archival records, though he apparently never submitted them as evidence in the trial—he detailed how his colleagues had impersonated telephone company officials as they unlawfully forced their way into Bowe's and Collier's homes.[44]

In yet another blow to the defense, witnesses were blocked from testifying that Wood had a history of goading activists to commit violent acts. Lane offered an affidavit from CORE member Barbara Loeb recounting the conversation at the June 1964 vigil in Foley

Square in which Wood suggested that they "bomb the sewers in New York City." A skeptical Loeb had countered with the idea of blowing up the Statue of Liberty as an act of protest against American hypocrisy. It was a hypothetical conversation, and one that Loeb had not taken seriously at the time, but it suggested that Wood considered the idea of bombing the statue months before meeting Collier.[45]

Then, when CORE member Jeremiah Teahan appeared in court, repeated objections by the U.S. attorney paused his testimony before he could recount his own conversations with Wood at Foley Square. In a sidebar out of earshot of the jury, Lane informed the prosecution and judge that Teahan planned to share that Wood had tried to recruit him to blow up the Statue of Liberty the previous summer. But Herlands agreed with Kaufman that such testimony was irrelevant, and he barred any statement from Teahan that concerned events prior to Wood's first encounter with Collier in December 1964. By ruling that Wood's behavior in CORE had no bearing on his infiltration of BLF, Herlands provided the detective and his BOSS colleagues an extraordinary measure of protection for their legally questionable actions.

And yet, Wood still admitted under oath that he had taken multiple actions critical to advancing the alleged dynamite plot. He had provided Collier the Army explosions manual and the ingredients for Molotov cocktails, both without being asked; he had covered the majority of the cost of the dynamite with police funds; he had provided the car for the Montreal trip, when Collier had neither his own vehicle nor the funds to rent one; and he had served as the telephone contact for Duclos's dynamite delivery since Collier had no phone.

For all these reasons, defense attorneys accused Wood of entrapping the defendants. They cited the Supreme Court's 1958 ruling in *Sherman v. U.S.*, which identified the telltale sign of entrapment as criminal conduct that "was 'the product of the creative activity' of law enforcement officials." As Judge Herlands instructed jurors,

> If you find that Wood, the policeman, merely afforded a favorable opportunity or facilities to Collier and Bowe for the commission of the alleged crime, such conduct on the part of Wood does

not constitute entrapment. Entrapment would occur only if you find that Wood induced Collier and Bowe to commit the crimes charged in the indictment.

While the defendants were not required to prove entrapment, "the government must prove its absence beyond a reasonable doubt." If there was even a moderate possibility that Wood had entrapped the men, the jurors were to acquit them.[46]

"Their conspiracy could hardly have been followed through as far as it was if it had not been for the intervention and assistance of Raymond Wood," *New York World-Telegram* columnist Murray Kempton posited in a May 1965 column, "A Policeman's Plot." A former socialist, Kempton had examined informers who spilled on left-wing activists in his 1955 book, *Part of Our Time: Some Ruins and Monuments of the Thirties*, a meditation on Depression-era communists and the backlash they faced after the war. In his signature deadpan, Kempton characterized Bowe, Collier, and Sayyed as "the most inept of conspirators. So inept in fact that it is possible to wonder how much they meant to be conspirators at all." If most reporters were taken in by the official narrative of Wood's heroics, Kempton cast a skeptical eye on the police spy. "It is altogether hard to see where the revolution would have been without the help of the cops," Kempton mused in closing his piece.[47]

———

In the end, none of Wood's inconsistencies or BOSS's legally questionable actions made any difference. On June 14, after deliberating for a little over three and a half hours, the all-white jury of eleven men and one woman found Bowe, Collier, and Sayyed each guilty on two charges, one for conspiracy to destroy federal property and another for the importation of dynamite. The three men appeared "stunned and bewildered" upon hearing the verdict, the *New York Times* reported.[48]

Three days later, as both sides reconvened for the sentencing hearing, Kaufman insisted that the trio had disgraced the cause of racial equality. "They sought to exploit the program of the civil rights movement for their own nefarious purposes," the prosecutor charged, taking pains to construct an argument that condemned the three activists while showing deference to the movement as a whole. That spring, polls showed that Americans regarded civil rights as the country's most important issue, with respondents backing demonstrators in Selma by a two-to-one margin over police. Aware of how strong sympathies were for the movement at this moment, Kaufman did not condemn all civil rights protesters—an argument likely to fail in New York City, even with an all-white jury—but, instead, denounced the defendants as renegades who sought to exploit the movement's good name for their own evil intentions.[49]

Lane rejected the prosecution's claims. "No one has said from the first moment until this time that it would have been an act on behalf of the civil rights movement for the Statue of Liberty to have been blown up." Instead, an undercover police officer had attempted to exploit the movement's good name to convince activists to use violence. "The civil rights movement and the terror in those who participate in the civil rights movement was skillfully utilized by Mr. Wood," Lane contended, reminding the judge that the undercover officer had told Bowe he had a responsibility as a Black father to avenge the deaths of the young girls killed in the Birmingham church bombing.[50]

But Lane's arguments fell on deaf ears. Herlands ultimately saw no reason to consider Wood's role in furthering the plot as he determined the defendants' punishment. After hearing arguments from Lane and the U.S. Attorney's Office, the judge gave Bowe, Collier, and Sayyed the maximum sentences possible, ten years each in federal prison.

———

The so-called Statue of Liberty plot struck many observers as a bizarre scheme by extremists with communist ties but no connection to the civil rights movement. In some ways, this interpretation served the purposes of not only law enforcement, who had to contend with widespread positive feelings toward the movement in

1965, but also civil rights organizations, who feared that hysterical charges of Black radicals gone amok could damage their cause. Even much of the sensationalist reporting on the case resisted the idea that Bowe, Collier, and Sayyed's case had any bearing on the movement's leading groups.

But the case did provide activists with an urgent set of warnings. The movement now had good reason to watch not only for surveillance but for active infiltration by police masquerading as organizers. Wood had been convincing in his role as a devoted CORE member. Could officers in other cities do the same? One Black organizer in Brooklyn suggested that they could, pointing to his colleagues' failure to detect Wood's subterfuge: "In CORE we suspected the white folks as the cops or the organized leftists," he told *Village Voice* reporter Susan Brownmiller. "But who would have looked at him?"[51]

Wood's spy work also signaled that Northern police were poised to intensify their efforts against movement groups as they pressed further into their cities. Bill Mahoney, a former SNCC staffer turned writer, described the Statue of Liberty trial in the radical *Liberator* magazine as "the same old shit: southern shit, northern shit . . . American shit." But if BOSS's work was any example, Northern police were more sophisticated in undermining the movement than their colleagues in Alabama and Mississippi. Instead of condemning the civil rights movement as subversive, prosecutors and police in New York claimed a color-blind opposition to racial discrimination while they assailed the civil rights cause's purported bad apples, the activists who had drifted into violent extremism and threatened to take the movement with them. If they could be stopped, Kaufman and BOSS argued, citizens could be kept safe. And instead of deploying an all-white police force against the movement, the NYPD had assigned a Black undercover officer to police his own community, all the while hoping that an integrated detective corps would dispel any accusations of racism levied against the intelligence unit. In a word, New York police had devised a politically savvy blueprint for repression that other police departments would soon replicate.[52]

8

Traitor

U.S. News & World Report was eager to record Los Angeles police chief William Parker's reaction to the Harlem uprising in July 1964. Parker was the most prominent police official in the country, the head of the third-largest police department in the country and the longest-serving chief among America's ten largest cities.

Parker did not hold back. Asked whether the civil rights movement was responsible for that summer's uprisings, Parker decried civil rights activists who manipulated Black people, dupes who were easily fooled because they "account for a fair proportion of the nine million functional illiterates in the United States."

But ignorance was the least of the sins the chief assailed in the interview. "The continued attack upon the police in this country is one of the great tragedies of our time," Parker charged. Calling out CORE by name, Los Angeles's chief blasted organizations that "direct their attack upon this local department today and that local department tomorrow and another one the next day," as defenseless law enforcement officers had no choice but to "stand there without any voice whatsoever to move up and to meet this abuse."

In Parker's eyes, the nation's police faced a vicious onslaught from leading civil rights groups. Unimaginable to him was the possibility that any of his officers might sympathize with the civil rights struggle. Even his department's handful of Black officers, Parker believed, had little affinity for the movement because they were "treated with contempt by their own people."

The idea that an LAPD officer might not only respect the civil rights movement but join it never occurred to Parker. And yet, within a year, the LAPD's leadership would seek to remove one such officer from their department, a man who wore a police uniform but in his free time attended rallies and joined pickets for equal rights, who dared to condemn the LAPD in print as a racist police force, and who even joined CORE as it demanded Chief Parker's resignation.[1]

———

Mike Hannon once thought that the prospect of working for the Los Angeles Police Department was "kind of romantic." In 1958, he joined the LAPD at twenty-one, a father of three looking for adventure and something that paid more than his work as a draftsman. Tall and thin with blue eyes, blonde hair, and thick-frame glasses, Hannon had a bookish air to him. The son of a prosperous contractor who grew up in Los Angeles's Silver Lake neighborhood, his background was unlike that of his many working-class colleagues on the LAPD. Hannon's first year on the force was uneventful, but it was an exciting job, maybe even a calling.[2]

But when Hannon was transferred to the Newton Division in 1959, his real "education began." The division's station lay on Newton Street in the heart of the community that had attracted more than one hundred thousand Black new arrivals from Southern states since World War I. By the 1950s, as many middle-class African Americans and businesses departed the area for recently desegregated communities to the west such as Crenshaw and West Adams, impoverished residents with more limited job prospects stayed behind.[3]

Hannon and most of his colleagues at Newton were white, of course. Just 4 percent of the entire department's officers were Black, and they were restricted to working by themselves in segregated squad cars, as though they were incapable of doing the work of white officers. At the same time, the department patrolled the Newton Division much more aggressively than other parts of town; in 1961 it spent four times as much to police each resident of the area than it spent per capita in the predominantly white West Los Angeles district. "Negroes in Los Angeles never know where or at what hour may come blows from the guardians of the law who are supposed to protect them," the NAACP charged in a report on police violence the next year.[4]

Hannon's white colleagues celebrated these disparities, dubbing their jurisdiction "occupied Newton." Hannon regularly heard officers spew racist invective. One lieutenant maintained that Black people were naturally more violent than whites because they were "not far removed from the stench of decaying elephant meat." While the man's choice of words "was more picturesque" than that of most of his colleagues, Hannon observed, "his attitude was common" in the division.[5]

———

In June 1960, Mike Hannon received an outstanding evaluation from his commander, Captain Ed Davis, who rated Hannon's performance as "very good to excellent" and predicted that he would soon make "an outstanding officer." Yet, as Hannon's confidence grew, he earned a reputation as a difficult colleague who shared his opinions freely. In summer 1962, Hannon was disciplined for bickering with his peers and given what was thought to be an unpleasant punishment: an assignment to work with a Black partner in one of the department's newly desegregated squad cars.[6]

Like most of his white colleagues, Hannon had long viewed the problems plaguing the Newton district as the fault of its residents, not deeper systemic inequalities. Unemployment was the natural result of idleness and dissipation. But those views changed as he shared a patrol car with his new partner. "My previous experience, growing up and working in a white, middle-class community, had been so far removed from the experience of ghetto life that their grievances seemed unreal and exaggerated." Though he had long

believed in meritocracy, Hannon "learned that in this 'land of opportunity' the opportunities are largely conditioned and prescribed by
the accident of birth." Working in the Newton district with a Black
partner politicized Hannon. "I began to feel like, well, an officer in
an occupation army riding up and down streets in the Negro ghetto.
I began to learn how Negroes see police," Hannon told the Black-
owned *Los Angeles Sentinel*.[7]

Experiences away from work reshaped Hannon's understanding
of inequality as well. In his free time, Hannon discovered KPFK, Los
Angeles's fledgling station in the left-wing Pacifica radio network.
Hannon loved listening to Art Kunkin, a recovering Trotskyite who
hosted the Socialist Party's official show on the station—so much so
that he wrote to him and struck up a friendship. By late 1962, he had
joined the party. Mike Hannon was now a socialist cop.[8]

———

In spring 1963, as the police attacks in Birmingham made headlines
and ignited outrage around the globe, demonstrations erupted
across the United States. In Los Angeles, CORE organized a solidarity protest on May 10. Joining them were members of the Socialist
Party, including Hannon and his wife, Sylvia. The march was orderly,
the *Los Angeles Times* reported, and "attracted no unusual police
attention."[9]

When Hannon appeared for roll call the next day, he found a
handwritten sign at the station asking him if his "feets" hurt. He
recognized it as a crude attempt to mimic African American Ver-
nacular English and noticed that several officers were acting "almost
hysterically hostile" toward him. Hannon's colleagues viewed the
Birmingham police as their comrades, and they regarded his attendance at the protest as an act of betrayal.[10]

Two months later, Hannon received a blistering evaluation from
a supervisor highlighting his arguments with fellow officers on "con-
troversial subjects" that included "civil liberties and socio-economic
theories." Hannon's direct superiors had ordered the young officer to
avoid joining protests, claiming that they "increased the animosity

of his fellow officers" and sapped the department's resources by diverting his colleagues away from their normal duties. But to his surprise, Hannon's protest activities also made him a few new allies on the force, introducing him to "a lot of friends I never knew I had." Some of his Black colleagues told him that they admired his willingness to stand for racial justice, making him feel like an "honorary member of the 'Black police force.'" And yet, most officers in the Newton Division agreed with the report that Hannon's decision to march raised "serious doubts about his loyalty."[11]

If only Hannon had chosen to join the John Birch Society (JBS) instead. Founded in 1958 by Massachusetts candy manufacturer Robert Welch, the society's stated objective was to eradicate communism, wherever it found it. It found it nearly everywhere. The diplomatic hand-wringing of the United Nations and associated "one-worlders" was nothing more than Marxists' covert strategy for global domination. Water fluoridation was the U.S. federal government's attempt at mind control. Welch decried Dwight Eisenhower during his presidency as a traitor who was "consciously serving the Communist conspiracy." In the early 1960s, the Birch Society was arguably the most influential right-wing organization in the country. Affluent San Marino in Los Angeles County was home to the group's West Coast headquarters, while neighboring Orange County earned a reputation as a national center for rank-and-file Birchers.[12]

Hannon's colleagues flocked to the society. The Newton station's lunchroom was filled with far-right literature, including issues of the group's *American Opinion* magazine. Hannon described the room as "the annex to a Birch Society 'Americanism' center," one of the organization's many bookstores and recruitment offices scattered throughout the country. When Hannon posted left-wing literature at the station, by contrast, it was quickly removed.[13]

As civil rights protests accelerated in 1963, JBS emerged as a prime antagonist of the movement and defender of police. In an unsigned July 1963 editorial, the society urged support for local law enforcement "now that Communist-inspired racial riots are getting to be a regular part of the American scene." The civil rights movement was pushing its own Big Lie. Even Bull Connor had been slandered, the article's anonymous author insisted, claiming that he had done a "superb job of maintaining law and order in the midst of a hot situation, while letting thousands of Negroes march and hundreds of white people protest all they wished." Movement groups, in fact, had exaggerated the police assaults on protesters in Birmingham. With the media watching, "one or more hotheads or dupes among the Negroes went up to the line and deliberately kicked one or more of the dogs." The image of Officer Dick Middleton's German shepherd biting the arm of young Walter Gadsden had been staged.[14]

The Birch Society's far-fetched claim—that irrefutable evidence of Birmingham police's brutality could actually be refuted—served as an announcement for the group's newest organizing campaign: Support Your Local Police. The country's leading far-right activists had thrust themselves into the raging national debate on how police should handle civil rights demonstrators. Mike Hannon's colleagues loved them for it.[15]

———

Not long after receiving his reprimand, Hannon became a dues-paying member of Los Angeles CORE. The chapter's leadership had no objections to Hannon's work as a police officer, which he disclosed on his membership application. Unlike Hannon's LAPD colleagues, who denounced his civil rights activities, CORE welcomed a police officer into its ranks at a time when much of the movement was losing faith in law enforcement.[16]

Los Angeles was one of the most fertile cities for CORE in the country. When the organization launched the Freedom Rides in 1961, more people joined them from L.A. than any other metropolitan area except for New York. The Los Angeles chapter was one of the most racially mixed in CORE; its membership was three-quarters white but led by Earl Walter, a Black social worker and Louisiana native who had chaired the chapter since 1951. Chief Parker, for his part, did not think that racial discrimination was common enough in his jurisdiction to justify the activities of a group such as CORE. "In this struggle for civil rights, it must be recognized that many of the conditions complained of in other sections of the United States do not exist in Los Angeles," Parker claimed to an audience at the annual conference of the International Association of Chiefs of Police in 1964.[17]

Just as Hannon joined CORE, the Los Angeles chapter was accelerating its organizing work against police violence. In early 1964, the chapter announced their agenda in a slim pamphlet titled "Our Proposal to Make a Dream Come True," which identified the fight against "police malpractice" as one of six target issues. "Our files are full of verified case after case of instances of minority persons brutally beaten, and with no legal help," the pamphlet declared, below a picture of three police officers standing over a man lying face down on the ground. The chapter's "dream," in a word, was "to guarantee each person full protection by the police."[18]

That spring, while visiting Los Angeles, CORE national director James Farmer joined a local picket line outside the Newton precinct station where Hannon worked (see figure 8.1). Inside the jailhouse, CORE activists were being held days after their arrest at a protest against the Van De Kamp's bakery chain for its discriminatory hiring practices. "How can Negroes respect the police?" Farmer asked a *Los Angeles Times* reporter at the scene. After all, he explained, the CORE members' arrests for peaceful protest signaled that "the police do not respect the Negro's rights as a citizen." Farmer remarked further that these protests represented a mild critique of police compared with how many Black people felt about them. "The feeling in the Negro community, especially in the North, is stronger against police brutality than anything else," Farmer observed. "Unless something is done, it's going to be a longer and hotter summer than ever."[19]

The LAPD was disturbed by CORE's campaigns that spring against police violence and discriminatory hiring in Los Angeles. Inspector Ed Davis—later the LAPD's chief—denounced organizers in a talk to business leaders as "second generation Communists" looking for "an excuse for anarchy." The week after Davis's harangue, the department dispatched "undercover operator #1" to a CORE general membership meeting. The spy issued a report to superiors naming five members in attendance, with a promise to identify

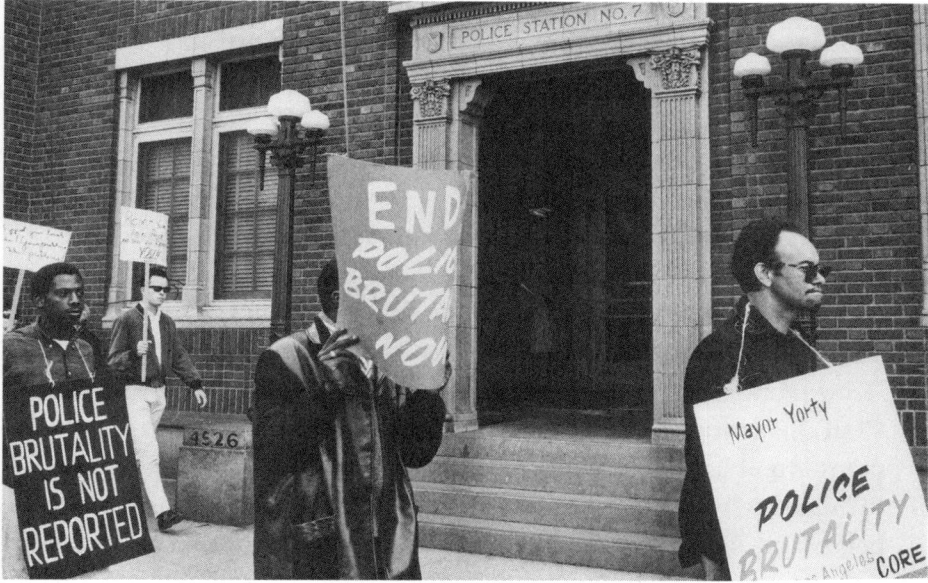

FIGURE 8.1. CORE protest against police violence outside an LAPD precinct station, February 27, 1965. Charles Brittin Papers, Getty Research Institute, Los Angeles (2005.M.11).

additional individuals based on photographs. Dated April 17, 1964, it was the first of a series of reports from Los Angeles CORE meetings by an undercover officer. Just as the chapter was organizing a campaign against police violence, the LAPD had infiltrated it.[20]

———

The next month, twelve CORE chapters in Southern California held a joint press conference calling for Chief Parker's resignation, amid a crackdown on activists and continued police brutality against Black citizens. The chief, CORE charged, had "shown himself to be emotionally and philosophically unfit to carry on his duties in this city with its two large minority communities." Three days later, Robert Cutts—an LAPD lieutenant and the president of the National Conference of Police Associations—condemned the organization, arguing that LAPD officers were "trained to enforce the legal rules of conduct upon all people, regardless of their ethnic origin." Not only that, but CORE was committing its own form of violence against the police, who had been "reviled, spat upon, injured, and hospitalized" while working at protests. "Now we find our officers being the victims of brutality," Cutts insisted, "while at the same time they are accused of inflicting it."[21]

As the war of words between CORE and the LAPD raged into the fall, a curious editorial appeared in the October issue of the *Los Angeles CORE-Lator*, the newsletter of the organization's Southern California chapters. The unsigned opinion attacked the LAPD as "Chief Parker's bastion of bigotry" but claimed that recent efforts by CORE had proved that political pressure could influence the department. The planned promotion of an LAPD detective—one of the "all time high record holders for citizens' complaints"—had recently been cancelled, for instance. Right-wing literature posted at police headquarters had disappeared as well. The author did not reveal how they had obtained such intimate knowledge of the department's promotional practices and interior decorating choices.[22]

Accompanying the editorial was a hand-drawn sketch of a police officer, and it was not pretty. Titled "Florida Justice—The Law Comes to St. Augustine," the cartoon skewered police who had recently attacked civil rights activists in the historic Southern beach town (see figure 8.2). With a cigarette hanging out of his mouth and a whiskey bottle tucked into his jacket pocket, the unshaven lawman carried a service pistol and a two-by-four studded with a nail. The implication was clear: though the LAPD and St. Augustine PD were two police departments on two sides of the country, one in a segregated Southern town and the other in the country's third-largest city, they had much more in common than many might realize.[23]

Meanwhile, questions about the propriety of police participating in the JBS mounted in Los Angeles and across the country. In late 1964, officials of the Anti-Defamation League had written to the International Association of Chiefs of Police to warn them that "infiltration of local police departments by the John Birch Society represents a threat to proper police work and protection of law and order." In response, the association's president, Atlanta police chief

FIGURE 8.2. The LAPD offered this unsigned cartoon from the
Los Angeles *CORE-Lator* newspaper as evidence of an act
demeaning law enforcement in disciplinary proceedings against
Michael Hannon. *Los Angeles CORE-Lator*, October 1964, 2.

Herbert Jenkins, maintained that his organization had no reason to
root out Birch members from police forces, since the organization
did not appear on the federal government's official list of subversive
groups.[24]

The LAPD made a similar argument that they had no right to prohibit officers from joining the society. Parker claimed that he "didn't

know anything about the society" and did not believe he knew any-one who belonged to the group—less than a month after receiving a letter from Black councilman and former police officer (and future mayor) Tom Bradley warning the department about Birch propa-ganda in its stations. Playing dumb, Parker gave his tacit approval to the organization. But those feelings were not universally shared by local officials throughout the country. In Philadelphia, Mayor James Tate condemned fourteen Birch-affiliated officers as members of secretive "cells," remarking that "this is the way the Nazi Party began and this is the way the Communist Party operated." The controversy only seemed to bring attention to the society, and in the wake of Lyn-don Johnson's resounding electoral victory running on a civil rights and antipoverty platform that November, JBS reported a surge of new members from law enforcement. As it turned out, officers in California, Philadelphia, and across the country were embracing an organization that celebrated police for brutalizing civil rights activ-ists in the name of racial segregation.[25]

———

"RIGHTS MELEE HERE JAILS 98," screamed the headline on the *Los Angeles Times* front page on March 11, 1965. Among those in attendance at the so-called melee was Mike Hannon—not as an offi-cer but as a protester carrying a sign reading, "Evacuate Vietnam—Occupy Alabama." The city's U.S. Federal Building had just been the site of three consecutive days of protests, in what may have been the most tumultuous civil rights demonstration in Los Angeles to that point.

Four nights earlier, on March 7, millions of households were watching the film *Judgment at Nuremberg* on ABC television, when an unscheduled news update from Selma, Alabama, flashed across their screens. Earlier that day, officers from the Alabama Highway Patrol and the Dallas County sheriff's office had brutalized civil rights marchers attempting to cross the Edmund Pettus Bridge on their way to the state capitol in Montgomery. Officers forced march-ers to the ground, beating them with clubs. Anguished screams filled the air. Those who tried to run were chased. Mounted patrolmen from Sheriff Jim Clark's office raced back and forth, assaulting Black men, women, and even children from horseback.[26]

By the next day, protesters were gathering at federal offices across the country demanding that President Johnson deploy troops to Selma and that Congress pass legislation protecting Black voters in the South. In Los Angeles, roughly 150 picketers assembled outside the U.S. Federal Building to demand federal intervention. Two lines of protesters locked arm in arm blocked the building's entrances, trapping roughly two thousand employees inside. The city had seen larger crowds of protesters before, but civil disobedience tactics of this kind were an unfamiliar sight. Uniformed and plainclothes U.S. Marshals swarmed the barricaders to make arrests, dragging protesters who resisted by their hands and feet and in some cases their necks. Many of those arrested screamed in pain as they were pulled away, while their comrades who watched from the sidelines chanted "non-violence, non-violence" and "freedom, freedom."[27]

Hannon was not one of the individuals who cordoned off the building—but he did not try to stop them, either. At one point, Hannon pointed out a plainclothes officer to his fellow demonstrators, urging them to keep their distance. That, Hannon's law enforcement colleagues later argued, was indefensible. The most volatile moment came when three uniformed members of the American Nazi Party appeared. Hannon urged his fellow demonstrators to ignore the "swine" that had come to heckle them, but protesters broke away and scuffled with Ralph Forbes, self-styled commander of the party's Western Division, who was carrying a sign reading, "Put the reds underground—six feet under." When a trio attacked the Nazi and a larger group followed, Hannon inserted himself between the Nazi and the crowd to prevent an all-out brawl.[28]

That spring, an LAPD undercover agent continued to attend CORE meetings and record the names and activities of dozens of chapter members in reports to superiors. The department wanted more. In late April, the officer noted with regret that he had failed to obtain the chapter's full membership list, even though he had earned enough trust within the chapter to be assigned chair of its membership committee.

The undercover officer dismissed the activists he endeared himself to as disorganized and incapable. "As far as strategy is concerned, there is no such thing in the CORE office and I personally am convinced that Dr. King himself has to consult with others as far as his notions are concerned and that there is someone directing him." The movement's organizers, the officer contended, were so aimless that their political victories could only be explained by some hidden hand or external power guiding them. Their work was the product of a larger plan, a coordinated conspiracy.[29]

———

As Hannon attended more and more of those same meetings, he developed a close relationship with the local CORE chapter's leaders. But at least one activist began to question his loyalties—Mario Sampson, a Nicaraguan student and newcomer to CORE's meetings that spring. In May 1965, two days after attending a protest with Hannon, a bewildered Sampson called the officer at his home to confirm that he was not a cop ordered to spy on organizers.

"Are you on the level?" an incredulous Sampson asked. "How come the police let you get away with something like this?" As Hannon explained, he had never hidden his job with the LAPD from his CORE colleagues.

"Your camps are so completely opposite," Sampson pushed back. "Don't you find that this conflicts a little bit?" Because police work was so menial, Hannon reasoned, he did not need to renounce his politics, even as colleagues on the force gave him the cold shoulder. The department could not fire him, because he had not broken any laws. He was very careful about that—though when Sampson pressed him on whether he had organized any arrestable activities, Hannon remarked he would "rather not talk about it on the phone."[30]

Three weeks later, on June 1, Hannon received some unpleasant news: a two-page complaint from Chief Parker charging him with ten counts of misconduct. The immediate punishment was suspension from the department, followed by a trial with the Board of Rights, the administrative body that adjudicated officer misconduct in the LAPD. Hannon soon learned that the charges carried a maximum penalty of removal from the force. As it turned out, Sampson had known all too well that the department would not let Mike Hannon continue his organizing work.[31]

———

Hannon had first realized how much trouble he was in when he ran into Sampson at LAPD headquarters one day that May. For months, the two men had encountered each other on picket lines around the city. But now, as Hannon stood across from Sampson, the man he believed to be a Nicaraguan student activist was wearing a police uniform. "He told me he was assigned to me—it was nothing personal—he was just doing his job," Hannon later recalled.[32]

The next month, on the morning of June 14, Hannon reported for trial at the Police Administrative Building wearing a gray business suit with a silver Congress of Racial Equality lapel pin. Hannon was appearing before the LAPD Board of Rights at the department's eight-story modernist headquarters, popularly known as the Glass House and dubbed by *Popular Mechanics* "the most scientific building ever used by a law-enforcement group." Presiding over the board was Ed Davis, the LAPD's second-in-command who had once predicted that Hannon would become "an excellent officer." Hannon was accompanied by ACLU attorney and longtime police critic A. L. Wirin. Hannon's charges included two instances of falling asleep on a shift; one of authoring an editorial "impugning the character, policies and practices of the Los Angeles Police Department" and another of drawing a cartoon that demeaned law enforcement, both of which appeared in a CORE newsletter; a charge of making a statement "designed to demean, vilify and calumniate the President of the United States" at a protest against the U.S. invasion of the Dominican Republic; and four counts alleging that Hannon "aided, abetted, and participated in a planned demonstration requiring the diversion of Los Angeles police personnel from their normal function of community security."[33]

Chief Parker had drawn up the charges against Hannon himself. In fact, Parker had authored the entire Board of Rights system upon assuming the top position in the department in 1950. Though the department's prosecutor, Lieutenant Robert Hill, revealed plans to call thirty-two different officers to testify against Hannon, there was at least one officer with intimate knowledge of Hannon's political activities whom Hill hoped to prevent from testifying, and that was the man who identified himself as Mario Sampson. As the lieutenant informed the board on the first day of Hannon's hearing, the undercover officer's face and real name—which Hannon still did not know—were "not to be exposed" in the press. But exposing the inner workings of the LAPD's surveillance operations and the department's racist, right-wing culture was just what Hannon wanted to do.[34]

Remarkably, Hannon was believed to be the first Los Angeles officer in history to exercise his right to an administrative trial. This was before the days when police unions blanketed trial boards with lawyers to defend officers against disciplinary proceedings. Parker celebrated his Board of Rights as a judicial body that afforded LAPD officers the opportunity for a full and fair hearing, with the right to review evidence and appeal. In reality, however, the board did little more than rubber-stamp Parker and the LAPD leadership's disciplinary decisions. Upon realizing that Hannon planned to mount a vigorous defense complete with extensive discovery proceedings, Hill complained that "the twisting of this administrative tribunal in[to] a court of law has completely flustered its function." Hannon, for his part, was eager not only to defend himself but to put the entire LAPD on trial.[35]

———

As preparations for the hearing were underway, a coalition of CORE members and other Los Angeles activists created the Michael Hannon Defense and Support Fund. "The action against officer Hannon constitutes a grave violation of his civil liberties," a letter from the fund informed would-be supporters. "A dangerous precedent, it is all the more alarming in view of the fact that right-wing political activities are not only tolerated by chief Parker, but are in many ways fostered by the Police Department itself." The committee's honorary chairs included James Farmer and perennial Socialist Party presidential candidate Norman Thomas—both of whom had played key roles in the 1962 Committee of Inquiry into police crimes against the Freedom Riders—as well as A. Philip Randolph, the venerable Black labor leader and founder of the March on Washington movement. Hannon's case was now a movement cause.[36]

Virulent hate mail from across the country poured into Hannon's mailbox, much of it racist. In a letter lacking a return address, Mrs. C. R. Brown offered her opinion that "you not only should be kicked off the Police Force—but tried for <u>Treason</u> and I do <u>not</u> mean maybe. Your 4 children should be taken away from you—and put in a school—as they will grow up with <u>no respect</u> for a Cain—you are a Red Rat." Another message came in the form of an unsigned and marginally literate postcard from Chicago telling Hannon that he was a

> dirty n____r loving RAT. Get of the good Police Force in L.A. and let some good red blooded American Boy have your Job. You do not deserve it. Only Americans belong on our Police Force, not commie-rats like you. Go some where and drop dead will you, do us all a favor. Included your family.

It was one thing for Hannon to be a police officer who criticized his coworkers. Worse to his detractors was that he was a white cop, betraying other white cops.[37]

"Police officers and officials all over the nation are watching the case of Michael B. Hannon," the *Christian Science Monitor* told readers, while newspapers across the country picked up coverage of his case from the Associated Press and United Press International wire services. *Newsweek*, then the third-most-read news weekly in the country, published a brief profile of the embattled officer. Speaking to a meeting of the California Peace Officers Association on June 16, Parker predicted that the outcome of Hannon's trial "will affect every police department in the nation," warning that if the officer prevailed, "we might have hundreds of policemen demonstrating" for political causes. Even as the chief maintained that Hannon's affiliation with CORE and the Socialist Party "is not at issue nor a cause for disciplinary action," Parker insisted that a police officer could not remain loyal to his department if he took part in civil rights work. "Can a man serve masters engaging in police activities at one point and activities inimical to the force while off duty" at another, Parker asked. As the chief saw it, "If we have come to the point where a police department is no longer a quasi-military organization that can decide the code of conduct for its members, we ought to find it out and find it out now."[38]

Among Hannon's reasons for requesting a trial was to simply not get fired from his job. Hannon, who had been attending law school at night for several years, had one semester left to complete his degree, and he was already making plans to quit the force. In the meantime, he had a family to support. Not only would he lose his ability to earn as long as he was suspended from work, but if he was fired, he would surrender an accumulated $2,000 in his pension fund, or more than $20,000 in 2025 dollars.

The nature of Hannon's charges ensured that a vigorous defense would have to confront the ills of the Los Angeles Police Department. Joining Wirin on the defense was his ACLU colleague Hugh Manes, author of a detailed report on police brutality against Black Angelenos two years earlier and an outspoken critic of surveillance abuses. If calling the LAPD a "bastion of bigotry" impugned the integrity of the department, as officials claimed, Hannon's team would show just how racist Parker's force was. Since Hannon was charged with improper political activity, he would show that the department itself permitted on-duty officers to indulge in right-wing political attacks on its critics. And if secret recordings of conversations were to be weaponized against Hannon, his defense would call the department's surveillance operations into question.[39]

First and foremost, Hannon sought to assert his right to demonstrate against racial discrimination. "If you are balancing an officer's desire to take part in the most serious social crisis this country faces against the police department's public relations image, certainly the public relations image is of minor importance in that balance," he reasoned to the Board of Rights. Hannon stressed that he had never broken any laws while picketing, not even traffic laws. As Manes told the Board of Rights, "We have nothing to hide about his politics, and I want to make it clear to the board we are not ashamed of any politics or political involvement."[40]

Most galling for department officials was Hannon's claim that the LAPD was racist to its core. Black leaders and civil rights organizers had of course long accused Parker's force of racism. But until that point, Parker had found great success dismissing his African American critics as antipolice hysterics who knew nothing about law enforcement. It was another matter altogether, however, for a white LAPD officer to assert that his nearly seven years on the force led him to conclude that the police force was anti-Black. Hannon laid bare the plague of racist policing in a way that perhaps no white police officer ever had.

The defense focused not on individual bigots in the department but on a pervasive culture of racism perpetuated by leaders in the organization. Hannon reminded the board that the department had segregated its patrol cars along racial lines until just three years earlier. He also recalled the not uncommon use of the n-word in the Newton Division, including instances of officers who addressed Black residents as such to their faces, as well as a flyer at the station denouncing Eleanor Roosevelt as a "n____r lover." When Inspector Davis asked Hannon why he had failed to report these occurrences, accusing him of having been "derelict in your duties," Hannon replied that he had kept silent because the offenders were unlikely to be disciplined. After all, he argued, "the same attitudes represent the feelings of the administration of the Police Department." Hannon estimated that more than two-thirds of his colleagues "agree with the southern policies of segregation." The sum effect, he contended, "was the total hostility of the department to the civil rights group as a movement."[41]

Throughout his trial, Hannon highlighted the hypocrisy of his prosecution for political activity in a department where right-wing activists operated with impunity. At the Newton station, he had witnessed coworkers selling tickets to John Birch Society events. He had seen Birch literature posted on bulletin boards, including the inaugural "Support Your Local Police" article from July 1963 denouncing the Birmingham protests as a false flag operation and praising Bull Connor's officers for their brutal response. Chief Parker had appeared on the nationally syndicated radio show of Dean Manion, a Birch Society board member, though he claimed not to have known of Manion's affiliation at the time. LAPD officer and John Birch Society section leader Jesse Roth asserted that as many as two-thirds of the department's officers were JBS members, though without providing evidence. Hannon's point in all of this was that the LAPD could not allow far-right groups to organize on the job and then argue that his protest activities violated departmental policy.[42]

Hannon's defense also sought to expose the formidable surveillance apparatus wielded by the LAPD against residents, particularly those working with racial justice groups. This was a delicate issue, as department officials contended that nearly any discussion of its covert activities risked endangering undercover officers and was therefore illegal. But with Wirin heading up his defense, Hannon had a leading expert on unconstitutional surveillance in his corner, and by showing how much police officials' case relied on surveillance of one of their own employees, Hannon's team hoped to discredit the department's investigation of their client.[43]

Wirin wanted to obtain all documents pertaining to conversations between Hannon and undercover members of the LAPD, Mario Sampson or otherwise. As it turned out, the undercover officer who had assumed the role of Sampson and infiltrated the Los Angeles chapter of CORE was twenty-five-year-old Robert Arguello, the son of a Nicaraguan doctor and American mother and the nephew of a former president of Nicaragua. Born in California, Arguello had spent most of his childhood in his native country until his family fled in the wake of right-wing dictator Anastasio Somoza's assassination in 1956. But in the days leading up to Hannon's trial, a Superior Court judge barred the LAPD from introducing confidential records into the proceedings unless the defense could first inspect them. This included surveillance or any other evidence resulting from undercover investigations. Parker's department was so intent on shielding Arguello's espionage from exposure that they opted not to call their undercover officer to testify in the trial, and they suppressed the secret recordings of his conversations with Hannon.[44]

With that evidence off-limits, Hannon's defense team illustrated the staggering scale of the department's surveillance operations by calling non-undercover officers to testify. Police photographer John Bigham admitted that he had standing orders to take pictures of "all the persons who may participate in a particular demonstration during an assignment." When Bigham had been dispatched to the Federal Building for the first two days of protests demanding a government intervention in Selma, he was supposed to capture images of each of the more than one hundred demonstrators, either on print film or on motion picture footage.

As for Hannon, at least eight different members of the LAPD had tracked him at protests—some by filming or recording him, some by watching from afar, some by tailing him on foot. At more than one protest, the plainclothes officers following Hannon were so obvious that he pointed them out to his fellow demonstrators as harassers intent on intimidating the crowd, not actually spying on them. And although Hannon recalled first meeting Arguello in April 1965, the LAPD had assigned an undercover operator—left unnamed in department documents—to infiltrate the Los Angeles CORE chapter at least a year earlier. The more than a dozen reports of CORE meetings produced by the spy were never made available to Hannon's defense. The LAPD had no intention of revealing its long record of political policing against the movement.[45]

———

Hannon's decision to challenge his punishment in administrative court outraged LAPD leadership. Past hearings had functioned as pro forma confirmations of the department's disciplinary decisions. But Hannon's defense was a direct challenge to Parker's authority. Throughout the trial, the prosecution and board's unrelenting hostility toward the embattled officer and his attorneys signaled that the defense had succeeded in throwing officials off-balance, no matter the case's outcome (see figure 8.3). The LAPD had no experience rebutting sworn testimony from a sitting officer at an administrative trial, especially not as he painted a vivid picture of

FIGURE 8.3. Michael Hannon at his police disciplinary trial, seated center at the table, with ACLU attorneys Hugh Manes, left, and A. L. Wirin, right, and LAPD chief William Parker in the foreground, July 13, 1965. *Los Angeles Times* Photographic Archive, Charles E. Young Research Library, UCLA.

the racism, right-wing extremism, and invasive political policing that pervaded the department. And nowhere was police officials' lack of preparation for this challenge more apparent than when William Parker sat for his interrogation by A. L. Wirin.

Here was a longtime critic of police abuses questioning America's most influential police official in his department's own headquarters. Two decades earlier, Wirin had triggered a federal investigation when he alleged he was kidnapped by a gang of strikebreakers led by the chief of the LAPD's red squad; in the 1950s, he had sued Parker for illegal surveillance practices and won before California's highest court. The men's low regard for each other became apparent soon after Wirin began his questioning. "You are a master of taking things out of context. I have watched you for years," Parker scolded the sixty-five-year-old ACLU attorney. While he may have meant to use the term figuratively, "watching" had the air of a Freudian slip, a reference to the department's monitoring of the left-wing groups to which Wirin belonged. But as much as Parker might have wished to project control of the situation, he could not help but let some of his unease with the interrogation show. "This is an odd situation. This is the first time I have ever sat in this chair all of the fifteen years. This is the first time I have had direct conversation with the Board on rulings so this is a unique situation as far as I'm concerned," the chief admitted. Five years younger than Wirin, Parker appeared every bit his senior, slouching and ruffled as he tried to parry the lawyer's questions. When Parker ridiculed the defense's charges of racism, Wirin gave as good as he got, as one sarcastic and uncomfortable exchange made clear.

> PARKER: "I will be in uniform Friday when we bring in a new group of bigots in the department."
> WIRIN: "I suggest you don't bring in anymore. You have enough now."
> PARKER: "We can use all we can get."[46]

In the end, none of this had a substantive impact on the trial's outcome—not the disclosures of surveillance, not the eyewitness accounts of racist acts by LAPD officers, and not even the exposure of the department's coddling of far-right activists. If anything, the very fact that Hannon had challenged—and embarrassed—Parker and the LAPD in their own administrative hearing system may have guaranteed the board's ultimate verdict. On July 23, 1965, twenty-five days and some 1,400 transcribed pages of testimony after the trial had begun—in what was the longest trial in department history—the LAPD Board of Rights found Hannon guilty on nine of ten counts of misconduct. Only on the charge concerning his actions on the first day of the Selma protests at the Federal Building did the three-man tribunal acquit Hannon, as they determined that the prosecution had failed to prove he had committed any crime or infraction in that instance. In the trial's final moments, Deputy Chief Thad Brown announced Hannon's sentence: expulsion from the LAPD.[47]

But to Hannon's surprise, after two dozen of his fellow officers testified against him and the Board of Rights recommended his removal from his job, Parker overruled the firing. Instead, the chief chose to suspend him for six months. This revised punishment still meant a loss of more than $4,400 in income for Hannon, or more than $44,000 in 2025 dollars. Yet the end result was that Hannon could return to his job half a year after his original citation, as well as keep his pension. Parker offered a flimsy explanation of his decision as the result of "a lack of communication of the charges to the board from myself." The more likely reason is that he hoped to ward off a challenge by Hannon in civil court, where firing a public employee was harder to defend than a temporary suspension.[48]

Unimpressed, Hannon insisted that the reduced penalty "in no way changes my position that the department has no right to discipline me for speaking out on political matters, especially in light of the ultra-right-wing activities of some police officers." Either way, he made it known that he intended to return to the force, if only temporarily to support his family while he completed his law studies. By December, Hannon had come back to the LAPD, but not to walk a beat. Instead, he was ordered to work as a security guard in a four-by-five-foot locked booth in the city's Treasury Building, an assignment designed to humiliate him. Within weeks, Hannon sued the city challenging his suspension and loss of pay. Six months later, on June 9, 1966, a Superior Court judge not only rejected Hannon's suit but overruled Parker and upheld the Board of Rights decision to dismiss him. That day, Hannon resigned from the LAPD and announced that he was launching a law practice, having recently passed the California bar. Parker and the department had gotten their way—they had driven out the so-called civil rights policeman. In the end, Hannon had been purged for betrayal.[49]

———

Three weeks after Hannon's original Board of Rights trial had concluded the previous summer, the LAPD were confronted with a far more serious challenge to their authority. On August 11, 1965, California Highway Patrol officer Lee Minikus pulled over a pair of Black men, brothers Marquette and Ronald Frye, on a corner in Los Angeles's Watts community. Minikus accused Marquette of driving drunk and ordered him and his brother out of their car. As officers kicked and clubbed the Frye brothers before arresting them, a restless crowd of more than two hundred people gathered. Soon Minikus called for backup, and additional Highway Patrol and LAPD officers arrived on the scene. When an onlooker spit at the officers, they chased her down and restrained her by her neck. Reports of police brutality quickly swept through the South Los Angeles community, and as the crowd grew to some 1,500 spectators, officers retreated under a hail of rocks and bottles.

Over the next five days, the events stemming from Frye's arrest spiraled into a full-fledged uprising by Black residents in Watts against Los Angeles police. In the wake of widespread looting and arson, officers carried out mass arrests of nearly four thousand people. More than one thousand individuals were injured, and thirty-four were killed, almost all by the LAPD. A coroner's report later conservatively determined eight of those deaths to not be justifiable homicides. Property damages approached $40 million.

With the assistance of the National Guard, the LAPD regained control of the city while exacting brutal retribution on Black residents. Parker claimed victory for his department on the fifth day of the riots, boasting as though he had triumphed on the battlefield, "We're on the top and they're on the bottom." But by calling in the National Guard, authorities had determined that Parker's officers were outmatched. Of the many outcomes of the events in Watts, one of the most immediate was the embarrassment of the LAPD on a scale that it had never experienced under William Parker. That humiliation was augmented by how unprepared Parker had been for civil disorder. Just one year earlier, the chief had predicted in a speech that riots "can't happen here." The reason, Parker explained, was that Black Angelenos had little reason for discontent.[50]

Hannon, by contrast, understood the uprising as a predictable response of Black residents to the continued violence they faced at the hands of the LAPD. "Policemen generally tend to see themselves as public servants in middle class, white communities and as an army of occupation in lower class or Negro neighborhoods," Hannon wrote four days after the riots had subsided, offering a withering critique of his employer in the *Los Angeles Free Press*. "In the South-Central area, the motto on the radio car doors, 'to protect and to serve,' has a particularly ironic note because both police and public know that the community is not the one being served." But as Black residents intensified their criticisms of the LAPD—whether through demonstrations or uprisings—police officials had no response other than violence. "The department's single answer to the rising hostility between the police and the Negro community has been force and more force," Hannon wrote, pinning the blame for Watts squarely on his colleagues.[51]

————

Hannon's editorial and the defense fund's activities represented the culmination of his battles with the LAPD. Among the questions Hannon had raised for years—first privately and then during his trial—was whether the Los Angeles Police Department, or any other law enforcement agency for that matter, was willing to recognize the racism inherent in their treatment of Black communities. Now, after the LAPD had lost control of their city for nearly a week in the face of the country's largest Black uprising in decades, some wondered whether a small opening for change would emerge in Los Angeles. If there was ever a moment for this to happen, it was on the heels of the Watts uprising, the preceding three years of local protest campaigns against police brutality, and, perhaps most unexpectedly, the public trial of a white police officer who championed the civil rights movement while excoriating his colleagues for their unrepentant racism.

Los Angeles mayor Sam Yorty, however, blamed the ongoing organizing against police abuses for the uprising. "For some time there has existed a world-wide subversive campaign to stigmatize all police as brutal. The cry of police brutality has been shouted in cities all over the world by Communists, dupes and demagogues irrespective of the facts," Yorty contended. Here was the mayor of America's third-largest city embracing a conspiracy theory championed not only by the LAPD but also by police in Birmingham and

Danville as they waged open warfare on civil rights organizers. Yorty maintained that the Watts uprising was not only a violent outburst lacking any basis in meaningful social grievance but also the fault of all the organizations—most of all CORE—that had long demanded an end to police malpractice in Los Angeles.[52]

Indeed, in the aftermath of Watts, a key question emerged for the movement: Could its growing efforts to end police abuses withstand the charge that their work was not a campaign for equality and freedom but, rather, a covert strategy to spur violent revolt? Since the start of the decade, white liberals in public office and the media had praised the movement for its fight against segregation and voting restrictions. But as 1965 turned to 1966, would they do the same for organizers' expanding campaigns against police violence—or would they denounce them as invitations to disorder that demanded an even more forceful counterresponse from law enforcement?

9

Deacons and Dynamite

Klantown, USA. That's what *The Nation* magazine called Bogalusa, Louisiana. Tucked into the state's southeastern corner on its border with Mississippi, Bogalusa was a hardscrabble mill town of 21,000 dominated by white segregationists and the company that employed most local residents, San Francisco–based paper manufacturer Crown Zellerbach. In his searing exposé for the publication in February 1965, journalist Paul Good estimated that Bogalusa's population included some eight hundred Klan members. With research based on figures from city officials, Good concluded that the town "has possibly the largest Ku Klux Klan concentration per capita of any community in the South." By all appearances, the group was operating with the approval of local government. As one townsperson remarked, it could "not survive here unless it has official sanction. The headquarters of the Klan, if anywhere, is at the fire station across from City Hall"—a building that also housed the town's police department. A federal report later confirmed that at least eighteen city police officers belonged to the Klan.[1]

At the start of that year, the Bogalusa Civic and Voters League (BCVL), the political standard-bearer of the Black community, had initiated its first ever campaign to desegregate the town's public facilities, aided by a pair of organizers dispatched by CORE's national office. Police and their Klan allies wasted little time attacking them. On the evening of February 2, police chief Claxton Knight and a deputy went to the home of BCVL members Bob and Jackie Hicks, who had invited white CORE organizers Bill Yates and Steve Miller for dinner and to stay the night. It was believed to be the first time a Black family had housed white people in the town's history—and many white locals were unhappy with the news. Knight informed Hicks that a mob had gathered nearby and was planning to apprehend the two guests, so the two civil rights workers and the Hicks family should leave town immediately. "We have better things to do than protect people who aren't wanted here," Knight snapped.

Instead of fleeing, the Hickses summoned more than two dozen armed Black men from CORE to guard their family and their guests. They also contacted CORE's national office in New York, setting into motion a chain reaction of hundreds of phone calls by the organization's members to reporters and federal and local officials. Finally, at around 4:00 in the morning, police returned to stand guard. The next day, Yates and Miller conferred with Black leaders at the town's Negro Union Hall. A police escort accompanied the pair as they left the hall, only to peel off as soon as a car with six white men arrived in pursuit.

The car pursued Yates and Miller on a high-speed chase into the town's Black community, where the two civil rights workers hoped to find refuge. As the CORE staffers rushed out of their car, a mob of angry whites grabbed hold of Yates and beat him, breaking one of his hands and causing internal injuries. After shots were fired, a group of Black residents managed to pull Yates free from the crowd and safeguard him in a neighborhood café where Miller had holed up moments earlier.

Bogalusa police and state officers arrived—but not to break up the mob, just to watch. One officer was sighted two blocks away in his patrol car speaking with a Klan leader. An FBI agent summoned by CORE officials made his way into the restaurant to take witness statements from the besieged organizers, only to leave without dispersing the crowd. Finally, a large group of armed Black residents arrived to escort Yates and Miller out of the café. Hours later the

FBI official and a colleague met the men at a private home with four
police cars and escorted them out of Bogalusa; state police replaced
the FBI at the city limits and drove with the CORE officials all the
way to Baton Rouge.[2]

This was yet another variety of political policing. Like the John
Birch members in Los Angeles and the red squads across the country, Bogalusa's local force was dedicated to undermining civil rights
organizing. The main difference was just how unabashed the Bogalusa force was, not even showing the slightest care if the whole town
knew it was a Klan-infested accomplice to violent mobs. But unlike
in Birmingham, where police coordinated mob attacks on defenseless Freedom Riders in 1961, in Bogalusa activists took up arms to
protect themselves.

Two weeks after the attacks, on February 21, a trio of community
members from the town of Jonesboro on the other side of the state
drove the better part of a day to meet with the Hicks's contingent at
their union hall in Bogalusa. In the wake of attacks on CORE staffers
in Jonesboro the previous year, local teacher and minister Frederick
Kirkpatrick had obtained permission from the town's white police
chief to organize a Black auxiliary unit to patrol the Black community.
After just half a year, however, the department dissolved the unit,
arguing that it was no longer needed now that demonstrations in
town had ceased. Undaunted, Kirkpatrick's auxiliary unit met with
local Korean War veteran Earnest Thomas at the encouragement
of CORE staffer Charlie Fenton. Thomas had assembled a group of
armed Black residents to protect CORE organizers in Jonesboro. Fenton, a twenty-three-year-old civil rights worker who later enrolled as
the first white student at Grambling College, recommended that the
men unite to form a "protective association" focused on self-defense
and political organizing. Equipped with walkie-talkies, citizens band
radios, and licensed firearms, the men incorporated as a chartered
organization in Louisiana with officers and regular dues. Although
they were not an official CORE project, they soon operated with the
quiet assistance of the organization's staff.[3]

According to a police informant's account of the meeting in
Bogalusa, Thomas proposed "roving patrols" in their respective

towns to shadow law enforcement and to "defend the position" of any Black person who was arrested, even if it meant blocking the arrest. Thomas advised the group to purchase two-way radios for their cars, ammunition, and a variety of long arms. The next day, Hicks instructed his colleagues in Bogalusa to obtain guns so that they could "defend themselves by converging on police officers at the time the arrest of a Negro is being made." Hicks and his allies were ready to expand their experiments in self-defense into a full-fledged unit aimed at monitoring the police and their collaborations with the Klan. These two groups had come together to protect themselves and their allies in the civil rights movement. Today, many would call this mutual aid. The men in Bogalusa followed the lead of their comrades from Jonesboro as they settled on a different name for their effort: the Deacons for Defense and Justice.[4]

———

Brewing conflict between police and the Deacons in Jonesboro and Bogalusa soon caught the attention of CORE's national office. In March 1965, James Farmer announced that the organization was targeting the Louisiana towns for its next major demonstration campaign. Responding to the recent attacks facilitated by law enforcement, Farmer demanded an increased federal presence in Bogalusa, stating that "FBI agents and federal marshals should make on-the-spot arrests when they see police brutality and the rights of people being violated." A series of protests featuring Farmer escalated the campaign in April, including one in which more than four hundred people marched through Bogalusa, fending off assault from white onlookers.[5]

The Deacons continued their armed protection of the protests as police persisted in allowing violent attacks on marchers. At the same time, CORE's national leadership avoided public comment on the Deacons, signaling that while they accepted the group's assistance, they wanted to do so without raising questions about their own organization's historic commitment to nonviolence. As both CORE and the Deacons increased the political pressure on

Bogalusa authorities, no fewer than eighteen police officers formally renounced their Klan membership in April so that they could keep their jobs. The move suggested that Bogalusa police had to at least start pretending to reject white supremacy, but it raised a more pressing question: Did anyone really think that officers who belonged to the Klan would now change their racist ways even if they left the terror group?[6]

The answer came on May 19 when a handful of CORE organizers and about seventy-five Black residents held a picnic at the city's Goodyear Park. Rita Marsh, a white staffer with the Committee of Concern for Bogalusa, a CORE offshoot based in San Francisco, watched as a group of twenty-five white men showed up at the park not long after the picnic party arrived. City police stationed at the park spoke with the men, some of whom were carrying pistols, and then allowed them to advance.

When one of the men hit a seven-year-old child with a belt, pandemonium ensued, and the white vigilantes charged the mostly Black crowd and bludgeoned them with clubs. Police at first watched the melee, before choosing to club the picnickers themselves and release dogs into the crowd. As an officer pulled out his gun, at least two Deacons drew their pistols as well, including Jackie Hicks, as she and her husband watched in horror as a dog bit their son. A seventy-five-year-old woman was beaten unconscious, while a Deacon was arrested on assault charges for protecting children with a revolver.

Among those attacked was Marsh, who had a gun put to her face when she challenged one of the assailants to hit her. But neither she, nor her CORE colleagues, nor Black locals were going to abandon self-defense as they continued their protest campaign. "The only protection we have are the guns we have ourselves," Marsh explained to a United Press International reporter. "And the men are ready to use them."[7]

———

The rampage at Goodyear Park affirmed that local and state police were still colluding with white mobs to attack Black residents in public view. Months of protests and national press coverage had failed to break law enforcement's resolve to crush the movement in Bogalusa. Marsh's account of the attacks amounted to one of the first public acknowledgments by CORE that it was working with the Deacons for Defense. In the coming weeks, the national organization's leadership inched toward adopting a policy of full acceptance of armed self-defense against white violence, state-sponsored or otherwise. In early June, CORE's director in Louisiana, Richard Haley, issued an internal police memo regarding the Deacons. While Haley emphasized CORE's dedication to nonviolence and its refusal to take up arms against segregationists, he also stressed that it was "prepared to work with all organizations that are actively participating in the Negro's fight for freedom." The Deacons, as Haley pointed out, "advocate use of weapons and defensive measures only because there is negligent or non-existent police protection."[8]

Later that summer, Farmer issued a full-throated endorsement of the Deacons in his column for the *New York Amsterdam News*. "The Deacons don't replace legal law enforcement," Farmer informed readers.

> There is no such thing as legal law enforcement in much of the South that will protect a Negro citizen. In fact, there is [a] considerable amount of police complicity with the Klan assaults— enough so, that alarmed Negroes, fearful for the lives of their families armed, organized and walked a beat. And I can't blame them. I can't find fault with a man for exercising his constitutional right to protect his home, with weapons if necessary. Period.[9]

Perhaps the most compelling justification for the Deacons came from people in Bogalusa who enjoyed their protection. As *Ebony* magazine attested, Black "townsmen consider the Deacons a deterrent to violence in Bogalusa. For one thing, their very existence forces white troublemakers to think twice. For another, by giving the job to mature and restrained men, they discourage Negro hotheads who otherwise might trigger a racial bloodbath in the tense city." Even the most steadfast proponents of nonviolence had to concede that CORE's pacifism might offer only limited help in this particular

Louisiana town. "You never stop being afraid there," a white twenty-two-year-old CORE staffer said of her time in Bogalusa. Asked by *Ebony* whether she approved of the Deacons, the Californian gave a reply that was both contradictory and totally convincing. "Not really," she said. "But when you're down there, it's an irrelevant question."[10]

With the arrival of summer, the fight against police violence moved to the very top of the Bogalusa activists' priority list, eclipsing calls for desegregation and the vote that had once propelled the group. The first on a list of fifteen demands issued by the BCVL later that month was "fair and adequate police protection for the Negro citizens of Bogalusa in their daily activities as well as protection for demonstrators." A second called for the firing of officers who had assaulted Black residents and punishments for any police who perpetrated future attacks, and a third requested the hiring of Black police officers. In so doing, the BCVL was pushing Bogalusa police to emulate the parish sheriff's department, which the previous year had hired its first two Black deputies, Onneal Moore and David Creed Rogers.[11]

Yet some Bogalusa whites were so determined to retain their monopoly on local law enforcement that they were willing to kill to halt its desegregation. On June 2, 1965, almost to the day of Moore and Rogers's one-year anniversary at work, a car of white men shot the two deputies when they were off duty, injuring Rogers and killing Moore. Rogers broadcast a clear description of assailant Ernest McElveen, whom police soon arrested in Mississippi. A known member of the Citizens' Council and the National States' Rights Party, McElveen was found with a card designating him a special agent signed by Louisiana State Police director Thomas Burbank. But Mississippi police released him after detaining him briefly, claiming that they lacked enough evidence to bring charges.[12]

In the meantime, the Deacons set their sights beyond Louisiana, prompted by the growing attention they received from CORE and the national press. Bob Hicks made no apologies for the group's daring strategy to combat police violence. "We're gonna patrol. And like policemen who are running you down and say, 'You speedin'," then we pull up to them and say, 'What's the matter,' and the policeman say, 'He's speedin'. And we say, 'We didn't see him speed,'" the Bogalusa leader told the *Los Angeles Times*, adding, "When the policemen see we armed just like they is—a white man's just like anybody else—they gonna let you go when they see you gonna attack them back."[13]

That June, Bogalusa Deacon Charlie Sims ventured to California on a fundraising tour and press junket. As scattered Black community groups in the North and West expressed interest in the Deacons' work, Sims considered whether the self-defense group could export its work beyond the South. When Earnest Thomas made his own trip to California, he spoke to an audience in Oakland that included young activists receptive to the Deacons' ideas, including an antipoverty worker named Bobby Seale and his friend, twenty-three-year-old college student Huey Newton. "We liked what he said," Newton recalled later, reflecting on his and Seale's inspirations for establishing the Black Panther Party for Self-Defense in October 1966.[14]

The positive reception Sims and Thomas enjoyed on the West Coast fueled their organization's hopes of expanding. "I'd like to start a chapter of the Deacons in Los Angeles," Sims told the *Los Angeles Times*. He was confident that the city's Black residents could benefit from one, reasoning to a reporter, "Man, there's police brutality and people with that white supremacy stuff everywhere." In less than a year, the Deacons had made a name for themselves in civil rights circles with a bold vision for countering the twin scourges of police violence and white vigilantism. As it turned out, their choice to monitor police with armed patrols instead of picketing them appealed to activists far beyond Louisiana.[15]

One evening in June 1966, twenty Black men reported for duty at the South Central Los Angeles office of the United Civil Rights Committee, a local organization with a history of working with CORE. Ranging from eighteen years old to middle-aged, each man in the group was expected to demonstrate that he was sober and

FIGURE 9.1. Member of the Los Angeles Community Alert Patrol, a team of police monitors with ties to SNCC and CORE, 1966. Photograph by Gordon Parks, courtesy of and copyright by the Gordon Parks Foundation.

unarmed. From there the men followed a tightly scripted routine, breaking into pairs and filing into ten cars, each one equipped with an audio recorder, a film camera, and a movie camera, plus two-way radios supplied by local SNCC organizers. Every car was decorated with a white flag on its antenna and a cardboard sign attached to its driver-side door reading "Community Alert Patrol—To Protect and Observe," a clever reworking of the LAPD's famed vow to "protect and serve" (see figure 9.1). Joining the patrol caravan that evening was Betty Pleasant, a reporter for the Black-owned *Los Angeles Sentinel* newspaper.

As they left the United Civil Rights Committee, the cars split into pairs to complete their rounds. When Unit #6 witnessed a police squad car racing after a woman driving on Central Avenue, they radioed headquarters to let them know they were pursuing the officers. As police caught the woman, Unit #6 pulled up behind them with plans to step out of their car to observe the interaction and, if necessary, take pictures and make recordings.

Almost as soon as officers saw the Community Alert Patrol (CAP) team arrive, they let the woman drive off without further action. Skeptical of the rationale for the traffic stop, the observers wondered whether the officers had released her only because they were being watched (see figure 9.2). "Through some strange procedure in Los Angeles, the police are always right and the citizens are always wrong," Pleasant quipped to readers. The mission of the community patrol, she explained, was "to find out if the man with the stitches in his head was brutally beaten by a cop as he claims or was as the cop says, 'resisting arrest and had to be restrained.'"[16]

Some LAPD officers made disparaging comments to the monitors; others wrote them traffic tickets for trivial infractions. Still others tried to foil the patrol's work, shining their spotlights on them as they took pictures. None of this dissuaded CAP members from their work. "Our local law officers maintain they are not harassing, bullying and beating people," Pleasant noted. "If they are not, good; the Community Alert Patrol cannot cramp their style. But if they are, the community alert patrol can save a lot of heads."[17]

The idea of unarmed citizen patrols monitoring police for misconduct was not new. In July 1965, Seattle's CORE chapter joined with the city's Central Area Committee for Civil Rights to launch what they called "freedom patrols." Following an inquest jury's refusal to charge an off-duty police officer in the fatal shooting of Robert Reece, a local Black contractor, more than two hundred people volunteered for nightly shifts to trail Seattle police on foot and take notes of any improper actions. If police used "abusive language, smile at them and write down their badge numbers," one of the organizers advised patrol members. "If there is unwarranted use of force, let them push you backward so you can write down their names and badge numbers."[18]

Unlike the Deacons for Defense, the freedom patrols in Seattle were unarmed and adhered to nonviolent principles. A freedom patroller, their guidelines suggested, might use their "body as a shield between an attacker and his victim," but under no circumstances were patrol members to make physical contact with law enforcement officers. While the freedom patrols might seem cautious compared

GUILTY OF
MURDER

Police murdered 34 of our brothers and sisters last August!

How many of us will they kill this year?

Stop the murder and beating of innocent people by the Los Angeles police and sheriffs!

Stand together against lawless police.

Support and work in your Community Alert Patrol.

Phone CAP at 750-5048

FIGURE 9.2. Los Angeles Community Alert Patrol poster, May 1966, featuring the black panther symbol popularized by the SNCC-affiliated Lowndes County Freedom Organization prior to the founding of the Black Panther Party for Self-Defense in October 1966. Charles Brittin Papers, Getty Research Institute, Los Angeles (2005.M.11).

with the Deacons, Seattle police officials viewed them as no less radical. Chief Frank Ramon claimed that "good sympathetic people are enraged at the idea of the Freedom Patrols," deriding them as a "retrogression of the Negro movement."[19]

If Black citizens and organizers hoped to stem the tide of police violence, perhaps they had no choice but to conduct surveillance on the police themselves. "The police department investigating itself is a joke in a democracy," one patrol member remarked. The *San Francisco Chronicle* described the patrols as a "surveillance demonstration," a clunky but apt turn of phrase suggesting a role reversal for the Seattle department, which, like most urban departments, operated an intelligence unit that spied on activists. With six-hour nightly shifts that lasted until 2:00 in the morning, the freedom patrols were difficult to sustain. Seattle CORE organized the patrols far less often than it liked, and it appears to have suspended them by summer 1966. But the Seattle project helped to popularize the idea of community activists monitoring police on the West Coast.[20]

Before winding down operations, Seattle's patrol organizers took the time to advise their counterparts in Los Angeles in CAP. As in Seattle, the patrols in L.A. were organized by an umbrella organization of community groups, in this case the Temporary Alliance of Local Organizations, better known as TALO. One activist described it as "the only organization in the history of Los Angeles that succeeded in getting the bourgeois Negro, CORE and SNCC, US, SLANT, Peter Salem, the Afro-American Cultural Association, the Slausons and the Businessmen to sit down and try to do something positive for this community and the way of keeping violence down." Stated otherwise, it brought together the traditional African American leadership class with civil rights groups, Black nationalists, and, in the case of the Slausons and Businessmen, gangs.[21]

As in Seattle, CAP formed in the wake of a fatal police shooting of a Black man, in this case Leonard Deadwyler, killed by Officer Jerold Bova in May 1966 after he pulled him over for speeding as he rushed his pregnant wife to the hospital. A coroner's inquest several weeks later drew one thousand spectators. Many in the Black community were bitterly disappointed when the jury ruled Deadwyler's death an accidental homicide, dismissing eyewitnesses who described seeing a cold-blooded murder.

CAP formed less than two weeks after Bova was exonerated. On June 10, 1966, TALO members arrived at LAPD headquarters for a Police Commission meeting devoted to community relations with Black residents. Once there, they announced a boycott of the proceedings because police had handpicked Black residents but excluded the fledgling coalition. As the meeting was underway, TALO activists directed attendees' attention to four cars circling the building outside, each flying a white handkerchief in honor of Deadwyler, who was flying a similar white fabric from his car as he rushed his wife to the hospital. The next night, CAP volunteers shadowed LAPD squad cars for the first time.

Beyond deterring police violence, CAP hoped to forestall any uprising that might arise in response to such attacks. Riots played into the hands of an LAPD that was glad to have an excuse to institute martial law after Watts the previous August. "Black folks are last hired and first fired AT in a riot situation," CAP organizer Louis Gothard remarked to SNCC's San Francisco newspaper, *The Movement*. Or as CAP volunteer Chester Wright told the paper, the patrols put to work "people who were throwing Molotov cocktails in the last riot, people who have gone through the daily grind of having police on their backs and on their children's backs every time they moved. For the first time in their lives, they got a chance to actively do something to alleviate this."[22]

————

Five days after the Community Alert Patrol debuted in Los Angeles, Stokely Carmichael found himself in jail in Greenwood, Mississippi. Active in the movement since the Freedom Rides, the SNCC chairman had been arrested more than two dozen times. Earlier that month, on June 5, James Meredith had set out on foot on a 220-mile solitary trek through his home state of Mississippi. The first ever Black student to enroll at the University of Mississippi in 1962, Meredith now intended to prove that if an unarmed Black man could traverse the state on his own—he had explicitly asked civil rights organizations not to accompany him—Black Mississippians had no reason to fear registering to vote, even in the face of threats from the Klan and outright defiance from white officials.

On the second day of his march as he walked south of the town of Hernando, Meredith was shot by an unemployed hardware contractor from Memphis named Aubrey Norvell. Photographs of Meredith stretched out on the road and screaming in pain made front-page news across the country. In response to the shooting, which Meredith survived, all four of the leading national civil rights organizations—CORE, SNCC, the SCLC, and the NAACP—converged on Mississippi to organize a procession across the state they christened the March Against Fear.

Eleven days after Meredith started his march, on June 16, organizers arrived in Greenwood, the seat of Leflore County on the eastern periphery of the Delta. As they had done on previous stops, marchers erected tents on town property, in this case at the Stone Street Negro School. But when police commissioner B. A. Hammond and a group of officers arrived, they instructed the group to disassemble the tents, claiming that they lacked permission from the school board to stay there. Carmichael, who happened to drive past the scene, jumped out of a car to tell the officers that they had no right to evict the group, and after he ignored Hammond's orders to not touch any of the tents, the commissioner had him arrested, along with SNCC staffer Robert Smith and CORE staffer Bruce Baines. The trio were taken to the city jail and held there for six hours. Upon their release, they headed to a nighttime rally where Carmichael was scheduled to be the final speaker.

Much has been made of the SNCC chairman's words at the mass outdoor meeting. As Carmichael reached the climax of his speech, he called out a phrase that mesmerized his audience, one that had been quietly circulating in SNCC but was foreign to the white reporters in attendance: "We want Black power!" With each declaration of the phrase, the overwhelmingly African American crowd roared back in approval, "Black power!"

In the weeks that followed, many journalists characterized Carmichael's speech as a decisive and abrupt rejection of multiracial organizing in favor of Black nationalism. But his words that night in Greenwood were only the first public pronouncement of SNCC's long, gradual shift away from desegregation campaigns in the South to an emphasis on Black community organizing and institution-building nationwide. SNCC executive secretary James Forman later observed that the rallying cry "merely shortened the phrase 'power for black people'—a goal of SNCC since 1961."[23]

But Carmichael's remarks earlier in his speech—long treated as little more than a preamble to his famous refrain—distilled SNCC's evolving analysis of the criminal justice system. "This is my 27th time I have been arrested. I ain't going to jail no more," he told the audience. "I ain't going to jail no more." After calling for Black power, Carmichael offered one more proposal: "Every courthouse in Mississippi ought to be burned down to get rid of the dirt." The crowd cheered in approval.

If Carmichael's demand for Black power signaled an ongoing shift in SNCC with long roots, his rejection of jail indicated a rethinking of incarceration's place in a movement that was becoming more radical, especially in its understanding of political policing. Since its inception in spring 1960, SNCC had celebrated doing time as a strategic tool of nonviolent resistance. A paraphrase of the famed exhortation of "jail, no bail" was even written into the organization's founding documents.[24]

Filling the jails was an idea grounded in Gandhian principles of nonviolence and embraced by SNCC, CORE, and the SCLC as a critical weapon against segregation. In the first half of the decade, the movement had treated jail time as a necessary rite of passage for organizers. SNCC volunteer and writer Sally Belfrage described getting arrested as a "fate almost universally considered desirable" by civil rights workers. Organizers were jailed so often that they tracked how many times they had been locked up. That Carmichael knew he had been in jail exactly twenty-seven times was a result of a mindset in the movement that treated incarceration as a matter of pride.[25]

Then why was Carmichael now renouncing jail time? The reasons are complex, but it is clear that SNCC and CORE were reconsidering how much incarceration served the movement's evolving goals. By

1966 there was a growing realization within SNCC that jail time was even more dangerous than originally thought. Fannie Lou Hamer's account at the 1964 Democratic National Convention of her physical and sexual assault by police in a Winona, Mississippi, jail was just one unforgettable reminder of these dangers. Surrendering one's bodily autonomy behind bars was at odds with the notions of self-defense and resisting police violence that were gaining traction within the movement. Indeed, the stakes of incarceration for activists appeared higher than they had been just a few years earlier. Compared to when Black students staged sit-ins across the South in spring 1960, police were more eager to charge organizers with felonies that could result in years in prison, not just weeks or months in a county facility.

As the idea of Black power made national headlines in summer 1966, police departments grew ever more zealous and sophisticated in their drive to incapacitate activists who took up Carmichael's call for increased defiance. Earlier in the decade, as sit-ins and Freedom Rides swept the South, young activists had regarded filling the jails as a strategy to bring attention to their cause and strain law enforcement's resources and resolve to defend segregation. But now, as organizers in SNCC and CORE broadened their conception of political repression, they came to understand incarceration less as an opportunity for tactical gain and more as an act of slow violence that threatened to destroy the movement.

———

One year earlier, in summer 1965, SNCC organizers in Philadelphia established the group's first ever community campaign outside the South. Their initial objective was to build a "Freedom Organization," a political network for working-class Black Philadelphians that was independent of leading churches, the NAACP, and elected officials. SNCC's arrival unsettled Mayor James Tate and his fragile Democratic coalition of white bosses who oversaw a municipal patronage system designed to extract votes from Black residents.[26]

In July 1966, with SNCC's work only slowly taking shape in Philadelphia, Chairman Stokely Carmichael visited the city to promote the project. Barely a month after his Black Power speech, a torrent of negative press trailed Carmichael to town. Appearing at the Church of the Advocate in North Philadelphia, Carmichael repeated his calls for Black power alongside Nina Simone to an audience of more than one thousand people. A reporter at the rally for the Black-owned *Philadelphia Tribune* quoted SNCC worker Morris Ruffin's bold, if metaphorical, declaration that "if it is necessary to use dynamite to blow down bastions of segregation, then we must blow them up and start over again." Tate blasted Carmichael as "not good for Philadelphia" in response and warned him to "stay out of Philadelphia and other big cities."[27]

Since February 1963, the city's police department had operated the Civil Disobedience Unit, an intelligence squad promoted not as a surveillance unit but as a socially aware community relations division. Public relations efforts notwithstanding, the CDU was still a red squad, and a very sophisticated one at that. Unlike most of its counterparts, it made no secret of its existence, as its agents strived to develop rapport with organizers so that they would give advance notice of their demonstrations. The unit was praised by officials as "color-blind" and composed of equal numbers of Black and white officers at a time when the Philadelphia police department was 80 percent white. The NAACP even invited CDU members to speak at its national convention in 1965, and the unit's second-in-command, George Fencl, had been friendly with Philadelphia NAACP president Cecil Moore since their days serving in the Marines. But more radical activists in Philadelphia remained unconvinced of the CDU. By 1970, the unit's files contained information on 28,000 individuals and five hundred organizations. Spencer Coxe, executive director of Philadelphia's ACLU, contended that the CDU's mission was to "give the demonstrators a sense of being watched."[28]

One individual who noticed he was being monitored by the CDU was Barry Dawson, a nineteen-year-old Philadelphia native and SNCC staffer committed to deploying the tactics of the Southern movement in his hometown. Dawson had volunteered for CORE in Cambridge, Maryland, and Chester, Pennsylvania, in 1964 and then completed a stint as a full-time staffer for SNCC in southwest

Georgia the following year. In late 1965, he returned to Philadelphia to work for SNCC's new community organizing campaign.[29]

By the following summer, Dawson regularly observed officers tracking him. In the wake of Carmichael's visit, the CDU conducted surveillance of the SNCC office and several other locations available to staffers. Late on the evening of August 10, Dawson was walking to a meeting when a group of white men jumped out of a car and approached him, addressing him by name. Within moments, the trio attacked Dawson and beat him to the ground, leaving him on the street unconscious. Once he awoke, Dawson sought refuge at his friend George Brower's nearby apartment. Brower was involved in Operation Alert, a campaign organized just weeks earlier to send teams of activists from SNCC, CORE, and the Communist Party's W.E.B. Du Bois Club onto Philadelphia's streets to monitor the city's police for any acts of violence they committed against Black residents. The effort was not unlike CAP in Los Angeles or the Freedom Patrols in Seattle.[30]

Dawson was convinced that his assailants had been police. The men had driven a car that resembled one he had seen plainclothes officers in earlier that day, and he was certain police were the only white people who knew his name. Several hours later, early on the morning of August 11, Dawson arrived at a police precinct to make a formal complaint in person. Although the department was adamant that their officers had nothing to do with the attack, police officials alerted the FBI to Dawson's complaint, likely hoping to preempt SNCC before they contacted federal authorities. While Bureau agents seemed to think little of Dawson's claim, the Department of Justice's Civil Rights Division thought it necessary to make plans to interview him about his allegations in the coming weeks.[31]

The next day, on August 12, Special Agent Irving Dean in the FBI's Philadelphia field office obtained a warrant to search Brower's apartment, where Dawson had fled after the beating. Issued by Leo Weinrott, a staunch law-and-order judge on the city's Common Pleas Court, the order permitted the seizure of "any and all dynamite, blasting caps, percussion caps or any other explosive material" in the apartment. In his warrant application, Dean stated that an informant had seen "a quantity of dynamite" at SNCC headquarters that the group's staff intended to divvy up and plant throughout the city with the goal of triggering "civil disturbances." Acting police commissioner Frank Rizzo—who later served two terms as Philadelphia's mayor—claimed that his colleagues believed the informant only after he brought them several sticks of dynamite.[32]

Dean assured the court that the unnamed source had provided "information concerning criminal activity on more than 200 occasions which has invariably proven to be accurate." If true, the agent was describing a seasoned informant with intimate knowledge of SNCC's activities. As the evening of August 12 approached, Philadelphia police finalized their plans for action.[33]

———

"4 RACISTS HELD, DYNAMITE SEIZED IN SNCC RAIDS," screamed the top headline on the cover of the *Philadelphia Daily News* tabloid the next morning. Hours earlier, police had raided SNCC's local headquarters just after midnight. A total of eighty officers with bulletproof vests and machine guns stormed the organization's office as well as three more properties linked to activists. An additional total of 1,500 officers assembled as backup in the four predominantly Black neighborhoods surrounding the raids. By "confiscating 2 1/2 sticks of dynamite and arresting four members of the Student Non-Violent Coordinating Committee," the *Daily News* informed readers, officers had "crushed a planned militant 'black power' movement in the city."[34]

At George Brower's apartment, police searched in vain for explosives for ten minutes. Then, when another colleague joined them inside the home, he somehow managed to spot several sticks of dynamite under a sofa within seconds. Police arrested Brower and two friends who were visiting him, Eugene Dawkins and Carol West. As a crowd of neighbors gathered outside, CDU chief Millard Meers announced over a loudspeaker that officers were searching for explosives. "I think it had a very sobering effect on them," Meers remarked to a *Daily News* reporter. Several years before Los Angeles police established the nation's first SWAT team, these raids by Philadelphia police resembled a military strike more than a law enforcement raid. "These people will be dealt with harshly," Rizzo declared, promising continued surveillance of SNCC's activities in the city.[35]

Before long, police outside the building had also arrested Dawson, the purported mastermind of the conspiracy, on his way to meet up with Brower, West, and Dawkins. The *Philadelphia Inquirer* repeated police claims that the four arrested were "cop watchers detailed to keep police activities under close surveillance to spot so-called 'police brutality.'" Indeed, each one of them was involved in the fledgling Operation Alert campaign. Within days of the raid, police arrested two more individuals and announced that they were seeking three additional activists at large. SNCC staffers Fred Meely, Morris Ruffin, and George Anderson had disappeared hours after the police raids, triggering a fourteen-state manhunt. Presiding again at a hearing for those arrested was Weinrott, who set the bail for each defendant at $50,000, or nearly half a million dollars adjusted for inflation. "These people were nothing but thugs and hoodlums," an irate Rizzo charged. "The civil rights movement would be a lot better off without them."[36]

Prosecutors' key evidence was a statement from Dawson confessing to transporting dynamite to Brower's apartment a few days earlier. In a convoluted narrative riven with contradictions and transcribed by a police stenographer, Dawson recounted how he dissuaded a friend from hiding the dynamite at Brower's apartment because it was too risky, only to take it upon himself to move it to SNCC headquarters. Two days later, the explosives somehow reappeared in Brower's apartment, an occurrence that Dawson could not explain. Dawson described SNCC in the confession as a group of agitators seeking to "start sit-ins [and] bus riots throughout the South," echoing language of the movement's segregationist critics. He sounded unlike any other civil rights organizer in his statement—so much so that his colleagues had to wonder whether he had given the confession at all.[37]

———

"I consider this assignment the most serious I've done for SNCC," James Forman soon concluded. "The importance of the situation in which SNCC finds itself in Philadelphia derives from the fact that this is the first attempt, in a major metropolitan area, to develop the concept of a national Freedom Organization," the organization's executive secretary reasoned. "We shall not allow the Philadelphia police force to destroy us."[38]

Hours after the police raids on August 13, SNCC's Central Committee dispatched Forman to leave the national office in Atlanta to help their beleaguered colleagues in Philadelphia. As soon as he and two SNCC staffers arrived at their hotel outside the city, they were alarmed to discover plainclothes police officers staying in the room adjacent to theirs. After refusing to answer their questions, the SNCC contingent snuck out of the hotel and made their way to a friend's house, now aware that their preparations for the trip had been compromised by surveillance.

Among the most pressing tasks was to find a new lawyer for Barry Dawson. To Forman and his colleagues' surprise, local NAACP leader Cecil B. Moore, a man with no connection to SNCC or to its Philadelphia staff, had volunteered to represent the young activist and encouraged him to make a full confession to police. Even more perplexing, Moore chose to abandon Dawson in the interrogation room just as an assistant district attorney and two police officers began their questioning. In a move that would boggle the mind of most defense attorneys, the young activist was left to fend for himself.

Just before jumping town, SNCC Philadelphia director Fred Meely urged his colleagues to "extricate Barry Dawson from the tentacles of Cecil Moore, primarily on the grounds that Dawson wouldn't get good representation and that Moore would try to kill what SNCC was trying to do in Philadelphia." Meely feared that the NAACP leader was capitalizing on the indictments to push a rival organization out of the city. Within days, SNCC replaced Moore with Len Holt, who could bring to bear his extensive experience defending activists, including in the Statue of Liberty case the year before. Joining him was local attorney Bill Akers, a CORE member who had run an unsuccessful campaign against Moore for the Philadelphia NAACP presidency in 1962.

Akers blasted Moore's spotty representation of Dawson as "service to the interests of 'white power,'" incredulous that the NAACP leader had abandoned his client in the interrogation room. Forman for his part insisted that police had planted the dynamite in Brower's apartment as part of "a frame up." Gullible local media who parroted police talking points instead of questioning the case's glaring inconsistencies only made matters worse. If the dynamite defendants stood any chance of getting a fair trial, Dawson's comrades reasoned, they would need to present a different narrative, one that exposed the case for what it was, an attack not only on SNCC but on all Black Philadelphians.[39]

———

At a press conference just six days after the raid, Jim Forman condemned Philadelphia police for planting evidence and orchestrating a slander campaign against SNCC activists. The majority of the nine indicted individuals were not even involved with the organization, Forman assured gathered reporters, and he rebutted claims repeated by the press that police had raided four SNCC offices. Forman clarified that the organization had only one office in Philadelphia, and FBI agent Dean's warrant request had been for just a single property, Brower's apartment. Police never disclosed warrants for the other locations, including SNCC's office, so three of the four raids on August 13 were likely illegal.

In the days leading up to the case's first major hearing, SNCC allies distributed literature in Black neighborhoods amplifying this message. "Don't let white power lynch the brothers," one flyer pleaded, above photographs of CDU lieutenant George Fencl and Chief Rizzo with Klan hoods drawn atop their heads. "PHILADELPHIA'S WHITE POWER IS FRAMING SNCC WITH RACIST RIZZO'S LIES," another blared, urging residents to "witness against the dynamite frame up" by attending the hearings and calling on Mayor Tate to get the charges dropped (see figure 9.3). "The tactics of the Philadelphia cops directed by Rizzo are as barbarous as those of Alabama or Philadelphia, Mississippi," the flyer charged,

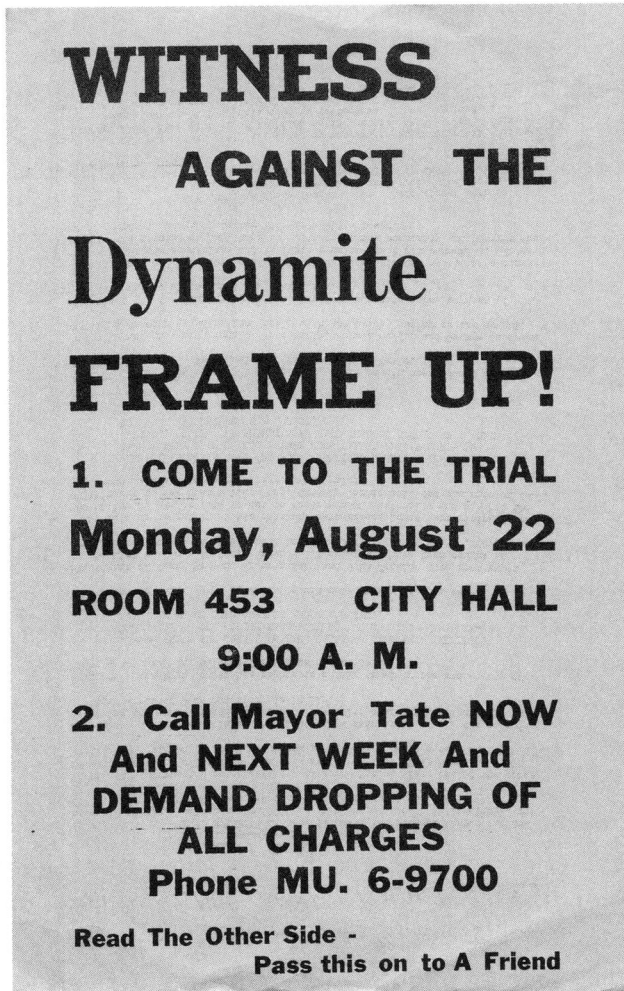

FIGURE 9.3. Flyer distributed as part of a defense campaign for four SNCC workers and additional activists charged by Philadelphia police with a dynamite plot in August 1966. James Forman Papers, LOC.

referencing the murder of Chaney, Goodman, and Schwerner. Rizzo's police force, in other words, was no better than its segregationist counterparts in the South.[40]

The crisis in Philadelphia was "symptomatic of the increasingly open and avowed fascist tactics of police departments," Forman maintained, and it augured an escalation of attacks on SNCC across the country. "The police will operate to suppress the legitimate aspiration of people within the inner city—and that mainly means the legitimate aspirations of Black people."

The indictments pushed SNCC to develop a campaign against police repression. In the weekend before the hearing, activists estimated that they distributed 45,000 copies of their flyer. They also spoke at multiple churches and staged impromptu rallies on street corners with megaphones. Philadelphia police showed their displeasure with the campaign and its allegations of police corruption by arresting and even physically attacking organizers. A plainclothes officer served Forman with a subpoena that, as Rizzo told the press, would allow him to prove his claims that the defendants had been framed.

As they made their way to the initial court hearing on August 22, SNCC organizers were unsure whether their days of organizing had aroused any meaningful community support. But as Forman and his colleagues arrived at the courthouse, they were stunned to see seven hundred supporters waiting for them. "We saw some of our brothers and sisters in their African dress, and we knew that it was going to be a very exciting morning," Forman later recalled with pride.[41]

Inside the hearing, CDU officials offered a surveillance photograph taken outside the SNCC office as proof that Dawson and Ruffin had handled dynamite. The only problem was that the picture showed the pair carrying two paper bags, with no indication as to their contents. No forensic evidence linked the activists to the dynamite, either. And while Dawson had confessed to handling explosives, he had recounted plans to dispose of them "so no one would get hurt." Pennsylvania law at the time defined possession of explosives as a crime only if accompanied by "the intent to use the same unlawfully against the person or property of another." In a word, Dawson's confession might not have been so incriminating after all.[42]

Rizzo was unconcerned with such evidentiary shortcomings. "I'm both disgusted and appalled that outsiders would come into our community and deliberately try to inject race into matters which involve danger to the lives and damage to the property of all our citizens," the police chief remarked to reporters, alleging that activists such as Dawson were Black supremacists crying discrimination in a color-blind city. Unbowed, SNCC's supporters assembled outside city hall after the day's hearing to cheer on Forman as he set his summons on fire, declaring "like trash it should be burned."

The following week, on August 30, more than a thousand SNCC supporters gathered at the Church of the Advocate for a mass meeting headlined by Carmichael in support of the defendants, filling the sizable gothic chapel beyond capacity before moving outdoors to transform the event into a public rally. Philadelphia was "run by a gestapo police force," the SNCC chair proclaimed. "What we need is control of the police precincts in our community," he continued, because "we are the only people who have to protect ourselves against our protectors."[43]

The *Daily News* described the rally with alarm, caricaturing Carmichael as something akin to a charismatic cult leader who brought to Philadelphia "robes, complex secret handshakes and fiery oratory that police say could start a riot." Fortunately, the paper noted, the vigilant Civil Disobedience Unit had kept the peace. When Carmichael had arrived for the mass meeting on a bus from New York, plainclothes CDU officers were there to greet him, and as he moved throughout the city, they followed him and observed his activities. At the rally later that day, at least a half dozen plainclothes officers mixed with the crowd, ejecting attendees they considered too supportive of what the *Daily News* described as Carmichael's "recruiting slogans for an army of rioters." As the rally came to an end, CDU officers followed individuals they deemed suspicious.[44]

———

On November 10, attorneys for Meely, Ruffin, and Anderson notified the CDU's George Fencl that their clients were ready to surrender after nearly three months on the run. A *Daily News* photographer captured the trio's "perp walk" outside police headquarters, handcuffed and with their heads bowed. By the end of the year, hearings for the SNCC workers had been postponed at least three times, with Fencl telling the court that "sudden illness" had stricken

Barry Dawson each time, preventing the prosecution's supposed star witness from appearing in court. All the while, Dawson faced continued harassment. In one incident, police arrested him on suspicion of assault and transported him to a precinct station, where an officer proceeded to knock out two of his teeth.[45]

In February 1967, just half a year after the raid, SNCC closed its Philadelphia office. Two months later, a judge granted a request from the same assistant district attorney who had interrogated Dawson to drop the charges against Meely, Ruffin, and Anderson after Dawson had refused to testify. Finally, in March 1968, Akers struck a plea deal for Dawson to escape prison time by completing probation and a rehabilitation program.

In the final analysis, authorities never produced any evidence of criminal wrongdoing other than an ambiguous surveillance photograph and a questionable confession Dawson had given after his attorney Moore had abandoned him in the interrogation room (see figure 9.4). It was not even clear whether the questioning had been legal. Of the nine original defendants, Dawson alone was convicted. "The power structure had pulled out a quintuple-barreled shotgun with which to blast SNCC away," Forman concluded. The "dynamite frame-up was one of the first acts of massive repression in the urban North against the current black movement." It would not be the last.[46]

The campaign against SNCC in Philadelphia exposed the organization's vulnerability to political policing disguised as colorblind riot prevention. In addition to the surveillance it conducted on the group prior to the arrests, the CDU seized extensive records from the chapter office during the office raid. With their files missing and SNCC staffers on the run, the local organization was paralyzed. The raids and records seizure scared off prospective recruits and gave pause to confirmed supporters who worried that police had found their names in SNCC's papers. This was as much an act of intimidation as an investigation.

"What took place in Philadelphia was a well planned operation," Fred Meely insisted in May 1967, looking back on the coordinated campaign of four raids and nine indictments that culminated in the collapse of SNCC in Philadelphia. "It didn't just happen." For Jim

FIGURE 9.4. SNCC report on Philadelphia authorities' failed felony indictments of four of its workers and additional activists on explosives charges. James Forman Papers, LOC.

Forman, the saga proved that staffers had to do more to protect themselves from law enforcement—everything from avoiding gambling and drugs to installing scramblers on their phones and searching their offices for "planted dynamite and SHIT."[47]

If there was anywhere in the country where SNCC affiliates stood to benefit from Forman's advice, it was Houston. Just as in Philadelphia, political and business leaders in the South's largest city claimed a record of harmonious race relations. But in fall 1966, as activists affiliated with SNCC began to confront racism in the Texas metropolis, the response from Houston police would make the actions of Philadelphia authorities appear tame by comparison.

10

Retaliation

Federal lawmakers vowed that the Civil Rights Act of 1964 would ensure racial equality in the United States. Two years later, many Black Americans remained unconvinced—and Houston's African American community was no exception. More than three hundred thousand strong, it was the largest of any city in the South and the eighth biggest nationally. "The downtown restaurants, theaters and hotels are open to him now, but this means little to him, where he remains segregated from decent wages, decent housing, and white schools, except in the most token way," the white liberal *Texas Observer* remarked in a report on "the Negro" in Houston in May 1966. Wilhelmina Perry, an African American sociologist at Texas Southern University (TSU), the state's foremost historically Black college, offered a dire assessment. "The whole community is a bomb," Perry contended. "Negroes are repressed and there is this latent anxiety."[1]

According to Perry, Black Houstonians had two pressing concerns above all others. One was educational inequality, and the other was police brutality. Racism found open expression among the city's officers. It was not unusual for radio dispatchers to use the n-word to describe Black suspects or for officers to employ the slur in recounting arrests. In the twelve-month period starting in July 1966, the Houston Police Department (HPD) disciplined fifty officers for various acts of disrespect and misconduct toward Black community members.

Houston employed not many more than a dozen Black officers, and it treated them terribly. One was E. J. Stringfellow, who joined the force with high hopes in 1954. "I thought the Police Department would be the fairest place you could find. But I found it was just the opposite. Segregation was worse here than anywhere else," Stringfellow told the *Houston Post* in 1980. As in most Southern cities and many Northern ones as well, Black officers had been discouraged or prohibited from arresting white citizens before the passage of the Civil Rights Act.[2]

Chief Herman Short had not created these conditions, but he did little to nothing to ameliorate them. Born in West Virginia in 1918, Short joined the Houston police force as a twenty-seven-year-old Coast Guard veteran just three months after the end of World War II. By 1964, he had risen to the rank of inspector. That October, Mayor Louis Welch fired the city's police chief and replaced him with Short, believing that he would work more aggressively than his predecessor to decrease the city's rising crime rate. Short was stocky, with dark hair and a square jaw. One reporter described him as "a broad-shouldered, brusque, perpetually frowning man," while an HPD officer who worked under Short remembered him as "respected, if not always loved," with a managerial style he characterized as "dictatorial."

Within six months of becoming chief, Short reconstituted the department's red squad as the Criminal Intelligence Division (CID) in March 1965. Short chose Joe Singleton, a detective from the HPD's robbery division, to lead the reimagined unit. As he told a reporter a decade later, the CID "worked around the clock, undercover, covering what we considered radical-type meetings, taking numerous pictures, taking notes and keeping track of people coming and going." Though its civil rights movement was dwarfed by those in other Southern cities such as Nashville, Atlanta, and New Orleans, Houston authorities went all in on political policing, concluding that the safety of their city depended on it.[3]

City of Houston Police Department
Intelligence Report
Subject: James Forman (SNCC)
Report Written By: F-12

On Tuesday, October 4th, 1966, officer attended an assembly
in the Auditorium at T.S.U. Dr. Thomas F. Freeman presided
over a discussion of "BLACK POWER, A NEW RELIGION."
    James Forman, who is the manager of the main office
in Atlanta, Georgia, was allowed to speak ten minutes to a
crowd of approximately 1,000 persons, mostly students. . . .
Forman said Black Power to him means wresting the black
slave concept from the white power. "Man, look around
you, look at the library here compared to Harvard," he said.
He stated, "SNCC has gotten us out of most of our problems
because it has unchained us from the white man, who has
been operating on us all these years."

SNCC executive secretary James Forman's visit to Houston in fall
1966 gave Houston police all the reason they needed to start monitoring the group in the city. Some of those attending his assembly
speech set about obtaining formal recognition as a Friends of SNCC
campus chapter from university officials. Unlike CORE and the
NAACP, SNCC was not an organization of paid staff, with no dues-
paying members. The Friends of SNCC was a coalition of chapters
concentrated on college campuses in the North and West supporting
their parent organization's Southern field campaigns with protests
and fundraising.
    Following the talk by Forman, which drew repeated cheers, Offi-
cer F-12 noted that "a program of the events and participants will be
placed in the brown envelope behind file for further use." Houston
police considered Forman and his comrades people to keep an eye
on, and at least three officials read the account of the rally: Short,
Singleton, and someone in the office of Mayor Louis Welch, who
kept a copy of the report.[4]

Surviving records from the CID suggest that the unit's intelligence operations in its first two years were broad but scattershot. Officers monitored the NAACP and SCLC, as well as the ACLU. One agent infiltrated local Klan gatherings. Another observed a Young Democrats meeting at the University of Houston where atheist Madalyn Murray O'Hair spoke. Majority-white leftist groups such as the Houston Socialist Forum and the Houston Citizens for Actions on Vietnam also appeared in the CID's files. Bill Lawson, a young Black minister affiliated with the SCLC, was a recurring subject of surveillance reports, as were representatives of the federal War on Poverty, both local organizers and visiting dignitaries such as Sargent Shriver, President Johnson's appointed director of the Office of Economic Opportunity.[5]

For a team of just half a dozen officers, the unit monitored a huge array of individuals and organizations. Most reports were based on public meetings, instead of undercover informants or other sources with access to private discussions. Spotty intelligence meant that the CID struggled to understand organizations that had operated in Houston for years, and the division's analysis of its subjects was rudimentary and shallow.

As 1966 came to a close, the CID was surprised to witness SNCC's ascent in Houston. On December 13, Mayor Welch appeared before a student assembly on TSU's campus to promote Project Partner, an initiative designed to show Houston's Black communities "a city that cares." While the city's *Chronicle* newspaper fawned over Welch's speech as a "major policy statement on Houston's race relations," the mayor's proposals were underwhelming. They included a pledge to persuade landlords to supply paint for their properties and a program inviting young Black residents to speak with police and ride in their patrol cars, so that they might "start looking upon the officers as their friend rather than someone to fear."[6]

TSU students were unimpressed. Three hundred protesters greeted Welch with chants of "Freedom Now!" and signs reading "Black Power Now" and "Stop Lies and Tricks, Deceitful Mayor Welch." Leading the demonstration was one Frederick Kirkpatrick, a founder of the Deacons for Defense and now a graduate student on campus. "The football season is over and we do not want any pep talks today," Kirkpatrick told the crowd, in anticipation of the mayor's boosterish attempt at addressing racial inequality.[7]

The protest shocked Welch and came as an embarrassing rejoinder to his meager efforts to assist Black neighborhoods. "None of our sources of information had any advance knowledge of the picket plans," the CID later admitted sheepishly. Two days after the protest, the intelligence unit reported to the mayor that Forman had met with some forty to fifty people interested in SNCC's organizing efforts when he visited TSU.

In closing, Singleton offered a stern warning that had up to that point appeared in none of the division's extant memos. "Information in this report was obtained from a highly confidential source and its contents should not be disclosed to <u>anyone</u> other than the mayor unless absolutely necessary." The unit had already secured an informant within SNCC.[8]

———

One day in late February 1967, a touring group of gospel singers from Houston was stopped by the State Highway Patrol in Livingston, a small town about eighty miles northeast of the city. A patrolman charged the four Black men with "making obscene gestures to a woman driver." When he attempted to arrest the men, the officer explained, they resisted, leaving him no choice but to club them. The quartet, whose names and home addresses were printed in the *Chronicle*, rejected the officer's account, saying that they had been beaten at jail long after they were arrested, two of them so badly that they checked into a hospital upon returning to Houston.[9]

TSU's Friends of SNCC resolved to force white Houstonians to confront what had happened. On the morning of March 11, a group of sixty marchers took off from campus on foot to protest police violence. Organizing the march were Kirkpatrick and Lee Otis Johnson, a charismatic student who had emerged as a new leader in the group. By the time the marchers reached the city's downtown commercial district, their numbers had swelled to more than one hundred. Their destination was the M & M Building, home to the state attorney general's offices in Houston. There they had plans to meet with several officials scheduled to receive them—but when they arrived, they found the doors locked.

Kirkpatrick taped a numbered list of thirteen demands to the front door. "1. Draft executive orders which would facilitate the obliteration of police brutality in Houston and on the state highways and byways," the group's instructions to the attorney general began, followed by calls for the hiring of more Black officers on the State Highway Patrol and Houston's police force, as well as a civilian review board to probe state law enforcement abuses.

After a string of a half dozen legal requests, the orders reached an emotional crescendo. "7. DEMAND THAT RACIST PATROL-MEN WHO BRUTALLY BEAT NEGROES FOR VIOLATION OF TRAFFIC LAWS BE EXPENDED [sic] AND DENIED THE OPPORTUNITY OF BECOMING ENFORCERS OF THE LAW," and, finally, "13. ACT NOW ON THE AFOREMENTIONED DEMANDS AND NOT LATER!!!!!!!!!!!!"

White Houstonians were unaccustomed to Black protesters marching through their main commercial district and making demands of officials. "Negroes Stage Noisy Rally Downtown," a headline on the front page of the *Post*'s Sunday edition reported, in seeming disbelief as it described how "a chanting, singing group of negroes known as the Friends of SNCC marched down Main Street Saturday protesting alleged police brutality." Dumbfounded white shoppers gaped at the procession in silence. Far from the TSU campus and the predominantly Black Third Ward, this was most white residents' firsthand introduction to SNCC.[10]

The CID sent three officers in an unmarked car to observe the march. Their overriding interest was in the various messages the protesters displayed on their placards, and the report they produced offered a verbatim inventory of twenty-one different signs, with messages including "I'm nonviolent ha ha. Until my people are beaten by a white cop"; "Mr. Charlie you best stop police brutality or burn baby burn"; and "Welch stop police brutality or we can turn Houston into a billion dollar graveyard." Another sign captured by a *Houston*

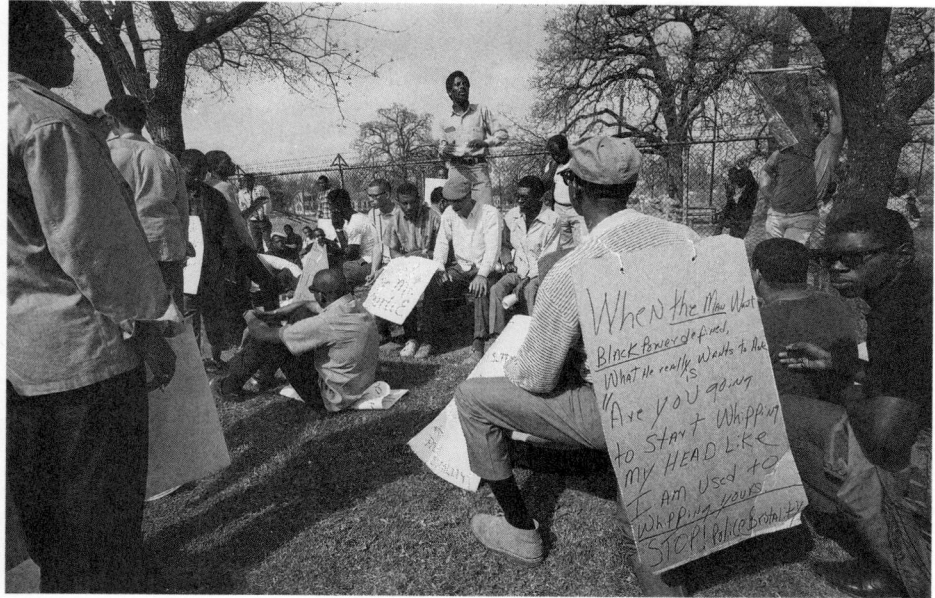

FIGURE 10.1. SNCC protest against police violence in Houston, March 11, 1967. RGD0006N-1967-0979, HHRC.

Post photographer offered a creative explanation of the movement's recent ideological turn: "When the Man want Black Power defined, what he really wants to ask is 'Are you going to start whipping my head like I am used to whipping yours'" (see figure 10.1).

This was tough talk in a city with little recent history of protest. In a copy of the CID's report sent to the mayor, Chief Short added a handwritten assurance to Welch that "pictures were taken of all the signs." While marchers' suggestions that they might riot if police brutality continued were almost certainly exaggerated, police were taking SNCC's rhetoric seriously.[11]

The two Friends of SNCC members of greatest interest to Houston police offered a study in contrasts. Frederick Kirkpatrick cut an imposing figure at six feet, two inches, and 275 pounds. He was a lay preacher who took to calling himself "Reverend" and a gifted guitarist with a powerful singing voice who knew how to work a crowd. As the son of sharecroppers from Haynesville, Louisiana, Kirkpatrick had gained admission to Grambling College, where he played football and graduated with a degree in education. After college, he played briefly with the American Football League's Dallas Texans, before taking a job teaching and coaching high school football in Jonesboro, Louisiana, where he helped establish the Deacons for Defense. In fall 1966, Kirkpatrick went to TSU to complete a master's program.[12]

Lee Otis Johnson had grown up in Houston's Third Ward, where his family had lived for some time in the city's first public housing, the Cuney Homes—a project that decades later would be home to a young George Floyd. From an early age, Johnson strived to earn money however he could. In his early teens he was sentenced twice to a state reformatory for truancy, and at sixteen he was convicted of interstate automobile theft and sent to a federal youth prison in Colorado, where he served three years. Johnson spent one more year in his middle twenties in state prison in Texas, again for automobile theft. But in fall 1966, a year after his release, he enrolled at the age of twenty-seven in his first semester of college at TSU. At five feet, eleven inches tall and just over 150 pounds, Johnson was wiry and muscular, and while he was not an experienced leader like Kirkpatrick, he was quick to immerse himself in the Friends of SNCC's activities, projecting a confident intensity that impressed younger activists on campus.[13]

As SNCC accelerated its work on TSU's campus, the chapter became a matter of civic concern for the city's police, its political leadership, and its white press. On March 20, 1967, nine days after the downtown police brutality protest, TSU officials notified the Friends of SNCC that they were no longer welcome on campus. In addition, the school informed SNCC faculty adviser and political science professor Mack Jones that his contract would not be renewed for the coming year. Two days later, on March 22, more than two hundred students held a protest against Jones's dismissal.[14]

Then, on the morning of March 28, the Friends of SNCC called for a student strike to demand that administrators grant them full

rights to operate at TSU. By that afternoon, the protests had grown
to roughly 1,500 students, more than a third of the campus's total
enrollment. Kirkpatrick and Johnson addressed a rally and were
joined by organizers from groups beyond TSU, including Franklin
Alexander, a traveling representative of the W.E.B. Du Bois Clubs,
the youth arm of the Communist Party USA.

"I am developing some concern over the influence of outside
elements," dean of students James B. Jones told the *Chronicle*. Jones
explained that he would discipline any students who participated in
an unsanctioned organization on campus. He hoped not to have to
involve law enforcement—unless the situation worsened. "But if it
gets too disruptive, we'll holler for help," the dean warned.

The administration's resistance encouraged the students to
organize for bigger changes. They called for campus security guards
to forgo pistols, just as unarmed guards did at white universities.
Students took to Wheeler Avenue and blocked any cars from entering, demanding that the treacherous thoroughfare bisecting campus
be shut down permanently to protect pedestrians.[15]

The following week, around midnight on April 4, officers raided
the YMCA near campus where Kirkpatrick and Alexander were living. They arrested the two men and announced that they were seeking Johnson as well. As it turned out, university president Joseph
Pierce had asked police to arrest the trio in the hopes that removing
them from campus would quell the protests. Though Johnson was
still unaccounted for, all three were charged with blocking access to
public buildings, disturbing the peace, and making threats to both
students and police officers.

As the news spread throughout the morning of April 4, the situation reached a boiling point. A crowd of five hundred took over the
university's main auditorium and insisted on meeting with Pierce.
When he arrived, the crowd demanded that he ask authorities to
drop the charges, but Pierce refused. The crowd stormed out of the
auditorium and headed to the Harris County Courthouse, where
Alexander and Kirkpatrick were being held, marching in pairs in a
line that extended two whole blocks. At the front of the procession
leading the demonstrators was Lee Otis Johnson.

A few blocks from TSU, the marchers approached Jeppesen Stadium, on the campus of the University of Houston. There they encountered about 150 helmeted members of the police riot squad. A line of about twenty service vehicles, each with six officers inside, began to follow the march. When several officers attempted to arrest Johnson, he struggled until about eight men subdued him and pulled him into a waiting car, as two intelligence officers stood guard over the crowd, one with a shotgun and another with a submachine gun.

Undaunted, the students proceeded to the courthouse. There they confronted another one hundred helmeted members of the riot squad carrying billy clubs, along with, in the words of Austin's *Rag* newspaper, "a police dog, tear gas, machine guns and shotguns, three paddy wagons, and fifty brown-shirted Harris County Deputies." If the students were intimidated, they did not show it.

As many as one hundred students held vigil outside the courthouse through the night in solidarity with their three jailed comrades. Their protests soon appeared to have borne fruit. A hearing scheduled for the next week that would have kept the three men in jail over the weekend had been moved up to the following day. A justice of the peace determined that the three men's bond, which had totaled a hefty $75,000—or more than $700,000 in 2025 dollars—should be reduced to $1,000 per person. The men could secure their release if they raised the funds, but they would only remain free as long as they adhered to a strict set of legally questionable conditions, including avoiding "any assembly of three or more persons with the purpose or intent to use loud language, or to yell or shriek, or use any electrical voice amplifier in any such manner as to disturb any person attending or at the campus." If any of the men failed to abide by these strictures, they would forfeit the bond and spend a year in jail.

The Friends of SNCC had turned their fight for survival into a rallying cry in the face of white authorities who weaponized arrest powers against the activists. When they marched on the courthouse, they encountered police assembled like a military force, armed to the teeth and ready for battle. But as students stood, sat, and slept outside the city's legal nerve center, they remained undeterred and unafraid.[16]

———

Not all Black leaders agreed with the Friends of SNCC's challenge to law enforcement. On April 18, two weeks after students had marched on the courthouse, four NAACP representatives met with Chief Short and the mayor's aides to propose a set of modest reforms for improving relations between police and the Black community. While SNCC had demanded a civilian board to review police misconduct, this NAACP contingent called only for a police community relations unit and a race relations committee in city hall. It also recommended that Short's department enlist TSU to offer continuing education for police officers. The sole major point that the NAACP delegation agreed with SNCC on was the idea that local law enforcement needed to hire more Black officers.

But even by the standards of 1967, even in Houston, these were timid, superficial proposals that failed to address police abuses head-on. They were the types of policies that most other major American cities had long since implemented. None of the reforms directly responded to police violence. Instead, NAACP representatives had come up with a set of diplomatic recommendations, under the mistaken belief that police would treat Black Houstonians more humanely if only they interacted with them more.

The delegation declared in a press statement that it was "seeking to establish wholesome communications between our city officials, concerned with the Police Department, [so] that immediate steps may be taken to correct this cancer tearing at the heart of Houston." But if the NAACP overestimated police's willingness to change, it still understood Black Houstonians' concerns. "Something must be done to calm this fear. It must be done in the midst of peace before this evil system breeds an unruly upheaval that may bring disgrace to our lovely city." Indeed, Black Houstonians were going to continue protesting as long as the police perpetrated violence against unarmed citizens in their city.[17]

———

Nearly a month later, on May 15, Friends of SNCC members immersed themselves in two more protest campaigns. In Sunnyside, a middle-class Black neighborhood five miles southwest of TSU, Black community members hoped to shut down a toxic sanitation dump and incinerator where a young boy had fallen into a garbage pit and drowned. After hours of protests, riot police and K-9 units broke up the picket. That same day, a SNCC contingent organized a demonstration with teenagers at suburban Northwood Junior High, a newly desegregated school where Black students were being disciplined much more harshly than white ones following interracial fights. After the crowd refused to disperse, police called in the riot squad, accompanied by dogs.

When protesters returned the next morning to Northwood, they confronted no fewer than 225 county sheriff's deputies. "The riot squad and sheriff's deputies advanced on the peaceful picket line, billy clubs and rifle butts swinging. Every demonstrator was arrested. Many were beaten. All were roughed up," Kirkpatrick later recounted. Law enforcement charged the crowd with unlawful assembly. Meanwhile, HPD officers at the Sunnyside dump arrested thirty-six demonstrators among hundreds gathered as they blocked garbage trucks from the site.[18]

The Friends of SNCC activists returned to TSU with visible lacerations and wounds law enforcement had given them. Some of their peers saw the arrests on television. With spring finals set to begin the next day, one of the protesters, Douglas Waller, urged his fellow students to head with him back to the city dump, where demonstrators had resumed their pickets.[19]

As a crowd began to grow around Waller, a twenty-one-year-old veteran who had served in Vietnam, four intelligence officers pulled up in unmarked cars. Searching him, they found a pistol on his body. Students heckled the officers as they placed Waller under arrest, and someone tossed a watermelon rind at a squad car as they took him away. When the same unmarked car returned moments later, students hurled rocks and bottles, and the officers called for backup. Soon enough, nine more officers arrived. Unbeknownst to the students, even more had gathered in riot gear at nearby Jeppesen Stadium.[20]

Mayor Welch's office soon appealed to three Black leaders to plead with students to de-escalate the situation: Bill Lawson, the reverend affiliated with the SCLC; Earl Allen, a staffer for a local federally funded antipoverty organization; and Kirkpatrick, who commanded the students' respect as an older activist and leader. But as the three men arrived on campus, Lawson realized that they had arrived too late to stave off a confrontation. Dozens of helmeted officers had blocked off Wheeler Avenue and were standing with their guns aimed at the student dormitories.

Two mayoral advisers soon arrived to urge the officers to leave campus while the three leaders spoke with students. The police refused, insisting that they needed to stay because a muzzle flash sighted from a distance suggested that students were armed. The negotiators reported back that protesters were calling for police to leave campus and for Wheeler to be converted immediately into a pedestrian zone. The mayor's advisers ordered that Wheeler be kept closed, but when Chief Short arrived, he instructed his officers to clear the street and reopen it to traffic.

Short then had his officers retreat but only pulled them back a few blocks so that the dozens of heavily armed officers were out of view of the dorms. Frustrated by the reopening of Wheeler, students responded by tossing corrugated metal sheets into the street and setting buckets of tar soaked in kerosene ablaze. Before long, police thought they heard gunfire coming from one of the dorms.

———

Douglas Waller had been arrested by Robert Blaylock, a white police intelligence officer who had earned a reputation as an imposing martinet quick to issue orders to Black students. As the night wore on, he joined the assembled officers positioned within sight of the dorms, ready to strike. Blaylock later told a reporter that a sniper positioned on the second floor of a dormitory fired on him shortly before midnight. After returning several shots, Blaylock was hit by a bullet near his groin.[21]

At about 2:00 a.m. Short ordered his men to open fire on two men's dorms. They unleashed some three thousand rounds of ammunition into Lanier and Jones Halls. "Young rookies who had never seen real danger fired wildly," Reverend Lawson later recounted. "The chief had lost control of them, for he could not reach them to give further commands. They shot through windows despite instructions to shoot high." They kept firing when students inside pleaded for the chance to bring out a wounded classmate. Another officer, Alan Dugger, was shot in the face, while a third, Louis Kuba, lay on the ground, struck down by a bullet—though the source of the shot was unclear.[22]

At around 3:00 a.m., police raided the dorms. Nearly fifty officers charged into the male students' residences. Joining them were canine units, and several students were mauled by dogs. Officers burst into the room of the residential supervisor, forty-nine-year-old Mattie Harbert, knocking her to the ground and trampling her.

With their official mission to turn up weapons, the officers trashed the dorms. Instead of using Harbert's passkeys to access students' rooms, officers broke down doors with their axes, stripping tiles from the ceiling and smashing mirrors. They destroyed a staggering variety of residents' possessions: televisions, eyeglasses, amplifiers, record players, books, clothing, radios, lamps, guitars, band instruments—even Harbert's sewing machine. Officers tried to arrest Harbert, but she insisted that as a state employee hired to manage university property, she would not be leaving the premises. Though the dorm supervisor would later be hospitalized for several days, she made sure to record an account of the residences' condition in a handwritten note signed by two witnesses: "This is to certify students did not break locks on doors, push out the ceiling, break out window panes, or disorganize and upset the rooms." Harbert already knew how the police would try to explain the damage.[23]

The officers arrested every student in sight in the dorms and ordered them outside. Many wore nothing but underwear. Officers clutching shotguns had the barely clothed students lie face down in long rows on the ground. Just under five hundred young men were arrested and taken to jail, where they were photographed, finger-printed, and questioned. In all, officers turned up just three weapons in the students' dorms: a rifle, a pistol, and a shotgun—hardly the ideal weapons for long-range sniping.[24]

Officer Kuba was declared dead later that morning, barely a month after he had joined the force. Prosecutors filed felony riot charges against five students involved in the local Friends of SNCC chapter and the previous day's protests: Trazawell Franklin, Floyd Nichols, John Parker, Charles Freeman, and Waller. The *Chronicle* printed the young men's names, home addresses, and grade point averages in that day's edition. Short said that he was "heartbroken that such a tragedy could happen in this city"—but he resented TSU's students for their protests. "It's my hope and prayer that this will serve as a deterrent to the acts of any individual who might foster similar action in the future," the chief remarked.[25]

Mayor Welch announced that as many as sixteen more suspects might be charged, including one for Kuba's murder. And yet, officials were mum about who had killed Kuba. Initial reports emphasized that he died as a result of a riot, but they avoided stating who had fired the fatal shot. With thousands of bullets shot by police and only three guns confiscated from students, ballistics tests were needed to deter-mine how the officers had been shot and by whom. Ten days later, in the Black-owned *Forward Times* newspaper, Bill Lawson published an account of watching an army of officers running toward the dorms and unleashing "a salvo of shots that sounded like 100 machine guns as over 5000 rounds of ammunition were poured forth. They were in each other's way. Young rookies who had never seen real danger fired wildly." Without naming names, the reverend shared a final, startling bit of testimony: One police officer had accidentally shot another.[26]

Lawson later insisted that Short could have de-escalated the con-flict. Officers in protective riot gear could have surrounded the dorms and ordered the students to walk outside; if students resisted, officers could have used tear gas to force them out without ransacking the dormitories. Lawson wondered whether the mass arrests were even necessary, considering how few guns were confiscated. If so, it was because Houston police had wanted to teach defiant Black people a lesson, he lamented—that they "needed to be kept in their place." This had been a full-scale military assault on a Black university, one that would have been unthinkable on a predominantly white campus. Hoping to eradicate SNCC from their city, Houston police had treated the students as enemy combatants.[27]

———

"Officer Slain, 3 Wounded, 488 Arrested; Welch Urges Restraint— Mayor Blames Minority Group." So read the *Chronicle*'s front-page headline on May 17, below which appeared a photograph of an officer clutching a pump shotgun while ordering more than a dozen barely dressed young Black men to lie face down on the ground (see figure 10.2). Another headline assured readers, "Police 'Did Right Thing,' Says Leader," in a dubious article that portrayed the SNCC leader as backing the officers' actions. They had done "the only thing they could do," Kirkpatrick was quoted as saying, having committed "no police brutality in rounding up the students." The veracity of the comments was highly questionable, considering that the SNCC leader would weeks later publish a graphic eyewitness account condemning the brutal raid.[28]

The *Chronicle* laid the responsibility for the violence squarely at the feet of campus militants.

> Students, armed with guns and Molotov cocktails, rioted today on the Texas Southern University campus. One police officer was shot and killed, and two other officers and a student were wounded. For more than 40 minutes the students held at bay with sniper fire about 200 police officers. Finally, police, infantry style, stormed dormitories and flushed out the rioters.[29]

Black Houstonians' account of the Texas Southern raid could not have been more different. As the Black-owned *Informer* newspaper's

FIGURE 10.2. Houston police arrested nearly five hundred students and fired more than three thousand shots on student dormitories in their raid on Texas Southern University on May 19, 1967. Officer Louis Kuba was shot and killed in the melee, though police never determined the source of the fatal bullet. AP Photo / *Houston Chronicle*, Blair Pittman.

top headline announced to readers on May 20, "Students Describe 'Nightmare' During All-Out Assault on T.S.U., Blame Wrecked Dorm as Work of Police." The paper repeated eyewitness testimony from a mass meeting two days earlier, where students rejected "media reports that they were responsible for the destruction of their own possessions in the dorms." More than eight students recounted "how they were herded like cattle after the building had been riddled with machine guns and rifles, beaten, kicked, forced against the walls and searched—how they were made to lay face down on the ground, stepped on and over, even spat on, before being carried half-dressed to the police station."[30]

In Bill Lawson's eyes, the city's white media had done little more than transcribe police officials' account of their raid. The town's leading news outlets had "seriously misrepresented the facts, partly because the aim of their stories has been to persuade the public that the acts of the police were 'prudent' and 'commendable.'" Chief among the department's most fawning defenders was the city's leading newspaper, which offered readers a terse, twenty-word statement printed in a front-page inset on the morning following the raid: "The *Chronicle* Believes—The Houston police this morning handled the Texas Southern University riots well. Law and order must prevail."[31]

Lawson charged city officials and the HPD with a cover-up, proposing a theory that Houston police were never able to refute: as officers had showered thousands of bullets on TSU dorms, friendly fire—and not a shot from a student's gun—had struck down their colleague. City officials did "not want to bear on their hands the guilt of the blood of young Louis Kuba, and they must wipe it off on somebody," Lawson contended. "The most obvious scapegoat is the university, whose administration may be degraded, and whose students, defenseless and half naked in packed patrol wagons, may be portrayed as 'villainous' and 'criminal.'"[32]

SNCC supporters meanwhile collected testimonials from dorm residents in the aftermath of the raid. A white exchange student described how

> when we heard machine guns outside, we stuck close to the floor, we heard megaphones and crawled into the bathroom for protection and heard two dudes come in with raised shotguns, shocked (at the fact that we were white) and stated, "well, what have we got here?" Their demeanor suggested that they were obviously having fun.

Another student gave a harrowing account of being transported in police vans.

> They were cramming the wagons full and beating the boys in line, trying to make them push up on those inside. There really wasn't enough room for all those they were trying to force in,

but they just kept pushing us and piling us on top of each other, just like in a slave boat or something—that's exactly what it was like, a slave boat.[33]

Even if police were suppressing a riot, as they claimed, few of the officers were trained to handle civil disturbances. If snipers were really defending the dorms, Lawson asked, why would Short send officers down an empty street where they could be easily fired upon, leaving them no option but to shoot to protect themselves? And why hadn't police faced resistance as they charged the students' living quarters?

While police and the mayor accused a permissive TSU administration of enabling a riot, campus officials were quick to fault student activists. The school expelled fifty-two students, including all of the known members of Friends of SNCC, barring them from campus under threat of arrest for trespassing. But for Freeman, Franklin, Nichols, Parker, and Waller—the five SNCC activists charged with inciting a riot—matters only got worse in the weeks ahead.[34]

———

"Murder Is Charged in Riot at TSU, Police Cleared of Blame by Jury," announced the top headline in the evening edition of the *Chronicle* on June 2. Earlier that day, a grand jury convened by District Attorney Carol Vance issued felony indictments for the five TSU students. Each one was charged with murdering Louis Kuba and with assaulting Officers Robert Blaylock and Allen Dugger with the intent to murder. The grand jury's foreman told reporters that despite "numerous rumors of police brutality, we find that the law enforcement officers acted in the best interests of the community." While Vance conceded that the students may not have fired the shots at the three men, he argued that they had prompted a civil disturbance in which the officers had been shot, and he pointed to a state antiriot law that made them criminally liable for the murder and two shootings. The five indicted men would be held until their trials unless they could each pay a bond of $10,000, or nearly $100,000 in 2025 dollars.[35]

Many Black Houstonians were left unconvinced. In his published account of the raid, Lawson had demanded that Welch and Short answer two urgent questions: What caliber bullet had killed Kuba? And had it been matched to a weapon found in the police's exhaustive search of the dorms? Most importantly, why had Short's officers fired thousands of rounds of ammunition as they stormed the residences in a full-scale military assault? The students sitting in jail charged with Kuba's murder—now referred to as the TSU Five in the Black press—must have shared these very questions. But these were questions that Welch, Short, the police, and the local white press all refused to answer.

By summer, SNCC was spiraling into crisis in Houston. In July, the organization's national newsletter featured a headline that contemplated the worst: "WILL THEY DIE? Five Texas Students Face Death." It was a fair question to ask about five Black men charged with murder in a state that had executed more people than any other that decade except California.[36]

With five of its most active organizers facing felony indictments, the Houston Friends of SNCC chapter turned their focus to organizing a legal defense campaign. For weeks, bail bondsmen in Houston had refused to do business with the TSU defendants, forcing them to find a Black-owned company two hundred miles away in San Antonio. Nichols and his SNCC colleague Trazawell Franklin were fired from their jobs with a federally funded antipoverty agency, casualties of political pressure from local white leaders, including congressman and future president George H. W. Bush. Fearing for their lives, several of the defendants went into hiding. In the aftermath of the murder indictments, Kirkpatrick withdrew from SNCC, leaving Lee Otis Johnson to replace him as its unofficial leader in Houston. In the year following the TSU raid, Houston's intelligence unit targeted Johnson with regular surveillance. In one incident, Johnson was pulled over in his car by a group of police that grew to no fewer than thirty-five officers.[37]

And yet, the prosecution of SNCC members in Houston gave the local organization a reason to fight, and the TSU Five drew the support of activists and left-wing media across the country. SNCC's national office showered supporters with appeals for financial aid to the five men, and the NAACP Legal Defense Fund headed the defendants' legal team. A SNCC press release insisted that the stakes could not have been higher: "FIVE BLACK STUDENTS CHARGED WITH MURDER IN HOUSTON—Indictments of SNCC-Affiliated Youths Form Part of Continuing Efforts to Destroy the Organization."[38]

As SNCC redoubled its efforts to wage a media campaign ahead of the TSU defendants' first trial, so, too, did the Houston police. Three months after the TSU raid, members of the city's red squad volunteered to testify before the U.S. Senate's Permanent Subcommittee on Investigations in November 1967. Chaired by devoted segregationist John McClellan of Arkansas, this was the same committee that Joseph McCarthy and his staff attorney Roy Cohn had made famous as a feared tool of political persecution the previous decade.

Houston intelligence chief Joe Singleton contended that SNCC's arrival in town had triggered the events culminating in the brutal police attacks on TSU's campus. Texas Southern, in Singleton's words, "had been the site of unrest since the first part of October 1966 when Frederick Douglass Kirkpatrick and Millard Leon Lowe joined forces supposedly to organize a chapter of the Student Non-Violent Coordinating Committee (SNCC)." Singleton let the word "supposedly" hang in the air without further clarification, but the implication was obvious. SNCC's name suggested that the organization was dedicated to peaceful protest, but their true objective was sparking violence.[39]

Singleton's testimony contradicted the accounts of numerous students and organizers—but it also conflicted with the FBI's analysis on at least one major count. "No info was developed to establish riot resulted from specific advanced planning by any organizational group," a July 1967 teletype summarizing the Bureau's own investigation stated plainly. Conveniently for Houston police—and for McClellan and his Senate colleagues who coveted their testimony as justification for a federal antiriot bill—the Bureau does not appear to have disclosed these doubts about SNCC's culpability to the public.[40]

Back in the Senate, members of McClellan's committee inquired about the source of Houston police information. Singleton contended that it was detailed in "a file in the possession of Lee Otis Johnson"—claiming that "we could not obtain the document itself without disclosing our informants." As it turned out, the purported smoking gun on SNCC's plans for wreaking havoc in Houston was one informant's transcription of a document that no authorities may have ever laid eyes on. Yet again—as in Philadelphia and New York—police intelligence had insisted that evidence documenting a violent plot by a civil rights group could not be revealed, lest an unnamed source or infiltrator be endangered.[41]

Liberal senators on the committee peppered Singleton with more pointed questions about his claims. Jacob Javits of New York expressed a marked skepticism of the five SNCC members' murder charges.

> JAVITS: So the evidence against them was that they were the activists in the demonstration which preceded the riot?
> SINGLETON: Yes, sir.
> JAVITS: But you had no evidence that they had actually engaged in unlawful conduct, other than activists, stimulation of the demonstration, if that was any unlawful conduct. I am just trying to pinpoint this.
> SINGLETON: Yes, sir.

Ed Muskie of Maine meanwhile questioned Singleton about his department's arrest of nearly five hundred young men on the morning of the raid. "At the time you picked them up, you did not know whether or not they were involved in any lawbreaking activity?" the senator probed. "No sir; other than being present there in the dormitory where the shooting was coming from," Singleton admitted, giving no indication that he believed any harm had been done to the students.[42]

At one point, Singleton argued that SNCC's efforts to get justice for victims of police violence in Houston as early as January 1967 amounted to "attempting to incite a riot." As he described a church meeting where organizers had denounced an assault on a pregnant Black woman by police, Singleton took particular issue with flyers distributed at the gathering that depicted a police officer "beating what appears to be a female." Fred Harris of Oklahoma, who at the time was serving on the National Advisory Commission on Civil Disorders, betrayed palpable disbelief as he returned to those comments and asked Singleton, "You feel that calling for a demonstration was, in fact, inciting to riot?" The Houston intelligence commander's reply was direct and unapologetic: "I feel like to a certain degree it was yes, sir."[43]

Despite all these inquiries, it was striking how many other questions were implied but left unasked in the hearings and how many questionable claims went unchallenged. For starters, the cache of weapons police found in Lanier Hall was limited to just a pistol, a rifle, and a shotgun. Could these three weapons have sustained the sniper fire that Houston police blamed on the students? Police maintained that some dorm residents had escaped undetected "out the back and over a large cyclone fence carrying several rifles prior to the policemen completely surrounding the area." But again, this information was nothing more than an unverifiable claim from a confidential source, and police insisted that disclosing his name would endanger him. And how certain were police that all the loud noises they heard were actually gunfire? One witness accompanying Singleton at the Senate hearing—local television news cameraman Robert Wolf—recounted that he and several officers had stood under a tree for ten minutes thinking they were listening to firecrackers go off in the distance before realizing that they were actually hearing gunfire, as evidenced by branches that fell from the tree, presumably because they were hit by bullets. But how confident could they be that the gunfire had come from students without seeing the source of the bullets?

Another nagging question concerned the issue of ballistics. Wolf and police referred to several cars that displayed bullet holes by the end of the night of the raid. Strangely, either no ballistics tests had been conducted, or if they had, police did not want to reveal their results. It was unclear whose bullets had damaged the vehicles. Both Javits and even McClellan—no friend of SNCC—pushed Singleton to shed light on the details of the shot that killed Kuba, but the intelligence chief could only share that fragments of a bullet had been found in the slain officer's head and that the department's investigators "were never able to determine what caliber it was." How could Houston police be certain that the slain officer had not been hit by one of the thousands of bullets his own colleagues had shot? Despite all these uncertainties, Singleton was confident that Kuba had been "mortally wounded by sniper fire." When Singleton eventually shared with the committee his colleagues' analysis of Kuba's fatal injuries, that information was inexplicably withheld from the public record.

At one point, Charles Howard, a Black intelligence officer testifying alongside Singleton, claimed that Kirkpatrick had accused students of shooting at him when he tried to negotiate with them on behalf of the city shortly before the police raid. It was a stunning allegation that appeared nowhere else in Kirkpatrick's many comments on the night's events, not in the suspicious *Chronicle* story the morning after the raid that quoted him as saying that officers "did the right thing" or in a detailed account of the evening he later penned for the Socialist Workers Party newspaper, *The Militant*.[44]

Singleton and his men were incapable of fathoming the terror experienced by hundreds of students as a militarized police force raided their campus. On at least one occasion, Howard referred to the local sheriff's department men assisting police as "troops," suggesting his view of the raid as an act of war, not civilian law enforcement. Officer James Norris seemed to find humor in an incident during the raid in which "we got approximately 15 subjects out of the shower, all with their clothes on. The water was not running. They were actually in the shower." McClellan crowed in reply, "They didn't have much of a place to hide, did they, once you got in the building?" What was entertaining for police and senators had been terrifying for students unsure of whether they would make it out of the building alive.[45]

Then there was the question of racism. It is inconceivable that Houston police would have handled students on a predominantly white campus as brutally as they had the students at TSU. Both the composition of Houston's intelligence squad and their choice of witnesses joining Singleton in Washington reflected an attempt by police to suggest that racism played no role in their actions. At the time, just

1 percent of Houston police officers were African American, but three of the intelligence squad's eleven members, or roughly 27 percent, were Black. Even more disproportionately, half of the officers who joined Singleton in testifying to the Senate were Black.[46]

In a pattern repeated by several other departments in congressional hearings, Houston police stacked the delegation they sent to testify with Black officers. For the most part, they sat silently as their white colleagues offered their testimony, only occasionally invited to add their own commentary. A Black police officer could not possibly do harm to another Black person, white officials seemed to stop just short of saying, hoping to project the image of integrated, color-blind intelligence squads.

And yet, it was apparent that white police were not alone in their ability to hurt Black community members. Celebrated as pioneers in desegregating municipal jobs, Black officers were now coveted by intelligence squads whose white officers were likely to arouse the suspicions of Black activists. Just as Ray Wood had infiltrated CORE and encouraged the Black Liberation Front to hatch a bomb plot, Black officers in Houston and Memphis would soon demonstrate their indispensability to police seeking to break up Black activist groups in their cities.

When police accused SNCC of inciting a riot in Atlanta in August 1966, staffer Bill Ware had condemned Black officers as "white men with Black skins" and insisted that they were "as much our enemy as any white Klu-Klux-Klansman [sic]." This represented one of the movement's more radical sentiments on African American police. But even if Ware was more scornful of Black cops than most in the movement, activists were growing increasingly weary of them. As James Baldwin had written of Harlem a dozen years earlier, "Negro policemen are feared more than whites, for they have more to prove and fewer ways to prove it." By 1967, many in the movement had reason to believe that Baldwin's words applied to the Black police in their cities as well.[47]

11

Provocateurs

Uprisings broke out in nearly one hundred Black communities across the United States in July 1967. In Detroit's riots alone, police made seven thousand arrests, and forty-seven people lost their lives. Law enforcement there killed twenty-eight unarmed African Americans. On July 27, President Lyndon Johnson opened an address on national television with somber words. "My fellow Americans: we have endured a week such as no nation should have to live through, a time of violence and tragedy."[1]

Six days later, on August 2, 1967, Captain John Sorace of the Nashville Police Department testified before the U.S. Senate Judiciary Committee, chaired by Mississippi's segregationist stalwart James Eastland. It was the opening day of the upper chamber's hearings for House Resolution 421, a so-called anti-riot bill conceived to bar anyone from crossing state lines to incite a civil disturbance. Only thirty years old, the Nashville captain had already enjoyed a charmed career. Described by various reporters as "youthful, articulate," and "darkly handsome," the Italian American Brooklynite was just twenty-seven when Nashville police named him the inaugural commander of their intelligence division in January 1965, not even three years into his law enforcement career.[2]

Now, as he addressed one of the Senate's most powerful committees, reporters for national news outlets listened in rapt attention
as Sorace made a shocking claim: SNCC had orchestrated riots in
Nashville. Though once respectable, the organization had, in Sorace's words, "literally turned into a Black Ku Klux Klan." Boasting
that his department had a "very active intelligence squad," Sorace
shared that an informant at the start of the year had discovered
Operation Nashville, a plot by SNCC to "organize the juvenile
elements in the neighborhoods into juvenile gangs and work
with them, teach them hatred of the white man, teach them judo
tactics . . . [and] how to manufacture what we commonly call the
Molotov cocktail."[3]

When Stokely Carmichael came to speak at local college campuses in the first week of April, authorities dispatched officers in
riot gear to serve on standby duty in North Nashville, the heart of
the city's Black community. Attending Carmichael's speech to a large
audience at Vanderbilt University were some eighty police officers,
more than half of them in plain clothes.

As Sorace explained, police realized that Operation Nashville
was underway later that evening as they witnessed a SNCC staffer
lead two dozen demonstrators in a protest outside a restaurant
where the proprietor had ejected a Black customer. Before long, a
crowd of 150 bystanders had gathered to watch. Soon police heard
shots fired, and the SNCC staffer threw a rock at the windshield of
a bus passing through the area. In Sorace's telling, that spark ignited
a three-day riot that saw twelve police injuries, thirty-five civilians treated in hospitals, nineteen arsons, and sixty-eight arrests—
although no fatalities.[4]

"If there is anything that these riots are teaching the municipal
police organizations, it is something that we very luckily had to
begin with, and that is to build a very strong intelligence operation," Sorace told senators. But police needed more help. Asked
by Eastland whether Nashville police had "the facilities to trace
these agitators from state to state and to trace guns that are brought
in from Atlanta and other states for the purpose of riots, killing

people," Sorace replied in the negative. "There is no local, municipal or state police organization in the country that does. They are not designed for this nationwide activity and investigation." But Sorace was optimistic that the bill under consideration could provide a remedy by making "it more difficult for these kinds of organizations that are hell bent on destruction and segregation, whatever they are called, that it is much more difficult for them to operate in this country."

"I do not think it is unreasonable to hope the federal government will turn its prosecutive agencies into looking into these problems," the Nashville intelligence chief continued, emphasizing that the proposed crackdown on agitators would follow the law. "We don't disregard the constitution of the United States, and we are not advocating that anyone else does."[5]

In the coming days, police officials from seven different cities joined Sorace in testifying that SNCC and its allies had provoked riots in their jurisdictions. Despite their pleas, the anti-riot bill stalled in the months ahead. But the FBI was unwilling to wait on legislators' approval to escalate its efforts to combat Black activists. Barely three weeks after testimony in favor of the bill concluded, the Bureau launched a new major counterintelligence program aimed at Black nationalists. Unlike the overt law enforcement response to urban uprisings proposed by the anti-riot bill, this would be a covert response, concealed from the American people for years. FBI officials dubbed the secret program COINTELPRO.

Six months later, in February 1968, researchers contracted by the National Advisory Commission on Civil Disorders released a field report on the Nashville uprising that contradicted Sorace's allegations. SNCC staffers told researchers that they had noticed plainclothes police following them and discovered tangible evidence of their office's phone being tapped in the early months of 1967. As for the Nashville captain's claims, commission researchers "found no evidence of any of these training activities having taken place, and the sequence of events during the time of the disturbances does not show the mark of a singular plan." Sorace's sworn testimony that

SNCC had organized riots in Tennessee's capital was false, investigators insisted. But the damage had already been done.[6]

———

The explanation of the Nashville uprising offered by Sorace was a popular one, an example of what we might call the agitator riot theory. Its adherents contended that most Black people would not start uprisings of their own accord. Rather, they were prompted into rebellion by organized Black militants who traveled the country sparking riots as part of a larger strategy of political subversion.

The theory of agitator riots was rooted in right-wing narratives about communists fomenting disorder in American cities. One of its leading proponents was W. Cleon Skousen, a former Salt Lake City police chief who had gained prominence in right-wing circles with his 1958 book, *The Naked Communist*, in which he accused liberals and leftists of planning a Marxist takeover of the United States on behalf of the Communist Party. Since 1960, Skousen had edited *Law and Order*, a monthly "independent magazine for the police profession," where he promoted his conspiratorial worldview and warned of the dangers of political demonstrations with articles such as "Planned Riots—What Can the Police Do About It?" In 1966, Skousen expanded his writings for the magazine into a book, *The Communist Attack on U.S. Police*. In one chapter, "The Communist Plan to Fight Police Through Civil Rights Riots," Skousen blasted SNCC as "substantially under the influence of the Communist Party" while attacking CORE as the organization that "has instigated more racial violence and disobedience than any other civil rights group."[7]

Liberals were skeptical of the agitator theory. Their preferred explanation for urban uprisings was grounded in social inequality, as epitomized by the Kerner Commission's report released in February 1968. After seven months of research, the commission argued that stifling racism and economic discrimination were the ultimate drivers of riots. "Segregation and poverty have created in the racial ghetto a destructive environment totally unknown to most white

Americans," the commission stated on the first page of its report. The study further asserted that "white racism is essentially responsible for the explosive mixture," and it pinpointed law enforcement as a significant exacerbating factor. "Almost invariably the incident that ignites disorder arises from police action," which in Black communities had "come to symbolize white power, white racism, and white repression."

And yet, these same liberals also argued for an expansion of police powers to respond to riots, including the establishment of red squads. Citing law enforcement's frequent lack of sound information during civil disturbances, the report insisted that in every city "an effective police intelligence unit trained and equipped to gather, evaluate, analyze, and disseminate information is needed." Among other things, this supposedly necessitated "the use of undercover police officers, reliable informants."[8]

But there was a third school of thought about urban uprisings, one beyond the political mainstream but embraced by various thinkers on the Left, including SNCC. That was the theory of the police riot, the idea that some law enforcement attacked Black communities with the hope of sparking riots, in turn giving officers license to carry out violent retribution in the name of the law.

In November 1967, SNCC organizer Fred Brooks voiced this theory at hearings before the Senate's Permanent Subcommittee on Investigations as he fended off accusations by Nashville police intelligence that he had orchestrated the city's riots. The committee had issued Brooks a subpoena to testify in hopes of humiliating, if not legally endangering, the SNCC staffer. Brooks met the challenge head-on and relished the opportunity to denounce the official police account of Nashville's uprising.

Sporting a large afro and dark sunglasses, a defiant Brooks smoked as he testified, telling the committee that "the news media's hysterical treatment of the appearance of Stokely Carmichael and hysterical attitude towards SNCC, together with the extreme reaction by the Nashville Police Department were the most significant, immediate causes of the disturbance." By dispatching hundreds of officers in response to what was a small, peaceful protest, Brooks contended, the police had antagonized the North Nashville community to the point of explosion, a point that McClellan pushed Brooks to justify in a heated exchange.

MCCLELLAN: They encouraged them to stay? Didn't they try to get the crowd to leave?

BROOKS: No.

MCCLELLAN: You mean the police did not get the crowd to leave?

BROOKS: No.

MCCLELLAN: They encouraged them to riot? According to your testimony the police are wholly responsible for the riot?

BROOKS: That is exactly correct.

Later in the hearing, Brooks suggested how police could have de-escalated the crisis, telling the committee, "The only way you were going to quiet this disturbance down is that you were going to have to get the policeman out of there and they refused to do that."[9]

Brooks was hardly the only organizer in SNCC—or in America for that matter—who argued that police started riots. The idea had a long lineage on the American left. In 1908, W.E.B. Du Bois wrote of a "police riot against Negroes" in New York City in which dozens of Black residents were killed, an incident that white observers had described as a "race riot." Four years later, in 1912, Black anarchist Lucy Parsons recounted Chicago's "eight hour strike of 1886" for the Industrial Workers of the World's newspaper, proclaiming that "there was no riot at Haymarket, except a police riot." In the following decades, "police riot" appeared from time to time in the Communist Party's *Daily Worker* newspaper as well, though the term enjoyed little currency outside left-wing circles.[10]

Since the outbreak of the direct action phase of the Black freedom struggle in the early 1960s, civil rights groups had come to embrace the term, too. In 1962, CORE gestured toward the theory with its Committee of Inquiry into law enforcement's handling of the Freedom Rides and its censure of Southern police for their "complicity in white mob violence." In April 1965, SNCC's California newspaper,

The Movement, wrote that "the Negro communities of Birmingham and Albany are two of the most well armed in the U.S. Sporadic police riots break out, particularly in Albany. They only serve to tear the lives of the people who are involved in them."[11]

Two years later, in July 1967, SNCC devoted nearly an entire issue of an eight-page newsletter to the police riots thesis, with a boldfaced question appearing on its front page: "COPS RUN WILD—WHERE WILL THEY STRIKE NEXT?" (see figure 11.1). The headline appeared below the newsletter's masthead as part of a collage made up of the names of more than fifteen cities that had experienced uprisings, including many of the towns that would send officers to testify to Congress.

An article in the issue on yet another uprising law enforcement blamed on SNCC—this time in Atlanta, the site of the organization's national office—advanced the police riot theory as well. "Police forces specially trained in Gestapo-like tactics, using the latest and most advanced 'riot equipment,' which is being purchased by all city governments in America, are standing by and on special alert as they move to provoke incidents which they know will incite black people to defend themselves and retaliate."[12]

SNCC and its allies argued that the underlying cause of many riots was not all that different from what motivated the infiltration of their organizations. In both cases, they believed that police provocateurs sought to manipulate Black people enraged by injustice into carrying out their own self-destruction. As urban uprisings spread across the country, more than a few activists would insist that police had escalated these tactics, if not perfected them.[13]

———

In June 1967, the national leadership of SNCC and CORE came together to issue a rare joint statement decrying the wave of police repression engulfing the movement. SNCC's new chair, Rap Brown, joined CORE's Floyd McKissick as they condemned the ongoing "effort by the white power structure to threaten and intimidate black militants, to curb protest, to discredit the rising tide of black

FIGURE 11.1. *SNCC Newsletter* cover, June–July 1967. Courtesy of the SNCC Legacy Project.

consciousness, to begin a new form of McCarthyism directed at the voices of dissent coming from the ghetto and enraged black youth."[14]

The pair rattled off a litany of questionable charges brought by police against movement activists. They lambasted the TSU case as an "indictment of five SNCC people on trumped up charges of murder, assault to murder, and inciting to riot in Houston." There was the dynamite case in Philadelphia, where "after a massive trial by headline, resulting action disclosed that police had framed the members of SNCC." And in the Statue of Liberty case in New York, "police planned and attempted to execute the plot, but implicated and convicted black men on trumped up charges."[15]

But almost no one was listening. When police had first announced arrests in these cases, reporters clamored to expose the villains behind the purported plots. Now, when SNCC and CORE came together to charge police misconduct, the media ignored the groups' counterclaims; not a single reference to the press conference turns up in searches of digitized newspaper and magazine coverage. If journalists even caught wind of the press conference, they likely believed that the accusations of frame-ups and character assassination strayed too far beyond the bounds of plausibility. And yet, much of what Brown and McKissick claimed would turn out to be true. None of the felony charges in Houston or Philadelphia would stick. And even Ray Wood himself had admitted under oath that he played a critical role in planning the purchase and detonation of explosives for the Statue of Liberty.

But the civil rights movement's critics—chief among them New York police—were quick to celebrate Wood as a hero whose exploits signaled the triumph of color blindness. A racist police force, they seemed to suggest, would not hire a Black man as an undercover detective and then award him with a medal and promotion ten months later. Never mind that red squads had come to admit that they could not infiltrate certain Black-led groups with white officers. The reality was that they badly needed young Black officers to assume false identities on the department's behalf. If red squads were color-blind, it was only because their plots for disrupting and spying on Black groups depended on it.

Though Wood had mostly stayed out of the news since the arrest of Walter Bowe, Khaleel Sayyed, and Bob Collier in February 1965, he, too, testified to Congress in November 1967. That month, Wood spoke at hearings on "subversive influences in riots, looting, and burning" held by the infamous House Un-American Activities Committee. Wood's testimony recapitulated his performance in federal court, though in this case it was carefully choreographed in practice runs with HUAC staffer Herbert Romerstein the week before his committee appearance. Notably, Wood admitted in his public testimony that he had infiltrated CORE and carried out a citizen's arrest of Mayor Wagner with Herb Callender and John Valentine, though he gave no reason for these actions. He also claimed that CORE had tasked him with coordinating protests during the July 1964 uprising, to "draw the New York city policemen out of the Harlem riot area" and to "weaken the powers of the New York City Police Department by dispersing its forces." In other words, he made a bold and unsubstantiated claim that CORE had attempted to weaponize peaceful demonstrations to sabotage the police response to the riots.[16]

But the most telling moment of Wood's testimony was when yet another ardent segregationist, HUAC chair Edwin Willis of Louisiana, made a point of praising the Black detective at the end of his appearance. "In penetrating, as you did, a group of ultra-radical, revolutionary, hate-America types, you certainly stuck your neck out," Willis complimented Wood. "Your action, the evidence indicates, saved some of this country's most precious monuments from destruction. For all this America is indebted to you." At the very end of his statement, Willis offered Wood one more word of praise, though its significance was not quite clear: "I wish we had more like you." What did he mean by that—more police to infiltrate activist groups? More Black police officers? Or simply more Black people who met his approval? Whatever he was getting at, one thing was sure—white opponents of the civil rights movement were doing their utmost to provide platforms to Black police working against racial justice groups.[17]

These congressional hearings confirmed that most Black intelligence officers were treated as tokens by their white colleagues and elected officials, limited in how much they could speak, and given careful guidance when they did. When Houston's Black intelligence officers spoke before McClellan's committee, their testimony filled in occasional gaps left by Houston police intelligence chief Joe Singleton, who dominated the proceedings. But one exchange was revealing. Of the three officers joining Singleton on his second day of testimony, two were Black. One of the men from the intelligence unit was Albert Blair, a ten-year veteran of the force and one of a pair of Black graduates from the department's 1957 academy class. Until around 1962, Blair and all other Black officers were generally prevented from making arrests of white suspects. Four years later, in 1966, Blair was transferred from patrol to the Criminal Intelligence Division, most likely as Singleton and his colleagues sought to expand their investigations of the growing number of Black activists in the city.

Now, sitting before the Permanent Investigations Subcommittee, Blair fielded questions from the segregationist McClellan about his work during the purported riot at Texas Southern.

MCCLELLAN: So this is your alma mater?

BLAIR: That is correct, sir.

MCCLELLAN: I imagine it wasn't very pleasant for you to have to go in there and perform a duty like this, was it?

BLAIR: Not pleasant. It is just a job, sir.

McClellan likely had conceived his question as an opportunity for Blair to express his displeasure over the current generation of Black radicals. But in the process, the senator from Arkansas may have tapped into something less favorable to his cause—a Black intelligence officer's misgivings, even embarrassment, about his role in a militarized assault on the university he had attended a decade earlier.[18]

———

The cumulative effective of the congressional hearings on riots in late 1967 was an unprecedented wave of public praise for police intelligence units' work against civil rights organizers. Never before had red squads so openly and unapologetically heralded their work against organizers for racial justice on the national stage. This was the "exposure system" at work yet again, as reading the names and addresses of suspected subversives into the legislative record triggered a cascade of public opprobrium that torpedoed individuals' careers and reputations, even if such revelations brought no legal consequences.

Intelligence officers were arguing that Black activists demanding equality in 1967 had little integrity compared with their less radical peers who had desegregated lunch counters and marched on Washington. These individuals could not be trusted to act nonviolently, and if they were not monitored carefully, they were likely to spread their chaos and destruction to any city that tolerated them. Sorace, Singleton, Wood, and all their brethren appearing in Congress maintained that they were pulling back the curtain on a once honorable movement gone bad, revealing how it had traded peaceful disobedience for violent subversion.

Harry Fox, the chief inspector overseeing Philadelphia police's intelligence unit, captured the mood at the annual meeting of the International Association of Chiefs of Police held in Kansas City in September 1967. "Civil disorder is the number one police problem today," Fox told his audience in a workshop titled "Community Tensions and Civil Disturbances," the conference's best-attended session and one featuring a U.S. Army general and police chiefs from San Francisco and Boston.[19]

"Good intelligence in this field is urgently needed to prevent tension and demonstrations from maturing into fires, snipers, looting, destruction and death," Fox warned, drawing a straight line from peaceful protest to bloody anarchy. Intelligence units had a variety of means at their disposal if they wished to prevent riots, the inspector noted. But in a rare acknowledgment of police departments' growing inclination to dispatch spies in Black communities, Fox was unequivocal: "Infiltrating with undercover men is the best way."[20]

———

Marrell McCollough did his best to make himself useful. When he started attending meetings of the Invaders in Memphis in March 1968, he had little to offer the fledgling offshoot of the Black Organizing Project, a new community group in the city hoping to emulate SNCC's work. But Mac possessed two things that quickly earned him the favor of the Invaders and the Black Organizing Project: an enthusiasm for almost any activity proposed by their leaders and a blue two-door 1967 Volkswagen 1600 Fastback coupe. As the only person in their group to own a car, Mac earned the unofficial title of the Invaders' "minister of transportation."

That February, Memphis sanitation workers had gone on their first ever strike to demand raises and improvements to their miserable conditions. In the weeks that followed, hundreds of local clergy rallied under the leadership of SCLC veteran and former SNCC adviser James Lawson to form Community on the Move for Equality in support of the strikers, virtually all of whom were Black. The campaign drew movement leaders to Memphis, including King, who headlined a march through city streets on March 28. Though the march drew more than twenty thousand people, organizers canceled it after violence broke out. In response to the looting of stores along the route, police chased marchers back to their headquarters at the African Methodist Episcopal Church's Clayborn Temple, where officers filled the chapel with tear gas and clubbed protesters as they sought cover. One officer sprayed Mac in the face with Mace. Officers also shot and killed Larry Payne, a Black sixteen-year-old who had surrendered peacefully when police stopped him on suspicion of looting.[21]

The following week, on April 4, Mac and one of King's lieutenants, the Reverend James Orange, had returned from a shopping trip when they ran into James Bevel, another of King's right hands, at Clayborn Temple. Bevel asked for a ride to the Lorraine Motel, where the SCLC was staying, and Mac was happy to oblige.

When they reached the motel's parking lot, King was standing outside his second-story room, leaning on the balcony and speaking with a few people. A few minutes later, Mac heard what he later described as a "loud explosion." As he looked to the balcony, he saw King collapse.

Mac rushed up the stairs and crawled to the SCLC leader on the balcony. He was the first person to reach the injured minister. Mac found him with a large wound running along the right side of his face down to his neck. As he applied a towel to stanch the bleeding, Mac was joined by the SCLC ministers Ralph David Abernathy, Jesse Jackson, and Andrew Young, who stood on the balcony, pointing to what they believed to be the source of the shots, a building across from the motel.[22]

Then, a South African photographer assigned to cover King named Joseph Louw stepped out of his hotel room, just sixty feet from the SCLC leader, and captured the harrowing scene in an unforgettable picture. Although Mac was not identified when the photo was picked up by the Associated Press wire service, he was visible as he crouched over King. Hundreds of thousands, if not millions, of Americans saw the photograph. But what virtually no one realized was that the man they saw kneeling over King was a Memphis police spy.[23]

A decade later, McCollough was called to testify by the House of Representatives' Select Committee on Assassinations probing the murders of King and John F. Kennedy. The white supremacist drifter James Earl Ray had been convicted of killing King in 1969, but doubts about his culpability lingered. Though he admitted that he had been assigned by Memphis police to infiltrate the Invaders, McCollough adamantly denied that he had any role in King's death or even that he had monitored him at all. But skeptics of Ray's conviction remained, and in the years that followed, researchers intent on disproving that Ray had worked alone fixated on McCollough.

To this date, no solid evidence has emerged to support the far-fetched theory that McCollough participated in King's murder. But a sustained obsession among conspiracy theorists has obscured an urgent question that emerges from McCollough's extensive paper trail: How could a police spy earn the trust of Black activist groups so quickly that he made his way into King's inner circle after not even a month of undercover work?

———

Though he was only twenty-three, McCollough had already worked for the U.S. Army Military Police Corps for almost three years when he applied to Memphis's police force in June 1967. McCollough wrote in his application that "a desire to serve the people of Memphis and my country" drove his interest in the job. Soon he was enrolled in the department's academy, which had only integrated three years earlier and where just 5 percent of his fellow cadets were Black.

The Memphis Police Department established its red squad—officially the Inspectional Bureau—in 1965, joining a list of intelligence divisions formed at the height of the civil rights movement that included Philadelphia, Houston, Nashville, and Baltimore.

Leading the unit since 1967 was Ely Arkin, a veteran with more than a decade of experience on the force.[24]

Black organizers in Memphis knew all too well that they might be infiltrated by law enforcement. An FBI source reported to the Memphis field office that the city's "Negro community was particularly bitter because the Police Department had sent many Negro officers in plain clothes to strike support meetings, several of them thus far having been exposed." In one meeting at the United Rubber Workers of America union hall, strikers denounced an attendee as a police spy in front of the crowd of eight hundred. The man, likely given away by the pistol and Mace he was carrying, was paraded to the front stage so the crowd could see him before being stripped of his weapons. "The ladies at the meeting put our bodies between him and the crowd until one of the ministers could get him outside," strike leader Cornelia Crenshaw explained to the press, after she had helped hold off irate strikers from beating the man. Once ejected, the spy was delivered to two traffic patrolmen and asked to be returned to police headquarters.[25]

Though numerous sources provided information to the FBI on the Black Organizing Project and the Invaders, the Bureau did not have an agent inside the group. As in the case of nearly all investigations of activist groups, the FBI avoided placing its own undercover agents within organizations, preferring to pay private individuals to do that work. The FBI had five freelance informants providing reports on the Invaders, one of whom joined the group. But the only documented case of a law enforcement employee penetrating the Invaders was McCollough. In fact, the FBI relied on Arkin to provide regular updates on McCollough's work.[26]

Years later, McCollough insisted that his only undercover assignment had been to monitor the Invaders, not King. Yet the Invaders and the SCLC's leadership were working together so closely by April 4 that it was impossible to monitor one without the other. The SCLC had rented rooms for the upstart group in the Lorraine Motel to hold meetings on the nights of April 2 and April 3. McCollough even met face-to-face with King the day before he was killed, when SCLC leaders invited the Invaders to discuss strike strategy at the

Lorraine. Whether or not McCollough's remit included King, he entered the leader's orbit remarkably fast.

Overall, Mac accepted the rationale of this work, later recalling it as an assignment "to gather intelligence that would help the police better understand the Invaders' goals and methods, and to collect evidence of any crimes they committed for later prosecution." Yet McCollough was a bit torn about his job. He later claimed that he agreed with the sanitation workers' cause and their unforgettable rallying cry: "I AM A MAN." But if he sympathized with the strikers, he was not going to let those feelings stop him from spying on them, taking notes at their meetings, or passing names on to his superiors. Keeping tabs on the Invaders meant monitoring the strike and, regardless of the original assignment, monitoring King.[27]

Mac's best cover may have been engaging in illegal activities, most of them minor offenses such as smoking weed and buying up Robitussin at area drugstores to mix with Karo syrup for sale on the black market. But by his own admission, some crimes were far from victimless. Chief among them was an arson McCollough's daughter recounted years later in a book on her father's life. On September 10, 1968, Mac drove a group of Invaders to Ingle Avenue and a cluster of homes owned by state representative and developer A. W. Willis, a Black attorney, NAACP leader, and failed mayoral candidate. Using a federal program that offered 3 percent mortgages to developers renovating homes for low-income buyers, Willis's company promoted the properties as "built by Negroes for Negroes." Although Willis had welcomed the Invaders' support during his candidacy, after his loss he avoided them, and some Invaders embraced the rumor that he had been hired by white mayor Henry Loeb as a decoy candidate to draw Black voters away from another Black candidate. The Invaders, according to Mac, now viewed Willis as an "Uncle Tom."

When they arrived at Willis's rehab jobs, the Invaders broke into one of the homes. In Mac's retelling years later, two Invaders poured gasoline throughout the house before stepping outside. One Invader lit a match as the others watched. The home ignited instantly and then exploded, and the men were lucky to escape getting burned. Mac drove the men as they fled the scene. At the time, conspiracy to commit arson—including providing transportation for perpetrators—was a felony under Tennessee State law that carried a prison sentence of three to twenty-one years. According to McCollough, no Invaders ever faced charges for the arson or any other crimes he witnessed.[28]

"'Black Hoodlums' Blamed by Willis for 3 Fires of Homes He Financed," the front page of the local *Press-Scimitar* blared the day after the fires. Under the headline appeared a photograph of a forlorn Ollie Elliot standing in front of her burned-out future home with the caption "Dream House Ruined by Blaze" (see figure 11.2). Elliot and her husband, John, lived with their three children in the nearby Foote Homes public housing development but had purchased the house from Willis for $12,000. The Elliots had paid the last installment of their down payment just one week before the fire, and they had hoped to move in by Thanksgiving. Now they would have to wait much longer, as would the family scheduled to move into the neighboring home in the development destroyed by fire. "I just don't know what to say," Elliot told a reporter for the *Commercial-Appeal* as she held back tears.[29]

James Lawson did know what to say, however. "It is time for Black people to discipline these elements among us that are deliberately trying to create riot and disorder," Lawson declared, striking a tone that came unusually close to menacing for a man renowned for his strict adherence to Gandhian nonviolence. "Some of the persons extorting and firebombing are in the pay of white racists for purpose of increasing the repression of Black people," he charged.

Whoever the arsonists and their paymasters were, Lawson did not publicly speculate—though earlier in the year he had remarked to a reporter that he feared the Black Organizing Project "had been infiltrated by some government agency." In Lawson's eyes, it was the servants of white supremacy, not Willis, who had betrayed Memphis's Black community.[30]

———

On April 14, a crowd of some 2,500 people gathered in Houston's Emancipation Park to commemorate Martin Luther King, just ten

DREAM HOUSE RUINED BY BLAZE
Mrs. John Elliott stands in front of the ruins of what was to have been her new home at 95 Ingle.
—Press-Scimitar Staff Photo by Tom Barber

FIGURE 11.2. Ollie Elliot in front of her future home after it was burned by a group that included undercover Memphis police officer Marrell McCollough masquerading as an activist, September 11, 1968. *Memphis Press-Scimitar*, Special Collections Department, University of Memphis Library.

days after he had been slain. Among the guests at the rally were Mayor Louis Welch, who believed he had been invited to speak. When he was introduced by Barbara Jordan, the first Black woman elected to Texas's state senate, the crowd booed.[31]

As it turned out, Welch was "not invited as a guest but as a public servant who needs to hear what we have to say," as SNCC ally and rally speaker Earl Allen explained. "We want white Houston to know: we've lived in a police state long enough," Allen proclaimed to loud cheers, adding a call for the establishment of a civilian review board with one out of three members appointed by Black community members. "We demand that the charges against the five Texas Southern University students be dropped immediately or there will be no peace in Houston," he vowed further. At the same time,

Allen insisted that more Black officers be promoted in the Houston Police Department, but only on one condition that drew enthusiastic applause: "We are going to demand that you Black policemen treat us like men and with dignity."

If Allen stole the show, another speaker's words had even greater consequences—though not ones he intended. "King gave you a weapon to fight with, a weapon called love. We don't advocate violence—but we don't tolerate it either," Lee Otis Johnson proclaimed to the crowd, in a clear endorsement of self-defense.

The next day, Welch arranged a press conference. "The entire tone of the meeting was anti-white, anti-government, anti-any kind of control and discipline," the incensed mayor ranted to the reporters. "It was not a service to honor Dr. King in any way." Welch further rejected the speakers' calls for change, dismissing them as political delusions "no thinking person could consider." Then, just a few hours after Welch's press conference, Houston police arrested Johnson on charges of felony marijuana distribution.[32]

———

Black Houstonians were quick to question the police's motives. "The *Informer* is looking into the arrest of Lee Otis Johnson on charges of possession and sale of marijuana and has found many who view the arrest with suspicion," one of the city's two Black newspapers told readers on its front page five days after the arrest. "The answer to the question WHAT DO YOU THINK? is usually answered as follows: 'I don't believe that Johnson is that stupid.'" The newspaper quoted one unnamed person with connections to city government who professed the belief that "they are just trying to shut Lee Otis up."[33]

If anything, the byzantine circumstances around Johnson's arrest raised suspicions. Though he was apprehended on April 15, just hours after Welch's press conference and a day after his fiery speech at the King memorial rally, the warrant for Johnson's arrest had been issued by a judge ten days earlier, on April 5, the day after King's murder. By law, the warrant was to be served on Johnson immediately. What could explain the ten-day gap between when the warrant was issued and when it was served, and why had authorities let Johnson go through with his speech at Emancipation Park, allowing him to speak before an audience of thousands? To complicate matters further, the warrant alleged that Johnson had sold marijuana on March 8, more than five weeks prior to his arrest. So why the delay?[34]

Police offered a none-too-convincing explanation. As they alleged, an undercover officer had provided the evidence for the warrant after Johnson had tried to sell him weed. He was not a vice squad officer, however, but a member of Houston's Criminal Intelligence Division, and he had been assigned to infiltrate Johnson's circle of Black radical friends. Police claimed that they could not initially reveal this information because the officer was still embedded with Johnson through the middle of April, and they did not want to risk blowing his cover. At the time, Houston's white media accepted this account without questioning it. Years later, the real chain of events leading to Johnson's arrest would emerge in federal court proceedings.

Coverage of Johnson's arrest identified the undercover officer as Billy M. Williams. Williams's entrée into activist circles was to make himself useful, to offer his target something he needed—just as McCollough and Wood had. For Williams, all it took was an introduction by a mutual acquaintance to Johnson—using the false name Frank Nelson—and then an offer to give him a ride from the courthouse to his home. Williams was quick to earn Johnson's trust, later recalling how during his assignment, "practically all the time we spent together."

Testifying in court, Williams later admitted that intelligence officials—most likely CID chief Joe Singleton or possibly Albert Blair—had ordered him to befriend Johnson because they wanted an undercover to monitor "left-wings and radical people" who were "troublemakers." As it turned out, Houston police had obtained warrants for sixteen different Black activists on drug charges the day after King's assassination but saved them to serve at the time and date of their choosing. Most were never executed. In insisting that the warrants were held up to prevent Williams's exposure, Singleton gave away the fact that an intelligence officer assigned to infiltrate radical circles had caught activists using drugs but not much else.

Police and city officials made no objection when Johnson's attorney Will Gray argued in court that the warrants for drug arrests were conceived as a check against individuals thought likely to spark riots in the wake of King's murder. Johnson, in other words, had not committed a crime, nor was he about to commit a crime, as far as the police knew when they assigned Williams to assume a false identity and start spying on him. But on April 15, the day after the King memorial rally where activists blasted the police and booed Welch, Johnson was arrested.[35]

Days before his trial, Johnson's defense team took the bold step of issuing subpoenas to Welch and Chief Short as material witnesses to a conspiracy by Houston police to entrap him "solely because of his constitutionally protected activities as a member of the Student Non-Violence [sic] Coordinating Committee." For four days leading up to the trial, Houston's two most prominent city officials somehow managed to avoid the summonses. On the first day of the trial, Gray submitted three motions. One was for continuance, a request that the trial be delayed so that the subpoenas could be served. A second was a request for individual questioning of the jury panel, so that the attorneys could determine what prospective jurors did and did not know about Johnson. Third, and most significantly, Gray requested a change of venue because of his fear that the extensive press coverage Johnson had received in Houston would taint the jury pool. The *Chronicle* and *Post* in the preceding year and a half had made no fewer than fifty-four mentions of Johnson, the vast majority of them negative. But Judge Wendell Odom rejected all three requests, and the trial continued as scheduled.

Williams appeared as the prosecution's star witness, one of very few that it called. The now-surfaced undercover officer told a simple story. On March 8, just one week after he started his work as an undercover agent, Johnson asked for a ride to a house to buy marijuana. Once he returned to the car after making the purchase, Johnson handed Williams a rolled joint, warning him not to get caught with it because it could get him in serious trouble with police.

The city district attorney, Carol Vance, had chosen to personally prosecute Johnson, his first ever marijuana case. He appeared to be motivated by a thirst for both publicity and vengeance. Under Texas law, even a gift of a single joint constituted felony distribution, Vance explained. Jurors had no choice but to convict Johnson and sentence him to prison, and "anything less than twenty years" would be inadequate.

After fewer than four hours of evidence and arguments, jurors spent barely two more hours to settle on a guilty verdict for Johnson. An additional seventeen minutes of discussion sufficed for jurors to determine Johnson's sentence: thirty years in state prison.[36]

———

Why were a small handful of Black police officers willing to spy on activists in a movement fighting for racial equality? The backgrounds and career trajectories of Marrell McCollough and Billy Williams offer important clues. Like Ray Wood and his colleague Gene Roberts assigned to Malcolm X's Organization of Afro-American Unity, both were Black men who had experienced the small-town Jim Crow South before moving as young adults to big cities to secure positions with overwhelmingly white police departments. Of the four, all but Williams had learned to follow orders and defer to hierarchy in the military. All came from modest if not impoverished backgrounds and were eager for middle-class government salaries with benefits. All four were assigned as rookies by white superiors to infiltrate Black activist groups, and though none had formal training in undercover work or any meaningful input in their assignments, they seemed to recognize that intelligence work offered Black officers a rare pathway into the detective ranks.

None of these men seemed to understand what they were getting into when they went undercover. They did not appear to grasp that their commanding officers would bar them from resurfacing until they had produced arrests of activists—even if that required aiding activists in committing crimes. It would be fair to conclude that financial insecurity, professional ambition, and outright ignorance of the demands of undercover work led these men to assume alter egos and infiltrate a movement that vowed to make life better for Black people.

At the end of 1968, it was a Hollywood film, of all things, that perhaps best articulated Black activists' dismay about the police spies who monitored them. Premiering in New York that December, *Uptight* was a remarkable and unconventional movie. It was the product of a multiracial screenwriting team of filmmaker Jules Dassin, actress Ruby Dee, and journalist Julian Mayfield, all three of whom had long histories of left-wing political activity. Dassin, a Jewish New Yorker and former communist, had been blacklisted from the major studios in the 1950s after he fled to Europe to avoid testifying to HUAC. Dee had participated in CORE and the March on Washington, and both she and Mayfield had worked on behalf of radical NAACP self-defense advocate Robert F. Williams and later the Organization of Afro-American Unity as well. All three screenwriters had been the subjects of FBI surveillance, and both Mayfield and Dee had been the targets of BOSS in New York. Even the film's production fell prey to Bureau surveillance.[37]

An adaptation of the 1935 John Ford film *The Informer*, which was based on a novel of the same name by Irish communist Liam O'Flaherty, *Uptight* told the story of Tank—played by Mayfield—an on-again, off-again activist in Cleveland grappling with an existential crisis in the aftermath of Martin Luther King's assassination. When Tank's friend Johnny plots to rob a gun warehouse on behalf of a Black radical group the two men are involved with, Tank passes on the scheme. Too drunk to join, he instead stays home to watch a broadcast of King's funeral. During the robbery, Johnny shoots a white security guard and then flees into hiding. The radical group's leaders blame Tank for refusing to help with the raid and excommunicate him, reasoning that he is an alcoholic liability.

At this point *Uptight*'s most treacherous villain, Clarence, emerges. A Black police spy and self-described stool pigeon, Clarence dresses like a detective, sporting a trench coat and a trilby, and he seems at ease at the local police station, even as he taunts the white officers he works for. He is also an openly gay man who rejects the homophobic slights that come his way; though left unsaid, an implication of the storyline is that Clarence has made a pact with the police so that they leave him to do what he wants at a time when homosexuality was still criminalized.

Clarence attends a small protest organized by the Black radical group, slipping in unnoticed by all except Tank, whom he summons for a meeting in his apartment, a stylish bachelor pad presumably funded with payments from the police. "Nobody should be poor," Clarence muses. "How do you feel when you sell a man?" Tank pushes back. "You grew up around here. You knew Johnny." Unfazed by the insinuation of betrayal, Clarence responds with defiant nihilism: "I don't care what happens to Johnny. Or to you. Or to my whole useless existence."

From a sheath of photographs Clarence then produces a surveillance shot of Tank attacking a police officer. He offers to have police remove the incriminating picture from their files if Tank reveals where Johnny is hiding. Tank leaves the apartment distressed and undecided—but he ultimately tips off the police, cashing in on a $1,000 award.

Tank thus sets into motion his own demise. In the film's final scene, two members of the Black Power group track him down at an industrial scrapyard. They shoot him, and he falls to his death. In its final moments, the film underscored one of the movement's nagging fears by the late 1960s: if activists were not careful, police provocateurs could manipulate them into self-destruction.

12

The Unraveling

By the start of 1968, SNCC and CORE had transformed their understanding of police abuses. The two groups had begun the decade concerned about police who enabled violent mobs, sometimes through direct collaboration and sometimes by looking the other way. In 1963, in the wake of Birmingham, they had shifted their focus to law enforcement's physical brutality against the movement, with some in CORE adopting a theory of "police malpractice" that also encompassed illegal arrests and unconstitutional searches. By 1967, both organizations had embraced an even more expansive conception of coordinated political policing and legal sabotage.

At this time, SNCC in particular faced accusations of abandoning on-the-ground organizing work, from both contemporaries and later some historians. But that was not quite true. Though it had moved on from much of the community organizing in the rural South that had made it famous earlier in the decade, SNCC was nowhere near done with its work. Instead, it had embraced the immense duty of combating repressive political policing. While few contemporary observers saw this work as anything more than SNCC simply trying to stay alive, it was a critical form of organizing that would only become more important in the years ahead.

As ever more SNCC organizers and allies faced dubious charges of insurrection and rioting, the organization committed itself to political defense campaigns. More than merely offering legal representation, SNCC sought to transform the fight against criminal convictions into more ambitious organizing aimed at raising political consciousness about state repression. SNCC's campaign in 1966 in Philadelphia in the wake of the dynamite indictments exemplified this work. The following year, SNCC undertook an aggressive campaign against antiriot laws cited by police to arrest civil rights workers and challenged the constitutionality of their restrictions on political speech.

Political defense campaigns had a long history in left-wing movements committed to protecting their organizers from police repression. They were premised on the notion that the American criminal justice system was so corrupt that an indicted radical—especially if they were Black or working class—could only get a fair trial if mass mobilization brought tremendous political pressure to bear upon state officials. Not even expert legal representation or an individual's innocence could guarantee a just outcome in courts disfigured by the unspoken precepts of racism and capitalism. In the 1930s and 1940s, the Communist Party's International Labor Defense had gained renown for its efforts to organize in the face of unjust prosecution, most spectacularly with its campaign on behalf of the Scottsboro Nine in Alabama. After World War II, the party folded the International Labor Defense into the newly established Civil Rights Congress. As anticommunist hysteria engulfed the Left, most organizations retreated from the work of defense campaigns. After the Civil Rights Congress disbanded in the wake of the federal Subversive Activities Control Board designating it a communist front organization in 1956, the National Lawyers Guild remained almost alone as an active political defense organization, and it remained a beleaguered one at that for the rest of the decade.[1]

Then, in the early 1960s, the civil rights movement jolted the National Lawyers Guild back to life. Over the course of the decade, almost every attorney who represented SNCC and CORE organizers in suits challenging police abuses was either currently or formerly involved in the Guild, including Len Holt, William Kunstler, Arthur

Kinoy, A. L. Wirin, and Hugh Manes. While the NAACP and ACLU remained leery of communists and many socialists, Guild attorneys and their Committee to Assist Southern Lawyers worked with virtually any organizers, no matter how radical. As survivors of the Red Scare—and in Holt's case, direct attacks from law enforcement in Virginia—they brought to their work a left-wing conception of police repression few lawyers held. Whether they were filing SNCC's lawsuits against police in Nashville and Atlanta, representing the organization's field secretaries indicted on dynamite charges in Philadelphia, or defending the Statue of Liberty defendants against the accusations of the NYPD's red squad, National Lawyers Guild attorneys remained at the forefront of defense campaigns against law enforcement's most withering attacks on movement organizers.[2]

A distinguishing feature of these campaigns was collaboration between civil rights groups and leftists outside the movement, an attempt at building a popular front that could draw more political support and media attention than a single organization could. In the TSU case, SNCC worked closely with the Socialist Workers Party, whose *Militant* newspaper lavished attention on the campaign, printing more than a dozen articles on the defendants in the year and a half following the police raid on campus. TSU Five defendant Floyd Nichols also traveled to New York to discuss his case with the group's Militant Labor Forum speaker series. A Trotskyist organization based in Manhattan, the Socialist Workers Party had enjoyed the most success of any socialist party in building bridges to Black organizers in the first half of the 1960s, including Malcolm X in the final year of his life.[3]

The party also had an abiding interest in exposing the inner workings of political repression. In 1965, the Militant Labor Forum invited Mark Lane, a defense attorney from the Statue of Liberty case, to lecture on Ray Wood and BOSS's infiltration of Black activist groups. Decades later, in 1988, the Socialist Workers Party won a groundbreaking settlement against the FBI for targeting it in the Bureau's third Counterintelligence Program, launched in 1961 nearly six years before the more famous "Black Hate" COINTELPRO was initiated.[4]

Defense campaigns offered alliances to SNCC that the organization desperately needed. As Jim Forman argued in his pamphlet *1967:*

High Tide of Black Resistance, repressive police aimed not just to put organizers behind bars or to stifle them with court costs and legal fees. They also intended to cut them off from less radical allies who had the influence and resources to shape mainstream political discourse. In Forman's eyes, SNCC's avowal of Black Power had triggered three varieties of backlash. First, Lyndon Johnson's federal government had attempted to bolster the cause of integration advocated by moderate groups such as the NAACP as a means to isolate SNCC. Second, government officials and the media did as much as possible to characterize Black Power advocates as violent radicals. Finally, "a third form of attempted destruction was exemplified in Philadelphia, Pennsylvania when the local police planted dynamite in the SNCC office there," Forman told readers. The dynamite raid overseen by Frank Rizzo and the Civil Disobedience Unit had established a model of "cutting off financial support through the intimidation of donors, by the harassment of investigating committees, by jail sentences and phony indictments."[5]

Another example of this strategy played out in Houston, where Forman recounted how a "Friends of SNCC group was charged with the murder of one cop, found dead on the side of a building where there were no windows—a cop who had actually died from a ricocheting bullet of his fellow cop." The year 1967 had been momentous for an evolving Black movement, a "year when the pattern of resistance, countered by repression, which in turn stimulated new resistance, became clearer than ever." But as Forman saw it, "If black (and white) resistance grew in 1967, so did the forces of repression." A glaring example of this dynamic was how "the old McCarthy Committee was reactivated under the name of the McClellan Committee. But this time the committee was not looking merely for so-called Communists. It was out to get Black Power people—all of them—on a conspiracy charge."[6]

And yet, while SNCC faced an existential crisis in the form of unstinting repression, Forman did not despair:

> The technical destruction of a single organization such as SNCC would be unfortunate, but it can no more stop the black liberation

movement than the murder of Che Guevara can stem the tide of liberation in Latin America. We do not despair or fear the future. Too many brothers have taken up the cry: Freedom or Death.

SNCC's future was uncertain, but Forman recognized that the organization's fate and the full impact of law enforcement machinations against the movement would become apparent in the coming months.

The year 1968 will surely bring the greatest repression we have seen to date. We must organize to meet the new techniques and weapons of the enemy with new strategies of our own. It will be a crucial year, a year in which the solidarity of liberation forces around the world is of absolutely vital importance.

As he looked to the coming year, Forman could have hardly anticipated what lay ahead with more prescience.[7]

———

These were admittedly difficult times for SNCC and CORE. In the period since both organizations had endorsed Black Power in 1966, they had shed support, especially from white liberals in the press and politics, as well as from more moderate civil rights organizations such as the NAACP, the Urban League, and King's SCLC. The upshot was that both SNCC and CORE were experiencing marked financial difficulties, their donor bases drastically reduced as the groups fended off charges of being Black supremacists and insurrectionists. Both organizations were also riven with internal disputes as their leadership debated how much they should reorient themselves toward Black nationalism, self-defense, and the growing anti–Vietnam War movement. If these challenges were not enough, ongoing repression by police and federal law enforcement made running a functional organization close to impossible. For SNCC, which endured the worst of it, police attacks in Nashville, Houston, Philadelphia, and Atlanta had left little energy for anything beyond mere survival.[8]

In February 1968, SNCC's remaining staff announced a dramatic proposal for reinventing their organization: a merger with the Black Panther Party for Self-Defense. Though the Panthers had formed in October 1966 in Oakland, as 1968 began they were still upstarts with limited influence in Black activist circles beyond California. They were known nationally for their dramatic armed protest at the state capitol in Sacramento as legislators debated a gun control bill, but not much else. In fact, when Hoover launched the covert COINTELPRO operation against "Black Extremists" four months after the Panthers' dramatic action at the capitol, he had described SNCC, CORE, and the Revolutionary Action Movement as the nation's most dangerous Black activist groups—but he made no mention of the Black Panthers. Both law enforcement and left-wing organizers understood the party as a local phenomenon of the Bay Area, not a national powerhouse.[9]

That changed in 1968, and SNCC was part of that transformation. While some described it as a marriage of convenience, the merger between the two groups made sense on several levels. SNCC had already exerted a tremendous—if to this day still underacknowledged—influence on the Panthers, especially in their analysis of police violence, as had CORE to a lesser degree. Police patrols are a key example. Launched with logistical support from both CORE and SNCC, the Community Alert Patrol in Los Angeles preceded the inception of the Panthers by some four months. Huey Newton was likely aware of CAP's work, due to a cover story on the group in the August 1966 issue of *The Movement* newspaper, which he regularly read. And in Oakland, former CORE staffer Mark Comfort had led protests against police violence and organized police patrols as early as September 1966, before later joining the Panthers.[10]

Indeed, while many have emphasized the Panthers' rejection of the tactics of the early civil rights movement, their party very much reflected the influence of radical civil rights organizers from 1966 onward, essentially the period after the Civil Rights and Voting Rights Acts were passed. Former SNCC staffers had a hand in all but one of the Panthers' first four chapters, chief among them Oakland, where the party's national communications secretary was Kathleen Neal, who had worked in SNCC for more than a year before meeting her future husband, Eldridge Cleaver, at SNCC's Black Power conference in Nashville in spring 1967. "Everything I learned in SNCC I took with me into the fledgling Black Panther Party," she later recalled.[11]

But while the Panthers built on SNCC and CORE's ideas on police repression, they pushed them to a more radical point. Unlike unarmed police patrols in Seattle and Los Angeles, the Panthers required their members to carry guns on patrol, taking a page from the playbook of the CORE-affiliated Deacons for Defense, for whom Huey Newton expressed admiration. The Black Panthers' newspaper frequently voiced the party's unrelenting repudiation of police, as illustrated by a single issue from May 4, 1968, published shortly after party member Bobby Hutton was killed by Oakland police. The issue contains the following: the front-page headlines "Pigs Ambush Panthers," "Pigs Use Mace in False Arrest," and "Free All Black Political Prisoners"; multiple cartoons of police cast as swine by Panther artist Emory Douglas, including one showing a pig's corpse punctured by bullets in three places; another cartoon captioned "We Want an Immediate End to Police Brutality and Murder of Black People" portraying a Black man aiming a pistol at a uniformed pig with his foot on top of a bleeding Black man; five reproduced telegrams condemning the killing of Hutton, including three from SNCC staffers; a fourteen-point guide on what to do if arrested; and two large, half-page photographs showing police making arrests of Black Panthers, the officers' faces clearly visible, under the headline "Gestapo Tactics." All of this appeared in just twenty-seven pages.[12]

For years, SNCC and CORE had bravely condemned police abuses in street protests and in writing. But as powerful as they were, most of their criticisms did not pack the emotional punch of the Panthers' attacks on police violence. The Panthers' denunciations were of another order: visceral, graphic, audacious to the point of absolute fearlessness. Not only that, but by early 1968, SNCC's leadership spoke less about police violence and repression than they had in 1966 and 1967.

The Panthers, by contrast, placed the fight against police repression at the heart of their work, as they reminded audiences at a pair of rallies in Oakland and Los Angeles on consecutive days in

February 1968 where they marked their merger with SNCC. "Black people in their homes—put a shotgun in your homes. The cop's in your community. He's not off in the white community brutalizing white people, he's down in the Black community brutalizing Black people, so you can patrol him from your window," Seale explained to the crowd in Los Angeles, who replied with generous applause.[13]

Careful observers of the Panthers might have wondered why the seventh point of their Ten-Point Program—the demand for "an immediate end to police brutality and the murder of Black people"—was the first one the group sought to implement, with the police patrols they organized not long after their founding. Seale explained that the party's work against police abuses was, regardless of where it appeared in the Ten Points, fundamental to its entire political program. "The reason we really started on point number 7 is because if you wanted to hold a meeting or hold a demonstration concerning employment, housing, decent education, et cetera, the man will send down the pigs to intimidate you with his pistols," Seale reflected. "So, if we're going to hold a rent strike, we're going to hold a rent strike with brothers there with arms, et cetera, to make sure that the Black people be defended and not let those cops brutalize them just because the people want to redress their grievances." Combating police violence, in other words, had been the Panthers' most pressing business, something without which its overall work aimed at Black people's progress could not proceed.[14]

Inspired by SNCC's earlier analyses of police violence, the Panthers now surpassed the older group with their pathbreaking analysis and organizing around the issue. As Rap Brown and Stokely Carmichael headlined the joint rallies for SNCC, they said next to nothing about police abuses or even about their vision for a political program more generally. Years of political infighting, nonstop travel, and organizing against repression had taken their toll. In Oakland, the single concrete recommendation Carmichael offered for resisting police was that Black people should "off" undercover spies they found in their communities. It came across as hyperbolic big talk, a threat Carmichael and his audience were unlikely to carry out. But if taken literally, it was a destructive act that would invite only more severe violence and repression from law enforcement.[15]

These were early signs that the Panthers and SNCC's partnership was not meant to last. By July 1968, just five months after their announced merger, the two organizations went their separate ways. There had always been something transactional about their arrangement. Gerald Fraser, a pioneering Black reporter for the *New York Times*, maintained that "the purpose of the alliance was to blend S.N.C.C.—the organization with the image—with the Panthers—the organization with the program." That may have been true, but in the months that followed the two groups' fusion, the Panthers gained the national influence they had previously lacked. In 1968 alone, the Panthers established almost twenty new chapters, on both coasts as well as in interior cities such as Chicago and even Des Moines and Omaha.[16]

"S.N.C.C. in Decline After 8 Years in Lead," Fraser's headline declared that October. If the group's dwindling supporters found it easy to write off the *Times* as establishment liberals, commentary from their mentor Ella Baker must have been harder to stomach. "They were unable to sense that the milieu and factors of change were more than they had dealt with before," Baker told the *Times*. "And the frustration that came to individuals that had gone through the Southern experience rendered them unable to make a historical decision that perhaps their days were over."[17]

By year's end, the Panthers had established themselves as the country's most significant Black activist group, a pacesetter that both Black and white organizers looked to for leadership and inspiration. They were now the vanguard of the movement, and the analysis and organizing against police violence at the heart of their work attracted new recruits and generous media attention. But it would soon become clear that their audacity and radicalism also drew the ire of police and federal law enforcement, triggering a wave of repression far more destructive than even what other Black organizers had experienced earlier in the decade.

———

Amid a year marked by assassinations and violent attacks on protests, the legal slow violence SNCC leaders endured in 1968 barely

FIGURE 12.1. Lee Otis Johnson in H. H. Coffield Unit prison, Texas, 1970.
MSS 105-152 B6 45/303/c, HHRC.

made the news. In Houston, reports of Lee Otis Johnson's conviction were buried inside the city's leading papers (see figure 12.1). It was a striking contrast to the front-page stories about SNCC's demonstrations, the TSU raid, and supposedly antiwhite rallies featuring Johnson since the spring of the previous year. Nationally, the story barely registered. Scattered reports appeared in the Black press, left-wing publications, and a few Texas papers. But almost no major city newspaper outside Houston appears to have reported on Johnson's case.[18]

The one surprising exception to this was the *Wall Street Journal*, which published a lengthy report on its front page about police intelligence units across the country investigating Black activists. Mentioning Johnson's case in passing, the *Journal*'s focus was Houston's Criminal Intelligence Division. The city's red squad was unusually candid in disclosing its activities for a story that opened with reporter David Brand's description of "Charlie Smith," an undercover police "spy" who was posing as a student on Texas Southern's campus. As intelligence chief Joe Singleton told the paper, despite his unit's official name, "since 1965, we haven't put as much effort into criminal investigation because of this racial thing."[19]

Rarely had a major national publication written so plainly and in such detail about a municipal police intelligence unit's undercover work against racial justice organizers. In Houston, "civil rights activists are trailed, observed from parked cars, photographed by policemen posing as news photographers, tape recorded by informers and cultivated by undercover agents acting as businessmen or ex-convicts," the *Journal* reported. Reverend Bill Lawson—who had fearlessly recounted in the *Forward Times* the brazen acts of violence by Houston officers he witnessed at the TSU raid and suggested that police may have inadvertently killed Louis Kuba—charged that his home phone was tapped. "We know more about the police than they know about us," Johnson claimed to Brand, a boast that likely struck most readers as improbable, especially after they learned that weeks earlier Johnson had been sentenced to three decades in prison for selling marijuana.

Houston police, for their part, argued that the safety of their city—and even their country—depended on their infiltration of activist movements. In Chief Short's estimation, intelligence operations had "been very effective in combatting in criminal unrest," and as the undercover officer at TSU fretted, "I just don't want to see this country burn." Another officer, one Lin Fowler, claimed that he had come to understand in his eighteen months undercover in Houston's antiwar movement that any talk of "social change" by demonstrators was a giveaway of their communist leanings. The red squad's unmitigated animosity for the city's activists was apparent.

Houston's Black organizers, according to Singleton, were nothing more than "arrogant bastards looking for an issue."[20]

It was an astonishing story—and Houston officials tried to walk back most of it. Three days after its publication, the *Journal* printed a detailed rebuttal from Welch and Short qualifying many of the article's disclosures, stressing the city's efforts at racial reconciliation, and denying every single quotation from Short and Singleton included in the story. Despite these protestations, one thing was clear: Houston police had been caught showboating. Two weeks after Johnson's conviction, as five TSU students remained indicted for murder, the city's red squad was gloating over their success in destroying SNCC in Houston.[21]

The events of the last several months gave local Black organizers ample reason to worry. Not the least of their concerns was whether the TSU Five would meet the same fate as Johnson and receive decades-long prison sentences that exceeded even what a vindictive prosecutor recommended. The man who may have had the most to fear was Charles Freeman, considered by many to be the quintet's leader. His trial for murder was the first that was scheduled and set to begin the following month.

In at least one regard, Freeman had the opposite problem as the one faced by Johnson, whose attorney had failed to secure a change of venue. Houston prosecutors announced their intent to move Freeman's case out of Houston, arguing that press coverage of the TSU raid had saturated the city to the point that the case risked being influenced by political currents. SNCC organizers and many Black Houstonians suspected that this was an attempt to move to a whiter and more conservative jurisdiction far enough from Houston to discourage protesters from attending the proceedings.

City officials and police never admitted this, of course. But prosecutor Carol Vance later recalled under oath that his staff had met with Singleton and police officials and taken their advice against holding the trial in Houston because it could be "disruptive" and "give rise to even more publicity." In other words, the very intelligence officer who oversaw the surveillance of SNCC sought to preempt any protests the trial might attract, so he persuaded prosecutors to try to move it out of town. Decades later, Vance claimed that public safety was the motivation, remarking that he "did not want a trial in Harris County that might trigger another riot." It was an outlandish claim by the retired prosecutor, a blatant attempt to rewrite the history of his dealings with the civil rights movement. Twelve days after Johnson's marijuana arrest, Freeman's trial was ordered moved to Victoria, a town of some forty thousand residents more than two hours by car southwest of Houston.[22]

The TSU defendants' lives had been turned upside down since they were indicted in June 1967. All five men—Floyd Nichols, Douglas Waller, Trazawell Franklin, John Parker, and Charles Freeman—had been expelled from Texas Southern. It mattered little to school officials that no charges had been proved against the students; they had been among the most outspoken activists on campus, and the administration was happy to be rid of them. The TSU Five plus five additional students sued the university in federal court for readmission in fall 1967, but they lost their case. Meanwhile, police and city officials seemed content to leave the murder indictments hanging over the five men as long as possible.[23]

Nearly a year and a half had passed since the TSU raids when Charles Freeman's case finally went to trial in October 1968. Prosecutors tried Freeman for assault with intent to murder intelligence officer Robert Blaylock, with plans to later try him on additional felony charges for the injury of Robert Dugger and the murder of Louis Kuba. From the start of the trial, the state conceded that they could not prove that the bullets that injured Blaylock and Dugger and killed Kuba had been fired by Freeman—or any of the other four defendants, for that matter. But the state rationalized the charge by pointing to the felony murder doctrine, which holds that if someone commits a violent felony other than murder but inadvertently kills someone in the process, they have effectively committed murder. In the prosecution's eyes, the five defendants had instigated the so-called riot on TSU's campus during which Kuba was killed and two officers were injured, in turn committing assault with intent to murder.[24]

As they sat in the Victoria courthouse, Freeman and his supporters could have been forgiven for thinking they had seen this movie before. Deciding Freeman's fate was an all-white jury culled from a pool of 276 from which all six Black members had been struck. Two of the jurors worked full-time as private security guards, including the foreman—hardly people one might expect to deliberate on alleged acts of violence against police with studied neutrality. The judge was the town's former mayor, fifty-seven-year-old Joe Kelly, also white.[25]

To many observers' surprise, Judge Kelly displayed a measured skepticism of the state's case. Most significantly, he granted the defense its request to bar the prosecution from claiming that Freeman had incited a riot or even from using the word "riot" at all in the trial. Prosecutors had failed to show that Freeman was responsible for the riot, the defense contended, and Kelly agreed that to claim otherwise would prejudice the jurors. In their closing, the prosecution admitted that the evidence that Freeman had assaulted Blaylock with intent to murder was no more than circumstantial. "There are no eyewitnesses, and none are necessary. We can prove that he encouraged the shootings on the campus by words," Vance insisted.[26]

At the end of oral arguments, jurors deliberated on the case for nearly nine hours before the foreman sent Judge Kelly a note with a brief message: "Your honor: the jury is unable to agree on a verdict." The case was declared a mistrial. Though Freeman could be tried again, the failure to convict him in his first trial was an undeniable defeat for the prosecution. As it turned out, at least two people on the all-white jury had wanted to acquit Freeman. Vance later lamented that Kelly rejected the prosecution's riot thesis, complaining that "some members of the public did not comprehend the theory of the State's case." It must have been a painful realization for Houston's prosecutors and police to learn that even in a small, seemingly conservative town such as Victoria, not every single white person was convinced that SNCC had triggered a riot and killed and injured officers.[27]

Even if an all-white, small-town jury had refused to affirm the prosecution's convoluted felony murder theory, officials were not going to let the TSU Five off easy. Police and prosecutors in Houston knew full well that as the five young men remained indicted for felony murder, the demands of mounting legal defenses and fears of future arrest were enough to reduce or even stop their political activities. Any additional arrests at protests would only further imperil the men's defense. The questionable prosecutions were an effective form of slow violence, exerting no small amount of pain and social control on five men who otherwise would have been completing their college studies, launching careers, or immersing themselves in political organizing. Instead, each had to plan for the possibility of serving time in prison.

But Charles Freeman's case turned out to be the beginning of the end for the state's prosecution of the TSU Five. In the two years that followed the mistrial, no further trials were held for any of the men. Finally, in November 1970, three and a half years after Houston police had stormed TSU's campus, District Court Judge Wendell Odom dropped all felony charges against the Houston SNCC members. Recommending the dismissal of the charges was Vance, the district attorney who now admitted what the defense had insisted all along: there was no evidence to link the five men to the injured officers or Kuba's death. Only Douglas Waller was convicted, for possession of a pistol, which resulted in a year's sentence in jail. And yet, a nagging question remained: Who had killed Louis Kuba? Was it possible, as Bill Lawson had theorized, that the police had inadvertently shot one of their own? Whatever they thought, city officials would not say.[28]

———

With the dropping of charges against the TSU Five, it became clear that one Houston SNCC member had fared far worse than the others, and that was Lee Otis Johnson. At the start of 1970, the Texas Supreme Court rejected Johnson's appeal of his conviction for marijuana distribution without explanation, ordering that he be moved from the Harris County jail to the state penitentiary. But now, as Johnson faced twenty-eight more years in prison for passing a single marijuana joint to an undercover cop, a movement to have his conviction overturned was growing.

The Lee Otis Johnson Defense Committee had started in early 1969, drawing about one hundred people to its early meetings.

Members included SNCC veterans as well as the chair of the Houston chapter of the ACLU, a biology professor at Rice University. But the multiracial group gradually drew national and even international notice with their cries that Johnson was a Black political prisoner. The London-based human rights organization Amnesty International corresponded with Johnson's defense committee about his case. And perhaps most significantly, the committee had convinced the U.S. Commission on Civil Rights to request an investigation of Johnson's case by the Department of Justice.[29]

In a four-page profile in the *Village Voice* in February 1970, reporter Ron Rosenbaum described Johnson as "a casualty of one of those quick police search-and-destroy operations which often go unnoticed in the attention devoted to the Song Mys of the domestic pacification program," a reference to the village at My Lai where American troops had massacred as many as five hundred civilians in March 1968. "As far as blacks are concerned, Houston justice is about as genuine as Astroturf," Rosenbaum lamented after a visit to Johnson in prison.[30]

This was not an isolated case of a Texas frame-up, Rosenbaum warned. "We can no longer look at such examples of Southern justice as remnants of a dead past, but instead as the shape of things to come in the North. Repression works." As he languished behind bars, Johnson did not hold back on denouncing police misdeeds. "'Law and order' is just a subterfuge for maintaining a strong police power," Johnson bemoaned to another reporter. Whenever a Black person was killed by an officer, "the most that will happen is that the cop will get fired from the police department. Then they'll put him on the payroll of a sheriff's department."[31]

Houston's red squad remained unbowed. "I don't regard Lee Otis Johnson as a political prisoner. I regard him as a criminal," spat Joe Singleton, the man who had ordered Officer Billy Williams to infiltrate Johnson's circle. "He doesn't tell you that he and his friends were smoking marijuana, drinking Robitussin and stealing food, that they were trying to get dynamite to blow up major overpasses, power stations, telephone facilities and public buildings." Like intelligence officers in New York and Philadelphia before him, Singleton maintained that a civil rights activist had plotted major acts of terrorism with explosives, though he offered no evidence to support his claim.[32]

The first nationally prominent figure to champion Johnson and his release was Angela Davis, another incarcerated organizer who had once been affiliated with SNCC. In August 1970, seventeen-year-old Jonathan Jackson—brother of incarcerated *Soledad Brother* author George Jackson and a close friend of Davis's—took five people hostage at the Marin County courthouse. He was assisted by Ruchell Magee and William Christmas, two men incarcerated at San Quentin called to testify that day in the trial of another incarcerated man charged with stabbing a guard. In exchange for the courthouse captives, which included Judge Harold Haley, they demanded the release of George Jackson, Fleeta Drumgo, and John Cluchette, the three so-called Soledad Brothers who had been charged with killing a guard at Soledad State Prison. As the kidnappers attempted to escape in a van with the hostages, law enforcement opened fire on the vehicle. Jackson, Christmas, and Haley were all found dead in the aftermath; authorities claimed that the kidnappers had died from their own bullets. A week later, Marin County authorities issued a warrant for Davis, alleging that she had purchased the guns used in the hostage-taking, and that October, she was apprehended on the run by FBI agents.[33]

Davis's case became a national and international cause célèbre. Many of the calls for her exoneration came from the National United Committee to Free Angela Davis, a defense campaign initiated by the embattled activist's allies in the Communist Party. Cochairing the committee was Davis's sister Fania Jordan and longtime party official Franklin Alexander, who had been arrested with Lee Otis Johnson and SNCC organizers at protests on TSU's campus in April 1967 as he was traveling through Houston on behalf of the W.E.B. Du Bois Clubs.

Though best remembered as a communist with close ties to the Black Panthers, Davis had extensive experience in the civil rights struggles of the 1960s. As a young woman in her hometown of Birmingham, she had taken part in the SCLC's voter registration drives, and as a high schooler and a member of the communist youth group Advance, she had demonstrated outside Woolworth stores in New York City as protests against the company's segregated lunch counters swept through the South in the early months of 1960. Later in the decade, Davis immersed herself in SNCC, joining a contingent of the group organized by James Forman in Los Angeles.[34]

Davis's connections to the movement were on full display in *If They Come in the Morning: Voices of Resistance*, an essay collection she coedited in 1971 as she sat in the Marin County jail. The book centered on Davis's and Magee's cases and the broader question of political prisoners in America, with essays by Communist Party comrades as well as Black Panther leaders Huey Newton, Ericka Huggins, and Bobby Seale.

If They Come in the Morning bore a distinct seal of approval from civil rights veterans. Ralph David Abernathy, King's right hand in the SCLC and now the organization's director, contributed an essay titled "I Bring an Indictment Against the American System," a full-throated defense of Davis charging "the American system with conspiracy to repress and violently subjugate those who resist." Another contributor, Coretta Scott King, pleaded for a fair trial from a legal system whose handling of Davis's case "carried us a long way back to the agonizing inquisitions of the early fifties." Julian Bond, SNCC's former communications director and now a Georgia legislator, provided the book's forward. "It will not suffice to have this collection read and approved. It will not suffice even to mouth slogan and rhetoric. Even Richard Nixon now says 'Power to the People,'" Bond reminded readers. "What is wanted for the subjects of this book, and for the 'army of the wronged' not mentioned in these pages, is concerted and organized action."[35]

Among the individuals on whose behalf Davis urged action was Lee Otis Johnson, in a section titled "Realities of Repression" that summarized twenty-one cases of incarcerated activists. "It had been an open secret that Houston authorities were determined to crush the burgeoning political activity in the Black community," Davis told readers. "In Brother Johnson's case, the transformation of the courts into an overt instrument of political repression is patently and outrageously exposed." She also gave space to Johnson to speak on his own case: "I'm a Political Prisoner, victimized for none other than my organizing influential and effective Human Rights activities to cure the conspicuous and detestable ills of this society."[36]

Davis was just one prominent voice in a burgeoning defense campaign for Johnson by the start of 1972. Two more were John Lennon and Yoko Ono, who sang "They got ol' Lee Otis, too" in their anthem "John Sinclair," a demand for freedom for the two activists imprisoned for marijuana possession. Johnson's campaign was now drawing press coverage from across the United States and around the globe, including from England, Italy, and West Germany. The *Black Panther*—with a circulation of more than 140,000, the second-most read African American newspaper in the country—devoted two pages to Johnson in its March 4, 1972, issue.[37]

Most important of all, Johnson's defense team had persuaded the U.S. District Court of Southern Texas to consider their writ of habeus corpus. Johnson's petition contended that Texas state courts had violated his constitutional rights by denying him a change of venue and the chance to subpoena witnesses of his choosing, as well as by subjecting him to cruel and unusual punishment. Submitted in August 1971, Johnson's writ further maintained that Houston police had entrapped him with the explicit goal of ending his political activities, thus violating his right to free speech and assembly.[38]

Johnson's defense team took full advantage of the habeus corpus hearing to confront Houston police over their long-standing surveillance of civil rights activists, charging that it amounted to a pattern of prejudice that ensured Johnson's arrest regardless of whether he broke the law. Unlike in his first trial, this time Johnson succeeded in serving Mayor Louis Welch and intelligence chief Joe Singleton with subpoenas. Johnson's attorney William Walsh probed Welch as to why he had supported moving the TSU Five's trial out of Houston, months before Johnson's bid for a move was denied. The mayor conceded that in the case against the TSU Five, he had been "fearful that the demonstrations on the sidewalks and in the streets might affect the judgment of the jury." But the mayor denied ever thinking that Johnson's trial had posed any danger to Houston.

Remarkably, Singleton contradicted the mayor in his testimony. He took no issue with defense attorney claims that police had viewed Johnson as a "potentially dangerous person who bore watching . . . specifically as a black militant." But he only grudgingly admitted that "we maintain surveillance and files on the various radical revolutionary-type elements," conceding that he and his colleagues "take thousands of pictures."[39]

Oral arguments for the habeus corpus petition were heard in the first week of January 1972. Two weeks later, Judge Carl Bue offered his judgment. Bue was unconvinced that Houston's police and mayor had conspired to entrap Johnson with their years of surveillance against him. Nor did the judge believe that the length of Johnson's sentence offered evidence of cruel and unusual punishment, though he conceded that it was "unduly severe."

But Bue was unequivocal that Johnson had been denied due process, reasoning "that the outside influences affecting the community's climate of opinion as to petitioner were so inherently suspect as to create a resulting probability of unfairness." The very fact that Houston's intelligence division had kept a surveillance file on Johnson because they viewed him as a dangerous radical was, in Bue's eyes, evidence that he "had a bad reputation in the community" and was unlikely to get a fair hearing in Houston. The Texas trial court had never "recognized the degree of hostility toward petitioner which had apparently permeated the community by that time; otherwise, it would have undoubtedly employed one or more of the recognized safeguards to insure a fair trial free from the effects of racial prejudice." This included Johnson's demands for individual questioning of potential jurors during voir dire, another of his requests rejected by the original criminal court.[40]

Bue's remedy dealt a major blow to Houston police and prosecutors. The judge ordered that Johnson's case be remanded to the state, which now had just ninety days to retry him. If prosecutors did not give Johnson another trial, Texas had no choice but to release him from prison. The judge's order set into motion a series of legal

FIGURE 12.2. Lee Otis Johnson outside court in Houston moments after a federal judge ordered him released from prison, June 2, 1972. RGD0006N-1972-2600, HHRC.

wranglings between Johnson, Texas, and the federal appeals courts. Finally, on June 2, 1972, Bue ordered that Johnson be released on bail as prosecutors deliberated whether to try Johnson again or not. As it turned out, Johnson would never again face the 1968 charges.

The next day, Lee Otis Johnson walked out of a Houston court to a crowd of family, friends, and supporters celebrating his release (see figure 12.2). Though he flashed a smile in several press photographs, the *Houston Chronicle* described him as "solemn." Johnson projected a weariness that contrasted with the youthful defiance that came across in photos of him before his imprisonment. "I've changed in four years and perhaps certain things around here have changed," Johnson told the crowd. "It's hard to believe that I'm free."[41]

Two days later, on June 4, a jury in Marin County announced their verdict in Angela Davis's murder and conspiracy trial: not guilty on all counts. Two of the political prisoners featured in *If They Come in the Morning* had been set free in less than forty-eight hours—though most of those profiled in "Realities of Repression" remained behind bars.

———

In the nearly four years that Lee Otis Johnson had spent in prison, SNCC had come undone, and CORE had devolved into a shell of its former self. Observers, especially white liberals, pointed to King's murder as the moment the movement died. It was nowhere near as simple as that, of course. Countless Black organizers continued their work in the wake of his death, and new organizations emerged after King as well. The movement's survival and reinvention after the SCLC leader's death is one of the central tenants of the "long civil rights movement" thesis that historians have embraced in the last two decades. But SNCC and CORE did suffer their own forms of death by 1968. Both still existed in name, but by the end of the year neither group's national office could claim to do much community organizing or political defense work.

There was no denying that the civil rights movement of the 1960s had unraveled. Some left activism to focus on their careers or families, while others looked for new organizations and political struggles to join. But a subset of the movement believed that the work of confronting police abuses in its many forms was far from over. It was these activists, so many of them veterans of SNCC and CORE, who in the 1970s committed themselves to the monumental task of unmasking the slow violence of political policing.

13

The Unmasking

In April 1974, a forty-year-old Methodist minister and religious studies professor from Temple University named John Raines published a slim book titled *Attack on Privacy*. "Because of new technologies in the collection of personal data and because of a law-and-order mentality that views opposition as subversive, we are undergoing a sharply increased invasion of individual and group privacy," Raines warned readers in his preface. For those who wanted to fight back, there were "several practical actions in law and politics that need our corrective effort."

Widespread surveillance by law enforcement agencies was a form of entrapment "from which there was small chance of successful escape," Raines charged in his opening chapter, "Dossier Prisons." Calling out Philadelphia's police intelligence unit by name, Raines demanded strict civil oversight of red squads across the country, arguing that "the use of informers (and wiretaps and electronic bugging) is practiced more intensively by local police agencies, such as civil disobedience and intelligence squads, where the authorization, accountability, and record maintenance are less stringently regulated than at the federal level."[1]

It was an odd choice of topic for a theologian. Published with a small press operating out of suburban Philadelphia, *Attack on*

Privacy attracted a handful of reviews, most of them from religious and scholarly publications. It otherwise drew little attention from readers. But Raines omitted one detail from his 144-page book that might have vastly increased his readership had he included it— though it would have come at a great cost.

That detail was the fact that he and his wife, Bonnie, were two members of the Citizens' Commission to Investigate the FBI, a group of eight Philadelphia activists who had broken into a small Bureau office in the nearby town of Media, Pennsylvania, and stolen some one thousand documents on the evening of March 8, 1971. The files included what would be the first ever public revelations of COINTELPRO, before any Americans outside the FBI had the slightest idea what the code name meant. Of the many records the commission pilfered, one from 1968 described surveillance of CORE, the SCLC, and at least two of the individuals charged by Philadelphia police with plotting to dynamite the Liberty Bell in August 1966, under watch by the Bureau two years after those charges had amounted to nothing. Another file contained a detailed surveillance report on a Philadelphia demonstration authored by the Civil Disturbance Unit and shared with the Bureau.[2]

In an anonymous call to a Reuters reporter from a pay phone the morning after the burglary, Raines shared a statement from the Citizens' Commission taking credit for the break-in. The group's objective was to determine "the nature and extent of surveillance and intimidation carried on by this office of the FBI, particularly against groups and individuals working for a more just, humane and peaceful society." The burglars had set out to wage a resistance campaign against "law and order which depends on intimidation and repression to secure obedience" and to expose the FBI's "use of provocateurs and informers," especially while the U.S. government fought an undemocratic war in Vietnam "in defiance of the vast majority who want all troops and weapons withdrawn."

Eleven days after the break-in, Raines mailed two sets of photocopied FBI records to members of Congress and another three to reporters. All but one of the addressees returned the documents to the FBI within days of receiving the photocopies. The lone exception was *Washington Post* reporter Betty Medsger, who bravely published a selection of the files in the newspaper on March 24, over the objections of Department of Justice officials. "Copies of stolen FBI records sent to *The Washington Post* described the bureau's surveillance of campus and black activist organizations at one college as involving the local police chief, the postmaster, letter carriers, campus security officers and a switchboard operator," Medsger's story opened. The report ignited a media and political firestorm. Deeply embarrassed by the disclosure of both the files' contents and their theft, Hoover's agents spent five years searching for the thieves, as laid out in an investigative file on the burglars totaling 33,698 pages.[3]

But the agents never apprehended any of the perpetrators. In 2014, forty-seven years after the break-in, Bonnie and John Raines and three other members of the group revealed their identities, long after the statute of limitations for their criminal act had passed. At the time of writing, all but one of the Media burglars have gone public.

Like John Raines, the one burglar who continues to shield her identity as of 2025 had also taken part in the civil rights movement in the 1960s. Their encounters with police violence in the movement gave way to an acute awareness of the threat that law enforcement posed to democracy, setting them on the slow path to the FBI office break-in. In July 1961, Raines had joined CORE's Freedom Rides, boarding a bus in St. Louis bound for Arkansas. Upon their arrival in Little Rock, 250 white hecklers awaited Raines and his three companions at the bus station, and police chief R. E. Glasscock had the Freedom Riders arrested for creating "a threat to the waiting room" (see figure 13.1). The group was promptly sentenced to jail for six months, though after three days they were released because city officials decided that their incarceration would bring unwanted media attention. In Shreveport, Louisiana, the four Freedom Riders disembarked from their bus to find themselves surrounded by police snipers perched on the roof of the city's bus station, rifles pointed at them from above. The unspoken suggestion that police would shoot to kill convinced the group to forgo testing the station's segregated waiting rooms, and they instead sought refuge with a local Black minister in his home. Finally, five days after they had started,

FIGURE 13.1. John Raines's arrest as a Freedom Rider in Little Rock, Arkansas, in July 1961 inspired him to help organize the Citizens' Commission to Investigate the FBI that burglarized a Bureau office in Media, Pennsylvania, in March 1971. Box 906, Orval Eugene Faubus Papers, Series 25, Special Collections, University of Arkansas Libraries.

the group made it to New Orleans, where plainclothes officers were on hand to monitor the Freedom Riders and photograph them for their dossiers.[4]

A few years after the Freedom Rides, Raines joined a SNCC campaign in southwest Georgia and was jailed in notorious Baker County. There he languished behind bars until local Black residents raised his bail because they had heard that the local White Citizens' Council planned to attack him there with the sheriff's blessing. These experiences with police prompted an awakening.

"I began to see another face of law and order: control over power-less people, such as the black majority in the South that couldn't vote.

I began to get a different sense of how power is used in society. . . .
I saw the law used to inflict injustice upon many people," Raines
recalled years later. "Without that experience, without what black
people taught me about resistance . . . I would have been a very different person ten years later."[5]

The Media FBI office break-in a decade after the Freedom Rides
was the most spectacular event in what we might call the great
unmasking of the 1970s. In the parlance of intelligence services,
"unmasking" refers to an agency revealing the identity of one of its
secret agents. In the aftermath of the 1960s, a broad coalition of
organizers on the American left took it upon themselves to carry
out the work of unmasking, as they exposed not only individual
law enforcement agents but a wide array of secretive intelligence
services aimed at political activists. These were of course the years
of the Vietnam War, the *Pentagon Papers*, and Watergate, and anger at
the U.S. government for its deceptions—and especially the FBI and
Central Intelligence Agency (CIA)—had reached a high-water mark.

Largely forgotten today is how much activists did to unmask the
misdeeds of local police intelligence units throughout the country.
Notably, this work drew from a wide array of movements, attracting
antiwar organizers, Black Panthers, and veterans of the civil rights
movement, including former organizers from SNCC, CORE, and the
SCLC as well as key support groups such as the National Lawyers
Guild and the American Friends Service Committee. For people like
John Raines, the road to unmasking the slow violence of political
policing began years earlier, as officers pointed guns at their faces
for demanding desegregated transportation and as they sat in jail,
wondering whether they would suffer unspeakable violence at the
hands of vigilantes working in concert with their uniformed captors.

———

In the weeks following Martin Luther King's assassination in
April 1968, New Jersey's State Police Central Security Unit issued
a memorandum to police departments throughout the state urging them to compile information on any gatherings by political

organizations that contributed to inciting riots. According to authorities, such groups included any that could be classified as "Left wing, Right wing, Civil Rights, Militant, Nationalistic, Pacifist, Religious, Black Power, Ku Klux Klan, Extremist, etc."[6]

In response, a coalition of activists sued the New Jersey attorney general and Jersey City's police chief. The *New York Times* described *Anderson v. Sills* as "the first major court test in the United States of the constitutionality of current police practices of collecting and maintaining intelligence information." Plaintiffs included Denise Anderson, a twenty-one-year-old chair of Students for a Democratic Society at Saint Peter's College, the Jersey City chapter of the NAACP, and Robert Castle, a white Episcopal priest who had transformed Jersey City CORE into a major force against police violence in his city.[7]

In July 1969, Judge Robert Matthews of New Jersey's State Superior Court ruled in the plaintiffs' favor, arguing that the intelligence operations described in the memo had violated the U.S. Constitution and "by their very existence tend to restrict those who would advocate, within the protected areas, social and political change." In response to Anderson and her co-litigants' request that police agencies be restrained from using any intelligence they had attained in their spring 1968 activities, Matthews ordered officials to produce all files that were unrelated to specific crimes under investigation so that they could be purged.[8]

Outraged police chiefs in Jersey City and Camden announced that they would resist the ruling. Before any files were destroyed, a second Superior Court judge ordered a stay on Matthews's order, and state officials were granted an appeal, which was ultimately heard six months after Matthews's decision, in February 1970. Assisting in representing the plaintiffs were ACLU staffer Eleanor Holmes Norton, a former SNCC organizer and future member of Congress, and National Lawyers Guild veterans Arthur Kinoy and William Kunstler. After representing SNCC and other organizers challenging police abuses countless times, Kinoy and Kunstler had started their own legal advocacy organization focused on social justice, the Law Center for Constitutional Rights, in 1966.

Before the Supreme Court of New Jersey, however, the Jersey City plaintiffs' arguments fell on deaf ears, and the justices overturned the lower court's decision in a unanimous ruling. Unlike Matthews, the higher court did not foresee the threat of surveillance as discouraging constitutionally protected political activity. "The police function is pervasive," the court contended. "It is not limited to the detection of past criminal events. Of at least equal importance is the responsibility to prevent crime." Any restraining action or injunction, the justices reasoned, had to be "precisely limited to the offending material or practice," not to the theoretical possibility of injury. Denise Anderson's contention that her fellow student protesters had been photographed by plainclothes officers in an unmarked car, for instance, had failed to move the justices because she could not prove that the photographers were police.[9]

While the Jersey City activists vowed to petition the U.S. Supreme Court, they were never able to move their case to the federal system. Though they had lost on appeal, the original ruling represented civil rights organizers' first ever victory against political surveillance of activists by police. Even in ultimate defeat, the appeals ruling pointed to a pathway for future litigation against police spying by suggesting that a court could restrain documented instances of surveillance.

As the 1960s turned to the 1970s, and more and more activists were charged with felonies, heightened political policing was not without its risks for law enforcement. Because many such prosecutions relied on warrantless investigative work by red squads, police risked exposing the inner workings of intelligence units by giving defense attorneys opportunities to subpoena files, depose witnesses, and even compel undercover officers to testify in court. If faced with these demands, would police stonewall litigants, just as New Jersey police had before they prevailed in court? Soon enough activists across the country would find out.[10]

———

No case in these years did more to raise the prospect of legal defense exposing police intelligence abuses than the *People of the State of*

New York v. Lumumba Shakur or, as it became more widely known, the Panther 21 trial. On April 2, 1969, Manhattan's district attorney indicted nineteen male and two female Black Panthers on charges of planning an elaborate series of violent acts. The alleged plots were to bomb four police precinct buildings, the Bronx Botanical Gardens, and several department stores, as well as to kill any police officers caught fleeing the attacks. Among the indicted were Robert Collier, made deputy minister of education by the New York Panthers after he had completed his federal prison sentence for the conspiracy to bomb the Statue of Liberty. Another defendant was twenty-two-year-old Harlem Panthers section leader Afeni Shakur, who would later give birth to a son she named Tupac.[11]

In the days leading up to the trial, the defendants—now whittled down to a group of thirteen—were certain that prosecutors would rely on the testimony of undercover spies planted in the party, but they were unsure who those spies were. Only once the trial began did the identity of the prosecution's star witness become clear: Gene Roberts, an undercover BOSS agent who had served as a trusted lieutenant in the Panthers' security force since early 1968, his entry into the party eased by his childhood friendship with Panther leader William King.[12]

Roberts was light-skinned and slight, with sharp features, a mustache, and dark, penetrating eyes. Much of his background matched that of Ray Wood—both were Southerners who had served in the military and then moved to New York, bouncing from job to job in the city before landing their positions with BOSS. Perhaps the two undercover officers' most notable commonality was that they shared the exact same hiring date, April 17, 1964. Though they were never introduced, much less apprised of each other, Roberts and Wood were effectively hired by BOSS as a pair to infiltrate Black activist groups. Unlike Wood, who after ten months of undercover work surfaced in February 1965 after preempting the purported Statue of Liberty plot, Roberts stayed undercover for nearly five years. Remarkably, he did so while he worked under his real name and even lived with his wife and daughter.

Roberts was first assigned to embed himself in Malcolm X's circle, barely a month after the minister of Harlem's Mosque No. 7

announced his formal resignation from the Nation of Islam. Malcolm hired Roberts as a bodyguard, recognizing his abilities in first aid and martial arts. Five days after Wood made national headlines with the Statue of Liberty dynamite arrests, Roberts witnessed Malcolm's murder from the front row of the Audubon Ballroom in Harlem. As his boss lay bleeding on the stage, Roberts rushed to resuscitate him, as documented in a photo of him crouching over Malcolm's body that appeared in *Life* magazine.[13]

Decades later, historian Garrett Felber published activist Yuri Kochiyama's March 1965 notes describing an unnamed witness who had sighted Ray Wood rushing out of the Audubon before being taken into police custody. Other than Kochiyama's secondhand account, however, no other contemporary source has emerged to tie Wood to the scene. Kochiyama's own memoirs make no mention of him either. The question of whether Wood would have risked walking into Malcolm's Audubon rally just five days after he had been outed in the national press as an undercover cop remains a matter of conjecture.[14]

But Roberts's presence at the killing could not be denied. "Isn't it a fact that you helped murder Malcolm X?" attorney Gerald Lefcourt asked Roberts without warning in the midst of the Panthers' trial, drawing cheers from Shakur. Roberts denied any involvement in the assassination, expressing a convincing sorrow for the leader's passing, though without stating whether other law enforcement may have been involved. In a cross-examination that stretched into several days, Roberts revealed more about a police intelligence unit's work against Black activists than had ever been publicly shared anywhere in the country.

In the process, Roberts expressed an indifference toward his superiors at BOSS that bordered on disloyalty. He had deceived the Panthers, and he was now testifying that they had been poised to carry out violent acts. But Roberts also confirmed that he and his fellow Panthers had good reason to fear being attacked by the police. This was a risk the department ran in sending agents under deep cover—to remain protected, Roberts had sparing contact with just two or three superiors on the force. Having spent nearly half a decade immersed in Black activist circles, Roberts had become socialized to reject the legitimacy of the police. Roberts, journalist Murray Kempton observed, "indicated a prejudice against his commanders that had endured intact through most of the years he had served them." Though he was never truly a Panther, Roberts's testimony raised serious questions about whether he still fully identified as a police officer after masquerading as a radical for almost five years.[15]

On May 12, 1971, a jury acquitted all thirteen Panther defendants after eight months of trial, rejecting prosecutors' argument that the bull sessions intercepted by BOSS had amounted to an actionable conspiracy plot. It was a rare rebuttal to the dozens of prosecutions brought against Panthers across the United States that resulted in quick convictions and long prison sentences. And though the verdict marked the end of an ordeal that had sidelined more than a dozen Black activists for two years, it signaled the beginning of another struggle that would stretch on for decades.

———

Just six days after the Panther acquittal, a coalition of New York activists prompted by the trial's disclosures filed suit against the NYPD. High-ranking officials including police commissioner Patrick Murphy and Mayor John Lindsay were named as defendants, as was the Special Services Division (SSD), the secretive intelligence unit that had replaced BOSS. The plaintiffs sued under section 1983 of the federal code, claiming that authorities had deprived them of rights enumerated in no fewer than seven amendments of the Constitution. They brought the suit not only on their own behalf but as a class action representing all New York City residents "who object to governmental policies or social conditions or who hold and express beliefs and ideas which conflict with the ideas and beliefs currently dominant in the United States." As a result, they had endured at the hands of the NYPD "infiltration, physical and verbal coercion, photographic, electronic and physical surveillance, provocation of violence, recruitment to act as police informers and dossier collection by defendants and their agents." That class, complainants alleged, comprised a whopping one hundred thousand New Yorkers.[16]

Many of the plaintiffs in *Handschu v. Special Services Division* had ties to the civil rights movement. Abbie Hoffman had organized with CORE and SNCC years before he was charged with instigating riots at the 1968 Democratic National Convention in the Chicago Seven case. Another plaintiff, Ralph DiGia, had worked for more than a decade with Bayard Rustin when the two were on the staff of the War Resisters League, an organization that collaborated closely with civil rights groups such as CORE, which its members had helped found in the early 1940s. Three of the *Handschu* plaintiffs were New York Panthers acquitted the week before; their chapter's first office had operated out of SNCC's headquarters, and one of them, Curtis Powell, had worked briefly with the organization. Additional plaintiffs were affiliated with the Gay Liberation Front and a group of leftist tech workers called Computer People for Peace, as well as the first person named in the suit, Barbara Handschu, a twenty-eight-year-old attorney and National Lawyers Guild member whose clients included the Young Lords.[17]

At the heart of the *Handschu* complaint was the SSD's extensive surveillance files. Though the testimony of police spies had captured the biggest headlines in the Panther trial, the activists suing the NYPD were more interested in reports police had submitted into evidence describing indicted individuals as "carded." The plaintiffs alleged that the term referred to an elaborate indexing system of surveillance records weaponized by intelligence officers against activists to "damage their academic, occupational and professional lives" and to "demoralize and fragment organizations."[18]

The overall effect was to chill the plaintiffs' exercise of free speech, a violation of First Amendment rights as reaffirmed by the U.S. Supreme Court in a series of recent decisions. Most prominent among these was the 1965 case *Dombrowski v. Pfister*, in which the justices had ruled against New Orleans police and Louisiana authorities for a raid in which they seized the records of the Southern Conference Educational Fund, a radical civil rights organization closely allied with SNCC. In suing the NYPD, the *Handschu* litigants were asking a judge to order the department to deliver all its political surveillance files into the court's custody so that their attorneys could inspect them. Not only that, but they wanted the court to enjoin the NYPD from ever collecting these types of materials on activists and to bar its officers from infiltrating their organizations. These were no small demands. The plaintiffs' attorneys—all of whom were National Lawyers Guild members—were seeking to pierce the hitherto impervious wall of secrecy erected by New York's political police dating back to the founding of the Anarchist Squad in 1904.

Even some within the NYPD began to voice misgivings about the department's surveillance apparatus. Weeks after the *Handschu* plaintiffs filed suit against the NYPD, Inspector Anthony Bouza shared with a conference on law enforcement technology his concerns that the ever-increasing collection of information in the computer age meant "that we might be a great deal closer to 1984 than the 13 years on the calendar." Bouza would have known. As a lieutenant in BOSS he had enjoyed a front-row seat to Ray Wood and Gene Roberts's exploits and had even authored a thesis on the intelligence unit for his master's of public administration degree from City College in 1968.[19]

Then, in June, the National Council of Police Societies went even further in disavowing political surveillance. Representing an estimated 25,000 Black police officers, the group had emerged in recent years as a leading critic of policing from within the profession. Three hundred officers from nearly twenty cities passed a resolution at the group's annual meeting in Philadelphia against any Black officer who "accepts assignment in the Black community as an undercover officer dealing with investigation of politically oriented cases unless a violation of existing law occurs." NYPD Guardian Association president Howard Sheffey declared that he was now "advising my Black officers to inform people that they are assigned to inform on that 'I'm a police officer assigned to inform on you.'"[20]

This was nothing less than a total repudiation of the infiltration tactic red squads had weaponized against the movement. The National Council of Police Societies was condemning the work Ray Wood, Gene Roberts, Billy Williams, and Marrell McCollough had been assigned. But who was most culpable—the Black officers who went undercover in activist groups or the almost exclusively white men leading intelligence units who ordered Black officers into those assignments? Or were both at fault? And what was the role of police leadership at the very top of their departments?

Keenly interested in that final question, the attorneys for the *Handschu* plaintiffs subpoenaed Commissioner Murphy to give a deposition by the end of 1971. Murphy's responses to fifty-three written questions painted a portrait of a city in crisis that demanded aggressive intervention by intelligence officers. "In the 1960's this squad was confronted with furious exile activities in the city, racial conflicts, protests over the Indo-China war, student unrest on campuses, terrorist bombings, spiraling crime rates, and revolution and urban guerilla warfare by various groups," Murphy contended. Without making any explicit mention of the civil rights movement, the commissioner's oblique reference to "racial conflicts" suggested a deeply cynical view that antiracist demonstrations required the same law enforcement response as terrorism and revolutionary violence. Increased use of undercover operatives by the department was due to a rise in "groups that because of their conduct or rhetoric may pose a threat to life, property, or governmental administration." The commissioner also cited the murder of Martin Luther King as a rationale for BOSS's "surveillance of malcontents." But Murphy admitted no wrongdoing whatsoever by his department.[21]

Indeed, the Special Services Division had no intention of halting or even slowing its work. On May 18, the very day that the *Handschu* group had sued the department, SSD undercover officer Oswald Alvarez filed his inaugural surveillance report in a new assignment to infiltrate activist circles on the Lower East Side. His targets included Robert Collier. Not even a week before Alvarez had launched his investigation, Collier and his codefendants had been acquitted on all charges at the Panther trial.[22]

It may have been pure coincidence that the SSD launched a new spy operation in the same community where many of the *Handschu* plaintiffs lived and organized, on the exact same day they filed their lawsuit and less than a week after the conclusion of a failed prosecution that had embarrassed the NYPD's intelligence unit and exposed its agents. It may have been mere happenstance that this new investigation against one of the Panther defendants was launched on the same day that a trio of Panthers had filed suit against the department. But it would have been a truly extraordinary coincidence.

––––––

Following her acquittal in June 1972, Angela Davis announced that she would embark on an effort to build what she called "a National Defense organization for victims of repression." The first major step toward such a group came in May 1973 with a conference in Chicago that drew heavily from some two hundred Free Angela chapters scattered throughout the country. "Fabricated 'conspiracies' and other frame ups are employed to behead and crush our movements for change," read an appeal by organizers beckoning activists to attend the meeting, adding that "extensive police and army intelligence networks, legalized wiretapping, 'no-knock' laws and other repressive legislation have already eroded our rights." As Davis proclaimed in her keynote address at the founding conference of the National Defense Organization Against Racist and Political Repression, this was to be a group to "protect and defend all of those who are victims of the racism and class bias of police, courts and prisons."[23]

The organization's supporters included many veterans of the civil rights movement. Leading the organizing effort along was Charlene Mitchell, a longtime Communist Party official who had headed the National United Committee to Free Angela Davis. Mitchell had served stints with the NAACP's youth division in the 1950s and later helped organize the Community Alert Patrol whose street teams had monitored the LAPD in the wake of the Watts uprising. A mass rally in Chicago organized by the conference was headlined by Davis, Dolores Huerta of the United Farm Workers, Clyde Bellecourt of the American Indian Movement, and Ralph Abernathy of the SCLC, a group now showing much more interest in organizing against police abuses than it had in the previous decade. The conference's long list of supporters also included Fannie Lou Hamer, former SNCC staffers Julian Bond and John Lewis, and Frederick Kirkpatrick, previously of the Deacons for Defense and Houston SNCC. Workshops at the conference were filled with civil rights organizers who had long fought police abuses and the cruelties of incarceration, including Lee Otis Johnson, who appeared on a "Prisoners and Prisons" panel.

Renamed the National Alliance Against Racist and Political Repression, but known to its members simply as "the Alliance," the organization was the first major national front against political policing since the early Cold War years, when the Civil Rights Congress had defended Black Southerners facing trumped-up criminal charges and presented *We Charge Genocide* to the United Nations. The group's supporters spanned the American left: civil rights veterans, trade unionists, Black nationalists, pacifists, incarcerated individuals, free speech advocates, organizers in the Chicano and American Indian movements, and, most significantly, avowed communists.

Predictably, anticommunists were alarmed to witness this alliance. The House of Representative's Internal Security Committee—the successor to HUAC—scrutinized the Alliance in July 1973 in hearings devoted to "Revolutionary Activities Directed Toward the Administration of Penal or Correctional Systems." Committee investigator and former military intelligence official Richard Norusis testified that he had infiltrated the group's founding conference. Now, just as HUAC witnesses had done at the height of the Red Scare, Norusis regaled committee members with long lists of attendees who had previously been identified as communists, in the hopes of exposing them to reputational peril and alienating the organization's more moderate supporters.[24]

And yet, Norusis's testimony and the Internal Security Committee's attacks appear to have done nothing to slow the Alliance. For years, law enforcement officials had wielded the accusation of communist ties as a cudgel against organizers for racial equality. Just a few years earlier, staff from groups such as the SCLC had kept a careful distance from communists. But now, the SCLC under Abernathy embraced communists as allies against the slow violence of political policing.

The Alliance had emerged from Angela Davis's defense campaign, but now that she was exonerated, building a national movement against repression depended on organizing around cases of lesser-known individuals harmed by police, prisons, and the courts. Along these lines, the organization built a network of sixteen local chapters throughout the country.

It was North Carolina, above all, where the Alliance aimed its sights. At their founding conference, delegates had elected Ben Chavis as one of the group's vice-chairs. A former SCLC organizer, Chavis was one of ten activists—all but one of them Black—who were charged on thin evidence of burning down a grocery store in the aftermath of protests against racist public school policies in the coastal city of Wilmington in 1972. As someone who could testify to his personal experience as a victim of political policing, Chavis succeeded in drawing the group's attention to his home state as "a national pilot project for repression in its most comprehensive form." North Carolina had the "worst anti-labor repression, widespread police violence, the rise of vigilante terrorism, the largest death row in the nation, [and] the worst prison system with proportionally more political prisoners than any other state," the organization alleged in a poster promoting its first national march, scheduled for Raleigh on July 4, 1974.[25]

On Independence Day that year, between four and ten thousand protesters from across the country descended on downtown Raleigh, with the *Chicago Defender* repeating observers' claims "that this was the biggest demonstration in the South since the death of Dr. Martin Luther King, Jr." The procession wound its way past the state's Central Prison, where waving marchers were greeted with cascades of cheers and whistles from the facility. As though they were preparing for mass violence, no fewer than two hundred local police, three hundred state highway patrolmen, and an untold number of State Bureau of Investigation agents patrolled the two-mile parade route, with another one thousand National Guard members garrisoned at the nearby State Fairgrounds.[26]

Davis characterized the protest in her keynote speech as the launch of "a new Popular Front of the political left," a major national

FIGURE 13.2. Ralph Abernathy of the SCLC, Clyde Bellecourt of the American Indian Movement, and Angela Davis at the National Alliance Against Racist and Political Repression's demonstration in Raleigh, North Carolina, on July 4, 1974. NO_7-4-1974_murray001, PhC. *News and Observer* Negative Collection, State Archives of North Carolina, Raleigh. Do not duplicate without expressed permission from the *News and Observer*.

effort "to fulfill the legacy that was left by the civil rights movement of the 1960s." But no one cast the day's events as civil rights work more convincingly than Abernathy. "Pharaohs of this state: open your prison doors and free your prisoners," the SCLC reverend commanded North Carolina authorities (see figure 13.2). As he embraced his "communist brothers and sisters, red brothers and sisters, brown brothers and sisters" gathered on that hot Independence Day, Abernathy made an appeal to leftist unity against police repression that would have been unfathomable coming from a civil rights leader just a few years earlier: "I've come to the march because the same foot of iron that seeks to keep me down as a Black man is seeking to keep us all down, whether we be Christians or Communists."[27]

Photos from the day show a sea of people who came out to see Davis and Abernathy. But as one might expect with any large demonstration, not everyone who came to watch was a supporter. In addition to the many uniformed law enforcement officers on the streets, Raleigh's police chief Robert Goodwin admitted that there were even more present. Officers set up at least a half dozen observation stations atop buildings along the parade route, ostensibly for security purposes—but their vantage points were also ideal for long-distance political surveillance. Plainclothes intelligence officers from two other departments attended the march as well. One was from another city in North Carolina, while an unidentified source told a reporter that a pair of intelligence agents from the Los Angeles Police Department had also come, more than 2,500 miles from their jurisdiction, taking photographs of marchers, including ones they recognized from other assignments. Like so many of his colleagues before him, Goodwin saw no irony in plainclothes police officers surveilling protesters as they peacefully demonstrated against political policing. "Law enforcement people did a very fine job, a beautiful job," Goodwin observed, summing up authorities' handling of the day's activities without a hint of misgiving.[28]

———

Fourteen years since the sit-in movement had exploded across the South, the Alliance had fused the spirit of the civil rights struggle with a newfound coalition of leftists and liberals opposed to the violence of political policing. But most Americans by 1974 considered the civil rights movement a thing of the past. What was just beginning that summer, however, was a brief but powerful national reconsideration of the harm that law enforcement had exerted on the movements of the 1960s. While radicals such as the Media burglars and the *Handschu* plaintiffs had already commenced this process, a national reappraisal of intelligence abuses against activists owed much of its momentum to something that appeared to have nothing to do with the civil rights movement: Watergate.

The two-year saga culminating in Richard Nixon's resignation on August 8, 1974, exposed how the highest office in the land had embraced espionage as a political weapon. Until Watergate, most Americans considered covertly recording conversations with one's coworkers or breaking into a political rival's office to install wiretaps the stuff of spy novels, not presidential politics. Cementing the perception of Watergate as the ultimate act of tradecraft was the fact that all but two of the seven men arrested for burglarizing the Democratic National Committee office had experience working for the CIA.[29]

Mostly forgotten today is the fact that two veterans of the NYPD's Bureau of Special Services were implicated in the cover-up as well. The first, Jack Caulfield, had worked as a BOSS detective for more than a decade before Nixon hired him to run his campaign security team in 1968. Upon Nixon's election, Caulfield hired his old colleague Anthony Ulasewicz, who had supervised Ray Wood and Gene Roberts when he was directing BOSS's undercover operations. Ulasewicz was assigned to launch an intelligence team that reported directly to the White House as it investigated activist leaders and the president's enemies. Following the Watergate break-in Ulasewicz had hundreds of thousands of dollars in hush money delivered to burglars G. Gordon Liddy and Howard Hunt, though he failed to buy off their coconspirator James McCord, who would go on to testify in court (see figure 13.3). Years later, Ulasewicz claimed that if he could have pulled off the burglary by himself, "there would have been no Watergate and Nixon would have finished his presidency." Indeed, if the CIA deserved some of the blame for Watergate, so, too, did BOSS and the various red squads across the country who had weaponized counterintelligence operations against activists for years, in the process producing a blueprint for political espionage embraced by Nixon's administration.[30]

The most significant attempt to investigate the culture of political spying undergirding Watergate was the U.S. Senate Select Committee to Study Governmental Operations with Respect to Intelligence Activities. Chaired by Idaho senator Frank Church, a foreign policy liberal and an early opponent of the American war in Vietnam, the committee launched in January 1975 in response to a raft of government surveillance scandals. In addition to Watergate, revelations emerged in 1974 that the CIA had spied on more than ten thousand antiwar activists on American soil in violation of its charter. From its

FIGURE 13.3. As an NYPD detective, Anthony Ulasewicz directed undercover officers to infiltrate Black activist groups. Later, he worked as a bagman for the Nixon White House and had hundreds of thousands of dollars in hush money delivered to Watergate burglars G. Gordon Liddy and Howard Hunt, as he testified to the U.S. Senate on July 18, 1973. AP Photo.

start, the committee sought to probe the CIA, FBI, Internal Revenue Service, and National Security Agency, in what would end up being the most consequential public investigation of federal surveillance practices in American history.[31]

But Church's official mandate extended beyond federal agencies. The Senate resolution establishing the committee targeted "any persons, acting individually or in combination with others, with respect to any intelligence activity carried out by or on behalf of the Federal Government." In other words, the committee had a clear charge to investigate anyone who worked in conjunction with federal agencies to monitor political activists. Chief among those collaborators were local police departments and their intelligence units.[32]

And yet, in what was perhaps its most unfortunate decision, the Church Committee passed on probing police departments and their red squads. Though its rationale was not entirely clear, the committee had come under tremendous pressure from defenders of the CIA and FBI—many of them Republicans—to limit the time and scope of its work. Church's investigators were denied access to countless witnesses and documents, and they struggled to investigate all that they had hoped to. Not only that, but Church may well have seen a focus on local police as less likely to ensure national media coverage; the senator was nothing if not press hungry.

The committee did not believe that the country's roughly 4,700 police intelligence officers merited attention, even though their numbers dwarfed the barely three thousand FBI agents dedicated to intelligence. In one particularly egregious misstep, Black committee staffer Arthur Jefferson was steered away from completing an investigation he started on Chicago police who had collaborated with FBI informants to monitor and kill Black Panther Fred Hampton in December 1969. Years later, former committee staffers maintained that they never understood why the probe was discontinued, but they suspected that Jefferson had been blocked by superiors from completing it.[33]

And still, it is undeniable that the Church Committee secured a major victory by drawing the public's attention to the flagrant abuses of the FBI and the CIA against left-wing movements. Much of what we know about J. Edgar Hoover's vendetta against Martin Luther King and about COINTELPRO, for example, stems from the work of Church's staff. One of the committee's most enduring legacies was to document the federal targeting of activists in the Black freedom and antiwar movements on the public record. These disclosures might otherwise have remained hidden.

But as the committee framed surveillance abuses as a federal problem, it drew Americans' attention away from the misdeeds of local police intelligence units. Additional actions by Congress in the immediate aftermath of Church's committee had a similar effect. The Federal Intelligence Surveillance Act of 1978 created a court designed to oversee any federal efforts to surveil foreign individuals on U.S. soil, but it said nothing about local police surveillance. That same year, the House of Representatives Select Committee on Assassinations completed a lengthy investigation of the murders of both

Martin Luther King and John Kennedy. Among their many unsettling findings was that Memphis officer Marrell McCollough had been at the Lorraine Motel kneeling by King's side as he lay dying. McCollough, who had since gone to work for the CIA, grudgingly acceded to a request to testify at hearings. The FBI also shared with investigators their extensive records documenting his frequent interactions with the Bureau in the weeks before and after King was killed. The committee found that while McCollough's undercover work was disturbing, it fell short of indicating police or FBI complicity in the leader's death. But like Church's investigation, the Assassinations Committee had missed a golden opportunity to probe a larger question: Why would Memphis police—or any other department—have ordered officers to assume fake identities to infiltrate and spy on civil rights organizations? That question, as it turned out, would be left primarily to activists themselves to answer through continued organizing in the 1970s and early 1980s.

14

The Unremembering

On September 10, 1976, Memphis mayor Wyeth Chandler called a meeting with the city's police chief and its head of domestic intelligence. The men had a political firestorm on their hands. Antiwar activist Rick Carter had requested that police provide him a copy of his surveillance file after a former roommate admitted that he had worked as an undercover officer assigned to spy on Carter when they lived together. After stonewalling the repeated requests for weeks, Memphis police informed Carter that they had destroyed the records.

The day before Chandler met with police, Carter's failed attempt to obtain the files was front-page news in local papers. "Any group that is out protesting and marching—you always need to check it out to see if anything radical is going on," the mayor insisted in the face of the revelations. One day later, the mayor had changed his tune. Now he was ordering police officials to disband Memphis's intelligence unit and to burn its surveillance files. Within hours, local American Civil Liberties Union attorneys obtained a federal court order protecting the files until a judge could review them. Ten minutes after the injunction was issued, an ACLU lawyer rushed to the mayor's office to deliver the order—but he was too late. Police had burned eighty trash bags of surveillance files dating back to 1965 in the less than five-hour window between the mayor's directive and the injunction. Chandler claimed that he had ordered the files destroyed to satisfy activists, remarking that he had gotten the idea by "listening to the so-called liberal establishment that they objected to having such files in the possession of police."[1]

Though the Memphis police chief later admitted that they had burned the files to preempt the injunction, that may not have been their only motive. Four days prior to the mayor's order, nationally syndicated columnist Jack Anderson had reported that Coretta Scott King and the Congressional Black Caucus were lobbying legislators to investigate the April 1968 murder of King's husband. At that point it had not yet been publicly disclosed that Memphis intelligence officer Marrell McCollough had spied on Martin Luther King and penetrated the civil rights leader's inner circle. By the time that the House of Representatives announced the Select Committee on Assassinations on September 13, any records in the eighty trash bags related to their surveillance of King, the SCLC, and the Memphis sanitation workers strike were long gone. Two months later, a congressional investigator accused Memphis police of destroying documents relevant to the inquiry.[2]

Memphis police were far from the only department to dispose of surveillance records in these years. In February 1973, NYPD commissioner Patrick Murphy—a named defendant in the *Handschu* federal suit—held a press conference at police headquarters to announce that the department's red squad had taken "self-corrective measures" and trashed files containing the names of one million individuals and organizations since 1970, roughly 80 percent of the unit's records. Murphy noted that the purge had been informed by a four-day course on handling political intelligence records offered by the Central Intelligence Agency, a training completed by a dozen city police officers the previous September but only revealed months later by Congressman Ed Koch, who denounced it as a violation of federal law barring the CIA from performing law enforcement duties on American soil.[3]

The following year, in November 1974, local organizers aligned with the National Alliance Against Racist and Political Repression in Chicago calling themselves the Alliance to End Repression developed plans to sue their city's police intelligence unit. Before they could file suit, an undercover intelligence officer embedded in the Alliance warned his superiors of the organization's intentions, in turn prompting Chicago police to destroy files on more than one hundred thousand individuals and 1,300 organizations. In the wake of a fire started in a filing cabinet in police headquarters, a federal judge ordered a halt to the destruction of all Chicago police records for the duration of the case.[4]

And in Los Angeles, Mayor Tom Bradley—a pioneering Black LAPD officer before he entered politics—announced the destruction of 1.9 million intelligence records in April 1975. The purge accompanied the release of a new set of guidelines prohibiting Los Angeles police from monitoring individuals on account of their race, nationality, sexual orientation, or political activity. "This enlightened approach demonstrates that through a spirit of cooperation between agencies of government we can rebuild the public trust in our institutions which is so vitally needed in today's society," Bradley proclaimed. Never mind that the destroyed files, in the words of one LAPD official, covered some 55,000 individuals "extending from the Wobblies of the 20s to the labor agitators of the 30s, the interned Nisei of the 40s, the alleged subversives of the 50s and some anti-war demonstrators of the 60s." Los Angeles police had destroyed an irreplaceable archive of left-wing political activity in Southern California—and almost certainly documentation of untold civil rights violations by the LAPD, too.[5]

Police officials in each of these cities insisted that they were performing a public service by destroying millions of surveillance records that happened to be the subject of civil litigation. They did so amid an ongoing reappraisal by Americans of intelligence agencies. Although the FBI and CIA had long been revered as guardians of the public order and national security, by the middle of the 1970s a large portion of Americans had come to view them as corrupt and invasive.[6]

But while the misdeeds of federal intelligence agencies captured headlines, local political police attracted far less scrutiny, even as activists targeted them for reform. Without the glare of sustained national media, they had the freedom to play a longer game than their colleagues in the FBI and CIA. As they began to grasp that their actions against the civil rights movement would not age well, local law enforcement and their allies perpetrated a far-reaching erasure of history. Unlike the reckoning that federal intelligence agencies were forced to endure, police pulled off what we can call an act of great unremembering.

———

The most meaningful investigations of political policing came not from the federal government but from the activists who sued red squads. As they launched numerous lawsuits against urban police departments, organizers built a national antisurveillance network to trade information and tactics. Chicago became the unofficial headquarters of the movement, as litigation against political policing moved more quickly there than anywhere else. The Alliance to End Repression and other local activists organized conferences with names like the National Conference on Litigation Against Secret Police Spying and Harassment in 1976 and the National Conference on Government Spying in 1977. Members of the ACLU, National Lawyers Guild, the National Conference of Black Lawyers, and the American Friends Service Committee provided much of the organizational backbone for these efforts.

There were victories, to be sure. One of the first came in March 1975, when the historian Hayden White—represented by the veteran ACLU police critic A. L. Wirin—won a California State Supreme Court case against Los Angeles police for sending undercover agents onto the University of California, Los Angeles, campus to spy on him and other politically engaged students and faculty. The court ruled that the practice violated the state's privacy laws. The LAPD announced its destruction of nearly two million surveillance records the next month. Another milestone came in April 1981, when a federal judge in Chicago ruled in favor of the Alliance to End Repression. The decision placed the strictest controls on political spying in the country, abolishing Chicago's red squad and banning city police from collecting intelligence without concrete evidence of imminent criminal activity. And in 1985, the *Handschu* plaintiffs secured a settlement against the NYPD fourteen years after they had filed suit. As in Chicago, the case produced a requirement that the New York police demonstrate evidence of criminal misconduct—and not political dissent—to conduct surveillance.[7]

Veterans of the Black freedom struggle of the 1960s netted significant wins against police repression well into the early 1980s. But in that decade, as federal and state officials accelerated the War on Drugs, the issue all but disappeared from national politics and media. Not only that, but as political intelligence units came under greater scrutiny and were shuttered in many cities, their strategies of surveillance and undercover investigations moved to the center of American policing as they were embraced by narcotics squads and units devoted to combating organized crime. Just when red squads looked like they were a thing of the past, their preferred weaponry had become the wave of the future.[8]

While activists had embraced the civil rights movement's analysis of police violence as systematic injustice, most white Americans resisted the idea that it was anything more than a justifiable law enforcement response to crime. And when activists did zero in on cases of police violence, they struggled to garner national attention and in most cases even local sympathy and political momentum. The media's approach to police violence exemplified this white indifference.

Leading newspaper coverage of shootings by officers relegated victims and activists to the sidelines, relying far more often on police and city officials as sources. Only a tiny fraction of stories on police shootings in the *New York Times* and *Los Angeles Times*, for instance, treated them as a part of a larger crisis of state violence against Black people. Instead, the papers reported on police shootings as isolated individual incidents. And that was in the rare instances where newspapers even covered police violence at all. In 1991, the *New York Times* reported on only one of the 111 times the NYPD shot civilians that year, and in the rest of the early 1990s the paper covered just 5 percent of police shootings in the city.[9]

The transformative political and legal change that civil rights activists had demanded from police remained elusive. The 1980s, 1990s, and early 2000s witnessed scattered and brief individual campaigns focused on single cases of beatings or killings by police, especially in the country's largest cities, where sizable communities of left-wing activists brought horrific incidents of police violence into the national spotlight from time to time. In October 1984, a team of six NYPD officers on an eviction raid shot and killed Eleanor Bumpurs, a sixty-seven-year-old Black woman with a history of mental illness. The Bronx woman's death sparked protests in New York and captured national headlines. In an editorial syndicated in Black newspapers, SNCC veteran Charlie Cobb blamed the Reagan administration for "the kind of repressive climate which gives birth to such racist murders," declaring that Bumpurs's killing signaled the "need to strengthen the organization of our communities against these racist attacks." Within months, however, the political momentum generated by the tragedy had slowed. When the Bronx district attorney indicted the officer who twice shot the unclothed Bumpurs with a shotgun, five thousand members of the Patrolmen's Benevolent Association marched against him. Two years later, in 1987, the indicted officer was acquitted, and U.S. Attorney Rudy Guiliani declined activists' calls to launch a federal civil rights investigation of Bumpurs's death.[10]

In March 1991, Rodney King's name became the rallying cry for protests across the country, following the release of video footage of his brutal beating by the LAPD. When the four Los Angeles officers charged with assaulting him were acquitted a year later, on April 29, 1992, the outrage was immediate. In Los Angeles, the largest uprising in U.S. history broke out within minutes of the decision. In its wake, long-standing groups in the city organized against police violence, including the Coalition Against Police Abuse and the Labor/Community Strategy Center, the second of which was established by a former New York CORE staffer and later counted Patrisse Cullors as a member years before she cofounded Black Lives Matter. Then, in 1999, the fatal shooting by NYPD officers of the unarmed Guinean immigrant Amadou Diallo ignited days of protests in New York and became a topic of debate in the following year's presidential election and the U.S. senate race in New York.[11]

While each of these cases of police violence made headlines across the country, none sparked a durable national movement. That is not to say that activists were ignoring police violence by the late 1990s. In California, the group Critical Resistance emerged to confront the prison industrial complex and pinpointed policing's central role in expanding incarceration. In Chicago, the Black Radical Congress identified police violence as a primary concern of their "freedom agenda" in the late 1990s, while the nation's most prominent movement against police torture took shape at the same time in the city. But for all this essential work, nothing approached the groundswell of activism against police violence of the civil rights and Black Power struggles of the 1960s until the emergence of Black Lives Matter in 2013.[12]

The limited visibility of these movements was due in no small part to how the media misreported police violence. As legal scholar Franklin Zimring has noted, police kill roughly one thousand people in the United States every year, but each police killing "begins with a primarily local identity as a news story rather than being seen as part of a larger national or state phenomenon." Until protests in Ferguson, Missouri, against the killing of Michael Brown captured the nation's attention in 2014, media coverage in the early twenty-first century focused on incidents of police violence as isolated local occurrences, which in turn helped forestall the emergence of a national movement against police violence. But even after the emergence of BLM, in rare instances where commentators and public officials have admitted that police violence is due to more than a few bad apples, they might conceive of a particularly brutal police department as a rotten bushel. A contaminated orchard, however, might be a more fitting symbol of this national crisis.[13]

———

At the same time, Americans have fallen short in remembering the full power and promise of the civil rights movement in the twenty-first century, as politicians and commentators—especially those on the right—substitute nostalgia and color-blind nostrums for honest appraisal of the organized struggle to dismantle white supremacy. Misappropriation of the movement's legacy is a recurring problem, but at least one that is widely recognized by professional historians. The sheer volume and growing sophistication of new public historical work on the movement in the last decade and a half—from signage, to documentaries, to exhibits and new museums—has helped to stem such creeping amnesia.[14]

But even as Americans have made strides in how they remember and commemorate the civil rights struggle, police have succeeded in shifting attention away from their sophisticated repression of the movement. Not only have they concealed their record of political policing and slow violence, but they have done their utmost to obscure how activists in SNCC and CORE put the fight against police repression at the heart of the civil rights movement's work.

A chief example of this revisionist approach can be seen in the National Law Enforcement Museum (NLEM) in Washington, D.C. Authorized by Congress and opened in 2018, the NLEM is overseen by a board filled with representatives from police unions and advocacy organizations. Although it is privately funded, its congressional mandate and location mere blocks from the National Mall bestow it with an unofficial status as our country's national museum of policing.

Dishonesty pervades the NLEM's narration of the police role in the civil rights movement. "As Americans took to the streets to voice their opinions and demand their rights, and police sought to maintain order and enforce the law, some clashes turned violent," an exhibit on the 1960s tells us, avoiding the question of whether police attacked peaceful protesters. Bull Connor appears as a rogue police chief who was "widely condemned by law enforcement" for attacking protesters with dogs and fire hoses, a dubious claim considering how many law enforcement officials refused to speak out against the Birmingham police. As the museum reassures us, "Thankfully, with the 1970s came efforts to repair the rift, as many police departments renewed their commitment to diversity and community engagement." As far as the National Law Enforcement Museum is concerned, police may have retaliated against protesters in the past—but not anymore.[15]

Leading college textbooks reveal how police attempt to sanitize their relationship to the civil rights movement as well. One such title is *An Introduction to Policing*, a widely assigned text published by Cengage currently in its ninth edition. The book's primary author, John Dempsey, completed a twenty-four-year career with NYPD that began in 1964, the same year that Ray Wood infiltrated CORE and other civil rights groups in New York. In his textbook's second edition, published in 1999, Dempsey wrote of the "adversaries on the street" whom he encountered early in his career as he "policed antiwar marches, civil rights demonstrations, and urban riots." Like the National Law Enforcement Museum, Dempsey and his coauthors minimize and conceal the active role police played in sabotaging the movement. A recurring strategy is to collapse any difference between peaceful protest and urban rebellions, describing how "the struggle for racial equality reached its peak, accompanied by marches, demonstrations, and riots that burned down whole neighborhoods in U.S. urban centers" in the 1960s.

Another strategy is to cast police as unwitting political victims forced to carry out the orders of corrupt officials against protesters. "The police were caught between those fighting for their civil rights and the government officials (the employers of the police) who wanted to maintain the status quo, between demonstrating students and college and city administrators," Dempsey and his coauthors tell readers. "The police received much criticism during these years. Some of it was deserved, but much of it was for circumstances beyond their control." Police, in other words, were not active combatants against the civil rights movement but, rather, mere spectators conscripted into action by paymasters who did not have their backs. Such far-fetched claims of political neutrality are contradicted by the long record of police attacks on civil rights activists.

In clear acts of projection, Dempsey's textbook and the NLEM decry the surveillance and invasions of privacy perpetrated by federal law enforcement against activists. Just as Dempsey condemns the "ugly political underside to Hoover's expanded role for the FBI," the museum disavows COINTELPRO as "inconsistent with American principles." Both omit the fact that countless police departments across the country not only committed similar abuses but assisted with the Bureau's counterintelligence efforts. Lest anyone doubt the NLEM's embrace of political policing, the museum's "covert ops" exhibit features a cheery graphic titled "How to Set Up a Wire Tap," while its research center is endowed by the J. Edgar Hoover Foundation and named for the FBI director.

To their credit, Dempsey and his coauthors admit at least one truth about this history in their most recent edition published in 2019. "Although the civil rights movement was necessary in the evolution of our nation," they concede, "the use of the police by government officials to thwart the movement left a wound in community relations that still has not healed." For once, police and their backers have admitted their profession's sabotage of the movement.[16]

———

When U.S. congressman and former SNCC chairperson John Lewis died on July 17, 2020, Americans commemorated his passing with an outpouring of celebrations of his life and the civil rights movement. That summer, as the COVID pandemic raged, an estimated 15 to 26 million people protested for Black lives across the United States in the wake of the killings of George Floyd in Minneapolis and Breonna Taylor in Louisville and too many other acts of police violence to name. It would prove to be the largest wave of sustained political protest in American history, drawing frequent comparisons with the civil rights struggle of the 1960s.[17]

Just one day after completing a round of chemotherapy, an emaciated Lewis made his last public appearance with a visit to the massive Black Lives Matter mural painted directly on Sixteenth Street in Washington, D.C., on June 7. Days earlier, crowds of protesters had been tear-gassed there by U.S. Park Police and Secret Service so that they could clear a path for Donald Trump to display an upside-down Bible at a press conference in front of St. John's Episcopal Church.[18]

Six weeks later, Lewis's passing prompted countless commentators to place Lewis's experience as a victim of police violence at the center of his story. Television coverage of his death almost invariably featured footage of law enforcement officers assaulting Lewis and his fellow protesters in Selma at the foot of the Edmund Pettus Bridge. Indeed, the very first sentence of the *New York Times* obituary identified him as "a son of sharecroppers and an apostle of nonviolence who was bloodied at Selma and across the Jim Crow South in the historic struggle for racial equality." Likewise, the opening line of the *Washington Post* obituary described Lewis as "a civil rights leader who preached nonviolence while enduring beatings and jailings during seminal front-line confrontations of the 1960s."[19]

The implication was that suffering through police violence—and not resisting it—defined Lewis and the movement. In his time as SNCC chairman, Lewis was among the movement's most prominent critics of police violence. Curiously, when he passed almost no one remembered him that way. Though recollections of Lewis made liberal reference to ongoing Black Lives Matter protests, their message was clear: the departed civil rights leader had passed the torch to a new generation of activists who, unlike those in the 1960s, could finally confront that brutality head-on.

Fixated on the televised assault at Selma, Lewis's obituaries overlooked the full array of slow violence Lewis had endured at the hands of police. Although some obituaries referenced the white mobs that set upon the Freedom Riders in Montgomery with baseball bats and metal pipes, knocking Lewis unconscious, virtually none mentioned that the attacks had been coordinated by members of the Montgomery police or that a federal court had ruled that officers had "acted in concert with the Klan groups herein named to commit acts of violence" (see figure 14.1). Lewis's obituaries also failed to note the pervasive surveillance that SNCC endured during his chairmanship—not only by the FBI but also by local police in New York, Philadelphia, Chicago, and Danville, Virginia. Indeed, the biggest speech of Lewis's life, at the March on Washington, was surveilled by multiple police departments.[20]

FIGURE 14.1. Flanked by Martin Luther King Jr., Ralph Abernathy, and James Farmer, twenty-one-year-old Freedom Rider John Lewis spoke at a press conference on the brutal assault he sustained outside the bus station in Montgomery, Alabama, in May 1961, an attack that a federal judge later faulted local police for planning with Klan members. AP Photo.

Some obituaries noted that movement leaders had forced Lewis to censor his own speech at the March because they feared that his criticisms of Kennedy's civil rights bill threatened the legislation's passage. But obituaries mentioned neither that the SNCC chairman's address repeatedly denounced police violence—from physical brutality to retaliatory prosecutions—nor that those charges elicited loud cheers from the crowd of some 250,000 attendees. Lewis had brought his message condemning police violence to the largest audience that had ever gathered as part of the movement.[21]

Indeed, it was during Lewis's chairmanship that SNCC made combating state-sponsored violence a focal point of its work. Chief among these efforts was SNCC's campaign against police in Americus, Georgia, in 1963, where police chief Ross Chambliss jailed a quartet of SNCC and CORE organizers on felony insurrection charges carrying the death penalty. "Legal terror is an old problem in the Black Belt communities of southwest Georgia," Lewis remarked at a press conference publicizing affidavits from Americus residents who had been beaten by police and crammed with as many as thirty-four other protesters into tiny jail cells without beds. "The police state atmosphere that prevails in Americus today makes that city a little South Africa for Negroes," Lewis protested further in a telegram to the U.S. Justice Department that August. Lewis did not reserve his criticisms for Southern police, either. "The use of police and military power to try to solve problems that Negroes are confronted with in the ghettoes and slums of our cities is an unspeakable mistake," he warned in August 1965 as the LAPD and National Guard imposed martial law on Black Angelenos during the Watts uprising.[22]

By ignoring this work, the coverage of Lewis's life perpetuated two dangerous myths: one, that civil rights organizers with saintlike perseverance suffered through police violence without fighting back and, two, that physical attacks such as those at Selma were the dominant form of violence perpetuated by police against the movement. In fact, many police understood the political risks of naked physical brutality and attacked the movement in ways more acceptable to the political mainstream. Retaliatory prosecutions, invasive surveillance, and covert collaborations with vigilante mobs were all more effective means of undermining the movement while minimizing political damage to police.

The public's virtual amnesia about the slow violence by police that SNCC both experienced and resisted stands in marked contrast to the widespread fascination with the FBI's actions against Martin Luther King. If historians in recent years have succeeded in dislodging King as the overwhelming focus of movement histories, we have failed to decenter him in our accounts of repression of the Black freedom struggle. Again and again, that story is told as a battle between two men, King and J. Edgar Hoover. In these stories, Hoover is the ultimate law enforcement villain against whom all others are measured. Meanwhile, Lewis and his comrades are remembered as victims who endured police brutality—not organizers in a broader fight against state repression.

———

Americans' conception of police violence against antiracist movements remains impoverished. We pay close attention when citizens are physically assaulted or even murdered by police on camera. But viral footage of the most gruesome acts of police violence may inadvertently reinforce the "bad apples" framing that emphasizes individual acts of police wrongdoing while sidestepping the larger problem of systematic culpability. As we are transfixed by the spectacle of physical violence by police, especially against Black people, we lose sight of less conspicuous but no less brutal forms of harm carried out by police and the carceral system. Ultimately, the slow violence of police may prove the most destructive to organized movements.

In 2020, Americans—and the world—were horrified by the video of George Floyd's murder by Minneapolis police officer Derek Chauvin. Similarly, the video of Ahmaud Arbery's murder by white vigilantes captivated the nation. In both cases, it is doubtful that the murderers would have faced any consequences had it not been for the videos that were captured. The footage of Floyd's murder galvanized millions to protest. And yet, there is a growing body of criticism that the viral distribution of these videos fuels a spectacle of death that veers into anti-Black exploitation—not entirely unlike the commercial marketplace for images of lynching that flourished in the Jim Crow era.[23]

Physical attacks against antiracist activists captured on video have triggered outrage and, in a few instances, consequences for individual law enforcement officers. Acts of slow violence perpetuated against organizers garner far less attention and result in far fewer consequences for police. Along these lines, the retaliatory filing of felony charges against those who protest police has seen a marked resurgence. Since 2017, twenty-one different states have criminalized various aspects of peaceful protest. Florida and North Carolina now consider some nonviolent blocking of streets as rioting, and South Dakota and Arkansas have increased civil liability for protesters and organizers. Oklahoma has gone as far as enacting anti-racketeering statutes against acts of so-called unlawful assembly.[24]

The expansion of political organizers' civil liability is especially troubling. In 2016, the prominent Black Lives Matter activist DeRay Mckesson was named as a defendant in a federal lawsuit filed by an unnamed Louisiana police officer. The officer alleges that Mckesson is responsible for injuries sustained at a protest organized by Mckesson, even though the activist had no hand whatsoever in the injuries. The case has wound through the legal system for nearly a decade and is still unresolved at the time of this writing. Whatever the ultimate outcome, the extended litigation makes it clear that federal courts remain divided on whether the First Amendment protects protest organizers against liability when those attending their protests violate the law—even in cases when organizers have not directed or intended the illegal acts.[25]

Further, in summer 2020 police weaponized unfounded felony charges to retaliate against Black Lives Matter organizers in cities across the country. In Nutley, New Jersey, a protester who posted a photo of a masked officer to Twitter and asked his followers for identifying information was charged with fourth-degree cyber harassment, a felony with a maximum of eighteen months in prison. In Miami, a BLM protester who removed a Trump flag from a car in a pro-police parade was slapped with robbery charges that carried up to fifteen years in prison. And in New York City, a protester who yelled with a megaphone into the ear of an NYPD officer later found himself surrounded by two dozen officers and a police helicopter outside his apartment, though they had no warrant for his arrest. When he surrendered himself at a police station, he was arrested on second-degree felony assault charges with a maximum penalty of seven years in prison.[26]

Ultimately, the felony charges in all three cases were dropped. But considerable harm was done—slow violence that took a tremendous toll on the finances, time, and emotional well-being of those arrested. Police achieved their goal of sabotaging those who would dare protest them, making it clear that they might pay an extraordinary price for their political activities.

The possibility of even worse consequences faces activists working to halt the massive $109 million training facility for Atlanta police known as Cop City. At the time of this writing, more than sixty individuals face state racketeering charges carrying maximum sentences of two decades in prison for their work with the Defend the Atlanta Forest movement, while more than forty more face domestic terrorism charges with a penalty of up to thirty-five years in prison for alleged minor property crimes. Another three organizers operating a bail fund for those arrested in this campaign were charged in March 2023 with money laundering, felonies carrying a combined twenty-five-year prison sentence for each defendant. State officials only dropped the laundering charges in September 2024 after a judge expressed marked skepticism of the indictments.[27]

At the same time, police surveillance of antiracist movements continues apace. In fall 2020, Los Angeles police hired a Polish company to track and collect millions of messages from Twitter users, thousands of which pertained to BLM and other organizers against police violence. In Atlanta, Stop Cop City organizers have caught undercover police attempting to infiltrate their encampments and impersonate protesters. And in Minneapolis, a consortium of local law enforcement agencies working with federal assistance created Operation Safety Net, a response to protests during and after the

2021 murder trial of Derek Chauvin, which included an ambitious surveillance component utilizing social media gathering and cell site simulators for capturing phone messages.[28]

Looking back, the police war on the civil rights movement of the 1960s presaged our current era of "big data surveillance" and "big data policing." On the one hand, it might seem as though we have entered uncharted territory, with the emergence of facial recognition software and camera drones that retail for less than $25. Civil rights activists of the 1960s could not have imagined that six decades later, police departments would monitor protesters against police killings of Black citizens with remotely piloted aircraft. "This is a local police department that increasingly acts like a national intelligence agency," Albert Fox Cahn of the Surveillance Technology Oversight Project said of the New York Police Department in 2024. "The idea that you can have a drone hovering over a protest, collecting the identities of every person there, without any oversight, without any protections? That's unbelievably chilling." And yet, police intelligence units in cities such as New York, Los Angeles, and Chicago have been acting like national intelligence agencies for decades. The red squads of the 1960s that stuffed file cabinets with millions of reports on their surveillance of protest movements were the original big data police, long before our current digital era.[29]

———

Whether one thinks that policing can still be reformed in America—or that nothing short of full defunding or abolition can bring meaningful change—one thing is undeniable: true justice cannot be achieved without police admitting their almost two centuries of violence against Black people and their left-wing political allies. As Americans cling to the idea that the civil rights movement set the country on the path toward democracy, achieving racial justice is impossible without exposing the historical truth of police attacks on antiracist activists.[30]

We cannot refrain from dredging up the history of police violence against the civil rights movement out of concern for so-called good cops. If acknowledging that violence exacerbates the already low levels of trust in the police—especially in Black communities and communities of color—so be it. The telling of these truths should not be avoided because police claim that they are busy at work repairing relations with these communities today. That is the excuse most city officials and their police departments have embraced as they work so hard to conceal this history. Why bring up the dark past when we are building a brighter future?[31]

Indeed, very few cities have made any meaningful effort to admit the violence their police committed against the movement. When the backlash against civil rights comes up, most Americans point to the South, and most Southerners point to Alabama and Mississippi. National police groups blame the FBI. It wasn't us, they all say. Sixty years later, no one has anything but kind words for the civil rights struggle.

Birmingham may be the only city in America to have even started the process of acknowledging the violence police did to the movement. Today, on the site where the city's officers brutalized Black protesters in 1963, Kelly Ingram Park is a memorial to the movement, with statues of Martin Luther King Jr. and Fred Shuttlesworth and a quartet of stone monuments dedicated to the four girls killed in the 16th Street Baptist Church bombing. But the park's most powerful memorials may be its most unusual. One is James Drake's *Police Dog Attack* (1993), a pair of sculpted bronze and steel walls positioned some ten feet apart, out of which burst three snarling attack dogs on leashes that extend over a narrow footpath running below (see figure 14.2). The overall effect is that of a terrifying gauntlet through which one can barely pass without brushing against the metal German shepherds.

A second statue in the park, Ronald Scott McDowell's *Dogs* (1995–1996), re-creates the photo of officer Dick Middleton and his canine attacking Walter Gadsden (see figure 14.3). Though McDowell takes considerable artistic liberty by erasing Gadsden's resistance to the assault, his message is no less powerful: when Black people demanded an end to Jim Crow, police terrorized them. The statue makes plain a truth that no other city has so publicly

FIGURE 14.2. James Drake, *Police Dog Attack*, 1993, Kelly Ingram Park, Birmingham, Alabama. Photograph by Joshua Clark Davis.

acknowledged. Granted, these two sculptures do not convey the full breadth of Birmingham authorities' long legacy of slow violence—their surveillance of Black citizens, their collusion with the Klan, and their authoritarian policing of free assembly. But they are none-theless unparalleled in this country as municipal commemorations of police violence against the civil rights movement.[32]

Of course, monuments can only do so much. One form of remem-bering that would do even more to document police violence against the Black freedom movement would be a national truth commis-sion. Such commissions have proliferated in countries transition-ing to democracy in the aftermath of authoritarianism, including South Africa, Chile, and Argentina. They have been less common in the United States. In a sense, the Church Committee approached something of a truth commission, as it sought to expose the FBI and

FIGURE 14.3. Ronald Scott McDowell, *Dogs*, 1995–1996, Kelly Ingram Park, Birmingham, Alabama. LC-DIG-highsm-05100, Prints and Photographs Division, Carol Highsmith Collection, LOC.

CIA's attacks on democracy through its sweeping investigation and public hearings. Police, however, have faced nothing approaching this level of scrutiny.[33]

A truth commission would be a major stride toward Americans admitting a painful reality: our nation's police, as primary antagonists of racial justice movements, have represented one of the foremost barriers to democracy in this country. A rare example of an American inquiry into police attacks on activists is the Greensboro Truth and Reconciliation Commission of 2004 to 2006, a local probe of the Ku Klux Klan killing of Communist Workers Party members in the North Carolina city in November 1979. As the commission found, Greensboro police knowingly allowed an armed Klan caravan to proceed to an antiracist protest, holding back officers from the scene after Klan members had fatally shot activists. Greensboro officers had borrowed a page from the playbook of police who had coordinated the brutal Klan attacks on the Freedom Riders in Montgomery in 1961. Though the full impact of such commissions is still up for debate, numerous survivors of the Greensboro massacre have endorsed their city's truth and reconciliation commission as a powerful exercise in healing and truth-telling.

A national truth commission on police crimes against the civil rights movement could take several forms. The most consequential— though improbable in our current political context—would be a congressional investigation with subpoena powers, a wide-ranging probe like the Church Committee that attracts national media coverage and produces tangible restrictions on law enforcement abuses. A more likely commission would be along the lines of Greensboro, an initiative spearheaded by racial justice organizations but boycotted by public officials. A commission organized by some combination of the Movement for Black Lives, the National Lawyers Guild, the Equal Justice Initiative, and the American Civil Liberties Union would come closer to the truth than one compromised by legislative niceties.[34]

Whatever form such a commission would take, America's police are long overdue for a reckoning on their history of attacks on antiracist movements. Hopefully this book makes a modest contribution toward the telling of that truth. Just as was the case six decades ago, police who attack these movements stand as a major barrier to racial justice in the twenty-first century.

Indeed, the words of SNCC mentor Ella Baker ring as true today as they did in August 1964 in the wake of the murders of James

Chaney, Andrew Goodman, and Michael Schwerner, murders that Mississippi police helped coordinate in a treacherous act of state-sanctioned violence often misremembered as mere Klan killings. Baker, whose organizing work against police violence stretched back to the early 1950s, offered a powerful message at the Mississippi Freedom Democratic Party convention in Jackson just two days after the young men's bodies had been unearthed by the FBI. "Until the killing of a black mother's sons becomes as important as the killing of a white mother's son," Baker urged her audience, "we who believe in freedom cannot rest." Today, more than sixty years later, in a nation where police kill some one thousand people per year—a vastly disproportionate number of them Black—and where police continue to retaliate against antiracist activists with countless acts of slow violence, those of us intent on justice would be wise to abide by Baker's words.[35]

ABBREVIATIONS

Select Archives

APRI	A. Philip Randolph Institute, New York
BPL	Birmingham Public Library, Department of Archives and Manuscripts
HHRC	Houston History Research Center, Houston Public Library
LOC	Library of Congress
MHPP	Michael Hannon Personal Papers
MLK	Martin Luther King, Jr. Center, Atlanta
NARA-A	National Archives and Records Administration, Atlanta
NARA-CLA	National Archives and Records Administration, Center for Legislative Archives
NARA-CP	National Archives and Records Administration, College Park
NARA-FW	National Archives and Records Administration, Fort Worth
NARA-NYC	National Archives and Records Administration, New York City
NYCMA	New York City Municipal Archives
PQHV	ProQuest History Vault
RCPOR	Roper Center for Public Opinion Research, Cornell University

SHC Southern Historical Collection, University Libraries, University of North Carolina at Chapel Hill

UCLA University of California, Los Angeles, Library Special Collections

UW University of Washington Special Collections

WHS Wisconsin Historical Society

WUL Washington University Libraries, Film and Media Archive

Selected Newspapers, Magazines, and Journals

AC *Atlanta Constitution*

ADW *Atlanta Daily World*

BAA *Baltimore Afro-American*

BG *Boston Globe*

BN *Birmingham News*

BP *Black Panther*

BPH *Birmingham Post-Herald*

BS *Baltimore Sun*

CD *Chicago Defender*

DW *Daily Worker*

FT *Forward Times*

HC *Houston Chronicle*

HP *Houston Post*

IT *Irish Times*

JBSB *John Birch Society Bulletin*

LAFP *Los Angeles Free Press*

LAS *Los Angeles Sentinel*

LAT *Los Angeles Times*

MCA *Memphis Commercial Appeal*

MPS *Memphis Press-Scimitar*

NG *National Guardian*

NJG *New Journal and Guide*

NOTP *New Orleans Times-Picayune*

NYAN *New York Amsterdam News*

NYDN *New York Daily News*

NYHT *New York Herald Tribune*

NYT *New York Times*

PC *Police Chief*

PDN *Philadelphia Daily News*

PEB *Philadelphia Evening Bulletin*

PI *Philadelphia Inquirer*

PT *Philadelphia Tribune*

RNO *Raleigh News & Observer*

TO *Texas Observer*

VT *Valley Times*

VV *Village Voice*

WP *Washington Post*

WSJ *Wall Street Journal*

NOTES

Introduction

1. Rob Nixon offers a working definition of this concept in *Slow Violence and the Environmentalism of the Poor* (Cambridge, Mass.: Harvard University Press, 2011), 2. See also Rory Kramer and Brianna Remster, "The Slow Violence of Contemporary Policing," *Annual Review of Criminology* 5 (2022): 43–66; and, on the violence of surveillance, Simone Browne, *Dark Matters: On the Surveillance of Blackness* (Durham, N.C.: Duke University Press, 2015), 9–17.

2. Michael A. Fletcher and Janell Ross, "Attack at Church Evokes Dark Days from Nation's Past," *WP*, June 19, 2015, 1; Robin Abcarian, "What We Learned from a Year of Living Pandemically," *LAT*, March 14, 2021, A19.

3. Frank J. Donner, *Protectors of Privilege: Red Squads and Police Repression in Urban America* (Berkeley: University of California Press, 1992), 7–43; Matthew Guariglia, *Police and the Empire City: Race and the Origins of Modern Policing in New York* (Durham, N.C.: Duke University Press, 2023), 107–134; Charisse Burden-Stelly, *Black Scare/Red Scare: Theorizing Capitalist Racism in the United States* (Chicago: University of Chicago Press, 2023); Sidney L. Harring, *Policing a Class Society: The Experience of American Cities, 1865–1915* (New Brunswick, N.J.: Rutgers University Press, 1983), 101–148; Christian Davenport, *How Social Movements Die: Repression and Demobilization of the Republic of New Africa* (New York: Cambridge University Press, 2015), 61–79. On red squads and student activists, see also Gregg L. Michel, *Spying on Students: The FBI, Red Squads, and Student Activists in the 1960s South* (Baton Rouge: LSU Press, 2024).

For conceptual explorations of the nature of political policing, see Jennifer Earl and Jessica Maves Braithwaite, "Layers of Political Repression: Integrating Research on Social Movement Repression," *Annual Review of Law and Social Science* 18, no. 1 (2022): 227–248; Jennifer Earl, "Political Repression: Iron Fists, Velvet Gloves, and Diffuse Control," *Annual Review of Sociology* 37, no. 1 (2011): 261–284; and Mark Mazower, ed., *The Policing of Politics in the Twentieth Century* (Providence, R.I.: Berghahn Books, 1997).

For the purpose of this work, I've settled on the "civil rights movement" as the best, though imperfect, term for racial justice activists from the 1940s until the late 1960s engaged in the Black freedom struggle, a much longer arc of activism that spans virtually the entirety of U.S. history. This work treats the civil rights movement and Black Power movement as briefly overlapping in the late 1960s, before the latter transcended the former in popularity toward the end of the decade. However, historians have debated for years whether the "long movement" civil rights framework includes Black Power activists or whether civil rights and Black Power represent two distinct movements. See Jacquelyn Dowd Hall, "The Long Civil Rights Movement and the Political Uses of the Past," *Journal of American History* 91, no. 5 (March 2005): 1233–1263; as well as a counterargument offered by Sundiata Keita Cha-Jua and Clarence Lang in "The 'Long Movement' as Vampire: Temporal and Spatial Fallacies in Recent Black Freedom Studies," *Journal of African American History* 92, no. 2 (2007): 265–288.

4. Elizabeth Hinton and DeAnza Cook, "The Mass Criminalization of Black Americans: A Historical Overview," *Annual Review of Criminology* 4, no. 1 (2021): 261–286, offers a valuable overview of the vast literature, as does a more general historiography of policing and inequality provided by Max Felker-Kantor, "To Protect and to Serve: Police, Power, and the Production of Inequality in the United States," *Crime and Justice* 53, no. 1 (2024). A far from exhaustive list of historical works on the long arc of the anti-Black punitive tradition in American policing includes Keeanga-Yamahtta Taylor, *From #BlackLivesMatter to Black Liberation* (Chicago: Haymarket Books, 2016); Elizabeth Hinton, *From the War on Poverty to the War on Crime: The Making of Mass Incarceration in America* (Cambridge, Mass.: Harvard University Press, 2016); Elizabeth Hinton, *America on Fire: The Untold History of Police Violence and Black Rebellion Since the 1960s* (New York: Liveright, 2021); Heather A. Thompson, *Blood in the Water: The Attica Prison Uprising of 1971 and Its Legacy* (New York: Pantheon Books, 2016); Heather A. Thompson, "Why Mass Incarceration Matters: Rethinking Crisis, Decline, and Transformation in Postwar American History," *Journal of American History* 97, no. 3 (2010): 703–734; Khalil Gibran Muhammad, *The Condemnation of Blackness: Race, Crime, and the Making of Modern Urban America* (Cambridge, Mass.: Harvard University Press, 2010); Margaret Burnham, *By Hands Now Known: Jim Crow's Legal Executioners* (New York: Norton, 2022); Simon Balto, *Occupied Territory: Policing Black Chicago from Red Summer to Black Power* (Chapel Hill: University of North Carolina Press, 2019); Stuart Schrader, *Badges Without Borders: How Global Counterinsurgency Transformed American Policing* (Oakland: University of California Press, 2019); Max Felker-Kantor, *Policing Los Angeles: Race, Resistance, and the Rise of the LAPD* (Chapel Hill: University of North Carolina Press, 2018); Dan Berger, *Captive Nation: Black Prison Organizing in the Civil Rights Era* (Chapel Hill: University of North Carolina Press, 2014); Melanie Newport, *This Is My Jail: Local Politics and the Rise of Mass Incarceration* (Philadelphia: University of Pennsylvania Press, 2022); Garrett Felber, *Those Who Know Don't Say: The Nation of Islam, the Black Freedom Movement, and the Carceral State* (Chapel Hill: University of North Carolina Press, 2020); Orisanmi Burton, *Tip of the Spear: Black Radicalism, Prison Repression, and the Long Attica Revolt* (Oakland: University of California Press, 2023); Donna Murch, *Assata Taught Me: State Violence, Racial Capitalism, and the Movement for Black Lives* (Chicago: Haymarket Books, 2022); Kelly Lytle Hernández, *City of Inmates: Conquest, Rebellion, and the Rise of Human Caging in*

Los Angeles, 1771–1965 (Chapel Hill: University of North Carolina Press, 2017); Kali N. Gross, *Colored Amazons: Crime, Violence, and Black Women in the City of Brotherly Love, 1880–1910* (Durham, N.C.: Duke University Press, 2006); Shannon King, *The Politics of Safety: The Black Struggle for Police Accountability in La Guardia's New York* (Chapel Hill: University of North Carolina Press, 2024); Carl Suddler, *Presumed Criminal: Black Youth and the Justice System* (New York: New York University Press, 2019); Jeffrey Adler, *Murder in New Orleans: The Creation of Jim Crow Policing* (Chicago: University of Chicago Press, 2019); Thomas Aiello, ed., *The Routledge History of Police Brutality in America* (New York: Routledge, 2023); Andrew Baer, *Beyond the Usual Beating: The Jon Burge Police Torture Scandal and Social Movements for Police Accountability in Chicago* (Chicago: University of Chicago Press, 2020).

5. On COINTELPRO and political policing by the FBI, see David Cunningham, *There's Something Happening Here: The New Left, the Klan, and FBI Counterintelligence* (Berkeley: University of California Press, 2004); Beverly Gage, *G-Man: J. Edgar Hoover and the Making of the American Century* (New York: Viking, 2022); Kenneth O'Reilly, *Racial Matters: The FBI's Secret File on Black America, 1960–1972* (New York: Free Press, 1989); Daniel S. Chard, *Nixon's War at Home: The FBI, Leftist Guerrillas, and the Origins of Counterterrorism* (Chapel Hill: University of North Carolina Press), 2021; Athan G. Theoharis, *Spying on Americans: Political Surveillance from Hoover to the Huston Plan* (Philadelphia: Temple University Press, 1978); Ward Churchill and Jim Vander Wall, *Agents of Repression: The FBI's Secret Wars Against the Black Panther Party and the American Indian Movement* (Boston: South End Press, 1988).

6. Sarah Brayne, "Big Data Surveillance: The Case of Policing," *American Sociological Review* 82, no. 5 (2017): 977–1008; Andrew Guthrie Ferguson, *The Rise of Big Data Policing: Surveillance, Race, and the Future of Law Enforcement* (New York: New York University Press, 2017); Mark Andrejevic and Kelly Gates, "Big Data Surveillance: Introduction," *Surveillance and Society* 12, no. 2 (2014): 185–196.

7. John Edgar Hoover, *Annual Report* (Washington, D.C.: Federal Bureau of Investigation, 1966), 43; *Surveillance: Who's Watching?* dir. Richard McCutchen (New York: National Educational Television, 1972), https://americanarchive.org /catalog/cpb-aacip_516-5m6251gg0m; Paul Cowan, Nick Egleson, and Nat Hentoff, *State Secrets: Police Surveillance in America* (New York: Holt, Rinehart and Winston, 1974), 16–17, 22.

8. *Intelligence Activities and the Rights of Americans: Book II. Final Report of the Select Committee to Study Governmental Operations with Respect to Intelligence Activities, Senate,* 94th Cong., 2d sess. (Washington, D.C.: Government Printing Office, 1976), 84; David Alan Sklansky, "Not Your Father's Police Department: Making Sense of the New Demographics of Law Enforcement," *Journal of Criminal Law and Criminology* 96, no. 3 (Spring 2006): 1214–1216.

9. William C. Sullivan, with Bill Brown, *The Bureau: My Thirty Years in Hoover's FBI* (New York: W. W. Norton, 1979), 158–159; Cowan et al., *State Secrets*, 18–19; Gary T. Marx, *Undercover: Police Surveillance in America* (Oakland: University of California Press, 1988), 4–5.

10. On undercover detectives and the Freedom Riders, see chapter 3; on police intelligence and the March on Washington, see chapter 5; on Memphis police's surveillance of King in 1968, including at the moment of his murder, see chapter 11; and on New York police surveillance of Malcolm X at the moment of his murder, see chapter 13. On Chicago police monitoring of King, see Chicago, Illinois, Folder 564, Taylor Branch Papers, 1865–2013, SHC. See also Balto, *Occupied Territory*, 180–187, on the Chicago police response to King.

11. Almond-Verba Survey: Civic Culture Study, 1959–1960, Question 34, "Suppose several men were trying to influence a government decision . . ." (June 1, 1959–March 1, 1960); Gallup Organization, Gallup Poll #646, Question 9, "Do you approve or disapprove of what the 'Freedom Riders' are doing?" (May 28, 1961–June 2, 1961); and Gallup Organization, Gallup Poll #709, "How much respect do you have for the police in your area—a great deal, some or hardly any?" and "In some places in the nation, there have been charges of police brutality. Do you think there is any police brutality in this area or not?" (April 2–7, 1965)—all in the iPoll database, RCPOR. Ramon Geremia, "Appeal of False-Report Sentence Cites 'Grave Constitutional' Issues," *WP*, February 5, 1964, C20; "Local NAACP Produces Brutality Witness," *Michigan Chronicle*, October 3, 1964, 1.

12. Almond-Verba Survey: Civic Culture Study, 1959–1960, "If you had some trouble with the police—a traffic violation maybe, or being accused of a minor offense—do you think you would be given equal treatment, that is, would you be treated as well as anyone else?" iPoll database, RCPOR.

13. *We Shall Overcome* (New York: National Educational Television, 1963), https://americanarchive.org/catalog/cpb-aacip_15-13zs9fcr.

14. Lorraine Hansberry, *The Movement: Documentary of a Struggle for Equality* (New York: Simon and Schuster, 1964), 60; Lance Brisson, "Parker, CORE Chief Predict More Anti-police Outbreaks," *LAT*, April 27, 1964, A1.

15. Local case studies of activism against police brutality include Marilynn S. Johnson, *Street Justice: A History of Police Violence in New York City* (Boston: Beacon Press, 2004); Leonard N. Moore, *Black Rage in New Orleans: Police Brutality and African American Activism from World War II to Hurricane Katrina* (Baton Rouge: Louisiana State University Press, 2010); and Clarence Taylor, *Fight the Power: African Americans and the Long History of Police Brutality in New York City* (New York: New York University Press, 2019). For key works that touch upon activism against police violence more briefly, see Megan Ming Francis and Leah Wright-Rigueur, "Black Lives Matter in Historical Perspective," *Annual Review of Law and Social Science* 17 (2021): 441–458; Robin D. G. Kelley, *Hammer and Hoe: Alabama Communists During the Great Depression* (Chapel Hill: University of North Carolina Press, 1990); Faith S. Holsaert, Martha P. Noonan, Judy Richardson, Betty Garman Robinson, Jean Smith Young, and Dorothy Zellner, eds., *Hands on the Freedom Plow: Personal Accounts by Women in SNCC* (Urbana: University of Illinois Press, 2012); Dan Berger, *Stayed on Freedom: The Long History of Black Power Through One Family's Journey* (New York: Basic Books, 2023); Jeanne Theoharis, *A More Beautiful and Terrible History: The Uses and Misuses of Civil Rights History* (Boston: Beacon Press, 2018); James Forman, *Locking Up Our Own: Crime and*

Punishment in Black America (New York: Farrar, Straus and Giroux, 2017); Fran-çoise N. Hamlin and Charles Wesley McKinney Jr., eds., *From Rights to Lives: The Evolution of the Black Freedom Struggle* (Nashville, Tenn.: Vanderbilt University Press, 2024); Nishani Frazier, *Harambee City: The Congress of Racial Equality in Cleveland and the Rise of Black Power Populism* (Fayetteville: University of Arkansas Press, 2017); V. P. Franklin, *The Young Crusaders: The Untold Story of the Children and Teenagers Who Galvanized the Civil Rights Movement* (Boston: Beacon Press, 2021); Danielle L. McGuire, *At the Dark End of the Street: Black Women, Rape, and Resistance—A New History of the Civil Rights Movement from Rosa Parks to the Rise of Black Power* (New York: Alfred A. Knopf, 2010); Christina Greene, *Free Joan Little: The Politics of Race, Sexual Violence, and Imprisonment* (Chapel Hill: University of North Carolina Press, 2022); Thomas Sugrue, *Sweet Land of Liberty: The Forgotten Struggle for Civil Rights in the North* (New York: Random House, 2008); Jordan T. Camp, *Incarcerating the Crisis: Freedom Struggles and the Rise of the Neoliberal State* (Oakland: University of California Press, 2016); Brian Purnell, *Fighting Jim Crow in the County of Kings: The Congress of Racial Equality in Brooklyn* (Lexington: University Press of Kentucky, 2013); Hasan Kwame Jeffries, *Bloody Lowndes: Civil Rights and Black Power in Alabama's Black Belt* (New York: New York University Press, 2009); Akinyele Omowale Umoja, *We Will Shoot Back: Armed Resistance in the Mississippi Freedom Movement* (New York: New York University Press, 2013); Felker-Kantor, *Policing Los Angeles*; Balto, *Occupied Territory*.

16. Patricia Sullivan, *Lift Every Voice and Sing: The NAACP and the Making of the Civil Rights Movement* (New York: New Press, 2009), 347–349, 370. On the NAACP's strategy on police violence, see Jay Stewart, "NAACP v. the Attorney General: Black Community Struggle Against Police Violence, 1959–68," *Howard Scroll: The Social Justice Law Review* 9 (2006): 29–72; Silvan Niedermeier, *The Color of the Third Degree: Racism, Police Torture, and Civil Rights in the American South, 1930–1955* (Chapel Hill: University of North Carolina Press, 2019); Bran-don T. Jett, "'We Crave to Become a Vital Force in This Community': Police Brutal-ity and African American Activism in Birmingham, Alabama, 1920–1945," *Alabama Review* 75, no. 1 (2022): 50–72.

17. Rebecca Hill, *Men, Mobs, and Law: Anti-lynching and Labor Defense in U.S. Radical History* (Durham, N.C.: Duke University Press, 2009), 247–248, 272–273.

18. Burden-Stelly, *Black Scare/Red Scare*; Taylor, *Fight the Power*; Kelley, *Ham-mer and Hoe*; Gerald Horne, *Communist Front? The Civil Rights Congress, 1946–1956* (Rutherford, N.J.: Fairleigh Dickinson University Press, 1988); Erik S. Gellman, *Death Blow to Jim Crow: The National Negro Congress and the Rise of Militant Civil Rights* (Chapel Hill: University of North Carolina Press, 2012); Glenda Elizabeth Gilmore, *Defying Dixie: The Radical Roots of Civil Rights, 1919–1950* (New York: W. W. Norton & Co., 2008), 93–98; S. W. Gerson, "Cops Use of Stoolies Violates Constitution," *DW*, May 19, 1950, 7; Vern Smith, *The Frame-Up System* (New York: International Publishers, 1930); "Spies Versus People," *DW*, January 18, 1950, 7; "Detroit 'Loyalty' Spies Go but 'Red Squad' Remains," *DW*, September 16, 1962, 9. On an underrecognized alliance between socialists and civil rights organizers, see Matthew F. Nichter, "From the Ashes of the Old: The Old Left and the Southern

Christian Leadership Conference, 1957–1965," *Critical Historical Studies* 10, no. 1 (2023): 1–41.

19. On lynchings, see Equal Justice Initiative, *Lynching in America: Confronting the Legacy of Racial Terror*, 3rd ed. (Montgomery, Ala.: Equal Justice Initiative, 2017). On police-mob collaboration, see Hill, *Men, Mobs, and Law*; and *United States v. U. S. Klans, Knights of Ku Klux Klan, Inc.*, 194 F. Supp. 897 (U.S. District Court for the Middle District of Alabama, Northern Division, June 2, 1961).

20. Maryland State Senate, *Report to the Senate of Maryland: Senate Investigating Committee Established Pursuant to Senate Resolutions 1 and 151 of the 1975 Maryland General Assembly*, December 31, 1975; Sharon Rosenhause, "Controls on Police Intelligence Net Urged," *LAT*, August 8, 1979, B28. NYPD News (@NYPDnews), "Today we take time to celebrate the life of Martin Luther King, Jr.," X, January 15, 2024, https://perma.cc/WUN8-DK6X; LAPD HQ (@LAPDHQ), "Chief Moore & Commissioner Dale Bonner led a group of LAPD Officers," Twitter, January 16, 2023, https://perma.cc/HQ7W-HVCH; Chicago Police (@Chicago_Police), "During the observation of the Dr. Martin Luther King Jr Holiday," Twitter, January 20, 2020, https://perma.cc/E3TC-4P4N—all accessed August 7, 2024.

21. Vesla M. Weaver and Gwen Prowse, "Racial Authoritarianism in U.S. Democracy," *Science* 369, no. 6508 (2020): 1176–1178; Christopher Sebastian Parker and Christopher C. Towler, "Race and Authoritarianism in American Politics," *Annual Review of Political Science* 22 (2019): 503–519; Robert Mickey, *Paths Out of Dixie: The Democratization of Authoritarian Enclaves in America's Deep South, 1944–1972* (Princeton, N.J.: Princeton University Press, 2015).

22. Larry Buchanan, Quoctrung Bui, and Jugal K. Patel, "Black Lives Matter May Be the Largest Movement in U.S. History," *NYT*, July 3, 2020, https://perma.cc/B7FK-DUY2, accessed August 6, 2024; Juliana Menasce Horowitz, Kiley Hurst, and Dana Braga, "Support for the Black Lives Matter Movement Has Dropped Considerably from Its Peak in 2020," Pew Research Center, June 14, 2023, https://perma.cc/3ZDP-C9WH, accessed June 11, 2024.

1. Political Police

1. "Blind Man Slain; 4,000 in Protest," *NYAN*, September 27, 1933, 3; "Atlantans Protest Police Killing," *Birmingham Reporter*, September 9, 1933, 1; "Denied Chance to Preach Sermon, He Takes His Protest to Lord in Prayer," *NJG*, September 30, 1933, 3; "5,000 Attend Mass Funeral of Negro Killed by Police," *DW*, September 6, 1933, 2; Charles H. Martin, *The Angelo Herndon Case and Southern Justice* (Baton Rouge: Louisiana State University Press, 1976), 89, citing *ADW*, September 18, 1933.

2. "Additions to Force Asked by Sturdivant," *AC*, September 1, 1933, 5; "Dixie Whites Threaten to Disbar Davis," *BAA*, September 16, 1933, 3.

3. Gerald Horne, *Black Liberation/Red Scare: Ben Davis and the Communist Party* (Newark: University of Delaware Press, 1994), 43–45.

4. Affidavit, Patrick V. Murphy, May 18, 1971, 2, *Handschu v. Special Services Division*, 71 Civ. 2203, U.S. District Court, Southern District of New York, NARA-NYC;

"Kidnappers, in Fright, Let Banker's Boy Go," *NYT*, March 8, 1906, 3; "Emma Goldman Arrested for Talking Violence," *NYT*, January 7, 1907, 1; "Goldman Sees World Revolt," *Chicago Daily Tribune*, March 23, 1908, 5; Donner, *Protectors of Privilege*, 30–31; Guariglia, *Police and the Empire City*, 107–134; Robert Justin Goldstein, *Political Repression in Modern America from 1870 to 1976* (Urbana: University of Illinois Press, 2001), 68–69, 79, 94; Anthony Gregory, *American Surveillance: Intelligence, Privacy, and the Fourth Amendment* (Madison: University of Wisconsin Press, 2016), 27–31; Tim Weiner, *Enemies: A History of the FBI* (New York: Random House, 2012), 3.

5. Donner, *Protectors of Privilege*, 37, 41–42, 350; James Basil Jacobs, "The Conduct of Local Political Intelligence" (Ph.D. diss., Princeton University, 1977), 107–111; "Police Seize 19 Alleged 'Reds,'" *Daily Boston Globe*, November 13, 1933, 1; "Reds and the Schools," *LAT*, April 26, 1933, A4.

On the related phenomenon of police vice squads, which targeted queer people as sexual deviants with undercover officers and surveillance—not unlike how red squads targeted activists as political subversives—see Anna Lvovsky, *Vice Patrol: Cops, Courts, and the Struggle over Urban Gay Life Before Stonewall* (Chicago: University of Chicago Press, 2021).

6. Kenneth O'Reilly, *Hoover and the Un-Americans: The FBI, HUAC, and the Red Menace* (Philadelphia: Temple University Press, 1983), 45–47; *Investigation of Communist Activities, New York Area. Hearings Before the Committee on Un-American Activities, House of Representatives*, 84th Cong., 1st sess. (Washington, D.C.: U.S. Government Printing Office, 1955), 809–909.

7. Franklin D. Roosevelt, "The Federal Bureau of Investigation Is Placed in Charge of Espionage Investigation. September 6, 1939," in *The Public Papers and Addresses of Franklin D. Roosevelt: 1939 Volume—War and Neutrality* (New York: Macmillan Company, 1941), 478–479.

8. "500 Officers Are Urged to Give FBI Aid," *HC*, June 10, 1941, 27.

9. "Public Relations Squad Again Gets Name Change," *NYT*, April 14, 1946, 35.

10. Michael Kazin, *American Dreamers: How the Left Changed a Nation* (New York: Alfred A. Knopf, 2011), 172.

11. "Davis to Ask City Council Probe Police Brutality," *DW*, October 21, 1947, 4; Martha Biondi, *To Stand and Fight: The Struggle for Civil Rights in Postwar New York City* (Cambridge, Mass.: Harvard University Press, 2003), 73–74.

12. "Davis to Ask City Council"; Abner W. Berry, "Symonette Case Highlights 26 Cases of Police Brutality," *DW*, December 1, 1947, 5; Horace Marshall, *Police Brutality: Lynching, Northern Style* (New York: Office of Councilman Benjamin J. Davis, 1948), 6, 22.

13. John Hudson Jones, "Police 'Talking Through Hat,' Davis Declares," *DW*, August 14, 1946, 9; "Wallander Denies Police Are Brutal in Negro Arrests," *NYT*, August 8, 1946, 1.

14. Michael R. Belknap, "Cold War in the Courtroom: The Foley Square Communist Trial," in *American Political Trials*, ed. Michael R. Belknap (Westport, Conn.: Greenwood Press, 1994), 210–211; Norma Abrams and Neal Patterson,

"FBI Seizes 7 Top U.S. Reds," *NYDN*, July 21, 1948, 3; Horne, *Black Liberation/ Red Scare*, 210–211, 254–269.

15. "25,000-Man Force Urged by O'Brien," *NYT*, January 24, 1950, 32.

16. Horne, *Communist Front?* 13–15.

17. Civil Rights Congress, *We Charge Genocide; the Historic Petition to the United Nations for Relief from a Crime of the United States Government Against the Negro People* (New York: International Publishers, 1951), xi, 8–9; Horne, *Communist Front?* 153, 167–176.

18. "Text of Jackie Robinson's Testimony in DC," *NYAN*, July 23, 1949, 8.

19. Frederick Woltman, "Police Investigated by U.S. Grand Jury on Brutality Charge," *NYWT*, February 16, 1953, 1–2; "U.S. Probes 'Brutality' of N.Y. Cops," *NYDN*, February 17, 1953, 4; telegram, Ella Baker and Edward Jacko to Vincent Impellitteri, February 16, 1953, "New York City—Police Brutality, 1953–1954," Papers of the NAACP, Part 18, Special Subjects, 1940–1955, Series C: General Office, LOC, PQHV.

20. Barbara Ransby, *Ella Baker and the Black Freedom Movement: A Radical Democratic Vision* (Chapel Hill: University of North Carolina Press, 2003), 142–147; "Jackson Conviction Unthinkable: NAACP," *NYAN*, June 13, 1953, 34.

21. Memo, "Police Brutality Meeting," February 18, 1953; and press release, "Civic Groups Demand Action Against Secret Rights Pact," NAACP, February 19, 1953, "New York City—Police Brutality"—both in NAACP Papers, LOC, PQHV.

22. Ella J. Baker, interview by Lenore Bredeson Hogan, March 4, 1979, 25–28, Box 1, Folder 3, Highlander Research and Education Center Records, Highlander 50th Anniversary Files, WHS.

23. "Brutality a 'Red' Plot Says Police Assn.," *NYAN*, March 21, 1953, 2; Juan Williams, *Thurgood Marshall: American Revolutionary* (New York: Crown, 2000), 161.

24. Johnson, *Street Justice*, 227; "Police Unit to Scan Brutality Charges," *NYT*, May 23, 1953, 17; Luther A. Huston, "Memo Is Produced on City Police Deal," *NYT*, February 20, 1953, 14; "Police Begin Classes in Human Relations," *NYAN*, May 30, 1953, 2.

25. "James M. McInerney," Criminal Division, U.S. Department of Justice, https://perma.cc/9HUH-4N2G, accessed July 9, 2024; Johnson, *Street Justice*, 226.

26. Statements of William Parker and James E. Hamilton, in *Investigation of Organized Crime in Interstate Commerce. Hearings Before the Special Committee to Investigate Organized Crime in Interstate Commerce, U.S. Senate*, 82nd Cong., 1st sess., November 15, 1950 (Washington, D.C.: U.S. Government Printing Office, 1951), 165–166, 171–172.

27. Memo, Hoover to Special Agent in Charge (SAC) San Francisco, "Law Enforcement Intelligence Unit (LEIU)," October 19, 1960; SAC Letter No. 62-28, "Law Enforcement Intelligence Unit Conference, May 3–4, 1962," May 15, 1962; and memo, C. D. DeLoach to John Mohr, "Law Enforcement Intelligence Unit," May 7, 1962—all in FBI File 62-103117-42.

28. "U.S. to Probe Kidnaping of Lawyer Aide to Strikers," *Illustrated Daily News*, January 26, 1934, 3; "Federal Inquiry Ordered into Brawley Abduction," *San Bernardino County Sun*, January 26, 1934, 4; Fred Okrand, "ACLU Posed Challenge

to War Internments," *LAT*, January 9, 1995, F3; Myrna Oliver, "Al Wirin, First Full-Time ACLU Lawyer, Dies at 77," *LAT*, February 5, 1978, A3; "Judge Rules He Cannot Stop Police Microphones," *LAT*, July 1, 1955, 27; "History," ACLU Southern California, https://perma.cc/NFP6-GWBR, accessed July 9, 2024. On Wirin's kidnapping, see also File 95-12-14, Sections 1 and 2, Box 29, Class 95 (Miscellaneous Criminal Cases) Litigation Case Files, 1902–1987, Record Group 60: Department of Justice, NARA-CP.

29. Robert Blanchard, "Democratic Leader Raps Chief Parker," *LAT*, May 23, 1956, 1; "Ziffren Under Fire for Parker Attack: Censured by Police Board and on Floor of City Council," *LAT*, May 25, 1956, 2; *Wirin v. Parker*, 313 P.2d 844 (Cal. 1957).

30. Andrew Tully, *CIA: The Inside Story* (New York: Morrow, 1962), 25; Anthony Bouza, "The Operations of a Police Intelligence Unit" (master's thesis, City College of the City University of New York, 1968), 51.

31. *Yates v. United States*, 354 U.S. 298 (1957).

32. David A. Shannon, *The Decline of American Communism: A History of the Communist Party of the United States Since 1945* (New York: Harcourt, Brace and Company, 1959), 354–364.

2. Jim Crow's Cops

1. "Cars Not Boycotted," *Montgomery Advertiser*, August 16, 1900, 7.

2. Fred L. Shuttlesworth, "Birmingham Revisited," *Ebony*, August 1971, 114.

3. Andrew M. Manis, *A Fire You Can't Put Out: The Civil Rights Life of Birmingham's Reverend Fred Shuttlesworth* (Tuscaloosa: University of Alabama Press, 1999), 80–87; Glenn T. Eskew, *But for Birmingham: The Local and National Movements in the Civil Rights Struggle* (Chapel Hill: University of North Carolina Press, 1997), 105; Elliot M. Rudwick, *The Unequal Badge: Negro Policemen in the South* (Atlanta: Southern Regional Council, 1962), 6–7.

4. Hall, "Long Civil Rights Movement and the Political Uses of the Past"; Kelley, *Hammer and Hoe*.

5. Manis, *Fire You Can't Put Out*, 106.

6. "James Roberson—Birmingham, Alabama," in Ellen Levine, *Freedom's Children: Young Civil Rights Activists Tell Their Own Stories* (New York: Puffin Books, 1993), 6–7; Fred Shuttlesworth, interview by Blackside, Inc., November 7, 1985, for *Eyes on the Prize: America's Civil Rights Years (1954–1965)*, Henry Hampton Collection, WUL.

7. William A. Nunnelley, *Bull Connor* (Tuscaloosa: University of Alabama Press, 1991), 71–73.

8. Eskew, *But for Birmingham*, 53–60.

9. Roberta Senechal de la Roche, "The Sociogenesis of Lynching," in *Under Sentence of Death: Lynching in the South*, ed. W. Fitzhugh Brundage (Chapel Hill: University of North Carolina Press, 1997), 51, 57; Equal Justice Initiative, *Lynching in America*, 4, 29, 37, 39, 46.

10. Manis, *Fire You Can't Put Out*, 120; Southern Negro Leaders Conference on Transpiration and Nonviolent Integration, "A Statement to the South and Nation,"

Box 115, Folder 4, Martin Luther King, Jr., Papers, Howard Gotlieb Archival Research Center, Boston University.

11. Eskew, *But for Birmingham*, 118–119; Kelley, *Hammer and Hoe*, 72–73, 214–215, 227. See also Brandon Jett, *Race, Crime and Policing in the Jim Crow South: African Americans and Law Enforcement in Birmingham, Memphis, and New Orleans, 1920–1945* (Baton Rouge: Louisiana State University Press, 2021).

12. Report, C. B. Stanberry, April 29, 1960, FBI File 44-15668-5, NARA-CP; Manis, *Fire You Can't Put Out*, 13–15, 44–50.

13. Manis, *Fire You Can't Put Out*, 103, 164–167; "Negro Applicant Sues Personnel Board," *BPH*, April 22, 1958, 3.

14. "Connor, Shuttlesworth at Odds over the Hiring of Black Officers," *Birmingham World*, June 7, 1958, 1, 8.

15. Manis, *Fire You Can't Put Out*, 169–171.

16. Letter, Fred Shuttlesworth to Eugene Connor, August 9, 1958, Albert Burton Boutwell Papers, 1963–1967, Folder 264.12.43, BPL.

17. Manis, *Fire You Can't Put Out*, 179–184; "B'Ham Police Seize 3 Montgomery Ministers," *ADW*, October 28, 1958, 1; "Birmingham Police Jail 3 Followers of Dr. King," *CD*, October 28, 1958, 4; "Arrests Stir Inquiry," *NYT*, October 20, 1958, 64; "Ask Probe in Arrest of Negroes," *Detroit Free Press*, November 14, 1958, 5; "Connor Slams Door in Face of Rights Probers," *BN*, September 12, 1958, 21.

18. Transcript, *Reverend F. L. Shuttlesworth and Reverend Charles Billups v. Eugene Connor and Jamie Moore*, Civil Action 9751, 291 F.2d 217 (U.S. District Court, Northern District of Alabama, 1960), 31–32, Division Record Group 21, NARA-A; "Third Arrested in Boycott Case," *BPH*, November 27, 1958, 8.

19. Franklin McCain, interview in Howell Raines, *My Soul Is Rested: The Story of the Civil Rights Movement in the Deep South* (New York: Penguin, 1985), 75–77.

20. William Chafe, *Civil Rights and Civilities: Greensboro, North Carolina, and the Black Struggle for Freedom* (Oxford: Oxford University Press, 1980), 84; Christopher W. Schmidt, *The Sit-Ins: Protest and Legal Change in the Civil Rights Era* (Chicago: University of Chicago Press, 2018), 17–19.

21. *State v. Avent*, 253 N.C. 580 (Supreme Court of North Carolina, 1961); Schmidt, *Sit-Ins*, 93–94.

22. Tilman C. Cothran, "The Negro Protest Against Segregation in the South," *Annals of the American Academy of Political and Social Science*, January 1965, 70; Chafe, *Civil Rights and Civilities*, 71; *The Student Protest Movement: A Recapitulation* (Atlanta: Southern Regional Council, 1961), 14–15.

23. Almond-Verba Survey: Civic Culture Study, 1959–1960, Question 33, iPoll database, RCPOR.

24. Clayborne Carson, *In Struggle: SNCC and the Black Awakening of the 1960s* (Cambridge, Mass.: Harvard University Press, 1981), 20–21; *Student Nonviolent Coordinating Committee 50th Anniversary* (Washington, D.C.: SNCC, 2010), 35; Southwide Youth Leadership Conference, "Recommendations of the Findings and Recommendations Committee Are as Follows," April 15, 1960, SNCC

Correspondence, Folder 252253-011-0401, SNCC Papers, Martin Luther King (MLK), PQHV. See also Zoe A. Colley, *Ain't Scared of Your Jail: Arrest, Imprisonment, and the Civil Rights Movement* (Gainesville: University Press of Florida, 2012).

25. Complaint, *Reverend F. L. Shuttlesworth and Reverend Charles Billups v. Eugene Connor and Jamie Moore*, Civil Action 9751, 291 F.2d 217 (U.S. District Court, Northern District of Alabama, 1960), NARA-A.

26. "Norfolk Lawyer Joins CORE Field Staff," *NJG*, March 5, 1960, 10.

27. Transcript, *Shuttlesworth v. Connor*, 34.

28. *Browder v. Gayle*, 142 F. Supp. 707 (M.D. Ala. 1956); transcript, *Shuttlesworth v. Connor*, 34, 69, 71–72, 76; Nunnelley, *Bull Connor*, 51.

29. Transcript, *Shuttlesworth v. Connor*, 96.

3. Collusion

1. James Farmer, *Lay Bare the Heart: An Autobiography of the Civil Rights Movement* (New York: Plume, 1985), 175–179.

2. Raymond Arsenault, *Freedom Riders: 1961 and the Struggle for Racial Justice* (Oxford: Oxford University Press, 2006), 92–129; John Lewis, *Walking with the Wind: A Memoir of the Movement* (New York: Simon & Schuster, 1998), 133, 142–143.

3. Arsenault, *Freedom Riders*, 141, 143–146, 150.

4. Arsenault, *Freedom Riders*, 148–160.

5. Eskew, *But for Birmingham*, 159–160.

6. "People Are Asking: 'Where Were the Police?'" *Birmingham News*, May 15, 1961, 1.

7. Arsenault, *Freedom Riders*, 262, 271–274, 325, 349–350.

8. Colley, *Ain't Scared of Your Jail*, 5; Arsenault, *Freedom Riders*, 319.

9. James Forman, "1967: High Tide of Black Resistance" (New York: SNCC, 1967), 9; emphasis removed.

10. Howard Zinn, *Albany: A Study in National Responsibility* (Atlanta: Southern Regional Council, 1962), 1–4; David Miller, "A Loss for Dr. King—New Negro Roundup," *NYHT*, December 19, 1961, 1; "Albany Arrests 29 in 'Lie-Down': Police Literally Carry Negroes from Demonstration," *AC*, April 22, 1962, 44.

11. "Freed by Mystery Fine Donor, Rev. King Meets Police Chief," *AC*, July 13, 1962, 1, 14.

12. Martin Luther King Jr., *The Autobiography of Martin Luther King*, ed. Clayborne Carson (New York: Grand Central Publishing, 1998), 159; "Martin Luther King Jr. Released from Jail; Decries Paying of Fine," *LAT*, July 13, 1962, 14.

13. Taylor Branch, *Parting the Waters: America in the King Years, 1954–1963* (New York: Simon & Schuster, 1988), 601–606.

14. Miller, "Loss for Dr. King"; Charles Portis, "Gandhi and Albany, Ga.," *NYHT*, August 4, 1962, 1.

15. "Determined Police Chief: Laurie Pritchett," *NYT*, July 23, 1962, 13.

16. Zinn, *Albany*, 7; *Upside-Down Justice: The Albany Cases* (Albany: National Committee for the Albany Defendants, 1964), 4.

17. Portis, "Gandhi and Albany, Ga."; "Determined Police Chief."

18. Howard Zinn, *You Can't Be Neutral on a Moving Train: A Personal History of Our Times* (Boston: Beacon Press, 1994), 51.

19. Zinn, *Albany*, vi, 1–2, 5, 21–22; *Upside-Down Justice*, 3; James Bowers Wall, "'Settling Down for the Long Haul': The Black Freedom Movement in Southwest Georgia, 1945–1995" (Ph.D. diss., University of Georgia, 2018), 160–161.

20. Gallup Organization, Gallup Poll #646, Questions 7 and 9 (May 28–June 2, 1961), iPoll database, RCPOR.

21. Press release, "Civil Rights Hearings to Open," May 24, 1962, Folder 3—Committee of Inquiry into the Administration of Justice in the Freedom Struggle, April 16, 1962–August 12, 1964, CORE Papers, WHS, PQHV.

22. Allida M. Black, *Casting Her Own Shadow: Eleanor Roosevelt and the Shaping of Postwar Liberalism* (New York: Columbia University Press, 1996), 128.

23. Transcript, "Commission of Inquiry into the Administration of Justice in the Freedom Struggle," May 25–26, 1962, 141–142, 147–155, Folder 474—Vol. I Commission of Inquiry into the Administration of Justice in the Freedom Struggle, Series 5, CORE Papers, WHS, PQHV.

24. *Justice?* (New York: CORE, 1962), 30, Folder 474—Vol. I Commission of Inquiry into the Administration of Justice in the Freedom Struggle, Series 5, CORE Papers, WHS, PQHV.

25. *Justice?* 11; Committee of Inquiry, "Albert Bigelow," Folder 3—Committee of Inquiry into the Administration of Justice in the Freedom Struggle, April 16, 1962–August 12, 1964, CORE Papers, WHS, PQHV.

26. Transcript, "Commission of Inquiry into the Administration of Justice in the Freedom Struggle," 188–195.

27. *Justice?* 31–33.

28. Letters, Roosevelt, Eleanor, February 2, 1961–June 3, 1963, Folder 40, Series 2, CORE Papers, WHS, PQHV; "Teacher Says Southern Cops Tortured Him as Negro Aider," *BG*, May 26, 1962, 21; "Tortured for Helping Negroes, Says Teacher," *LAT*, May 26, 1992, 7; "Racial Probe Group Told of Harassment," *BS*, May 27, 1962, 19.

29. "Rights Leaders to Testify Before Mrs. Roosevelt," *CD*, May 22, 1962, 7; "Mrs. Roosevelt's Civic Unit to Eye Dixie Police Tactics," *BAA*, May 26, 1962, 16; T. R. Bassett, "Washington Panel Told of Brutality by Southern Cops," *The Worker*, June 3, 1962, 2; "Too Few Listen as Freedom Riders and Sit-In'ers Tell Their Dramatic Story," *I. F. Stone's Weekly*, June 4, 1962, 2–3; letters, Folder 3—Committee of Inquiry into the Administration of Justice in the Freedom Struggle, April 16, 1962–August 12, 1964, CORE Papers, WHS, PQHV.

30. Eleanor Roosevelt, *Tomorrow Is Now* (New York: Harper & Row, 1963), 51–55; letters, Folder 3—Committee of Inquiry into the Administration of Justice in the Freedom Struggle, April 16, 1962–August 12, 1964; "Too Few Listen as Freedom Riders and Sit-In'ers Tell Their Dramatic Story."

31. Robert E. Baker, "Albany Anti-Negro Tack May Set South's Course," *WP*, August 5, 1962, A1.

4. Freedom Now

1. Eskew, *But for Birmingham*, 266–272; Diane McWhorter, *Carry Me Home: Birmingham, Alabama, the Climactic Battle of the Civil Rights Revolution* (New York: Simon & Schuster, 2001), 366–376; Claude Sitton, "Violence Explodes at Racial Protests in Alabama," *NYT*, May 4, 1963, 1; "New Alabama Riot: Police Dogs, Fire Hoses Halt March," *LAT*, May 4, 1963, 1; "Fire Hoses and Police Dogs Quell Birmingham Segregation Protest," *WP*, May 4, 1963, A1; Martin Berger, *Seeing Through Race: A Reinterpretation of Civil Rights Photography* (Berkeley: University of California Press, 2011), 105; Hedrick Smith, "Foreign Reaction to Race Rift Mild," *NYT*, May 29, 1963, 16; Mary L. Dudziak, *Cold War Civil Rights: Race and the Image of American Democracy* (Princeton, N.J.: Princeton University Press, 2002), 168–169.

2. Diane McWhorter, "The Moment that Made a Movement," *WP*, May 2, 1993, C3.

3. CORE staffer Alan Gartner made the "police malpractice" concept the basis of his study *The Police and the Community: Police Practices and Minority Groups* (Waltham, Mass: Brandeis University, 1963), 1–4.

4. Kelley, *Hammer and Hoe*, 61, 81, 115–116, 120, 123.

5. Martin Luther King Jr., *Why We Can't Wait* (New York: Signet Books, 1964), 117; Eric Sevareid, *This Is Eric Sevareid* (New York: McGraw-Hill Book Company, 1964), 89.

6. Alvin Adams, "Picture Seen Around the World," *Jet*, October 10, 1963, 26.

7. "They Fight a Fire That Won't Go Out," *Life*, May 10, 1963, 36.

8. Eskew, *But for Birmingham*, 292–297.

9. Jerry Burns, "Baldwin Hits Whites for South Disorders," *VT*, May 16, 1963, A-11.

10. General Order 1-60, W. J. Haley to all members of the Police Department, June 22, 1960, January 6, 1960, to November 1, 1960, Folder, Department General and Special Orders Theophilus Eugene Bull Connor Papers, 1959–1963, BPL; Samuel Chapman, *Police Dogs in America* (Norman: University of Oklahoma Bureau of Government Research, 1978), 12–14; *Report of the Police Commissioner for the City of Baltimore to His Excellency the Governor of Maryland for the Year 1957* (Baltimore, MD: Baltimore Police Department, 1957), 59–60, Pullen Collection, University of Baltimore Special Collections and Archives; "Birmingham to Have Own K-9 Corps Soon," *BN*, November 23, 1959, 6; "K-9 Corps," in *Annual Report 1960* (Birmingham, Ala.: Birmingham Police Department, 1960).

11. "B'ham's Police Dogs Shock World," *BAA*, May 18, 1963, 5; Richard J. H. Johnston, "N.A.A.C.P. Urges Mass Picketing," *NYT*, May 8, 1963, 28; Lou Potter, "2,000 NAACP Pickets Demonstrate at City Hall Sat.," *PT*, May 14, 1963, 3; "Demonstrations Over Nation Back Birmingham Fight," *CD*, May 13, 1963, 1.

12. "Protesters March in N.Y.," *BS*, May 9, 1963, 14; "B'ham's Police Dogs Shock World"; report, "Protest Demonstration at City Hall Sponsored by the N.A.A.C.P.," May 8, 1963, NAACP Folder, 1961–1972, pp. 1–192, NYPD Intelligence Records, NYCMA.

13. Roger L. Abel, *The Black Shields* (Bloomington, Ind.: AuthorHouse, 2006), 465.

14. Letter to Roy Wilkins, September 12, 1956, Folder 001453-004-0465, Papers of the NAACP, Part 17: Supplement, National Staff Files, 1956–1965, PQHV; "369th Vets Re-elect De Fossett," *NYAN*, January 14, 1961, 5.

15. Reports, Box 36, New York City Bureau of Special Services Files, Series VI, Malcolm X Project Records, Archival Collections, Columbia University Libraries; David Garrow, "Malcolm X Under the BOSS's Prying Eyes," *Newsday*, June 10, 1993, 103; Mariame Kaba, *An (Abridged) History of Resisting Police Violence in Harlem* (Chicago: Project NIA and Chicago Prison Industrial Complex Teaching Collective, 2012), 9–12.

16. Reports, William K. De Fossett, BOSS, April 29, June 25, and June 28, 1961, and January 5, 1962, NAACP Folder, 1961–1972, pp. 1–192, NYPD Intelligence Records, NYCMA; "Two Harlem Leaders Clash to Control NAACP," *New York Age*, November 28, 1959, 3; "Sutton to Discuss NAACP Fight in NYC," *NYAN*, January 14, 1961, 3.

17. Len Holt, *An Act of Conscience* (Boston: Beacon Press, 1965), 4.

18. *Student Nonviolent Coordinating Committee 50th Anniversary*, 32; Barbara Carter, "A Lawyer Leaves Mississippi," *The Reporter*, May 9, 1963, 39; M.F. III, "The Negro Lawyer in Virginia: A Survey," *Virginia Law Review* 51, no. 3 (April 1965): 521; complaint, *Shuttlesworth v. Connor*; Jeffrey L. Littlejohn and Charles H. Ford, "'In the Best American Tradition of Freedom, We Defy You': The Radical Partnership of Joseph Jordan, Edward Dawley, and Leonard Holt," *Journal of African American History* 106, no. 3 (2021): 496–520; letter, Julian Bond to Ernest Goodman, TL, May 4, 1962, SNCC Papers, rl. 8, fr. 267, as cited in Tomiko Brown-Nagin, *Courage to Dissent: Atlanta and the Long History of the Civil Rights Movement* (Oxford: Oxford University Press, 2011), 184, see also 175–211.

19. Holt, *Act of Conscience*, 4.

20. Acts Passed at a General Assembly of the Commonwealth of Virginia, 1832 Va. Acts 20, 20–22; Brian McGinty, *John Brown's Trial* (Cambridge, Mass.: Harvard University Press, 2009), 85–86.

21. *Decisions of the Interstate Commerce Commission of the United States, vol. 271* (Washington, D.C.: U.S. Government Printing Office, 1950), 616; "Danville, Virginia" (Atlanta: SNCC, 1963), 3, 13.

22. Emily A. Martin Cochran, "'It Seemed like Reaching for the Moon': Southside Virginia's Civil Rights Struggle Against the Virginia Way, 1951–1964" (Ph.D. diss., University of South Carolina, 2021), 105–120, 140–148; Holt, *Act of Conscience*, 230.

23. Cochran, "It Seemed like Reaching for the Moon," 150; Danny Lyon, *Memories of the Southern Civil Rights Movement* (Chapel Hill: University of North Carolina Press, 1992), 63.

24. Lyon, *Memories of the Southern Civil Rights Movement*, 63.

25. Holt, *Act of Conscience*, 7–13, 149–154, 190–192; Lyon, *Memories of the Southern Civil Rights Movement*, 68.

26. "Martin Luther King, Jr., Speech, Danville, Virginia (WDBJ Television, Roanoke, VA)," July 11, 1963, *Television News of the Civil Rights Era*, http://t.ly/QFTZx, accessed July 16, 2024.

27. Ben A. Franklin, "Danville Method Studied in South," *NYT*, August 11, 1963, 71.

28. Holt, *Act of Conscience*, 198, 216–217; emphasis removed.

29. Wyatt Tee Walker, interview by Blackside, Inc., October 11, 1985, for *Eyes on the Prize: America's Civil Rights Years (1954–1965)*, Henry Hampton Collection, WUL; David Garrow, *Bearing the Cross: Martin Luther King, Jr., and the Southern Christian Leadership Conference* (New York: William Morrow, 1986), 228; Thomas Hargrove, "Walker Paved Way for King to Light Fuse," *BPH*, April 16, 1981, C1.

30. James Forman, *The Making of Black Revolutionaries*, rev. ed. (Seattle: University of Washington Press, 1997), 312.

31. "Danville, Virginia," 3.

32. "Five Arrested in Danville," *Student Voice*, December 16, 1963, 4; news release, "Danville Halts Trial Transfers," SNCC, October 1963, Mary E. King Papers, 1960–1999, Box 1, Folder 12, WHS; *We Shall Overcome.*

33. Juby E. Towler, *The Police Role in Racial Conflicts* (Springfield, Ill.: Charles C. Thomas, 1964).

34. Cochran, "It Seemed like Reaching for the Moon," 181–190, 198; order, Judge Glyn R. Phillips, Corporation Court of Danville, February 9, 1973, January–February 1973 Folder, 1963 Danville Civil Rights Case Files, Series V: Court Orders, Library of Virginia, Richmond.

35. "Negro Among Five Rookie Policemen," *Danville Bee*, October 17, 1963, 5; "Danville Ouster Move Is Planned," *Richmond Times-Dispatch*, November 18, 1963, 2; Cochran, "It Seemed like Reaching for the Moon," 183.

5. Up North

1. "Resolution," passed at the Twentieth Annual CORE Convention in Miami, Florida, June 28–July 1, 1962, Press Releases, Community Relations Department Publicity and Funding, December 5, 1960–February 28, 1966; and "CORE Action Council Maps New Plan—Attacks Brutality, State Bonds," December 27, 1962, Press Releases, Community Relations Department Publicity and Funding, December 5, 1960–February 28, 1966, both in CORE Papers, WHS, PQHV.

2. Alan Gartner, "Police Relations," June 21, 1963, Folder 300, Police Incidence [*sic*], June 21, 1963–February 26, 1964, Series 5 Departments and Related Organizations, Organization Department, 1947–1968, Correspondence by Subject, CORE Papers, WHS, PQHV.

3. Gartner, *Police and the Community*, 10–14, 37–39; *Justice: 1961 Commission on Civil Rights Report* (Washington, D.C.: U.S. Government Printing Office, 1961), 81–82.

4. Gartner, *Police and the Community*, 17–22, 24, appendix C; Justin McCrary, "The Effect of Court-Ordered Hiring Quotas on the Composition and Quality of Police," Working Paper 12368 (Cambridge, Mass.: National Bureau of Economic Research, July 2006), Table 1.

5. August Meier and Eliot Rudwick, *CORE: A Study in the Civil Rights Movement* (Urbana: University of Illinois Press, 1973), 215–216, 221–222; "Police Horses, Tear Gas Rout 1,000 Negroes," *LAT*, September 2, 1963, 2.

6. "A Negro Protest March vs. Police," *San Francisco Examiner*, October 27, 1963, 6; "Syracuse Police Picketed," *NYT*, March 1, 1964, 47; Frazier, *Harambee City*, 127–128.

7. Thomas J. Cahill, "Seminar: Police Training for Inter-racial Problems," *PC*, December 1963, 34.

8. "Negro Protest March vs. Police," 6; Cahill, "Seminar," 36. On police-community relations in the 1960s, see also Balto, *Occupied Territory*, 157–162; and Felker-Kantor, *Policing Los Angeles*, 143–144. On the International Association of Chiefs of Police, see Stuart Schrader, "To Protect and Serve Themselves: Police in US Politics Since the 1960s," *Public Culture* 31, no. 3 (2019): 601–623.

9. Ralph Kinney Bennett, "The Tinderbox Squad," *Greater Philadelphia Magazine*, October 1965, 48; memo, Sidney Rocker to George W. O'Connor, Police Operations Division, and Paul Estaver, Civil Disorders Program Division, "Philadelphia Civil Disobedience Unit," February 13, 1970, 5, National Criminal Justice Reference Service Virtual Library, U.S. Department of Justice.

10. Harry G. Fox, "The CD Man," *PC*, November 1966, 22.

11. Fox, "CD Man," 24; Bennett, "Tinderbox Squad," 123; George Lakey and Martin Oppenheimer, *A Manual for Direct Action* (Chicago: Quadrangle Books, 1965); George Lakey, *Dancing with History: A Life for Peace and Justice* (New York: Seven Stories, 2022), 102–104.

12. Fox, "CD Man," 24–25.

13. Bennett, "Tinderbox Squad," 128; Frederick Schauer, "Fear, Risk and the First Amendment: Unraveling the Chilling Effect," *Boston University Law Review* 58, no. 5 (November 1978): 685–689.

14. Committee for Emancipation March on Washington for Jobs, "This Is a Call to America for an Emancipation March on Washington for Jobs," May 7, 1963, Circular Letters [1963] Folder; and A. Philip Randolph, "We March on Washington for Jobs," Printed [1963] Folder—both in Chronological Subject File—March on Washington—1963, Bayard Rustin Papers, APRI, PQHV.

15. "Proposed Plans for March," July 2, 1963, https://perma.cc/HW2X-U4U2, accessed July 26, 2024.

16. Robert Shellow, "Reinforcing Police Neutrality in Civil Rights Confrontations," *Journal of Applied Behavioral Science* 1, no. 3 (September 1, 1963): 243–254.

17. McWhorter, *Carry Me Home*, 489; William P. Jones, *The March on Washington: Jobs, Freedom, and the Forgotten History of Civil Rights* (New York: W. W. Norton & Company, 2013), 193–194; Lauren Feeney, "Two Versions of John Lewis' Speech," July 24, 2013, Moyers & Company, https://perma.cc/496Z-S5ZR, accessed July 26, 2024.

18. "March on Washington for Jobs and Freedom; Part 6 of 17," August 28, 1963, Open Vault from GBH, https://perma.cc/QM4N-LDY8, accessed July 26, 2024; Aniko Bodrogkhozy, *Equal Time: Television and the Civil Rights Movement* (Urbana: University of Illinois Press, 2012), 89–90, 100–101; "March on Washington for Jobs

and Freedom: Lincoln Memorial Program," August 28, 1963, https://perma.cc/VBW3-8GPU, accessed July 26, 2024.

19. "D.C. Guide for a Day: The Civil Rights Way," *WP*, August 25, 1963, A18; Ernest B. Furgurson, "Million Turn Out to Watch Kennedy Inaugural Parade," *BS*, January 21, 1961; 1; "Jails Open, Bars Shut," *NYDN*, August 28, 1963, 8.

20. Les Matthews, "Bomb Scare Didn't Mean a Thing," *NYAN*, September 7, 1963, 49; "Chief Marshal of March Gave Up His Vacation Time," *BAA*, August 31, 1963, 5; James N. Reaves, *Black Cops* (Philadelphia: Quantum Leap Publisher, Inc., 1991), 109–116.

21. John Kinsella, "Railroad and Bus and Auto Transportation for the Civil Rights March on Washington on August 28, 1963," August 21, 1963; and Detective Kenneth Egan, "Railroad and Bus Transportation for the Civil Rights March on Washington on This Date," undated—both in March on Washington Folder, NYPD Intelligence Records, NYCMA.

22. "Landry, Lawrence—Investigator's Report," May 1968, Box 81, Folder 564, Chicago (2 of 4), Taylor Branch Papers, 1865–2013, SHC; "Photographs Related to the Civil Rights Movement," 1125.11.21A-1 to 1125.11M-1, Birmingham, Alabama, Police Department, Surveillance Files, 1947–1980, BPL.

23. Reaves, *Black Cops*, 110, 116.

24. Philip Benjamin, "Police Report Picketing at Peak in City in Last Hectic 10 Months," *NYT*, October 31, 1963, 29.

25. Richard H. Johnston, "Rallies Here Decry Suppression of Negro Protests in Alabama," *NYT*, May 9, 1963, 18; "Protesters March in N.Y.," 14.

26. Benjamin, "Police Report Picketing at Peak in City in Last Hectic 10 Months," 29.

27. Benjamin, "Police Report Picketing at Peak in City in Last Hectic 10 Months," 29; Jack Roth, "City Using Psychology," *NYT*, November 7, 1963, 39, 42.

28. Wayne Kinsler, Tina Lawrence, and Joe Sweeny, memo, November 1963, CORE 1 of 2, Large Organization Folders, NYPD Intelligence Records, NYCMA.

29. "Pickets, Cops Clash as Wallace Speaks," *NYDN*, November 7, 1963, 371.

30. Les Matthews, "Police Brutality Charged," *NYAN*, November 16, 1963, 4.

31. Kinsler et al., memo, November 1963.

32. Memo, Commanding Officer of Bureau of Special Services, "Picketing of Police Headquarters, 240 Centre Street, Manhattan, by Manhattan Chapter of Congress of Racial Equality (CORE)," November 19, 1963; and "Supplementary Report Persons Identified from Photographs Taken at This Demonstration"—both in CORE 1 of 2, Large Organization Folders, NYPD Intelligence Records, NYCMA; Kinsler et al., memo, November 1963.

33. Matthews, "Police Brutality Charged," 4; "130 Policemen in 'Line-Up' Studied by CORE Members," *NYT*, November 21, 1963, 60.

34. "Memo to Lt. Mulligan," November 20, 1963, CORE 1 of 2, Large Organization Folders, Folder 15, NYPD Intelligence Records, NYCMA.

6. Undercover

1. Ronald H. Bayor and Timothy J. Meagher, *The New York Irish* (Baltimore, Md.: Johns Hopkins University Press, 1996), 427; David W. Abbott, Louis H. Gold, and Edward T. Rogowsky, *Police, Politics and Race: The New York City Referendum on Civilian Review* (New York: American Jewish Committee, 1969), 22–23; Peter Kihss, "City Police Cheer Talk by M'Carthy," *NYT*, April 5, 1954, 12; Guy Passant, "P.B.A. to Apologize to Sheen and Wilson for Kennedy Talk," *NYT*, April 20, 1960, 23.

2. Harry Schlegel, "Boss Cop Warns Civil Rights Firebrands," *NYDN*, March 16, 1964, 3; R. W. Apple Jr., "The Chief Policeman Talks About His Beat," *New York Times Sunday Magazine*, June 21, 1964, 10, 34–35.

3. *Civil Rights and the Police: A Compilation of Speeches by Commissioner Michael J. Murphy* (New York: New York Police Department, 1964), 4; *Report of the National Advisory Commission on Civil Disorders* (Washington, D.C.: U.S. Government Printing Office, 1968), 169; Sklansky, "Not Your Father's Police Department," 1220; Emanuel Perlmutter, "Murphy Says City Will Not Permit Rights Violence," *NYT*, March 16, 1964, 1.

4. "Callender, Herbert Ebenezer," Criminal Record, Individual Files, NYPD Intelligence Records, NYCMA.

5. "Two Ford Workers Leave for 'Freedom Ride,'" *Paterson Evening News*, June 13, 1961, 7; "UAW Officers Join Freedom Ride," *Ridgewood Herald-News*, June 15, 1961, 29.

6. "Jury Selection Begins in Freedom Rider Appeal," *Corpus Christi Caller-Times*, August 23, 1961, 11; "Freedom Rider Trial in Ocala Postponed," *Orlando Sentinel*, September 27, 1962, 2; "Freedom Riders Day," *NYAN*, July 8, 1961, 1, 17.

7. Bronx Chapter of CORE, "Herbert Callender," October 15, 1966, Box 2R572, Records of Professional Activities—CORE—New York CORE—Correspondence Publications Folder, James Leonard Jr. and Lula Peterson Farmer Papers, Briscoe Center for American History, University of Texas at Austin; "Addendum—Congress of Racial Equality (CORE), New York City Metropolitan Area Chapters—C.O.R.E. Participation in N.Y.–Harlem–Bedford-Stuyvesant Riots, 1964," CORE Folders, NYPD Intelligence Records, NYCMA.

8. "CORE Fact Sheet & Memo from Herbert Callender, Chairman, Re: 'Police Brutality Case of Jesse Roberts,'" February 13, 1964, Box 3, Folder 4, Arnie Goldwag Brooklyn CORE Collection, Brooklyn Historical Society; Les Matthews, "PD Mouthpiece Knows It Not as 100 Picket," *NYAN*, February 29, 1964, 21.

9. "CORE Sounds Commissioner," *NYAN*, March 7, 1964, 7; Adolph "Abe" Hart, *Memoirs of a Spy* (Bloomington, Ind.: 1st Books, 2004), viii.

10. "7 Rights Demonstrators Get Suspended Sentences," *NYT*, July 14, 1964, 19.

11. Louis Lomax, *The Negro Revolt* (New York: Harper & Brothers, 1962), 59.

12. Taylor, *Fight the Power*, 71–73, 90–91, 94–95; Felber, *Those Who Know Don't Say*, 85–86, 130–131.

13. Matthews, "PD Mouthpiece Knows It Not as 100 Picket"; Leonard Buder, "Bridge Sitdown by CORE Blocks the Triborough," *NYT*, March 7, 1964, 1;

Jack Mallon and Edward Kirkman, "CORE Sitters Snarl Cop HQ and Triboro," *NYDN*, March 7, 1964, 3; Malcolm Nash, "Spring Bringing 'Open Season' On," *NYAN*, March 14, 1964, 50.

14. Richard J. H. Johnston, "Police Tighten Security Rules at Headquarters," *NYT*, March 11, 1964, 24; *The Militant*, March 30, 1964, 2; "Commissioner Murphy's House [Protest Against Segregation]," March 20, 1964, NYPD Surveillance Films, 1960–1980, Rec. 0063, nypd_f_0177, NYCMA.

15. Transcript, *U.S. v. Bowe*, Case 29881, 65 C.R. 1989 (U.S. District Court, Southern District of New York, 1965), 688, NARA-NYC; Susan Brownmiller, "View from the Inside: I Remember Ray Wood," *VV*, June 3, 1965, 3.

16. Kelly Wood, interview by the author, recording, March 6, 2021; "What Shapes a Hero? She Helped," *NYDN*, February 18, 1965, 362; "Raymond Wood's Road to Heroism," *News Journal* (Wilmington, Del.), February 21, 1965, 17.

17. *Report of the National Advisory Commission on Civil Disorders*, 169; Tony Ulasewicz, with Stuart A. McKeever, *The President's Private Eye: The Journey of Detective Tony U. from N.Y.P.D. to the Nixon White House* (Westport, Conn.: MAC-SAM Publishing Company, 1990), 146, 153–155.

18. Solomon Herbert, interview by the author, recording, August 24, 2020; transcript, *U.S. v. Bowe*, 2217.

19. "Job Bias Summonses in N.Y. Are Dismissed," *BS*, June 13, 1964, 7; memo, "Citizen's Arrests of Public Officials by Members of Bronx C.O.R.E.," June 18, 1964, Folder 19, CORE 1 of 2, NYPD Intelligence Records, NYCMA.

20. Seth Cagin and Philip Dray, *We Are Not Afraid: The Story of Goodman, Schwerner, and Chaney and the Civil Rights Campaign for Mississippi* (New York: Nation Books, 2006), 285–295; Taylor Branch, *Pillar of Fire: America in the King Years, 1963–65* (New York: Simon & Schuster, 1998), 361–368; Claude Sitton, "3 in Rights Drive Reported Missing," *NYT*, June 23, 1964, 1, 13.

21. M. S. Handler, "F.B.I. Augments Mississippi Force," *NYT*, June 25, 1964, 18; "Pickets Demonstrate at U.S. Courthouse in Foley Square," *NYDN*, June 25, 1964, 836.

22. "Mississippi Police Accused by CORE," *NYT*, June 28, 1964, 47.

23. "Supplementary Report Persons Identified from Photographs Taken at This Demonstration"; Kinsler et al., memo, November 1963.

24. Appendix, *U.S. v. Bowe*, U.S. Court of Appeals for the Second Circuit, June 8, 1965, 458b–459b, NARA-NYC.

25. "Callender, Herbert Ebenezer," Criminal Record; "Addendum—Congress of Racial Equality (CORE), New York City Metropolitan Area Chapters."

26. Will Lissner, "7 in CORE Guilty in Police Sit-In," *NYT*, May 21, 1964, 1; "7 Rights Demonstrators Get Suspended Sentences."

27. Press release, Bronx CORE, July 1, 1964, CORE, NYPD Intelligence Records, NYCMA; "Citizen's Arrests of Public Officials by Members of Bronx C.O.R.E.," June 18, 1964.

28. Bert S. Prunty Jr., Code of Criminal Procedure §183–§185, *New York Statute Law* (New York: Practising Law Institute, 1959), 12; "Re: Threatened Citizen's Arrest by Bronx C.O.R.E. of the Governor and the Mayor," July 9, 1964, CORE, NYPD Intelligence Records, NYCMA.

29. Edward O'Neill and Henry Lee, "It Just Wasn't Their Day to Go Mayor-Arresting," *NYDN*, July 16, 1964, 7; "CORE Member Is Accused of Trying to Arrest Mayor," *BAA*, July 25, 1964, 14.

30. L.E.J. Rachell, "Inconegro: How Law Enforcement Spies on Black Radical Groups," *History News Network*, October 16, 2019, https://perma.cc/8BA3-WGSV, accessed July 29, 2024; "City Hall; Herbert Callander Attempting to Make Citizens Arrest of Mayor Wagner," July 15, 1964, NYPD Surveillance Films, 1960–1980, Rec. 0063, nypd_f_0207, NYCMA.

31. "7 Rights Demonstrators Get Suspended Sentences"; "Tribute to Judge Edward D. Caiazzo," *Congressional Record* 110, no. 17, House (September 22, 1964): 22411; Jack Roth, "Judge Scolds Woman in Slacks and Charms Her with Gallantry," *NYT*, August 10, 1960, 33.

32. "7 Rights Demonstrators Get Suspended Sentences," 19.

33. "7 Rights Demonstrators Get Suspended Sentences," 19.

34. Janet L. Abu-Lughod, *Race, Space, and Riots in Chicago, New York, and Los Angeles* (Oxford: Oxford University Press, 2007), 171–173; Michael W. Flamm, *In the Heat of the Summer: The New York Riots of 1964 and the War on Crime* (Philadelphia: University of Pennsylvania Press, 2017), 10–16; Christopher Hayes, *The Harlem Uprising: Segregation and Inequality in Postwar New York City* (New York: Columbia University Press, 2021), 110–116.

35. Theodore Jones, "Teen-Age Parade Protests Killing," *NYT*, July 18, 1964, 1.

36. "Events Leading to Riots," Box 16, Harlem Riots, Folder 16, NYPD Intelligence Records, NYCMA. On uprisings in the 1960s, see Hinton, *America on Fire*; and Peter B. Levy, *The Great Uprising: Race Riots in Urban America During the 1960s* (Cambridge: Cambridge University Press, 2018).

37. Claude Sitton, "Chaney Was Given a Brutal Beating," *NYT*, August 8, 1964, 7; John Herber, "Philadelphia, Miss., Is Awaiting Arrests in Civil Rights Slayings," *NYT*, August 7, 1964, 13; Elliot Chaze, "Judge Mize Dismisses COFO 'Scattergun' Suit," *Hattiesburg American*, July 30, 1964, 1, 4; William Bradford Huie, *Three Lives for Mississippi* (New York: WCC Books, 1965), 198; Jack Nelson, "7 Guilty in Rights Conspiracy," *LAT*, October 21, 1967, 1; David Stout, "Cecil Price, 63, Deputy Guilty in Killing of 3 Rights Workers," *NYT*, May 9, 2001, B8.

38. SNCC, "Some Proposals for a Mississippi Summer Project," memo, 1964, https://perma.cc/J4PM-FSDW, accessed July 30, 2024; "Freedom Party Cracks Miss. Status Quo," *LAS*, August 27, 1964, A1.

39. Maegan Parker Brooks and Davis W. Houck, eds., *The Speeches of Fannie Lou Hamer: To Tell It Like It Is* (Jackson: University Press of Mississippi, 2011), 42–54.

40. Keisha N. Blain, *Until I Am Free: Fannie Lou Hamer's Enduring Message to America* (New York: Beacon Press, 2021), 53–58; Kate Clifford Larson, *Walk with Me: A Biography of Fannie Lou Hamer* (Oxford: Oxford University Press, 2021), 273; Maegan Parker Brooks, *Fannie Lou Hamer: America's Freedom Fighting Woman* (Lanham, Md.: Rowman & Littlefield Publishers, 2020), 78–80; Nan Robertson, "Mississippian Relates Struggle of Negro in Voter Registration," *NYT*, August 24, 1964, 17.

41. "Mississippi, Freedom Rally Series Subject," *NYAN*, July 25, 1964, 35.

42. Edward C. Burks, "Mississippi Negro Tells of Beating," *NYT*, August 21, 1964, 12.

43. "Commitment Scored in Callender Case," *NYT*, July 22, 1964, 20; "Accuser of Mayor Gets 60-Day Term," *NYT*, January 14, 1965, 41; "Civil Rights Leader out of Bellevue," *NYT*, July 21, 1964, 22; Ulasewicz, *President's Private Eye*, 157.

44. David Henderson, "Boston Road Blues," in *Black Fire: An Anthology of Afro-American Writing*, ed. LeRoi Jones and Larry Neal (New York: William Morrow, 1968), 233–238.

45. Brownmiller, "View from the Inside," 11.

46. Ulasewicz, *President's Private Eye*, 157.

7. Infiltration

1. Transcript, *U.S. v. Bowe*, 3388–3389.

2. Transcript, *U.S. v. Bowe*, 3388–3415.

3. "Narrative—C.O.R.E. Participation in N.Y.–Harlem–Bedford-Stuyvesant Riots, 1964," CORE Folders, NYPD Intelligence Records, NYCMA.

4. "Narrative—C.O.R.E. Participation in N.Y.–Harlem–Bedford-Stuyvesant Riots, 1964."

5. Manning Marable, *Malcolm X: A Life of Reinvention* (New York: Viking, 2011), 305, 335.

6. Transcript, *U.S. v. Bowe*, 912; Brownmiller, "View from the Inside," 3; Timothy Tyson, *Radio Free Dixie: Robert F. Williams and the Roots of Black Power* (Chapel Hill: University of North Carolina Press, 1999), 262–286; "Rally to Protest Police Terror in Harlem," *The Militant*, July 27, 1964, 1.

7. Leslie Evans, "Manifesto Issued in Capital for Freedom Now Party," *The Militant*, September 2, 1963, 1. See also Paula Marie Seniors, *Mae Mallory, the Monroe Defense Committee, and World Revolutions* (Athens: University of Georgia Press, 2024).

8. Ulasewicz, *President's Private Eye*, 153.

9. Transcript, *U.S. v. Bowe*, 2222; Brownmiller, "View from the Inside."

10. William Rice, "84 Pro-Fidel Students Home, Get Their Passports Lifted," *NYDN*, August 15, 1964, 3; File 105-100322-122, cited in "Correlation Summary—Robert Steele Collier," Bureau File 105-132441, September 17, 1971, FBI.

11. Memo, Boston SAC 105-BS-11873 to Director J. Edgar Hoover, "Robert Steele Collier," July 15, 1964, FBI.

12. Raymond Wood, transcript of interview with BOSS officials, 22, "Collier, Robert," File 66-M, NYPD Intelligence Records, NYCMA; transcript, *U.S. v. Bowe*, 1189; appendix, *U.S. v. Bowe*, 101b–103b.

13. Wood, transcript of interview with BOSS officials, 6; Raymond Wood, timeline of undercover activities, February 16, 1965, "Collier, Robert," File 66-M, NYPD Intelligence Records, NYCMA.

14. Appendix, *U.S. v. Bowe*, 185b–186b, 270b–286b; transcript, *U.S. v. Bowe*, 1123, 1153.

15. Wood, timeline of undercover activities, February 16, 1965.

16. Transcript, *U.S. v. Bowe*, 918–925; Wood, timeline of undercover activities, February 16, 1965; U.S. Department of the Army, *Explosives and Demolitions* (Washington, D.C.: U.S. Government Printing Office, 1963).

17. "N.A.G. Membership Roster," Folder 252253-060-0028, Nonviolent Action Group, June 4, 1964–November 18, 1965, SNCC Papers, King Center, PQHV; "Sayyed Held Before in Cambridge Fray," *Cumberland Evening Times*, February 19, 1965, 7; "Accused Plotter Called Strange," *BAA*, February 20, 1965, 13.

18. "Election Rally & Dance," *The Militant*, July 10–17, 1961, 3; telegram, Washington Freedom Riders Committee to John F. Kennedy, May 28, 1961, Folder 001349-003-0395, January 26, 1961–August 6, 1962, Civil Rights During the Kennedy Administration, 1961–1963, Part 1, White House Central Files and Staff Files and the President's Office Files, PQHV; "Freedom-Rider Sympathizers Demonstrate at White House," *NYT*, May 31, 1961, 22; Walter Bowe, interview with the author, recording, January 7, 2020, Brooklyn; Khaleel Sayyed, interview with the author, recording, June 15, 2019, Paige, Texas.

19. Memo, Herbert Romerstein to Donald T. Appell, "Riots—New York City—Statue of Liberty Case," September 20, 1967, "Riots—New York—General" Folder, HUAC Records, NARA-CLA; transcript, *U.S. v. Bowe*, 1354, 1370; appendix, *U.S. v. Bowe*, 138b–140b, 359b, 368b, 377b.

20. Transcript, *U.S. v. Bowe*, 1377; appendix, *U.S. v. Bowe*, 109b–115b.

21. Ken MacQueen, "Political Dynamite," *Ottawa Citizen*, February 9, 1995, 13.

22. Transcript, *U.S. v. Bowe*, 639; appendix, *U.S. v. Bowe*, 137b.

23. Transcript, *U.S. v. Bowe*, 3399, 1382; memo, J. A. Sizzo to W. C. Sullivan, "Robert S. Collier," February 3, 1965, FBI Record 157-2624-4; Hart, *Memoirs of a Spy*; Edith Evans Asbury, "Detective Defends Role He Played as a Panther," *NYT*, December 9, 1970, 64; Ulasewicz, *President's Private Eye*, 161–167; memo, SAC New York to SAC Albany, "Re: New York and Albany Telephone Calls 1/29/65, 2/2/65," February 9, 1965, FBI Record 157-1411-39.

24. Memo, "Illegal Sources of C-4 (Plastic Explosive) in the Metropolitan Area," February 10, 1965, "Collier, Robert," File 66-M, NYPD Intelligence Records, NYCMA; appendix, *U.S. v. Bowe*, 149b, 176b.

25. Transcript, *U.S. v. Bowe*, 2191, 653; appendix, *U.S. v. Bowe*, 150b–151b.

26. Appendix, *U.S. v. Bowe*, 195b–196b.

27. Appendix, *U.S. v. Bowe*, 376b; Raymond Wood, memo, February 3, 1965, "Collier, Robert," File 66-M, NYPD Intelligence Records, NYCMA.

28. Teletype, SAC New York to Director, February 13, 1965, FBI Record 157-1411-41; teletype, John Dennis O'Connell, "New York Teletypes to Bureau Dated 2/13/65, 2/10/65, and 2/4/65," February 19, 1965, FBI Record 157-1411-1211; O'Reilly, *Racial Matters*, 99.

29. Teletype, SAC New York to Director, February 13, 1965; appendix, *U.S. v. Bowe*, 202b.

30. Appendix, *U.S. v. Bowe*, 210b.

31. Report, Daniel J. Quigley, "Black Liberation Front," March 5, 1965, 19, FBI Record 100-15485; appendix, *U.S. v. Bowe*, 200b–212b.

32. Homer Bigart, "4 Held in Plot to Blast Statue of Liberty, Liberty Bell and Washington Monument," *NYT*, February 17, 1965, 1.

33. Bigart, "4 Held in Plot to Blast Statue of Liberty, Liberty Bell and Washington Monument," 1; "Sketches of Figures and Groups in Dynamiting Plot," *NYT*, February 17, 1965, 34; Edward V. McCarthy, "Terrorist Shrine Plot Unfolds," *BG*, February 17, 1965, 1; Phil Casey, "Monument Bomb Plot Foiled," *WP*, February 17, 1965, 1; "Hero Cop Foils Bomb Plot—Liberty Target; Girl & 3 Seized," *NYDN*, February 17, 1965, 1, 3–5; "4 Seized in Conspiracy to Blow Up Statue of Liberty," *LAT*, February 17, 1965, 1; "Nab 4 in Liberty Bell Blast Plot," *CD*, February 17, 1965, 1; "Statue of Liberty Bomb Plot Alleged," *IT*, February 17, 1965, 1; Michael Mok, "Plot to Behead the Statue of Liberty," *Life*, February 26, 1965, 38; "The Monumental Plot," *Time*, February 26, 1965, 22–23; "Conspiracies: The Dynamiters," *Newsweek*, March 1, 1965, 33–34.

34. U.S. Attorney for the Southern District of New York, "Press Release," February 16, 1965, *U.S. v. Bowe*, Case 29881, 65 C.R. 1989 (U.S. District Court, Southern District of New York, 1965), NARA-NYC; Frank J. Donner, *The Un-Americans* (New York: Ballantine Books, 1961), 54–98.

35. "Four Seized in Plot on U.S. Shrines," *NYDN*, February 17, 1965, 3–4; Theo Wilson, "Gold Badge of Courage for Cop; Dynamite Outplayed," *NYDN*, February 17, 1965, 3–4.

36. Bowe, interview with the author; Sayyed, interview with the author.

37. Brown-Nagin, *Courage to Dissent*, 175–211; testimony of Ernst H. Rosenberger, in *George Harrold Carswell. Hearings Before the Committee on the Judiciary, U.S. Senate*, 91st Cong., 2d sess., January 27–29 and February 2–3, 1970 (Washington, D.C.: U.S. Government Printing Office, 1970), 149–150. On Lane, see memo, Commanding Officer of Bureau of Special Services, "Picketing of Police Headquarters, 240 Centre Street, Manhattan, by Manhattan Chapter of Congress of Racial Equality (CORE)," November 19, 1963; "Police Brutality Charged by CORE," *NYT*, November 9, 1963, 21; Peter Kihss, "Lawyer Urges Defense for Oswald at Inquiry," *NYT*, December 19, 1963, 24.

In December 1963, Lane made international headlines when he submitted a ten thousand-word brief to the fledgling Warren Commission—reprinted in full by the left-wing *National Guardian* newspaper—urging it to appoint posthumous defense counsel to Lee Harvey Oswald, in what amounted to the first major critique of the lone gunman theory in Kennedy's assassination. See Mark Lane, "Oswald Innocent? A Lawyer's Brief," *NG*, December 19, 1963.

38. Transcript, *U.S. v. Bowe*, 3398; decision, *U.S. v. Bowe*, U.S. Court of Appeals for the Second Circuit, April 28, 1966, 1720, NARA-NYC.

39. Transcript, *U.S. v. Bowe*, 702, 2219, 945–946, 1289–1290; appendix, *U.S. v. Bowe*, 450b–451b.

40. Transcript, *U.S. v. Bowe*, 864, 459–460; *Report of the National Advisory Commission on Civil Disorders*, 169.

41. Appendix, *U.S. v. Bowe*, 286b; transcript, *U.S. v. Bowe*, 705–706, 1118–1122, 831.

42. Transcript, *U.S. v. Bowe*, 1141–1142, 1237, 1243, 1247–1248, 1306–1315; Exhibit XXVIII, *U.S. v. Bowe*, Case 29881, 65 C.R. 1989 (U.S. District Court, Southern District of New York, 1965), NARA-NYC.
43. Transcript, *U.S. v. Bowe*, 2191, 711, 1327–1330, 2191; Brownmiller, "View from the Inside."
44. Transcript, *U.S. v. Bowe*, 1419–1438; Wood, memo, February 3, 1965.
45. Appendix, *U.S. v. Bowe*, 458b–459b; brief, Walter Bowe and Khaleel Sayyed, appendix of appellants Bowe and Sayyed, *U.S. v. Bowe*, U.S. Court of Appeals for the Second Circuit, undated, 13.
46. Appendix, *U.S. v. Bowe*, 441b–457b, 469b–471b.
47. Murray Kempton, "A Policeman's Plot," *New York World-Telegram*, May 19, 1965, 29.
48. Richard J. H. Johnston, "3 in Shrine Plot Are Found Guilty," *NYT*, June 15, 1965, 7.
49. Gallup Organization, Gallup Poll #708, "What do you think is the most important question facing the country today?" (March 18, 1965); and Louis Harris & Associates Poll, "In the recent showdown in Selma, Alabama over Negro voting rights, have you tended to side more with the civil rights groups or with the State of Alabama?" (May 1, 1965)—both in the iPoll database, RCPOR.
50. Transcript, *U.S. v. Bowe*, 3401–3402.
51. Brownmiller, "View from the Inside," 3.
52. Bill Mahoney, "The Statue of Liberty Conspiracy Trial: No Hiding in Foley Square," *Liberator*, July 1965, 18.

8. Traitor

1. "A Police Chief Talks of 'Police Brutality,'" *U.S. News & World Report*, August 10, 1964, 34, 36.
2. Michael Hannon, "Socialist Patrolman Suspended," *New America*, September 17, 1965, 8.
3. Paul Robinson, "Race, Space and the Evolution of Black Los Angeles," and Reginald Chapple, "From Central Avenue to Leimert Park: The Shifting Center of Black Los Angeles," both in *Black Los Angeles: American Dreams and Racial Realities*, ed. Darnell M. Hunt and Ana-Christina Ramón (New York: New York University Press, 2010), 38, 60–73.
4. Sklansky, "Not Your Father's Police Department," 1216; Jill Leovy, *Ghettoside: A True Story of Murder in America* (New York: Spiegel & Grau, 2015), 157; "NAACP Claims Brutality by Police in L.A.," *LAT*, February 17, 1962, B3. On police brutality in Los Angeles in these years, see also Felber, *Those Who Know Don't Say*, 88–94, 120–150.
5. Hannon, "Socialist Patrolman Suspended," 8; John Bryan, "Why Is Cop a Dirty Word?" *LAFP*, May 14, 1965, 5. On the get-tough tactics of the LAPD in these years, see Felker-Kantor, *Policing Los Angeles*, 19–25.
6. Michael B. Hannon, Personnel Rating Report, LAPD, July 6, 1960, MHPP, in author's possession.

7. "UCRC Joins Policeman's Fight," *LAS*, June 10, 1965, A-4; Hannon, "Socialist Patrolman Suspended," 12.

8. Hannon, "Socialist Patrolman Suspended"; Michael Hannon, interview with Betty Egle, May 28, 1965, MHPP, in author's possession; Sean Stewart, ed., *On the Ground: An Illustrated Anecdotal History of the Sixties Underground Press in the U.S.* (Oakland, Calif.: PM Press, 2011), 10–12.

9. "500 March on City Hall to Protest Segregation," *LAT*, May 11, 1963, 8.

10. Hannon, "Socialist Patrolman Suspended."

11. Michael Hannon, Personnel Rating Report, LAPD, June 30, 1963, MHPP, in author's possession; Hannon, interview with Egle, May 28, 1965.

12. G. Edward Griffin, *The Life and Words of Robert Welch, Founder of the John Birch Society* (Thousand Oaks, Calif.: American Media, 1975), 239; Barbara Shell Stone, "The John Birch Society of California" (Ph.D. diss., University of Southern California, 1968), 1.

13. Hannon, "Socialist Patrolman Suspended"; Michael Hannon, "Encouragement of Rightwing Politics," undated, MHPP, in author's possession.

14. "Support Your Local Police," *JBSB*, July 1963, 12–14.

15. "Support Your Local Police," *JBSB*, September 1963, 88–90.

16. Hannon, interview with Egle, May 28, 1965, 2; transcript, recorded call between R. R. Arguello and Mike Hannon, May 10, 1965, 6, Box 28, Folder 6, Hugh Manes Papers, UCLA.

17. Mike Davis and Jon Wiener, *Set the Night on Fire: L.A. in the Sixties* (London: Verso, 2020), 51; "Memorial Rite Set Friday for Local CORE Founder," *LAS*, June 17, 1965, A1; Meier and Rudwick, *CORE*, 194; William Parker, "The Police Role in Civil Rights," in *The Police Yearbook 1965* (Washington, D.C.: International Association of Chiefs of Police, Inc., 1965), 280.

18. "Our Proposal to Make a Dream Come True," Los Angeles CORE, 1964, MHPP, in author's possession.

19. Brisson, "Parker, CORE Chief Predict More Anti-police Outbreaks," A1; Paul Weeks, "Parker Cites Figures on Recruitment," *LAT*, April 28, 1964, A1.

20. "Picketing in Valley Pinned on Reds by Police Inspector," *VT*, April 8, 1964, 2; "Transcript of Tape Recorded Confidential Report from Confidential Operator No. 1," April 17, 1964, Box 55, CORE Folder, Investigation Section, Organization Files, HUAC Records, NARA-CLA. The surveillance reports from the CORE meetings are blind memos printed in the same font and featuring the same heading ("TRANSCRIPT OF TAPE RECORDED") as the transcript of Arguello's conversation with Hannon, which is marked as an LAPD record. They also feature multiple references to "Chief Parker." See transcript, recorded call between Arguello and Hannon, May 10, 1965; and "Confidential Report from Confidential Reporter #1," January 8 and August 26, 1965, LAPD, CORE Folder, HUAC Records, NARA-CLA.

21. "CORE Groups Demand Parker's Resignation," *LAT*, May 5, 1964, A8; "Police Chief Unfit to Carry Out Duties," *LAS*, May 7, 1964, A2; "National Police Leader Assails CORE," *Los Angeles Herald-Examiner*, May 7, 1964, F-8.

22. "Pressure on Police Pays Off," *Los Angeles CORE-Lator*, October 1964, 2.

23. "Pressure on Police Pays Off," 2.

24. "Police and Free Choice," *PC*, February 1965, 8–9.

25. Harry Bernstein, "Extremism Now Laid to Police, Parker Charges," *LAT*, November 21, 1964, B10; letter, Thomas Bradley, agenda packet, October 28, 1964, Board of Police Commissioners Meeting, Box B-0259, Los Angeles City Archives; "Fate of 14 Policemen Hinges on Birch Political Status," *PI*, November 12, 1964, 6; "Mayor to Curb Duties of All Police Members in John Birch Society," *PI*, November 14, 1964, 17; "Phila. Birch Unit Lists More than 20 Policemen," *PI*, November 17, 1964, 42; "Rousselot Cites Big Gains by Birch Society," *LAT*, December 9, 1964, 26.

26. David J. Garrow, *Protest at Selma: Martin Luther King, Jr., and the Voting Rights Act of 1965* (New Haven, Conn.: Yale University Press, 1978), 78–85.

27. Walter Ames and Richard Main, "Rights Melee Here Jails 98," *LAT*, March 11, 1965, 1, 3; "Millions Roar Alabama Protest," *NJG*, March 13, 1965, C1; "Thousands Across Nation Protest Violence in Alabama," *AC*, March 10, 1965, 6.

28. Trial transcript, "Hannon, Michael B and the Police Board of Rights Hearing," 244, Box 35, Folders 3–6; and transcript, interview with Captain Al Trembley and Sergeant H. L. Hansen, March 12, 1965, 8–10, Box 28, Folder 6—both in Hugh Manes Papers, UCLA.

29. "Transcript of Tape Recorded Confidential Report from Confidential Operator #1," March 12, April 21, and April 26, 1965, CORE Folder, HUAC Records, NARA-CLA.

30. Transcript, recorded call between Arguello and Hannon, May 10, 1965.

31. William H. Parker, Complaint and Relief from Duty or Suspension in the Matter of M. B. Hannon #10139, No. 1970, LAPD, June 1, 1965, MHPP, in author's possession.

32. Howard Hertel, "Police Spy Infiltrated Civil Rights Activities," *LAT*, June 15, 1965, 3.

33. Trial transcript, "Hannon, Michael B and the Police Board of Rights Hearing," 1–2, 566; Jack B. Kemmerer, "The Jail that Modern Science Built," *Popular Mechanics*, July 1956, 79; Hannon, Personnel Rating Report, July 6, 1960; transcript, Al Wirin, interview by Joel Gardner, September 5, 1974, 22–23, Center for Oral History Research, Charles E. Young Research Library, UCLA; *Wirin v. Parker*.

34. Howard Hertel, "32 Officers to Testify Against L.A. Policeman," *LAT*, June 29, 1965, 3; trial transcript, "Hannon, Michael B and the Police Board of Rights Hearing," 11.

35. Parker, Complaint and Relief from Duty or Suspension in the Matter of M. B. Hannon, June 1, 1965; letter, M. B. Hannon to LAPD, June 4, 1965, MHPP, in author's possession; Ken Hansen, "Rank and File Police, Firemen Seeking Power," *LAT*, February 20, 1972, SF-A1; trial transcript, "Hannon, Michael B and the Police Board of Rights Hearing," 540–542, 1011; "Mike Hannon Board of Rights Hearing Continues," *LAS*, July 1, 1965, A2.

36. Letter, Bea Stanley, Michael Hannon Defense and Support Fund, June 1965, MHPP, in author's possession.

37. Letter, Mrs. C. R. Brown, July 27, 1965; and undated postcard, "Hi Brother Rat"—both in MHPP, in author's possession.

38. Curtis Sitomer, "Los Angeles Debates Policemen's Rights," *Christian Science Monitor*, August 11, 1965, 12; "Police May Fire Civil Rights Picket," *Detroit Free Press*, July 8, 1965, 18; "Officer Returned to Duty at Devil's Island Station," *Albuquerque Journal*, December 3, 1965, B-9; "Odd Cop Out," *Newsweek*, June 21, 1965, 30–31; *The World Almanac and Book of Facts* (New York: New York World-Telegram Corporation, 1965), 541; "Trial of Officer-Picket Seen as National Issue," *LAT*, June 17, 1965, 31.

39. Hugh Manes, "A Report on Law Enforcement and the Negro Citizen in Los Angeles," July 1963, Box 40, Folder 1, Hugh Manes Papers, UCLA; "Cops and the Courts," *Frontier*, August 1959, 11–12; "The Price Is Right," *Frontier*, April 1962, 13–14.

40. Trial transcript, "Hannon, Michael B and the Police Board of Rights Hearing," 182, 193, 723, 735, 791, 1441.

41. Trial transcript, "Hannon, Michael B and the Police Board of Rights Hearing," 658–659, 664, 790, 831.

42. "Support Your Local Police," July 1963; trial transcript, "Hannon, Michael B and the Police Board of Rights Hearing," 670–672, 975, 1029, 1068–1069, 1247, 1251, 1380, 1446. On Roth as a John Birch Society section leader, see letter, Jesse Roth to J. Edgar Hoover, March 11, 1965, FBI Record 62-104779-102.

43. Trial transcript, "Hannon, Michael B and the Police Board of Rights Hearing," 675–676.

44. Trial transcript, "Hannon, Michael B and the Police Board of Rights Hearing," 9; Corine Crawford, "Teatro Intimo Stages Spanish 'Inspector Calls,'" *LAT*, October 29, 1968, G8; Joseph Hanania, "On the Right Wavelength with Latinos," *LAT*, December 26, 1995; Paul S. Hospodar, "Speaking About L.A. Police Job Opportunities," *Valley News*, March 26, 1970, 2; "LA Officer Demands Look at Police Files," *Los Angeles Independent*, June 24, 1965, 1; "Court Limits Evidence in Police Case," *LAT*, June 25, 1965, 38.

45. Trial transcript, "Hannon, Michael B and the Police Board of Rights Hearing," 44, 467, 720, 747–748; "Transcript of Tape Recorded Confidential Report from Confidential Operator No. 1," April 17, 1964.

46. Trial transcript, "Hannon, Michael B and the Police Board of Rights Hearing," 998, 1017, 1072.

47. Trial transcript, "Hannon, Michael B and the Police Board of Rights Hearing," 1422–1425, 1462.

48. Eric Malnic, "Parker Orders Suspension, Not Dismissal, for Hannon," *LAT*, July 28, 1965, 3, 21.

49. Art Berman, "Hannon Found Guilty and Dismissal Asked," *LAT*, July 24, 1965, 1, 19; Howard Hertal and Art Berman, "Hannon Back with Police—in Locked Booth," *LAT*, December 2, 1965, 3; "Cop Reinstated After Suspension for Rights Work," *BAA*, December 11, 1965, 14; "Civil Rights Police Man Back—in Cage," *San Bernadino County Sun*, December 2, 1965, 1; "LA Civil Rights Policeman Loses Suit," *Sacramento Bee*, June 10, 1966, 9.

50. Felker-Kantor, *Policing Los Angeles*, 26–34; Gerald Horne, *Fire This Time: The Watts Uprising and the 1960s* (Charlottesville: University of Virginia Press,

1995), 54–60; "We're on Top, Says Chief," *BPH*, August 16, 1965, 12; Gordon Grant, "Parker Says Rioting 'Can't Happen Here,'" *LAT*, July 23, 1964, SF1.

51. Mike Hannon, "Hannon Describes Police Indifference to Poverty," *LAFP*, August 20, 1965, 9.

52. Erwin Baker, "Yorty Hits Brutality Charges as 'Big Lie,'" *LAT*, August 18, 1965, 3.

9. Deacons and Dynamite

1. Paul Good, "Klantown, USA," *The Nation*, February 2, 1965, 110–113; *Polk's Bogalusa (Washington Parish, La.) City Directory* (Richmond, Va.: R. L. Polk Publisher, 1965), 23–24; *Activities of Ku Klux Klan Organizations in the United States. Hearings Before the Committee on Un-American Activities, U.S. House of Representatives*, 89th Cong., 2d sess., January 6, 1966 (Washington, D.C.: U.S. Government Printing Office, 1966), 2549–2550.

2. Lance E. Hill, *The Deacons for Defense: Armed Resistance and the Civil Rights Movement* (Chapel Hill: University of North Carolina Press, 2004), 92–94. CORE, "Fact Sheet on Bogalusa," February 17, 1965; and "Bogalusa, Louisiana Incident Summary: January 25–February 21"—both in "Bogalusa, Jackson Parish (Jonesboro), Louisiana Local Chapter, Community Relations Department" Folder, CORE Papers, 1941–1967, PQHV.

3. Hill, *Deacons for Defense*, 24–26, 31–35, 41, 45; Justin Madden, "The Life and Times of Charles Fenton," *The Gramblinite*, February 28, 2013, https://perma.cc/X9CM-VZRS, accessed August 30, 2024.

4. Teletype, SAC New Orleans to J. Edgar Hoover, "Deacons for Defense and Justice," February 23, 1965, FBI File 157-2466-3. On self-defense in the civil rights movement, see Umoja, *We Will Shoot Back*; Charles E. Cobb, *This Nonviolent Stuff'll Get You Killed: How Guns Made the Civil Rights Movement Possible* (New York: Basic Books, 2014); Tyson, *Radio Free Dixie*; Kellie Carter Jackson, *We Refuse: A Forceful History of Black Resistance* (New York: Seal Press, 2024); Jasmin A. Young, "Gloria Richardson, Armed Self-Defense, and Black Liberation in Cambridge, Maryland," *Journal of African American History* 107, no. 2 (2022): 212–237.

5. "CORE Leader Likes Word by LBJ—but Awaits Deeds," *Louisville Courier-Journal*, March 15, 1965, 7; John Fahey, "CORE Director to Lead March," *NOTP*, April 9, 1965, 16; "Weary Bogalusa Quiet Today as Invaders Plan Picketing," *Crowley Post-Signal*, April 10, 1965, 1.

6. *Activities of Ku Klux Klan Organizations*, 2448, 2549–2550.

7. "Negroes, Whites Battle in Bogalusa City Park," *Dayton Daily News*, May 20, 1965, 3; "Bogalusa Attack Is Laid to Police," *NYT*, May 20, 1965, 29; "White Woman Tells of Beating in Bogalusa," *CT*, May 20, 1965, C6; Hill, *Deacons for Defense*, 126–127.

8. Richard Haley, "CORE Deacon Relationship," Addendum, 1944–1968, Folder 27—Deacons for Defense, Subgroup E. Community Relations Department, 1949–1968, CORE Papers, MLK, PQHV.

9. James Farmer, "The CORE of It: Deacons for Defense," *NYAN*, July 10, 1965, 15.

10. Hamilton Bims, "Deacons for Defense," *Ebony*, September 1965, 25–30.

11. Gene Roberts, "CORE Maps Drive in Bogalusa, La.," *NYT*, July 5, 1965, 1; "The Demands of the Bogalusa Voters' League," July 19, 1965, Addendum, 1944–1968, Southern Regional Office Field Reports: Bogalusa, Louisiana, CORE Papers, PQHV.

12. John Fahey, "M'Elveen Case Hearing Aired," *NOTP*, June 8, 1965; see also Stanley Nelson, *Klan of Devils: The Murder of a Black Louisiana Deputy Sheriff* (Baton Rouge: Louisiana State University Press, 2021).

13. "Negro 'Deacons' Claim They Have Machine Guns, Grenades for 'War,'" *LAT*, June 13, 1965, 1.

14. Huey Newton, *Revolutionary Suicide* (New York: Penguin Books, 1973), 118; Hill, *Deacons for Defense*, 218.

15. "The Negro Feared Most by Whites in Louisiana," *Jet*, July 15, 1965, 15–19.

16. Betty Pleasant, "Cop Watching Serious Business with Community Alert Patrol," *LAS*, June 16, 1966, B11.

17. Pleasant, "Cop Watching Serious Business with Community Alert Patrol," B11; Louis J. Gothard, "How to Organize a Community Alert Patrol," *The Movement*, February 1967, 11.

18. Lane Smith, "Better Police-Citizen Climate Is Goal, Says N.A.A.C.P. Aide," *Seattle Times*, July 11, 1965; Lane Smith, "Freedom Patrols to Watch City Policemen," *Seattle Times*, July 11, 1965.

19. "Non-violent Discipline for Patrols," Box 8, Freedom Patrols Folder, CORE, Seattle Chapter Records, UW; "Slaying of Negro by Drinking Cop Spurs Action," *Jet*, August 12, 1965, 18–19.

20. "Freedom Patrols Keep Cop Watch," *SFC*, July 26, 1965, 10; Robert Vernon, "Freedom Patrols in Seattle Trail Ghetto Cops," *The Militant*, September 6, 1965, 8; Seattle Chapter, CORE, *CORE-Lator*, July 24, 1966, Accession 1563, Box 2, "Newsletter CORE-Lator 1961–1968" Folder, Seattle CORE Papers, UW.

21. Pleasant, "Cop Watching Serious Business with Community Alert Patrol"; "We Have Got to Get the Police Off Our Backs," *The Movement*, September 1966, 5, 7.

22. Davis and Wiener, *Set the Night on Fire*, 236–242; Jack Jones, "Police Hearing Boycotted by Rights Groups," *LAT*, June 11, 1966, 3; Gothard, "How to Organize a Community Alert Patrol," 11; "We Have Got to Get the Police Off Our Backs."

23. Gene Roberts, "Mississippi Reduces Police Protection for Marchers," *NYT*, June 17, 1966, 1; Forman, "1967," 13.

24. Roberts, "Mississippi Reduces Police Protection for Marchers"; Southwide Youth Leadership Conference, "Recommendations of the Findings and Recommendations Committee Are as Follows."

25. Sally Belfrage, *Freedom Summer* (New York: Viking Press, 1965), 136; Colley, *Ain't Scared of Your Jail*, 1–9.

26. Matthew J. Countryman, *Up South: Civil Rights and Black Power in Philadelphia* (Philadelphia: University of Pennsylvania Press, 2006), 209, 211–214.

27. "Tate Says Carmichael Shouldn't Have Come," *PEB*, July 18, 1966.

28. "Jim Crow's Sweetheart Deal," *PT*, February 23, 1963, 4; "Philadelphia Civil Disobedience Unit," U.S. Department of Justice; Bennett, "Tinderbox Squad," 124, 126, 128; Fox, "CD Man," 25; *Report of the National Advisory Commission on Civil Disorders*, 169.

29. "Statement of Barry Dawson, 23-C," August 13, 1966, 6–9, Box 44, Folder 2, SNCC Subject File, James Forman Papers, LOC.

30. J. Donald Porter, "Beaten SNCC Worker Claims 'Harassment' After 'Wild Wednesday,'" *PT*, August 13, 1966, 1–2; statement, Arlene Alma Jones, Philadelphia Police Department, August 17, 1966, 2, FBI File 44-HQ-33870, NARA-CP; memo and summary of Operation Alert flyer, Special Agent Elmer E. Sussman to SAC, "Possible Racial Violence—Major Urban Areas—RM," September 1, 1966, FBI File 157-PH-2849, NARA-CP.

31. Memo, Sergeant Charles Bush, "Investigation Concerning Injuries of Barry Dawson Field Secretary of S.N.C.C.," Philadelphia Police Department, August 11, 1966; and memo, A. Rosen to Deke DeLoach, "Unknown Subjects; Barry Dawson—Victim Civil Rights," August 31, 1966—both in FBI File 44-HQ-33870, NARA-CP.

32. Search warrant for 909 N. 16th Street, No. 37066, Philadelphia, August 12, 1966, Box 44, Folder 2, SNCC Subject File, James Forman Papers, LOC; Richard Aregood and Jerry Oppenheimer, "Dynamite Found in Raids on 'Black Power' HQ," *PDN*, August 13, 1966, 3.

33. "Statement of Barry Dawson, 23-C," August 13, 1966; search warrant for 909 N. 16th Street, No. 37066, Philadelphia, August 12, 1966; Aregood and Oppenheimer, "Dynamite Found in Raids on 'Black Power' HQ"; "4 Racists Held, Dynamite Seized in SNCC Raids," *PDN*, August 13, 1966, 1.

34. "4 Racists Held, Dynamite Seized in SNCC Raids," 1.

35. "4 Racists Held, Dynamite Seized in SNCC Raids"; Aregood and Oppenheimer, "Dynamite Found in Raids on 'Black Power' HQ"; "SNCC Member Gives Up in Phila.," *Camden Courier-Post*, August 15, 1966, 3. On the long genealogy of SWAT teams, see Schrader, *Badges Without Borders*, 214–234.

36. "One of 4 in SNCC Raid Gives Self Up," *PI*, August 15, 1966; George J. Murray and Francis M. Lordan, "SNCC Aides Hunted After Police Raids," *PI*, August 14, 1966, 1; "Report from Fred Meely," August 13, 1966, Box 44, Folder 3, James Forman Papers, LOC; Donald A. McDonough and Dennis M. Higgins, "Rizzo Contends Dynamite Find Barred Incident," *PI*, August 16, 1966.

37. "Statement of Barry Dawson, 23-C," August 13, 1966.

38. James Forman, "Philadelphia Black Paper," draft and final versions, August 1966, Box 44, Folder 4, James Forman Papers, LOC; Bill Wingell, "SNCC in Philadelphia: The Cops Declare War," *NG*, August 27, 1966, 6.

39. Forman, "Philadelphia Black Paper," final version, 5–6; Art Peters, "Off the Mainstem: Local Legal Eagles Plan Move to Swank Suite on Market Street," *PT*, November 13, 1962, 5; Bill Wingell, "War on SNCC Pressed in Philadelphia Court," *NG*, September 3, 1966.

40. Forman, "Philadelphia Black Paper," final version, 6–7; flyer, "No Votes for White Power," FBI File 44-HQ-33870, NARA-CP; flyer, "Witness Against the Dynamite Frame Up!" August 1966, Box 44, Folder 4, James Forman Papers, LOC.

41. Forman, "Philadelphia Black Paper," final version, 1–2, 8.

42. J. Donald Porter, "SNCC Advised Not to Testify by Atty," *PT*, August 23, 1966, 1–2; "3 Dynamite Suspects Held in $50,000 Bail, 3 Released," *PI*, August 23, 1966, 1, 3; § 4417, Carrying Bombs or Explosives, in *Purdon's Pennsylvania Statutes Annotated: Title 18, Crimes and Offenses*, § 1 to 4700 (Philadelphia: George T. Bisel Company, 1963), 285.

43. Forman, "Philadelphia Black Paper," final version, 8; "SNCC Suspects Photographed with Dynamite," *PEB*, August 21–23, 1966; Dick Aarons, "SNCC 'Frame' Charges Fizzle; 3 Held in Dynamite Rap," *PDN*, August 23, 1966, 5; Forman, "Philadelphia Black Paper," draft version; "Stokely Carmichael Stirs Things Up in Philadelphia," *NG*, September 10, 1966, 6; "Black Power Rally—Flyer," Box 44, Folder 2, James Forman Papers, LOC; "SNCC Leader Tells 1000 at Phila. Rally 'Slave Period Is Over,'" *PI*, August 31, 1966, 5.

44. "How to Handle Racists? Some Say to Ignore Them," *PDN*, September 1, 1966, 5; Joe O'Dowd and Rich Aregood, "The Silent Six: Keeping Civility in Civil Rights Protests," *PDN*, September 26, 1966, 5.

45. "3 Hunted Leaders of SNCC Surrender," *PI*, November 11, 1966, 4; "Three SNCCers Surrender," *PDN*, November 11, 1966, 4; "Sudden Illness Forces 3rd Delay in SNCC Hearing," *PDN*, December 22, 1966, 25; "Cop Brutality Protests Flood Tribune Office," *PT*, November 21, 1967, 1; "Snick Aide Accused of Mule Kick to Cop Held for Jury," *PT*, November 26, 1966, 7.

46. "Snick Closes Office Doors 'Temporarily,'" *PT*, February 7, 1967, 4; "Court Dismisses SNCC Trio in Dynamite Case," *PI*, April 23, 1967, 37; William Akers, interview with the author, August 22, 2018; "Hid Dynamite in SNCC Office, Dawson Admits," *WP*, March 9, 1968, A5; Forman, *Making of Black Revolutionaries*, 471.

47. "Classic Frame-Up: SNCC Unit Dies," *NG*, May 27, 1967, 11; Forman, "Philadelphia Black Paper," final version, 11.

10. Retaliation

1. Larry Lee, "Black Houston," *TO*, May 13, 1966, 1–2.

2. "Fifty Officers Disciplined for Racial Disrespect," *HP*, June 30, 1967; Rob Meckel, "Black Ex-Policeman: 2nd-Class Days Remembered," *HP*, November 17, 1980; Rudwick, *Unequal Badge*, 10–11.

3. Tom Curtis, "Support Your Local Police," *Texas Monthly*, September 1977, 160; Larry Watts, "Herman Short—A Police Chief During Times of Change," *Crimes, Criminals and the Cops Who Chase Them*, July 2013, https://perma.cc /7TH9-WKW3, accessed February 3, 2025; Jack Weeks, "Evolution of Police Spy Unit in Houston," *HC*, January 12, 1975, 1, 20; Joe Singleton, interview by Louis Marchiafava, October 3, 1974, OH 166, Oral History Collection, HHRC. On

Houston's movement in the 1960s, see F. Kenneth Jensen, "The Houston Sit-In Movement of 1960–61," in *Black Dixie: Afro-Texan Culture and History in Houston*, ed. Howard Beeth and Cary D. Wintz (College Station: Texas A&M University Press, 1992), 211–222; Thomas R. Cole, *No Color Is My Kind: The Life of Eldrewey Stearns and the Integration of Houston* (Austin: University of Texas Press, 1997); and Brian D. Behnken, *Fighting Their Own Battles: Mexican Americans, African Americans, and the Struggle for Civil Rights in Texas* (Chapel Hill: University of North Carolina Press, 2011).

4. "James Forman," October 6, 1966, Box 31, Folder 1, Police Intelligence Reports, 1965–1967, Louis Welch Papers, HHRC; "A Note About the Friends of SNCC Groups—What Do They Do," ca. 1965, Press Releases, May 31, 1965–February 17, 1968 Folder, William Porter Papers, SNCC Papers, MLK, PQHV.

5. "Young Democrats," February 18, 1966; "American Civil Liberties Union Meeting on 02/27/66," March 4, 1966; "Ku Klux Klan," March 21, 1966; "KKK Meeting on 07/26/66," July 26, 1966; "NAACP Demonstration," March 7, 1966; "Booker T. Bonner's Activities," July 20, 1966; "Houston Citizens for Action on Vietnam," March 7, 1966; "Houston Socialist Forum Meeting on June 24, 1966," June 28, 1966; "Sargent Shriver's Visit to Houston 7/7/66 in Regards to Youth Program," July 8, 1966; "Activities of Rev. Wm. A. Lawson (7/23 & 24)," July 26, 1966; and "Activity of Rev. Lawson July 25th + 26th," July 27, 1966—all in Police Intelligence Reports, 1965–1967, Louis Welch Papers, HHRC.

6. "City Begins 'Partner' Plan in Negro Areas," *HC*, December 13, 1966, 1, 13.

7. "City Begins 'Partner' Plan in Negro Areas," 1, 13.

8. "Incident and Names of Subject at the Speech by Mayor Welch on 12/13/66 at T.S.U.," December 15, 1966, Police Intelligence Reports, 1965–1967, Louis Welch Papers, HHRC.

9. "Officer Says 4 Resisted Before Scuffle," *HC*, March 4, 1967, 25.

10. "Friends of S.N.C.C. Post Desires on Asst. Attorney General's Office," *The Informer*, March 18, 1967; "Negroes Stage Noisy Rally Downtown," *HP*, March 12, 1967, 1.

11. "Demonstration March by Negroes of the SNCC Group Protesting Police Brutality on 3/11/67," March 13, 1967, Police Intelligence Reports, 1967, Louis Welch Papers, HHRC.

12. Report, "Frederick Douglass Kirkpatrick," November 6, 1967, FBI File 100-HQ-448314, Section 1, Serials 1, NARA-CP; Hill, *Deacons for Defense*, 30–51.

13. Gethsemane Campbell, interview with the author, recording, October 21, 2020; Tracy Jan and Arelis R. Hernández, "Segregated from Opportunity," *WP*, October 15, 2020, http://t.ly/TXGM4, accessed September 22, 2024; "Johnson, Lee Otis," March 26, 1960, Department of Police, Bureau of Criminal Identification, Houston, Texas, FBI File 100-HQ-448069, NARA-CP; W. H. Stickney, "Ex-Gambler, Ex-Pimp, Ex–Car Thief Now Minister," *HC*, October 8, 1972, sec. 4, p. 4; Curtis Lang, "A Depleted Legacy: Public Housing in Houston," *Cite: The Architecture and Design Review of Houston* 33 (1995): 10–15.

14. "SNCC Unit Told to Meet Off Campus," *HC*, March 21, 1967, 8; "Protest Held in Support of Teacher," *HC*, March 23, 1967, 3.

15. Joyce Vane Weedman, "SNCC Members Bar Doors at TSU," *HC*, March 28, 1967, 1, 7; Joyce Jane Weedman and Ted D'Andriole, "Boycott at TSU Fizzles and Classes About Normal," *HC*, March 29, 1967, 8.

16. Charles M. Smith and Bill Moore, "In Houston . . . Black Student Power," *The Rag*, April 10, 1967, 11; "Friends of SNCC Bow to TSU Ruling, Ask Accreditation," *HC*, March 30, 1967, sec. 7, p. 3; "March Leader Arrested at TSU," *HC*, April 5, 1967, 1; Joyce Jane Weedman, "Two Protesters at TSU Jailed; Cafeteria Torn Up," *HC*, April 4, 1967, 1; "TSU Protesters Increase as Compromise Bid Fails," *HC*, April 5, 1967, 1, 10; Smith and Moore, "In Houston . . . Black Student Power," 3, 10–11; William C. Bryson, "Texas Southern University: Born in Sin, a College Finally Makes Houston Listen," *Harvard Crimson*, May 22, 1967; Joyce Jane Weedman, "Out of Jail, Demonstrator Says He's Through with TSU Protests," *HC*, April 7, 1967, 7; "A Question of Money," *HC*, May 24, 1967, sec. 3, p. 8.

17. "NAACP Offers Plan for Better Police Relation," *HC*, April 18, 1967, 2; Ethel Gray, "Houston NAACP Warns of Uneasiness due to Fear of Police Brutality," *FT*, April 22, 1967, 37.

18. Rev. F. D. Kirkpatrick, "The Police Attack at Texas Southern," *The Militant*, June 26, 1967, 8; "20 Marchers Stage Protest at NE School," *HC*, May 15, 1967, 1; "Sheriff Arrests 28 at School Protest," *HC*, May 16, 1967, 2; "36 Arrested at City Dump Protest," *HP*, May 17, 1967, 1.

19. "Field Research Report: Civil Disturbances in Houston, Texas, Spring, 1967," February 1968, 7–8, Box E 70, Records of the National Advisory Commission on Civil Disorders, Embargoed Series, LBJPL; Sonny Wells, "Dump Squabble in Sunnyside," *FT*, May 20, 1967, 7.

20. "Field Research Report: Civil Disturbances in Houston," 8.

21. "Field Research Report: Civil Disturbances in Houston," 8; Mary Jane Schier, "Officer Blaylock Feels He's Lucky," *HP*, May 18, 1967, 12.

22. Bill Lawson, "A Second Look at the 'TSU Riots,'" *FT*, May 27, 1967, 8.

23. "Field Research Report: Civil Disturbances in Houston," 5–11; Lawson, "Second Look at the 'TSU Riots,'" 8; "Dorm Matron's Account," *The Informer*, May 20, 1967, 7; Mattie Mae Harbert, "To Whom It May Concern," May 17, 1967, Texas Folder, Subgroup A. Atlanta Office, Series XV. State Project Files, 1960–1968, SNCC Papers, MLK, PQHV.

24. Zarko Franks and Lloyd Mathews, "Dorms Stormed to End TSU Riot," *HC*, May 17, 1967, 1, 16.

25. "Welch: Minority Group to Blame," *HC*, May 17, 1967, final edition, 1.

26. Lawson, "Second Look at the 'TSU Riots,'" 8.

27. "Welch: Minority Group to Blame," 1; "Five Charged in TSU Riot Fatal to Young Officer," *HP*, May 18, 1967, 13; "Campus Slaying Nearer Solution," *MCA*, May 19, 1967, 12; Lawson, "Second Look at the 'TSU Riots,'" 8.

28. "Officer Slain, 3 Wounded, 488 Arrested; Welch Urges Restraint—Mayor Blames Minority Group," *HC*, May 17, 1967, 1; Franks and Mathews, "Dorms Stormed to End TSU Riot"; David Beckwith, "Police 'Did Right Thing,' Says Leader," *HC*, May 17, 1967, 1.

29. "Officer Slain, 3 Wounded, 488 Arrested."

30. "Students Describe 'Nightmare' During All-Out Assault on T.S.U.," *The Informer*, May 20, 1967, 1.

31. Lawson, "Second Look at the 'TSU Riots,'" 8; "The *Chronicle* Believes," *HC*, May 17, 1967, 1.

32. Lawson, "Second Look at the 'TSU Riots,'" 8.

33. Willie Robinson and Gary Rutherford, statements, 11, 13, Texas Folder, Subgroup A. Atlanta Office, Series XV, SNCC Papers, PQHV.

34. Kirkpatrick, "Police Attack at Texas Southern," 8; Lawson, "Second Look at the 'TSU Riots.'"

35. Bob Tutt, "Murder Is Charged in Riot at TSU, Police Cleared of Blame by Jury," *HC*, June 2, 1967, 1–2; Sonny Wells, "Attorney for TSU Students Talks of Case," *FT*, June 17, 1967, 4.

36. "Police Riot in Atlanta," *SNCC Newsletter*, June–July 1967, 3; "Executions in the U.S. 1608–2002: The ESPY File. Executions by State," Death Penalty Information Center, https://perma.cc/Y9EF-V9FD, accessed June 14, 2024.

37. Trazawell Franklin and Floyd Nichols, interview by author, July 1, 2022, Houston; "Bond Made for Remaining 'TSU 5'—Public Mass Meet Set," *The Informer*, June 24, 1967, 1; Wesley G. Phelps, *A People's War on Poverty: Urban Politics and Grassroots Activists in Houston* (Athens: University of Georgia Press, 2014), 137–138. "Activities of Lee Otis Johnson," January 23, 1968; "Info. on Lee Otis Johnson," January 25, 1968; and "Activity of Lee Otis Johnson & Group," March 6, 1968—all in Police Intelligence Reports 1968, Louis Welch Papers, HHRC. "Charge Against Police to Be Probed," *HC*, August 24, 1967, sec. 5, p. 1.

38. "Special SNCC Report: Five Black Students Charged with Murder in Houston," June 1967, Texas Folder, Subgroup A. Atlanta Office, Series XV, SNCC Papers, PQHV.

39. Statement of M. L. Singleton, *Riots, Civil and Criminal Disorders. Hearings Before the Permanent Subcommittee on Investigations of the Committee on Government Operations, U.S. Senate*, 91st Cong., 1st sess., July 1–2 and 8, 1969, on S.R. 53 (Washington, D.C.: U.S. Government Printing Office, 1969), 146–147.

40. Teletype, Houston SAC 157-1017 to FBI Director, "Re: Texas Southern University (TSU) Riot, Houston, Texas, May Sixteen–Seventeen Last," July 27, 1967, FBI File 157-6-19.

41. *Riots, Civil and Criminal Disorders*, 148.

42. *Riots, Civil and Criminal Disorders*, 169, 184, 195, 200, 203–205, 215, 362, 368, 380–381, 384.

43. *Riots, Civil and Criminal Disorders*, 147–148, 169, 184, 195, 200, 203–205, 215, 362, 368, 380–381, 384.

44. *Riots, Civil and Criminal Disorders*, 147, 203–204, 362, 368; Beckwith, "Police 'Did Right Thing,' Says Leader"; Kirkpatrick, "Police Attack at Texas Southern."

45. *Riots, Civil and Criminal Disorders*, 359, 363, 172.

46. May Walker, *The History of Black Police Officers in the Houston Police Department* (Dallas: Taylor Publishing Company, 1988), 17.

47. SNCC, *Atlanta Black Paper* (Atlanta: Student Voice, Inc., 1966), 6; James Baldwin, *Notes of a Native Son*, 2012 ed. (Boston: Beacon Press, 2012 [1955]), 85.

11. Provocateurs

1. *Report of the National Advisory Commission on Civil Disorders*, 297, 324; "Fatalities and Victims," in *Detroit Under Fire: Police Violence, Crime Politics, and the Struggle for Racial Justice in the Civil Rights Era*, March 2021, https://perma.cc /KV7W-5W3G, accessed June 21, 2024.

2. Pat Harris, "Sorace: Portrait of a Cop," *Nashville Magazine*, November 1968, 11; John Herbers, "U.S.-Aided School Held Antiwhite," *NYT*, August 4, 1967, 1; Jim Squires, "Briley, Kemp Choose Sorace," *Nashville Tennessean*, December 8, 1967, 1, 14.

3. John Sorace, testimony, in *Antiriot Bill—1968. Hearings Before the Committee on the Judiciary, U.S. Senate*, 90th Cong., 1st sess., on H.R. 421, pt. 1 (Washington, D.C.: U.S. Government Printing Office, 1967), 137–138, 145.

4. Sorace, testimony, in *Antiriot Bill—1968*, 137–138, 145; Center for Community Studies, "Field Research Report—Civil Disturbances in Nashville Tennessee, Spring 1967," February 1968, 4, Box E71, Records of the National Advisory Commission on Civil Disorders (Embargoed Series), LBJ Presidential Library, Austin.

5. Sorace, testimony, in *Antiriot Bill—1968*, 137–138, 145, 148–149, 151, 161.

6. *Antiriot Bill—1968*, 31–134, 192–300, 353–477; Gage, *G-Man*, 682–683; O'Reilly, *Racial Matters*, 276–286; Center for Community Studies, "Field Research Report—Civil Disturbances in Nashville," 1.

7. W. Cleon Skousen, "Planned Riots—What Can the Police Do About It?" *Law and Order*, June 1962, 22–25, 47; W. Cleon Skousen, *The Communist Attack on U.S. Police* (Salt Lake City: Ensign Publishing Company, 1966), 26–27.

8. *Report of the National Advisory Commission on Civil Disorders*, 1, 91, 93, 173, 177.

9. *Riots, Civil and Criminal Disorders*, 646, 684, 710, 716, 746.

10. W.E.B. Du Bois, *Some Notes on the Negroes of New York City* (Atlanta: Atlanta University Press, 1908), 5; Lucy E. Parsons, "The Eight Hour Strike of 1886," *Industrial Worker*, May 1, 1912, 6; "Denver Police Attack Anti–Jim Crow Fight," *DW*, August 19, 1932, 3; "Bring Back the Bill of Rights to New York," *DW*, March 23, 1940, 6.

11. *Justice?* 2; "Who Decides?" *The Movement*, April 1965, 1.

12. "Cops Run Wild," *SNCC Newsletter*, June–July 1967, 1.

13. "Cops Run Wild," 1; "Police Riot in Atlanta," 3.

14. "Statement by CORE and SNCC by Floyd McKissick, National Director of CORE and H. Rap Brown, Chairman of SNCC," June 27, 1967, FBI File 100-HO-10390, Section 1, NARA-CP.

15. "Statement by CORE and SNCC by Floyd McKissick, National Director of CORE and H. Rap Brown, Chairman of SNCC," June 27, 1967.

16. Herbert Romerstein, "Suggested Questions for Raymond Wood," October 26, 1967, Riots—New York—General Folder, 1.57-75, HUAC Investigative General Organization Files, NARA-CLA; *Subversive Influences in Riots, Looting, and Burning, Part 2. Hearings Before the Committee on Un-American Activities, U.S. House of Representatives*, 90th Cong., 1st sess. (Washington, D.C.: U.S. Government Printing Office, 1967), 1034.

17. *Subversive Influences in Riots, Looting, and Burning*, 1045.

18. Walker, *History of Black Police Officers in the Houston Police Department*, 13, 16–17; *Riots, Civil and Criminal Disorders*, 374.

19. *The Police Yearbook 1968* (Washington, D.C.: International Association of Chiefs of Police, 1968), 172.

20. Ronald J. Ostrow, "Show a Big Stick to Rioters, Police Told," *LAT*, September 14, 1967, 22; *Police Yearbook 1968*, 177–182. On coordinated efforts of law enforcement to respond to uprisings, see Schrader, *Badges Without Borders*, 166–191; Hinton, *America on Fire*, 23–26; Felker-Kantor, *Policing Los Angeles*, 19–42; Balto, *Occupied Territory*, 213–216.

21. "Re: Black Organizing Project Racial Matters," May 6, 1968, 2–6, FBI File 157-ME-1067, Section 1; Leta McCollough Seletzky, *The Kneeling Man: My Father's Life as a Black Spy Who Witnessed the Assassination of Martin Luther King Jr.* (Berkeley: Counterpoint, 2023), 121.

22. Marrell McCollough, testimony, November 20, 1978; and Marrell McCollough, interview by Howell S. Love and William H. Lawrence, April 12, 1968, FBI File 44-ME-1987—both in *Investigation of the Assassination of Martin Luther King, Jr., Volume VI. Hearings Before the Select Committee on Assassinations of the U.S. House of Representatives*, 95th Cong., 2d sess. (Washington, D.C.: U.S. Government Printing Office, 1979), 418, 423, 425.

23. "I Knew I Must Record It for the World," *Life*, April 19, 1968, 3; *CT*, April 9, 1968, 1; *LAT*, April 9, 1968, 2; *NYT*, April 9, 1968, 35; *WP*, April 9, 1968, A7.

24. Application, "McCollough Marrell," June 19, 1967, Memphis Police Department, Weisberg Collection on the JFK Assassination, Weisberg Archive, Beneficial-Hodson Library, Hood College, https://perma.cc/87SV-E9R8, accessed June 21, 2024; Seletzky, *Kneeling Man*, 88; Gregg L. Michel, "Surveilling the Memphis Movement: Police Spying in Memphis, 1968–1976," *Journal of Southern History* 87, no. 4 (2021): 682 n. 19; "Eli H. 'Arch' Arkin, Jr.," *MCA*, December 29, 2006, 22; "Ex-Policeman Waves City Court Hearing," *MPS*, November 9, 1976, 6. On the Inspectional Bureau, see also Michael Honey, *Going Down Jericho Road: The Memphis Strike, Martin Luther King's Last Campaign* (New York: W. W. Norton & Company, 2007), 398–409. On the Memphis red squad, see also Gregg L. Michel, "Memphis," in *Spying on Students: The FBI, Red Squads, and Student Activists in the 1960s South* (Baton Rouge: Louisiana State University Press, 2024).

25. Airtel, SAC Memphis to Director, "Changed: Black Organizing Project," May 6, 1968, 27, FBI File 157-ME-8460; "Policeman Is 'Uncovered,'" *MCA*, February 25, 1968, 11; Joseph Sweat, "Strike Supporters Map Strategy in Face of Legal Action by City," *MCA*, February 25, 1968, 1.

26. Teletype, Memphis 157-1067 to Director, "Newsday Article Re Invaders," February 2, 1976; and memo, J. G. Deegan to T. W. Leavitt, "Newsday Article Concerning Invaders," March 2, 1976—both in FBI File 157-ME-8460. *Investigation of the Assassination of Martin Luther King, Jr.*, 428.

27. Application, "McCollough Marrell," June 19, 1967; Seletzky, *Kneeling Man*, 4, 108–109, 122.

28. Seletzky, *Kneeling Man*, 157–158, 180; Tennessee Code Annotated (1955), §§ 39–1106 (Supp. 1955).

29. "'Black Hoodlums' Blamed by Willis for 3 Fires of Homes He Financed," *MPS*, September 11, 1968, 1; Robert Samsot, "Dream of Home Consumed by Arsonists' Fury," *MCA*, September 11, 1968, 25.

30. Memo, "Re: Sanitation Workers Strike Memphis Tennessee; Racial Matters," March 13, 1968, 4–5, FBI File 157-ME-1092; Robert Kellett, "Civil Rights Leaders Urge Action Against Terrorism in Negro Areas," *MCA*, September 12, 1968, 1; memo, "Re: Black Organizing Project," June 6, 1968, 25, 47, FBI File 157-ME-8460.

31. Carroll Parrott Blue, "Emancipation Is a Park," *Houston History*, Summer 2012, 15–16; Ralph Williams, "2,500 Marchers Honor King," *HP*, April 15, 1968, 1, 16.

32. Williams, "2,500 Marchers Honor King"; Ellen Middlebrook, "Meeting Called Anti-white," *HP*, April 16, 1968; Edward Walsh and Ken Sheets, "Welch Says Tone of King Meeting Was Anti-white," *HC*, April 15, 1968, 1, 22; "Reverend Earl Allen at Houston MLK Memorial (1968)," April 14, 1968, KPRC-TV, Texas Archive of the Moving Image, https://perma.cc/9R5A-7ENP, accessed June 21, 2024; "Johnson Free on Charge of Narcotics Sale," *HC*, April 17, 1968, 1.

33. Bud Johnson, "Citizens Eye Johnson's Arrest with Suspicion," *The Informer*, April 20, 1968, 1.

34. "Petition for Writ of Habeus Corpus," August 19, 1971; and "Transcript of Proceedings," 149, 223—both in *Lee Otis Johnson v. George J. Beto*, Civil Action 71-H-909, U.S. District Court for the Southern District of Texas, Houston Division, 1972, NARA-FW.

35. "Transcript of Proceedings," *Johnson v. Beto*, 149–150, 154, 159–163, 181–183, 223–224.

36. "Petition for Writ of Habeus Corpus," *Johnson v. Beto*, 3, 8–9; docket sheet, *The State of Texas v. Lee Otis Johnson*, April 27, 1968, No. 132144, Civil Action 71-H-909, U.S. District Court for the Southern District of Texas, Houston Division, 1972, NARA-FW; Bob Tutt, "Johnson Claims Dope Conviction Trumped Up," *HC*, August 28, 1968, 33.

37. Christopher Sieving, *Soul Searching: Black-Themed Cinema from the March on Washington to the Rise of Blaxploitation* (Middletown, Conn.: Wesleyan University Press, 2011), 124–125, 129; "Negro Stars, CORE Picketing Shows: Ossie Davis, Ruby Dee, Cecily Tyson Take Part," *PT*, April 7, 1962, 1; Lula Patterson, "It Was No High Dress Affair, Reports Our Lula," *BAA*, September 7, 1963, 8; Tyson, *Radio Free Dixie*, 204–205; Manning Marable and Garrett Felber, eds., *The Portable Malcolm X Reader: A Man Who Stands for Nothing Will Fall for Anything* (New York: Penguin, 2013), 340; William W. Sales, *From Civil Rights to Black Liberation: Malcolm X and the Organization of Afro-American Unity* (Boston: South End Press, 1994), 60, 100; report, "Julian Mayfield—Security Matters," August 15, 1954, 6, FBI File 100-NY-120145; Ruby Dee, FBI Record 100-HQ-428507, NARA-CP; "Dee, Ruby," Box 6, Folder 37, Individual Files, NYPD Intelligence Records, NYCMA; Jules Dassin, FBI File 100-21689; memo, G. C. Moore to W. C. Sullivan, "Allegations Concerning Motion Picture 'Betrayal,' Also Known as 'Uptight,'" August 23, 1968, FBI Record 100-138754-1280.

12. The Unraveling

1. Hill, *Men, Mobs, and Law*, 247–248; Luca Falciola, *Up Against the Law: Radical Lawyers and Social Movements, 1960s–1970s* (Chapel Hill: University of North Carolina Press, 2022), 4–5.

2. *Brooks v. Briley*, Civil Action 4747, U.S. District Court for the Middle District of Tennessee, Nashville Division, October 9, 1967; *Carmichael v. Allen*, Civil Action 10421, U.S. District Court for the Northern District of Georgia, Atlanta Division, January 16, 1967.

3. See, for example, Dick Roberts, "Distortion of TSU-5 Case," *The Militant*, April, 29, 1968, 3; "Floyd Nichols Speaks in Defense of TSU 5," *The Militant*, December 4, 1967, 8; Elizabeth Barnes, "TSU Five Continue Fight Against Racist Frame-Up," *The Militant*, December 20, 1968, 8. Marable, *Malcolm X*, 302–304, 336–337, 377.

4. Nelson Blackstock, *COINTELPRO: The FBI's Secret War on Political Freedom* (New York: Pathfinder Press, 1988), 1–12; Margaret Jayko, ed., *FBI on Trial: The Victory in the Socialist Workers Party Suit Against Government Spying* (New York: Pathfinder Press, 1988).

5. Forman, "1967," 14–17.

6. Forman, "1967," 20.

7. Forman, "1967," 27.

8. Carson, *In Struggle*, 265–272; Meier and Rudwick, *CORE*, 414–425.

9. Joshua Bloom and Waldo E. Martin, *Black Against Empire: The History and Politics of the Black Panther Party* (Berkeley: University of California Press, 2013), 143–145, 159.

10. Bloom and Martin, *Black Against Empire*, 34–36; "Black Power Archives—Ron Wilkins on Community Alert Patrol," http://t.ly/lrmg4, accessed February 10, 2025; "Black Power Hour: Ron Wilkins Interview 2022," https://bit.ly/3F0sQNL, accessed February 22, 2025; Terence Cannon, "A Night with the Watts Community Alert Patrol," *The Movement*, August 1966, 1, 3. Copies of *The Movement*, including one from summer 1966, appear in Newton's personal papers, Box 9, Folder 13, Dr. Huey P. Newton Foundation Inc. Collection, Special Collections, Stanford University. "Freedom Patrols Keep Cop Watch"; "Six Pickets Arrested at Restaurant," *Oakland Tribune*, February 13, 1965, 5; "Civil Rights Marchers in Oakland," *Petaluma Argus-Courier*, February 20, 1965, 3; "Police Pressure Building Up in Oakland," *The Movement*, September 1966, 3.

11. Kathleen Cleaver, "Women, Power, and Revolution," in *Liberation, Imagination, and the Black Panther Party: A New Look at the Panthers and Their Legacy*, ed. Kathleen Cleaver and George Katsiaficas (New York: Routledge, 2001), 123–124; Bloom and Martin, *Black Against Empire*, 105–106. In addition, former SNCC worker Aaron Dixon headed up the Black Panther Party's first chapter outside California, in Seattle; in New York City, the first Panther chapter on the East Coast operated out of SNCC's national office; and its first captain, Joudon Ford, had also been affiliated with SNCC. See Aaron Dixon, *My People Are Rising: Memoir of a Black Panther Party Captain* (Chicago: Haymarket Books, 2012), 66–69,

76–77; Murray Kempton, *The Briar Patch: The* People of the State of New York v. Lumumba Shakur et al. (New York: E. P. Dutton Co., 1973), 43; and Bloom and Martin, *Black Against Empire*, 149.

12. "Pocket Lawyer of Legal First Aid" and other stories in *BP*, May 4, 1968.

13. "Free Huey Newton Los Angeles Part 1 February 18, 1968," http://t.ly/ylHPH, accessed February 10, 2025.

14. Newton, *Revolutionary Suicide*, 118; Hill, *Deacons for Defense*, 218; "Free Huey Newton Los Angeles Part 1 February 18, 1968"; "Bobby Seale Speech at the Oakland Auditorium," February 17, 1968, http://t.ly/0IUBc, accessed February 10, 2025.

15. "H. Rap Brown and Stokely Carmichael Address the Black Panthers," February 17, 1968, Pacifica Radio Archives, http://is.gd/AHEhLX, accessed June 27, 2024; "Free Huey Newton Los Angeles Part 2 Stokely Carmichael Kwame Ture February 18, 1968," http://t.ly/Cc7qP, accessed February 10, 2025; "Words We Love from Mr. Hydrogen Bomb, Mao Tse-Tung," *BP*, July 3, 1967, 4.

16. C. Gerald Fraser, "S.N.C.C. in Decline After 8 Years in Lead," *NYT*, October 7, 1968, 51; *Gun-Barrel Politics: The Black Panther Party, 1966–1971. Report of the Committee on Internal Security, U.S. House of Representatives*, 92nd Cong., 1st sess. (Washington, D.C.: U.S. Government Printing Office, 1971), 88–89.

17. Fraser, "S.N.C.C. in Decline After 8 Years in Lead," 51.

18. Tutt, "Johnson Claims Dope Conviction Trumped Up," 1; Ernest Bailey, "SNCC's Johnson Is Found Guilty," *HP*, August 28, 1968, 6.

19. David Brand, "Undercover Cops: Police Intelligence Units Step Up Their Watch on the Racial Situation," *WSJ*, September 10, 1968, 1.

20. Brand, "Undercover Cops," 18.

21. "Letters to the Editor: A Reply from Houston," *WSJ*, September 13, 1968, 14.

22. "Transcript of Proceedings," *Johnson v. Beto*, 167–169; Carol S. Vance, *Boomtown DA* (Houston: Whitecaps Media, 2010), 117.

23. Dave McNeely, "Readmission Denied to 10 TSU Students," *HC*, September 29, 1967, 3.

24. Criminal docket, *State of Texas v. Parker et al.*, Case 7553; court's charge, *State of Texas v. Parker et al.*, Case 7553; and letter, Carol Vance to Ronnie Dugger, January 11, 1971, *Texas v. Parker* Case File—all in Criminal District Court of Victoria County, Texas.

25. Sonny Wells, "Charles Freeman's Trial Causes Much Speculation," *FT*, November 2, 1968, 2; James Simons, "Jury Completed in Freeman Case," *Victoria Advocate*, October 29, 1968, 1; Selma Wells, "Keyhole Peek at a Lady Lawyer from New York," *FT*, November 2, 1968, 2.

26. Charles Freeman and Ned Wade, motion to restrict state's argument, October 30, 1968, *Texas v. Parker* Case File, Criminal District Court of Victoria County, Texas; "Field Research Report: Civil Disturbances in Houston," 7, 56–57.

27. James Simons, "Freeman Jurors Retire for Evening," *Victoria Advocate*, October 31, 1968, 1, 12; note, Alfred W. Parsons to Joe E. Kelly, October 31, 1968, *Texas v. Parker* Case File, Criminal District Court of Victoria County, Texas; "Jury Disagree

in TSU Student Trial," *The Informer*, November 16, 1968, 1, 3; letter, Vance to Dugger, January 11, 1971.

28. "Judge Drops All TSU Riot Charges," *HC*, November 5, 1970, 1.

29. Bob Tutt, "30-Year Pot Sentence: Justified or Political," *HC*, May 18, 1969, 41. See also Box 1622, Case File 144-74-1038; Box 3922, Case File 144-74-1434; and Box 3980, Case File 144-74-2263—all in Department of Justice Record Group 60, Class 144 (Civil Rights) Litigation Case Files and Enclosures, 1936–1997, NARA-CP.

30. Ron Rosenbaum, "Lee Otis Johnson Case: 30 Years for 'One Joint,'" *VV*, February 26, 1970, 12, 25.

31. Rosenbaum, "Lee Otis Johnson Case,'" 12–14, 25; Michael Adams, "Lee Otis . . . ," *TO*, September 4, 1970, 5.

32. Tutt, "30-Year Pot Sentence," 41.

33. John Leighty, "Shootout Kills Judge, Prisoners, Accomplice," *BAA*, August 15, 1970, 1; David Shaw and Jim Stingley, "Angela Charged in Judge's Murder," *LAT*, August 15, 1970, 1.

34. Ralph Abernathy, "I Bring an Indictment Against the American System," in *If They Come in the Morning: Voices of Resistance*, ed. Angela Y. Davis (New York: Third Press, 1971), 274; Angela Davis, *Angela Davis: An Autobiography* (New York: International Publishers, 1974), 111–112, 165–166.

35. Abernathy, "I Bring an Indictment Against the American System"; Coretta Scott King, "Statement by Coretta Scott King"; and Julian Bond, "Forward"—all in Davis, *If They Come in the Morning*, 282–283.

36. Davis, *If They Come in the Morning*, 87.

37. John and Yoko/Plastic Ono Band, "John Sinclair," *Some Time in New York City*, recorded December 1971–March 1972; "The Real Criminals in Society," *IT*, March 25–April 8, 1971, 16; "Questo è l' 'ordine' che dovremmo imparare dagli USA?" *l'Unita*, March 12, 1972, 6; "Rettet Angela vor dem Justizmord!" *Der Spiegel*, November 7, 1971; "Twenty-Eight Years to Go, Now," *BP*, March 4, 1972, 2, 6; *Black Panther Party—Part 1. Hearings Before the Committee on Internal Security, U.S. House of Representatives*, 91st Cong., 2d sess., March 4–6 and 10, 1970 (Washington, D.C.: U.S. Government Printing Office, 1970), 4992; Roland E. Wolseley, *The Black Press, USA*, 2nd ed. (Ames: Iowa State University Press, 1990), 90.

38. "Petition for Writ of Habeus Corpus," *Johnson v. Beto*, 13–14.

39. "Transcript of Proceedings," *Johnson v. Beto*, 132, 145, 159.

40. Opinion, *Lee Otis Johnson v. George J. Beto*, Civil Action 71-H-909, U.S. District Court, Southern District of Texas, Houston Division, January 19, 1972.

41. Fred Harper, "Lee Otis out of Prison on $10,000 Bond," *HC*, June 3, 1972, 1.

13. The Unmasking

1. John C. Raines, *Attack on Privacy* (Valley Forge, Pa.: Judson Press, 1974), 13–16, 32, 82, 125.

2. "The Complete Collection of Political Documents Ripped-Off from the F.B.I. Office in Media, Pa., March 8, 1971," *WIN: Peace and Freedom Through Nonviolent Action*, March 1972, 33–34, 37, 53–55.

3. Betty Medsger, *The Burglary: The Discovery of J. Edgar Hoover's Secret FBI* (New York: Vintage Books, 2014), 160–162, 167–178.

4. "Pastor from LI Jailed as Little Rock 'Rider,'" *Newsday*, July 11, 1961, 7; "Ex-LI Minister, 3 'Riders' Take Ark. Jail Term," *Newsday*, July 13, 1961, 4; Medsger, *Burglary*, 460–463; Van Savell, "Freedom Riders End Trip Through State," *Lake Charles American-Press*, July 18, 1961, 17.

5. Medsger, *Burglary*, 469–471.

6. "Secret Riot Dossiers," *Jersey Journal*, February 3, 1970, 1.

7. Ronald Sullivan, "Jersey High Court Backs Police Files on Activists," *NYT*, June 2, 1970, 1, 26; William Judkins, "Rudd Finds Large Audience but Few Revolutionaries," *Jersey Journal*, January 22, 1969, 3; David Carrad and Leon Zimmerman, "Jersey City Riot Area Under Tight Police Net," *Hackensack Record*, August 3, 1964, 12; "4,000 in March Hit Review," *Hackensack Record*, July 30, 1965, 18.

8. "Sills Studies Appeal of Ban Against Files," *Red Bank Daily Register*, August 7, 1969, 1; *Anderson v. Sills*, 106 N.J. Super. 545 (N.J. Superior Court, 1969); "Court Allows Use of Police Riot Files," *Camden Courier-Post*, October 2, 1969, 38.

9. "Nardi Sees Need for Police Files," *Camden Courier-Post*, August 12, 1969, 8; "Whelan Seeks Support to Fight Ruling on Dumping Riot Files," *Central New Jersey Home News*, August 13, 1969, 17; *Anderson v. Sills* (N.J. Superior Court, 1969); *Anderson v. Sills*, 56 N.J. 210 (N.J. Supreme Court, 1970).

10. Fred J. Cook, "Again the Hot Issue of Those Files on Dissenters," *NYT*, June 7, 1970, 154; Mark A. Chertok and Stanley Marcus, "Chilling Political Expression by Use of Police Intelligence Files: *Anderson v. Sills*," *Harvard Civil Rights–Civil Liberties Law Review* 5, no. 1 (January 1970): 71–88.

11. Report, "Robert Steele Collier," February 26, 1969, FBI File 105-NY-71003.

12. Donner, *Protectors of Privilege*, 187–188.

13. Edith Evans Asbury, "Police Agent in Panther Case a Boyhood Friend of Defendant," *NYT*, December 3, 1970, 32; "Wood, Raymond A.," Employment Record, NYPD, shown during a Facebook Live hosted by Abdur-Rahman Muhammad, March 8, 2021, screenshot in author's possession; Donner, *Protectors of Privilege*, 198–199; "The Violent End of a Man Called Malcolm," *Life*, March 5, 1965, 27.

14. Garrett Felber, "Malcolm X Assassination: 50 Years On, Mystery Still Clouds Details of Case," *The Guardian*, February 21, 2015, https://perma.cc/S3PK-STHB, accessed August 15, 2024; Yuri Kochiyama, *Passing It On: A Memoir* (Los Angeles: UCLA Asian American Studies Center Press, 2004). On an additional letter—purportedly written by Ray Wood and posthumously released by his relative Reggie Wood—that alleges Ray's involvement in Malcolm's assassination, see Sydney Trent, "Did a Black Undercover NYPD Detective Unwittingly Aid Malcolm X's Assassination?" *WP*, April 18, 2021, https://wapo.st/3X3kN9K, accessed August 15, 2024.

15. Kempton, *Briar Patch*, 200–203.

16. Complaint, *Handschu v. Special Services Division*, 71 Civ. 2203 (U.S. District Court, Southern District of New York, 1971), NARA-NYC.

17. Marty Jezer, *Abbie Hoffman: American Rebel* (New Brunswick, N.J.: Rutgers University Press, 1992), 52–67; John D'Emilio, *Lost Prophet: The Life and Times of*

Bayard Rustin (New York: Free Press, 2003), 210; Scott H. Bennett, *Radical Pacifism: The War Resisters League and Gandhian Nonviolence in America, 1915–1963* (Syracuse, N.Y.: Syracuse University Press, 2003), 216–224; "March on Washington for Jobs and Freedom: 1st Plan of Operation Submitted to Chairmen," July 8, 1963, 3, "Plan of Operation—1963" Folder, Chronological Subject File—March on Washington—1963, Bayard Rustin Papers, APRI, PQHV; Sekou Odinga, Dhoruba Bin Wahad, Shaba Om, and Jamal Joseph, *Look for Me in the Whirlwind: From the Panther 21 to 21st-Century Revolutions* (Oakland, Calif.: PM Press, 2017), 450; Bloom and Martin, *Black Against Empire*, 149; Frank B. Latham, *American Justice on Trial* (New York: Franklin Watts, 1972), 4–5; Falciola, *Up Against the Law*, 64.

18. Complaint, *Handschu v. Special Services Division*, 14, 17–18.

19. *Dombrowski v. Pfister*, 380 U.S. 479 (1965); complaint, *Handschu v. Special Services Division*, 20; David Burnham, "Moral Problems of Technology Cited," *NYT*, May 27, 1971, 41; Bouza, "Operations of a Police Intelligence Unit," 79–82, 87–88.

20. C. Gerald Fraser, "Black Policemen Dissent on 'Order,'" *NYT*, June 13, 1971, 25; C. Gerald Fraser, "Black City Policeman Assails Transfers to Political Infiltration," *NYT*, June 12, 1971, 30; "Black Policemen Bar Political Spy Role," *LAT*, June 14, 1971, 7.

21. Deposition, Patrick V. Murphy, December 9, 1971, *Handschu v. Special Services Division*, 71 Civ. 2203 (U.S. District Court, Southern District of New York, 1971), NARA-NYC.

22. *People v. Collier*, 85 Misc. 2d 529, 376 N.Y.S.2d 954 (N.Y. Sup. Ct. 1975).

23. "Miss Davis Plans Tour of Thanks," *BS*, June 7, 1972, A12; Angela Y. Davis, "Keynote Address to the Founding Conference for a National Defense Organization Against Racist and Political Repression," 1973, Unpublished Writings, Angela Y. Davis Collection, Stuart A. Rose Manuscripts, Archives, and Rare Book Library, Emory University.

24. Tony Pecinovsky, *Let Them Tremble: Biographical Interventions Marking 100 Years of the Communist Party, USA* (New York: International Publishers, 2019), 90–96; John Hart, "Unity + Struggle + Organization = Victory," *World Magazine*, May 31, 1980, 16; *Revolutionary Activities Directed Toward the Administration of Penal or Correctional Systems—Part 4. Hearings Before the Committee on Internal Security, U.S. House of Representatives*, 93rd Cong., 1st sess., July 25, 1973 (Washington, D.C.: U.S. Government Printing Office, 1973), 1506–1508; Richard G. Stahl, Agent Letter No. 10, February 15, 1971, in *Federal Data Banks, Computers and the Bill of Rights. Hearings Before the Subcommittee on Constitutional Rights of the Committee on the Judiciary, U.S. Senate*, 92nd Cong., 1st sess., pt. 2 (Washington, D.C.: U.S. Government Printing Office, 1971), 1467–1468, 1490.

25. Poster, "Stop Racism and Repression—National Demonstration," 1974, Box 3, Folder 156, Printed Ephemera of African American Political Activism and Arts Collection, JWJ MSS 36, Beinecke Rare Book and Manuscript Library, Yale University.

26. Ginny Carroll, "4000 March Here in Peaceful Protest," *RNO*, July 5, 1974, 1, 7; "10,000 in N.C. Protest March," *CD*, July 9, 1974, 4; Pat Stith, "Police, Patrol Keep Close Eye on March," *RNO*, July 5, 1974, 1.

27. Carroll, "4000 March Here in Peaceful Protest"; "Justice Assailed in North Carolina," *NYT*, July 5, 1974, 16; Kenneth Janken, *The Wilmington Ten: Violence, Injustice, and the Rise of Black Politics in the 1970s* (Chapel Hill: University of North Carolina Press, 2015), 116.

28. Stith, "Police, Patrol Keep Close Eye on March," 6.

29. Alfred Lewis, "5 Held in Plot to Bug Democrats' Office Here," *WP*, June 18, 1972, A1; Jefferson Morley, *Scorpions' Dance: The President, the Spymaster, and Watergate* (New York: St. Martin's Press, 2022), 2.

30. John Caulfield, *Caulfield, Shield #911-NYPD* (Bloomington, Ind.: iUniverse, Inc., 2008); Ulasewicz, *President's Private Eye*, 149–154, 175–180, 250–261; "Nixon Bagman Says He'd Redo Watergate Job," *Fort Worth Star-Telegram*, June 28, 1982, 9C.

31. Seymour M. Hersh, "Huge C.I.A. Operation Reported in U.S. Against Anti-war Forces," *NYT*, December 22, 1974, 1, 26.

32. U.S. Senate Resolution 21, 94th Cong., January 27, 1975, 1.

33. James Risen, *The Last Honest Man: The CIA, the FBI, the Mafia, and the Kennedys—and One Senator's Fight to Save Democracy* (Boston: Little, Brown, 2023), 320–324.

14. The Unremembering

1. "Councilmen Critical of Police Files," *MPS*, September 9, 1976, 16; Joseph Weiler, "File Burning Draws Mayor's Attention," *MCA*, September 9, 1976, 1, 10; ACLU of Tennessee, "Surveillance of Protected First Amendment Activities: *Kendrick v. Memphis Police Department*—History of the Lawsuit" (Memphis: ACLU, 1978), in author's possession; "Court Order Too Late; Police Burn Intelligence Files," *MPS*, September 11, 1976, 1.

2. "Memphis Denies Burning Data on King Slaying," *BS*, November 17, 1976, A8; Jack Anderson, "Many Fears Still Linger," *AC*, September 5, 1976, 22A; "House Panel Rejects Assassination Inquiry," *NYT*, April 1, 1976, 53; Norman Kempster, "New Probe of Assassinations," *LAT*, September 14, 1976, 1; "Subpoenas Issued in Kennedy Probe," *York Daily Record*, September 17, 1976, 1.

3. David Burnham, "Police Intelligence Records Here Are Purged of a Million Names," *NYT*, February 9, 1973, 73; "Police Remove Names of 1 Million from Files," *Ithaca Journal*, February 9, 1973, 9; David Burnham, "C.I.A. Discloses It Trained Police from 12 Agencies," *NYT*, February 6, 1973, 1.

4. "Cops Admit Destroying Records," *CT*, October 27, 1976, 5; "U.S. Court Halts Further Destruction of Police Files," *CT*, March 27, 1975, 1.

5. Bill Hazlett, "Police Purge Nearly 2 Million Dossiers: Files Gathered on 55,000 Persons, Groups Destroyed," *LAT*, April 11, 1975, C1; "Coast Police Unit Purges Its Files," *NYT*, April 13, 1975, 16.

6. Louis Harris & Associates Poll: "It was a violation of basic rights for the CIA and FBI to conduct spying on prominent Americans here at home," "It was wrong for the FBI to send a note to Martin Luther King suggesting that he commit suicide," and "How would you rate the job being done by . . . the FBI?"

(December 1975); and Gallup Organization, Gallup Poll: "Turning to some other agencies of our federal government, how much trust and confidence do you have in the Federal Bureau of Investigation, that is, the FBI?" (June 1976)—both in the iPoll database, RCPOR.

7. *White v. Davis*, Case 30348, 533 P.2d 222 (Cal. 1975); "A Notable Reversal: Holding the Chicago Red Squad Accountable," in *The Price of Dissent: Testimonies to Political Repression in America*, ed. Bud Schultz and Ruth Schultz (Berkeley: University of California Press, 2001), 430–434; *Handschu v. Special Services Division*, Case No. 71 Civ. 2203-CSH, 605 F. Supp. 1384 (S.D.N.Y. 1985).

8. Marx, *Undercover*, 1–11, 36, 59, 206–233.

9. Regina Lawrence, *The Politics of Force: Media and the Construction of Police Brutality* (Oxford: Oxford University Press, 2000), 28, 43–45.

10. LaShawn Harris, "Beyond the Shooting: Eleanor Gray Bumpurs, Identity Erasure, and Family Activism Against Police Violence," *Souls* 20 (January–March 2018): 86–109; LaShawn Harris, *Tell Her Story: Eleanor Bumpurs and the Police Killing that Galvanized New York* (Boston: Beacon Press, 2025); Keisha N. Blain, "'We Will Overcome Whatever [It] Is the System Has Become Today': Black Women's Organizing Against Police Violence in New York City in the 1980s," *Souls* 20 (January–March 2018): 110–121.

"On Combatting Police Abuse," *CD*, December 10, 1984, 11; Frank J. Prial, "Judge Acquits Sullivan in Shotgun Slaying of Bumpurs," *NYT*, February 27, 1987, B1; "U.S. Inquiry Ruled Out in Death of Bumpurs," *NYT*, August 5, 1987, B3. On police killings in New York City in the 1980s, see also Alphonso Pinkney, *Lest We Forget . . . White Hate Crimes: Howard Beach and Other Racial Atrocities* (Chicago: Third World Press, 1994); and Interference Archive, *Defend/Defund: A Visual History of Organizing Against the Police* (Philadelphia: Common Notions, 2023), 18–37.

11. Felker-Kantor, *Policing Los Angeles*, 218, 227, 232; *Reconstructing Los Angeles from the Bottom Up: A Long-Term Strategy for Workers, Low-Income People, and People of Color to Create an Alternative Vision of Urban Development* (Los Angeles: Labor/Community Strategy Center, 1992), 42–47; Eric Mann, "Black Led 'Defund the Police' Movement Wins Great Breakthrough in Los Angeles: An Organizer's Interpretation," *CounterPunch*, August 21, 2020, https://perma.cc/L4DF-TQQ6, accessed September 13, 2024; Howard Chua-Woan, "New York: Black and Blue," *Time*, March 6, 2000.

12. "The History of Critical Resistance," *Social Justice* 27, no. 3 (2000): 6–10; Baer, *Beyond the Usual Beating*, 165–199; "The Black Radical Congress: A Black Freedom Agenda for the Twenty-First Century," *Black Scholar* 28, no. 1 (1998): 71–73; Interference Archive, *Defend/Defund*, 38–45, 60–79, 111–115, 122–135. On histories of Black Lives Matter, see Taylor, *From #BlackLivesMatter to Black Liberation*; Murch, *Assata Taught Me*; Hamlin and McKinney, *From Rights to Lives*; Barbara Ransby, *Making All Black Lives Matter: Reimagining Freedom in the Twenty-First Century* (Oakland: University of California Press, 2018); Christopher J. Lebron, *The Making of Black Lives Matter: A Brief History of an Idea*, updated ed. (New York: Oxford University Press, 2023); Stefan M. Bradley, *If We Don't Get It: A People's History of Ferguson* (New York: New Press, 2025); Christopher Cameron

and Phillip Luke Sinitiere, eds., *Race, Religion, and Black Lives Matter: Essays on a Moment and a Movement* (Nashville, Tenn.: Vanderbilt University Press, 2021).

13. Franklin E. Zimring, *When Police Kill* (Cambridge, Mass.: Harvard University Press, 2017), 10, 24, 38–40.

14. On contemporary uses and misuses of the civil rights movement's legacy, see Hajar Yazdiha, *The Struggle for the People's King: How Politics Transforms the Memory of the Civil Rights Movement* (Princeton, N.J.: Princeton University Press, 2023). On public history of the civil rights movement, see Kim Severson, "Shining New Spotlight on Civil Rights Era," *NYT*, February 19, 2012, A8; Cynthia Fabrizio Pelak, "Institutionalizing Counter-memories of the U.S. Civil Rights Movement: The National Civil Rights Museum and an Application of the Interest-Convergence Principle," *Sociological Forum* 30, no. 2 (2015): 305–327; Marita Sturken, *Terrorism in American Memory: Memorials, Museums, and Architecture in the Post-9/11 Era* (New York: New York University Press, 2022), 221–264.

15. Panel, "Legacy of Slavery," NLEM, Washington, D.C., author visit, March 25, 2024.

16. John S. Dempsey, *An Introduction to Policing*, 2nd ed. (Belmont, Calif.: West/Wadsworth Publishing Company, 1999), 17; John S. Dempsey, Linda S. Forst, and Steven B. Carter, *An Introduction to Policing*, 9th ed. (Boston: Cengage Learning, 2019), 20–22; J. Edgar Hoover video and panel, and "How to Set Up a Wiretap," NLEM, Washington, D.C., author visit, March 25, 2024.

17. Buchanan et al., "Black Lives Matter May Be the Largest Movement in U.S. History."

18. Jada Yuan, "Documenting John Lewis's Last Public Appearance," *WP*, July 30, 2020, https://perma.cc/LW69-S7F5, accessed August 14, 2024.

19. Katharine Q. Seelye, "John Lewis, Towering Figure of Civil Rights Era, Dies at 80," *NYT*, July 17, 2020, http://t.ly/jli5B, accessed February 11, 2025; Laurence I. Barrett, "John Lewis, Front-Line Civil Rights Leader and Eminence of Capitol Hill, Dies at 80," *WP*, July 17, 2020, https://perma.cc/YGA5-A5LU, accessed August 14, 2024.

20. *United States v. U. S. Klans, Knights of Ku Klux Klan, Inc.*, June 2, 1961; "Ex-Reserve Policeman Is Charged," *Alabama Journal*, May 23, 1961, 1; Arsenault, *Freedom Riders*, 212; Reaves, *Black Cops*, 109–116; "Landry, Lawrence—Investigator's Report," May 1968; "Photographs Related to the Civil Rights Movement," 1125.11.21A-1 to 1125.11M-1, Birmingham, Alabama, Police Department, Surveillance Files, 1947–1980, BPL; surveillance records on SNCC, in *Chicago Police Department, Red Squad Selected Records, c. 1930s–86*, Abakanowicz Research Center, Chicago History Museum; "Student Non Violent Coordinating Committee" Folder, NYPD Intelligence Records, NYCMA.

21. "March on Washington for Jobs and Freedom; Part 6 of 17," August 28, 1963.

22. Stanley S. Scott, "Americus Demonstrators Charge Police Brutality," *ADW*, September 11, 1963, 4; "Henrietta Fuller, Duly Sworn Deposes and Says," September 13, 1963, and "3 SNCC Workers Face Death Penalty," August 1963—both in Folder 252253-037-0423, SNCC Files on Americus, Georgia, SNCC Papers, MLK, PQHV; "SNCC Head Hits Alleged Brutality in Americus, Ga.," *ADW*, August 17,

1963, 5; "SNCC Blasts Troop Use in Los Angeles," *AC*, August 17, 1965, 3; Ernestine Cofield, "SNCC Drive to 'Save Americus Four,'" *CD*, September 17, 1963, A10.

23. See, for instance, Rasul A. Mowatt, "Black Lives as Snuff: The Silent Complicity in Viewing Black Death," *Biography* 41, no. 4 (2018): 777–806.

24. "U.S. Protest Law Tracker," International Center for Not-for-Profit Law, https://perma.cc/SAC2-8G98, accessed August 14, 2024.

25. ACLU, "*Mckesson v. Doe*," https://perma.cc/ZYC6-MKWG; and Urooba Abid and Vera Eidelman, "The Supreme Court Declined a Protestors' Rights Case. Here's What You Need to Know," April 22, 2024, ACLU, https://perma.cc/4P45 -264D—both accessed February 11, 2025.

26. Amara Enyia and Jamecia Gray, "The GOP Has Declared a War on Protests," *In These Times*, June 9, 2021, https://perma.cc/9SYC-FJ5K; Mike Davis, "Cyber Harassment Charges Dismissed Against Tweeters, Retweeters of Nutley Cop Photo," *Asbury Park Press*, August 7, 2020, https://perma.cc/88US-8A7Y; and Adrienne Green, "The Room Where It Happened," *New York Intelligencer*, May 25, 2021, https://perma.cc/URH7-552N—all accessed August 14, 2024.

27. Christopher E. Bruce and Hina Shamsi, "RICO and Domestic Terrorism Charges Against Cop City Activists Send a Chilling Message," ACLU, September 21, 2023, https://perma.cc/4K5P-VDTA; Sarah Teitz and Shaiba Rather, "How Officials in Georgia Are Suppressing Political Protest as 'Domestic Terrorism,'" ACLU, March 24, 2023, https://perma.cc/AU7X-V3WR; and Matt Scott, "APD, GBI Raid Bail Fund, Arrest Three Organizers," *Atlanta Community Press Collective*, May 31, 2023, https://perma.cc/JNY7-K39L—all accessed August 14, 2024. Timothy Pratt, "Money-Laundering Charges Dropped Against Bail Fund in Cop City Protest Case," *The Guardian*, September 19, 2024, https://perma.cc/DU8V-KU74, accessed February 23, 2025.

28. Mary Pat Dwyer and José Guillermo Gutiérrez, "Documents Reveal LAPD Collected Millions of Tweets from Users Nationwide," Brennan Center for Justice, December 15, 2021, https://perma.cc/CVA6-BAYL; Cody Bloomfield, "Organizing in the Shadow of the Surveillance State," *Defending Rights and Dissent*, July 5, 2023, https://perma.cc/D3E8-GPCY; and Tate Ryan-Mosely and Sam Richards, "The Secret Police: Cops Built a Shadowy Surveillance Machine in Minnesota After George Floyd's Murder," *MIT Technology Review*, March 3, 2022, https://perma .cc/M2Y4-6X6J—all accessed August 14, 2024.

29. Brayne, "Big Data Surveillance"; Ferguson, *Rise of Big Data Policing*; Andrejevic and Gates, "Big Data Surveillance." Bahar Ostadan, "The NYPD Is Using Drones 3 Times More than Last Year," *Gothamist*, November 13, 2023, https://perma.cc/5XHB-T7K8; and Bahar Ostadan, "NYPD Will Deploy Drones to Respond to Gunshots in 5 NYC Precincts, Officials Say," *Gothamist*, May 16, 2024, https://perma.cc/T9W5-AABG—both accessed August 14, 2024.

30. On abolitionism, see Angela Y. Davis, *Freedom Is a Constant Struggle: Ferguson, Palestine and the Foundations of a Movement* (Chicago: Haymarket Books, 2016); Angela Y. Davis, *Abolition: Politics, Practices, Promises, Volume 1* (Chicago: Haymarket Books, 2022); Mariame Kaba, *We Do This 'Til We Free Us: Abolitionist Organizing and Transforming Justice* (Chicago: Haymarket Books,

2021); and Derecka Purnell, *Becoming Abolitionists: Police, Protests, and the Pursuit of Freedom* (New York: Astra House, 2021).

31. See Peter Pihos, "Good Cops?" in *From Rights to Lives: The Evolution of the Black Freedom Struggle*, ed. Françoise N. Hamlin and Charles Wesley McKinney Jr. (Nashville: Vanderbilt University Press, 2024), 71–98.

32. Dell Upton, *What Can and Can't Be Said: Race, Uplift, and Monument Building in the Contemporary South* (New Haven, Conn.: Yale University Press, 2015), 134–171.

33. Greg Grandin and Thomas Miller Klubock, "Introduction: A U.S. Truth Commission," *Radical History Review* 97 (Winter 2007): 99–101; Nicole Fox and David Cunningham, "Transitional Justice in Public and Private: Truth Commission Narratives in Greensboro," *International Journal of Transitional Justice* 16, no. 2 (2022): 235–253.

34. Spoma Jovanovic, *Democracy, Dialogue, and Community Action: Truth and Reconciliation in Greensboro* (Fayetteville: University of Arkansas Press, 2012), 172, 178–179; "Greensboro Truth & Reconciliation Commission Project," Beloved Community Center, https://perma.cc/PNB9-Z84V, accessed August 14, 2024; Sally Avery Bermanzohn, "A Massacre Survivor Reflects on the Greensboro Truth and Reconciliation Commission," *Radical History Review* 97 (Winter 2007): 102–109.

35. Claude Sitton, "Mississippi Rights Slaying Is Being Reconstructed—Arrests Awaited," *NYT*, August 7, 1964, 13.

INDEX

Page numbers in italics refer to figures.

A NOTE ON THE TYPE

This book has been composed in Adobe Text and Gotham.
Adobe Text, designed by Robert Slimbach for Adobe,
bridges the gap between fifteenth- and sixteenth-century
calligraphic and eighteenth-century Modern styles.
Gotham, inspired by New York street signs, was designed
by Tobias Frere-Jones for Hoefler & Co.